Hereward Tilton

The Quest for the Phoenix

Arbeiten zur Kirchengeschichte

Begründet von
Karl Holl† und Hans Lietzmann†

herausgegeben von
Christoph Markschies und Gerhard Müller

Band 88

Walter de Gruyter · Berlin · New York

2003

Hereward Tilton

The Quest for the Phoenix

Spiritual Alchemy and Rosicrucianism
in the Work of Count Michael Maier (1569 – 1622)

Walter de Gruyter · Berlin · New York
2003

BF
115
.A57
T558
2003

∞ Printed on acid-free paper which falls within the guidelines of the ANSI
to ensure permanence and durability.

ISBN 3-11-017637-8

Bibliographic information published by Die Deutsche Bibliothek

Die Deutsche Bibliothek lists this publication in the Deutsche Nationalbibliografie; detailed
bibliographic data is available in the Internet at <http://dnb.ddb.de>.

© Copyright 2003 by Walter de Gruyter GmbH & Co. KG, D-10785 Berlin

All rights reserved, including those of translation into foreign languages. No part of this book may
be reproduced or transmitted in any form or by any means, electronic or mechanical, including
photocopy, recording, or any information storage and retrieval system, without permission in
writing from the publisher.
Printed in Germany
Cover design: Christopher Schneider, Berlin.

Learn O ye students, that which the Philosophers have long since intimated, saying that truth is not discerned but by error, and that nothing begets more grief to the heart than error in this work; for when a man thinks he has done and has the world, he shall find nothing in his hands.

(Baqsam in *The Flying Atalanta*, discourse XXXIX)

Foreword

The following work is the fruit of research carried out in libraries and archives across Europe under the aegis of the Deutscher Akademischer Austauschdienst Forschungsstipendium and the University of Queensland Research Travel Award; in the course of my travels a number of people stepped forward to assist me. Amongst those I would like to thank here are Prof. Dr. Karin Figala and Dr. Ulrich Neumann of the Technische Universität München, for their readiness to impart knowledge and their generosity with the sharing of valuable primary sources related to Maier; Dr. José Bouman and Dr. Cis van Heertum of the Bibliotheca Philosophica Hermetica, Amsterdam, for their assistance with a beautiful collection; Dr. Jill Bepler of the Herzog August Bibliothek, Wolfenbüttel, for welcoming me to an illustrious institution; PD Dr. Carlos Gilly of Universität Basel, for sharing his knowledge of Rosicrucian matters; Prof. Antoine Faivre of the Sorbonne, for providing timely advice on methodology; Prof. Vladimír Karpenko of Charles University, Prague, for providing me with food for thought; Assoc. Prof. Michael Lattke of the University of Queensland, Brisbane, for help with logistics; Dr. Tara Nummedal of Brown University, Providence, for engaging in a fruitful dialogue; PD Dr. Heiko Droste of Hamburg, for his insistence that truth is founded only upon error; Dr. Sabine Horst of Stuttgart, for her invaluable language training; and Dr. Lisa Colledge of London, for her kind support during my research at the British and Bodleian libraries. My special thanks go to Assoc. Prof. Richard Hutch of the University of Queensland, Brisbane, for his sage advice; to my parents Harold and Hilary; and to my good friend and wife PD Dr. Michaela Boenke of Ludwig-Maximilians-Universität München, for her unwavering technical and personal support.

Table of Contents

IV. The Rosicrucian 'Imposture'

V. The Completion of the Work

VI. Conclusion: Maier and the Historiography of Alchemy

I. Introduction: Jung and early modern alchemy

1. The alchemical chimera

The early modern period witnessed the emergence of theosophy, Rosicrucianism and Freemasonry as esoteric currents with specifically 'alchemical' concerns. Nevertheless, the task of defining alchemy in this period is fraught with difficulties, and the relationship between the spiritual alchemies of the Western esoteric tradition and the laboratory quest for the alchemical agent of transmutation remains to be clarified. Indeed, the very term 'alchemy' had accumulated a variety of meanings by the turn of the sixteenth century, and the nature of the endeavours to be placed under its rubric remains a contentious issue to this day. Arguing against the implicitly religious interpretation of the ambiguous alchemical corpus put forward by the Swiss psychoanalyst, Carl Gustav Jung (1875-1961), Lawrence Principe and William Newman have recently contended that the symbolic literature of laboratory alchemy in the early modern period dealt primarily with code-names (*Decknamen*) for chemical processes, and for the greater part bore no relation to matters of spiritual or psychological transformation. Furthermore, Principe and Newman argue that Jung's schema falsely implies a discontinuity between alchemy and modern chemistry. In their view, there is a lack of any clear and widespread demarcation between the words *chemia* and *alchemia* in the early modern texts, and consequently they have recommended that we dispense with the term 'alchemy' altogether when referring to this period, utilising instead the more common early modern appellations of *chemia* or *chymia*, whilst reserving the term 'alchemy' for the medieval period alone.[1]

---

[1] Principe, Lawrence M. and William R. Newman. "Some Problems with the Historiography of Alchemy." In Newman, William R. and Anthony Grafton (eds.). *Secrets of Nature: Astrology and Alchemy in Early Modern Europe.* Cambridge, Ma.: MIT Press, 2001, pp. 385-431; "Alchemy vs. Chemistry: The Etymological Origins of a Historiographic Mistake," *Early Science and Medicine*, Vol. 3, No. 1, 1998, pp. 32-65; also Newman, William R. "*Decknamen* or Pseudochemical Language? Eirenaeus Philalethes and Carl Jung," *Revue D'Histoire des Sciences*, Vol. 49, No. 2, 1996, pp. 159-188.

Although Faivre has dealt extensively with the subject of alchemy from the perspective of the history of Western esotericism,[2] the primary historical enquiry into the status of laboratory alchemy in early modernity continues to take place amongst historians of science. As a consequence the following study enters both these arenas of discourse. Clearly the arguments of Principe and Newman deal not only with questions of historiography and nomenclature, but concern the very nature of laboratory alchemy in the sixteenth and seventeenth centuries and its relation to the esoteric traditions. These introductory pages constitute an extended theoretical preamble on this current controversy, which will serve as a prelude for an analysis of the concrete example of the alchemy of Count Michael Maier and his place in the history of early Rosicrucianism. In the course of that analysis it will be seen that the relation of Maier's religious sentiments to his laboratory practice – no less than his role in the history of Western esotericism – presents difficulties for the contentions of Principe and Newman. These difficulties will be detailed in the conclusion with the aim of defining alchemy as a subject of study in the field of the history of Western esotericism. There it will be shown that if the study of esoteric currents of thought (and hence the study of their categories) is taken seriously, the term 'alchemy' becomes entirely indispensable, and appears to refer to a broad yet coherent complex of ideas with precisely its origins in the early modern period and the work of alchemists such as Maier (that author's eschewal of the term 'alchemy' notwithstanding). Indeed, if Carl Gustav Jung's work is itself considered as a religious artefact, then he may be understood as only the latest purveyor of a 'spiritual alchemy' with expressly modern characteristics.

2. The reception of Jung amongst historians of alchemy

Whilst the ideas of Principe and Newman have attained a certain popularity at this point in time, the reception of Jung and his psychoanalytic approach amongst historians of alchemy has not always been negative. On the contrary, Jung's alchemical studies earned the controversial and mystery-mongering psychologist his closest encounter with academic respectability. Since his extensive work on the subject in the 1930's, 40's and 50's, Jung's belief that alchemical symbolism expresses psychological processes of an essentially

---

[2]   See, for example, Faivre, Antoine. *Access to Western Esotericism.* Albany: State University of New York Press, 1994, *passim.*; *The Golden Fleece and Alchemy.* Albany: State University of New York Press, 1993; "Mystische Alchemie und Geistige Hermeneutik." In *Correspondences in Man and World.* Eranos Yearbook, 1973. Leiden: E. J. Brill, 1975, pp. 323-360.

religious nature has held wide currency in the academic study of alchemy. In 1942 Jung published his *Paracelsica: Zwei Vorlesungen über den Arzt und Philosophen Theophrastus*,[3] in which he boldly declared that the Swiss alchemist Paracelsus (c.1493-1541) had anticipated the findings of twentieth century psychoanalysis:

I had long been aware that alchemy is not only the mother of chemistry, but is also the forerunner of our modern psychology of the unconscious. Thus Paracelsus appears as a pioneer not only of chemical medicine but of empirical psychology and psychotherapy.[4]

In Jung's opinion the symbols of Paracelsian alchemy, and of alchemical literature in general, make more or less veiled reference to the evolution of the individual psyche – a dialectical process of 'individuation' in which consciousness is confronted with the forces of the unconscious mind. Furthermore, Jung felt that alchemy was not only the precursor to the modern psychology of the unconscious, but also a bridge in the history of ideas between his own thought and the religion of the Gnostics.[5] Thus he spoke of Paracelsus as a man whose soul "was intermingled with a strange spiritual current which, issuing from immemorial sources, flowed beyond him into a distant future."[6]

Upon its first appearance Jung's understanding of Paracelsus was met with enthusiasm by historians of chemistry; in his 1946 review of *Paracelsica* for *Ambix*, Gerhard Heym wrote that no modern authority prior to Jung had been able to decipher the 'abstruse and obscure' vocabulary of the 'psychology' of Paracelsus.[7] Heym was joined in his praise by no less

---

3   A revision of two lectures: *Paracelsus als Arzt*, delivered to the Schweizerischen Gesellschaft für Geschichte der Medizin und der Naturwissenschaften at the annual meeting of the Naturforschenden Gesellschaft, Basel, September the 7th, 1941; and *Paracelsus als geistige Erscheinung*, delivered at Einsiedeln, the birthplace of Paracelsus, on October the 5th, 1941, at the celebrations marking the 400th anniversary of his death; Jung, Carl Gustav. "Studien über Alchemistische Vorstellungen." *C. G. Jung Gesammelte Werke*. Vol. 13. Freiburg im Breisgau: Walter-Verlag, 1978, p. 125.

4   Jung, Carl Gustav. "Alchemical Studies." *The Collected Works of C. G. Jung*. Vol. 13. Trans. R. F. C. Hull. Princeton: Princeton University Press, 1967, p. 189; Jung, "Studien über Alchemistische Vorstellungen," p. 209: "Es war mir schon lange bewußt, daß die Alchemie nicht nur die Mutter der Chemie ist, sondern auch die Vorstufe der heutigen Psychologie des Unbewußten. *So sehen wir Paracelsus als einen Bahnbrecher nicht nur der chemischen Medizin, sondern auch der empirischen Psychologie und der psychologischen Heilkunde.*"

5   *Ibid.*, p. 224.

6   *Ibid.*, p. 209: "...Paracelsus, dessen Seele verwoben ist in ein seltsames geistiges Leben, welches, aus ältesten Quellen entspringend, weit über ihn hinaus in die Zukunft strömt."

7   Heym, Gerhard. "Review. Paracelsica, Zwei Vorlesungen über den Arzt und Philosophen Theophrastus," *Ambix*, Vol. 2, No. 3, December 1946, pp. 196-198.

eminent a scholar of Paracelsianism than Walter Pagel, who likewise claimed that Jung's *Paracelsica* had finally made 'accessible' to him the obscure terminology of Paracelsian iatrochemistry.[8] Writing in *Isis* in 1948, Pagel described Jung as the creator of "an encyclopaedia, atlas and new interpretation of alchemical symbolism which will be fundamental for all future studies on the subject."[9] In the same place Pagel reviewed Jung's *Psychologie und Alchemie* (1944), a work based on two lectures delivered to the *Eranos Tagung* in 1935 and 1936.[10] In this work Jung attempted to correlate alchemical symbolism with motifs from the dream life of one of his patients – a man we now know to be Wolfgang Pauli, the Nobel prize-winning physicist and Jung's collaborator on the synchronicity theory. Having argued that both the alchemical corpus and the dreams of contemporary citizens express a psychological process of self-realisation, Jung embarks on an exploration of what he understands to be religious conceptions in alchemy, during which he sets forward a succinct account of his theory of projection and the historiography it entails:

What [the alchemist] sees in matter, or thinks he sees, is chiefly the data of his own unconscious which he is projecting into it. In other words, he encounters in matter, as apparently belonging to it, certain qualities and potential meanings of whose psychic nature he is entirely unconscious. This is particularly true of classical alchemy, where empirical science and mystical philosophy were more or less undifferentiated. The process of fission which separated the φυσιχα from the μυστιχα set in at the end of the sixteenth century and produced a quite fantastic species of literature whose authors were, at least to some extent, conscious of the psychic nature of their "alchymical" transmutations.[11]

---

[8]   Pagel, Walter. "Jung's Views on Alchemy," *Isis*, Vol. 39, No. 1, May 1948, pp. 44-48.

[9]   *Ibid.*, p. 48.

[10]   *Traumsymbole des Individuationsprozesses.* Eranos Yearbook, 1935. Zurich: Rhein, 1936; *Die Erlösungsvorstellungen in der Alchemie.* Eranos Yearbook, 1936. Zurich: Rhein, 1937. First published in English as *The Integration of the Personality*. New York: Farrar & Rinehart, 1939.

[11]   Jung, Carl Gustav. "Psychology and Alchemy." *The Collected Works of C. G. Jung.* Vol. 12. Trans. R. F. C. Hull. London: Routledge and Kegan Paul, 1968, p. 218; Jung, Carl Gustav. "Psychologie und Alchemie." *C. G. Jung Gesammelte Werke.* Vol. 12. Freiburg im Breisgau: Walter-Verlag, 1972, p. 267: "Was er im Stoffe sieht und zu erkennen meint, sind zunächst seine eigenen unbewußten Gegebenheiten, die er darein projiziert; das heißt es treten ihm aus dem Stoff diesem anscheinend zugehörige Eigenschaften und Bedeutungsmöglichkeiten entgegen, deren psychische Natur ihm gänzlich unbewußt ist. Dies gilt hauptsächlich von der klassischen Alchemie, in welcher naturwissenschaftliche Empirie und mystische Philosophie sozusagen ununterschieden vorliegen. Der mit dem Ende des 16. Jahrhunderts einsetzende Spaltungsprozeß, welcher die φυσιχα (das Physische) von den μυστιχα (das Mystische) trennte, hat nun eine wesentlich phantastischere Literaturgattung hervorgebracht, deren Autoren die seelische Natur der „alchymistischen" Wandlungsprozesse einigermaßen bewußt war."

It is this notion of the supposed post-Reformation 'fission' in the alchemical literature of the *physica* and the *mystica*, elements that were formerly unified in the 'classical' period of ancient and medieval alchemy, which Principe and Newman refute on the grounds that no clear distinction between *chemia* and *alchemia* arises in the literature prior to the eighteenth century.[12] In their eyes, any effort to distinguish a 'mystical' alchemy from a 'physical' chemistry in the seventeenth century is presentist – that is to say, it projects contemporary categories into a time in which such distinctions were alien. Furthermore, they argue that Jung's schema supports the false notion of a discontinuity in the evolution of chemistry, a disjuncture between a modern mechanistic science and an alchemy that is defined by its 'spiritual or psychic dimension'.[13]

Principe and Newman also see Jung as the chief progenitor of a tendency "to downplay or eliminate any natural philosophical or 'scientific' content in alchemy"[14] – and as we shall see, this has been a common criticism voiced by historians of science, be they partisans or foes of the Jungian approach. Indeed, in his review of *Psychologie und Alchemie* Pagel also stated that Jung was "prone to belittle the role of alchemy as a precursor to modern science" by overemphasising the psychological aspect of the texts he studied.[15] Nevertheless, he felt that Jung had revolutionised the academic study of alchemy:

[Jung] succeeds: (1) in placing alchemy into an entirely new perspective in the history of science, medicine, theology and general human culture, (2) in explaining alchemical symbolism, hitherto a complete puzzle, by utilising modern psychological analysis for the elucidation of an historical problem and – vice versa – making use of the latter for the advancement of modern psychology; and all this in a scholarly, well documented and scientifically unimpeachable exposition. If not the *whole* story of alchemy, he has tackled its "mystery," its "Nachtseite," i.e., the problem most urgent and vexing to the historian.[16]

Pagel was an early opponent of positivism in the field of the history of science; whilst many of his contemporaries had dismissed the magical and religious beliefs of pre-modern and early modern scientists as retrogressive, Pagel attempted to demonstrate the 'organic coherence' of such beliefs with recognisably 'modern' elements in the scientific worldviews he studied.[17] On

---

[12] Principe and Newman, "Some Problems with the Historiography of Alchemy," pp. 404, 407-408.

[13] *Ibid.*, pp. 417-418.

[14] *Ibid.*, p. 412.

[15] Pagel, "Jung's Views on Alchemy," p. 48.

[16] *Ibid.*

[17] On this subject, and on the historiography of alchemy in general, see Debus, Allen G. "Chemists, Physicians, and Changing Perspectives on the Scientific Revolution," History

this count he felt Jung's theories were an antidote to the positivist view of science as progress towards a truth divorced from its philosophical and psychological context.[18]

Another early contributor to the influence of Jung's ideas in the academic study of alchemy was the Swiss-educated John Read, who commented in 1947 that it had required 'the discernment of a master' to elucidate the intimate relationship of alchemy to psychology.[19] Soon the conception that alchemy had involved the projection of unconscious psychological processes into the objective world of the laboratory became a commonplace amongst academics in the field. Even those positivistic writers who were antagonistic towards the role of the irrational in alchemy referred to Jung's theories in order to demarcate the realm of 'genuine' science from mere superstition. Thus Eduard Farber in *The Evolution of Chemistry* (1952) scorned the 'mystical' class of alchemical texts as a collection of 'fantastic tales', devoid of both art and science, which might interest a psychoanalyst such as Jung but were of no use for the historian of chemistry.[20] In similar vein, Maurice Crosland wrote in his *Historical Studies in the Language of Chemistry* (1962):

The psychologist Jung considered the paradox as 'one of our most valued spiritual possess-ions' and stated that a religion 'becomes inwardly impoverished when it loses or reduces its paradoxes', because an unambiguous language is unsuited to express the incomprehensible. It seems clear that, whereas mystical alchemy may well have thrived on paradox, its existence in the literature was stultifying to alchemy as a science.[21]

Although more rationalistic sensibilities were offended by the mystically-minded 'adept', whose "cloud of obscure nomenclature and speculation contributed nothing to chemistry,"[22] other historians followed Pagel in an attempt to address the complete intellectual output of the alchemists. One such writer was Betty Dobbs, who – in stark contrast to Principe and Newman – utilised Jung's ideas to emphasise the continuity of the alchemical tradition with modern chemistry in her work *The Foundations of Newton's Alchemy* (1975). There she traced the influence on Isaac Newton's

---

of Science Society Distinguished Lecture, *Isis*, Vol. 89, No.1, March 1998, pp. 66-81; also Pagel, Walter. *William Harvey's Biological Ideas*. New York: Karger, 1967, p. 82.

18 Pagel, "Jung's Views on Alchemy," p. 48.

19 Read, John. *The Alchemist in Life, Literature and Art*. London: Thomas Nelson and Sons Ltd., 1947, p. 2.

20 Farber, Eduard. *The Evolution of Chemistry*. New York: The Ronald Press Company, 1952, pp. 39-40.

21 Crosland, Maurice. *Historical Studies in the Language of Chemistry*. New York: Dover, 1962, p. 27.

22 Farber, *Evolution of Chemistry*, p. 40.

intellectual development of alchemical writers such as Michael Maier, who inspired Newton to dabble with his 'chemical' interpretation of myth and hieroglyph and study the older texts of the alchemical canon.[23] Dobbs charted Newton's efforts to experimentally verify the notions of alchemy, particularly those of the Neoplatonist alchemists, and she described Newton's career as 'one long attempt to integrate alchemy and the mechanical philosophy.'[24]

Although she also criticised Jung's ahistorical approach, Dobbs followed Jung's historiography in the course of her work, describing an 'older' ancient and medieval alchemy in which psychological processes remained largely unconscious to the adept, and a 'newer' alchemy arising with the advent of the Reformation, in which divisions began to appear between a conscious alchemical mysticism and an experimentally-based alchemy.[25] Attempting to give some more historical grounding to Jung's schema, Dobbs called upon the ideas of the left-leaning psychoanalyst Erich Fromm.[26] According to Fromm, large-scale 'individuation' or reflexive personal development emerged in the wake of the collapse of medieval social structures; Dobbs suggested such a socio-historical process may have given rise to 'a more spiritual variety of alchemy'.[27] On the other hand, a more rigorous experimental study of alchemical processes also ensued:

That was excellent for chemistry, which was thereby enabled to incorporate into itself a rational alchemical paradigm, but it was deadly for the older alchemy. It had been too thoroughly chemicalised to carry out its older functions of a religious and psychological nature, for those functions required a considerable ignorance about the substances with which the alchemist worked. From that time on the intertwined halves of the older alchemy were irrevocably separated.[28]

So although Dobbs followed Jung in his distinction between a 'scientific' and a 'spiritual' alchemy in the late sixteenth and seventeenth centuries, she did not believe Jung's work supported the notion of a radical discontinuity in the evolution of chemistry. Rather, she believed modern chemistry had emerged from a new 'experimental alchemy' that was integrally linked to the scientific revolution of the Enlightenment:

---

[23] Dobbs, Betty Jo Teeter. *The Foundations of Newton's Alchemy*. Cambridge: Cambridge University Press, 1975, pp. 90, 192.

[24] *Ibid.*, p. 230.

[25] *Ibid.*, pp. 34, 42, 80.

[26] It should be said that Dobbs incorrectly refers to Fromm as an 'analytical psychologist', the term utilised by Jungian psychoanalysts.

[27] *Ibid.*, p. 42.

[28] *Ibid.*

...it seems clear that both the mechanical philosophers and the reformers who were descended intellectually from the mystical Rosicrucians contributed to the new alchemy which insisted upon full communication of alchemical secrets, experimental study of alchemical processes, and full description of experimental results in common chemical terminology... The function of the movement towards the rationalization of alchemy was to join alchemy to the mainstream of the scientific revolution, destroy its quasi-religious aspect, and set it on a path of gradual evolution into objective chemistry.[29]

The first major challenge to the historiography promoted by Jung came from the French historian of alchemy, Barbara Obrist. From the outset of her *Les Débuts de l'Imagerie Alchimique (XIVe – XVe siècles)* (1982), a study of alchemical illustration in the late medieval period, Obrist felt it necessary to dispense with Jung's perspective – a perspective which, she lamented, had acquired the status of a self-evident truth and was no longer questioned by historians of alchemy.[30] Arguing against its 'monopolisation' of the academic study of alchemy, Obrist described Jung's theory as an 'ahistorical vision' which does not take into account the specific political, social and intellectual contexts of the periods and societies in which alchemy has functioned. Whilst we have seen that this criticism had been voiced by earlier writers more sympathetic to the Jungian approach, Obrist extended her critique to the historiography proposed by Jung. Thus Jung's 'early' or 'classical' alchemy – to which Dobbs had recourse in her work – is an erroneous construct presented as a 'great timeless unit' framed by late antiquity and the seventeenth century. Obrist believed that Jung utilised his theory of universal archetypal propensities of the human psyche "in order to make products as strange as alchemical writings and illustrations, pertaining to fundamentally 'other' intellectual milieus, accessible to the reader of the twentieth century."[31]

According to Obrist, this ahistorical approach of Jung led him to propagate two mistaken conceptions regarding alchemy, which were later reinforced by the historian of religions, Mircea Eliade, in *The Forge and the Crucible* (1962): firstly, the fundamental religiosity of the alchemists, and secondly, their 'animistic' (that is to say, vitalistic) worldview.[32] With regard to the first error, Obrist cites Jung's attitudes towards Christological motifs in the late medieval literature, which she believes served the primarily rhetorical purpose of explaining purely chemical processes figuratively. Stating that the medieval alchemist possessed "a very developed consciousness of the levels of designations and strategies of language," she argues that there is nothing to

---

[29] *Ibid.*, pp. 80-81, 91.
[30] Obrist, Barbara. *Les Débuts de l'Imagerie Alchimique (XIVe – XVe siècles)*. Paris: Le Sycomore, 1982, p. 14.
[31] *Ibid.*, p. 16.
[32] *Ibid.*, p. 17.

justify the notion that laboratory workers of this time were engaged in a spiritual quest for selfhood.[33] Rather, she believes Jung projected the Protestant myth of the solitary, interior search into the Middle Ages, thus portraying the medieval alchemist as a lone pre-Reformer, and all alchemy as an enterprise opposed to the dogmas of the Church. These misconceptions of Jung, Obrist argues, are inspired primarily by the esoteric literature of the seventeenth century and its perpetuation into the nineteenth and twentieth centuries in the form of 'theosophy' – a literature in which mystical quests, religion and alchemy are indeed bound together.[34] As for the second error referred to by Obrist, the views of Jung and Eliade merely echo those of Hélène Metzger, who sought to distinguish alchemy from a mechanistic chemistry with reference to its supposed vitalistic and organic view of the cosmos – a distinction recently undermined by Newman's identification of a corpuscularian tradition within medieval and early modern alchemy.[35]

3. The arguments of Principe and Newman

In a manner similar to Obrist, Principe and Newman reject both Jung's historiography and his theory of projection, although their criticisms focus on the alchemy of early modernity rather than that of the medieval period. In his first foray into the subject of the Jungian interpretation of alchemy and its reception, *Decknamen or Pseudochemical Language? Eirenaeus Philalethes and Carl Jung* (1996), Newman draws upon the work of the pseudonymous seventeenth century author Eirenaeus Philalethes to demonstrate that the surreal symbols of seventeenth century laboratory alchemy are in fact "secretive names for mineral substances" rather than "parables of the psyche unfolding its own transformation," as Jung had proposed.[36] Newman cites the work of Obrist, as well as that of Robert Halleux, in support of his contentions, and states that in view of the rejection of Jung by such "serious historians of alchemy," his own critique could be considered 'otiose'.[37]

Whilst there is much that is to be commended in the extensive work of Principe and Newman on the subject of early modern alchemy, an even-handed appraisal of their contribution to the field requires that we sort the

---

[33] *Ibid.*, pp. 16, 20.

[34] *Ibid.*, p. 17.

[35] Metzger, Hélène. "L'évolution du règne métallique d'après les alchimistes du XVIIe siècle," *Isis*, Vol. 4, 1922, pp. 466-482; Newman, William R. "The Corpuscular Theory of J. B. Van Helmont and its Medieval Sources," *Vivarium*, Vol. 31, 1993, pp. 161-191.

[36] Newman, "*Decknamen* or Pseudochemical Language?," pp. 160, 174.

[37] *Ibid.*, pp. 160-161.

wheat from the chaff and dispense with a number of methodological and factual errors in their analyses from the outset. On this count, it must be stated that Halleux by no means holds "an overtly anti-Jungian position."[38] On the contrary, in the passage cited by Newman (and referred to again by Principe and Newman in their most recent work on the matter[39]) Halleux praises Jung's scrupulous adherence to the fruits of erudition concerning the dating and authorship of texts, and speaks of Jung's 'brilliant' exegesis of certain particularly 'mystical' texts such as the Hellenistic Egyptian *Visions of Zosimos*.[40] Indeed, Halleux draws directly from Jung's writings in his exposition of medieval alchemy; his only caveat is that put forward by those other partisans of Jung, Pagel and Dobbs – namely the ahistorical nature of the Jungian approach.[41] Contrary to Principe and Newman, Halleux's opinions on the matter of medieval alchemy are diametrically opposed to those of Obrist on precisely the subject of Jung; for example, Halleux refers to the corpus of pseudo-Arnoldus de Villanova to emphasise the close connection of religion with alchemy in the medieval period, and to show that the medieval adept was often concerned with 'a process of spiritual self-transformation'.[42] Obrist, on the other hand, refers to the same corpus in the following manner:

In the texts attributed to Arnold, the metaphor of Christ appears amongst others which are used as examples, helping to demonstrate chemical processes that are difficult to understand. They are metaphors like the others, and nothing but metaphors, a fact which Arnold and the authors who follow in his tradition explain extremely well, and which also applies to the illustrations of such treatises. Nothing allows us to speculate on the religiosity of an author when he uses a consciously rhetorical process.[43]

---

38 *Ibid.*

39 Principe and Newman, "Some Problems with the Historiography of Alchemy," p. 406: "...the historians Barbara Obrist and Robert Halleux have presented detailed arguments against Jung's interpretation based upon their extensive reading of late medieval and Renaissance alchemical texts, indeed, some of the very same figurative texts that Jung found most attractive."

40 Halleux, Robert. *Les Textes Alchimiques*. Brepols: Turnhout, 1977, p. 55.

41 *Ibid.*, pp. 140 ff.

42 *Ibid.*, p. 142.

43 Obrist, *Les Débuts de l'Imagerie Alchimique*, p. 21: "Dans les textes attribués à Arnaud, la métaphore du Christ figure parmi d'autres qui servent d'*exempla*, aidant à démontrer des processus chimiques difficiles à comprendre. Ce sont des métaphores comme les autres, et rien que des métaphores, ce qu'Arnaud et les auteurs qui le suivent dans la même tradition expliquent fort bien et qui vaut aussi pour l'illustration de tels traités. Rien ne permet de spéculer sur la religiosité d'un auteur lorsqu'il utilise consciemment un procédé rhétorique."

The misappropriation of Halleux by Principe and Newman could be explained as a simple matter of error in translation, and undoubtedly does not hinder the main thrust of their arguments; nevertheless, by exaggerating the weight of evidence in favour of their own ideas, newcomers to the subject are liable to gain a false impression concerning the acceptability of certain conceptions in the academic milieu. And here we must emphasise the importance of utilising an inclusive and ideally value-neutral language when dealing with the history of alchemy, lest we appear to repeat the positivist errors of authors such as Herbert Butterfield, who famously derided historians of alchemy as being "tinctured with the same type of lunacy they set out to describe."[44] On this count Newman caricatures the Jungian interpretation of alchemy by stating that the work of Eirenaeus Philalethes is not "the product of a disordered mind" or the work of "an irrational mystic unable to express himself in clear English."[45] It matters little that 'irrational mystics' have given rise to some of the finest literature in the English language; what is at stake here is the devaluation of religious sentiments – be they present in the work of Eirenaeus Philalethes or not. Furthermore, if we follow Principe and Newman in counterposing a positively valued 'correct chemical analysis'[46] carried out by 'serious historians of alchemy'[47] with a negatively valued 'analysis of unreason'[48], we not only run the risk of committing a violence against the texts at hand, but we also perform a disservice to contemporary scholarship on the subject of alchemy by excluding certain voices (principally those of the psychoanalysts) from the realms of valid discourse.

This initial criticism should serve to clarify the approach adopted by the current author – and it should also be abundantly clear that the criticisms I will shortly direct at the Jungian hermeneutic are not the work of a follower of Jung, lest I too should be accused of being "tinctured with the same type of lunacy" as the people I study.

The second error committed by Principe and Newman, and one that stands closer to the heart of their argument, is their fundamentally inaccurate portrayal of the Jungian theory of projection and its relation to the unconscious. Thus in their most recent work, "Some Problems with the Historiography of Alchemy," Principe and Newman make a general

---

[44] Butterfield, Herbert. *The Origins of Modern Science, 1300-1800*. New York: MacMillan, 1952, p. 98; cited in Principe and Newman, "Some Problems with the Historiography of Alchemy," p. 389.

[45] Newman, "*Decknamen* or Pseudochemical Language?," pp. 165, 188.

[46] *Ibid.*, p. 188.

[47] *Ibid.*, p. 161; Principe and Newman, "Some Problems with the Historiography of Alchemy," p. 401.

[48] Newman, "*Decknamen* or Pseudochemical Language?," p. 174.

description of Jung's approach to alchemy in which they portray the projection of the symbols of 'individuation' onto the elements in the alembic as a conscious process:

According to Jung, alchemists were concerned less with chemical reactions than with psychic states taking place within the practitioner. The practice of alchemy involved the use of 'active imagination' on the part of the would-be adept, which led to a hallucinatory state in which he 'projected' the contents of his psyche onto the matter within his alembic... the actual substances employed in a process made no difference at all to the alchemist so long as they stimulated the psyche to its act of projection.[49]

To state that the alchemists were 'concerned with psychic states', or that they utilised 'active imagination' – a Jungian psychotherapeutic technique involving a 'dialogue' between the conscious and unconscious minds – implies that they held a conscious understanding of self-transformation as the goal of their Art; according to Jung's theory of projection, the alchemists were by and large *un*aware of the course of their psychic life during laboratory practice, and were conscious only of the very worldly goal of the transmutation of metals. Thus Jung and his followers do not suggest the alchemists were indifferent to the chemical nature of the substances in their retort, as Principe and Newman expressly state.[50] Rather, Jung argued that the 'classical' alchemy he referred to was "a chemical research into which there entered an admixture of unconscious psychic material by the way of projection;" and on this point it is pertinent to note that Principe and Newman misrepresent Jung's declaration that the alchemists dealt "*not only* with chemical experiments," giving instead "*not* with chemical experiments *as such.*"[51] In Jung's view, only a minority of adepts through the centuries demonstrated a conscious understanding of the 'interior' dimensions of their work:

Certainly most of the alchemists handled their *nigredo* in the retort without knowing what it was they were dealing with. But it is equally certain that adepts like Morienus, Dorn, Michael Maier, and others knew in their way what they were doing. It was this knowledge,

---

49   Principe and Newman, "Some Problems with the Historiography of Alchemy," p. 402.
50   *Ibid.*
51   Jung, "Psychologie und Alchemie," p. 282: "Im alchemischen Opus handelt es sich zum größten Teil *nicht nur* um chemische Experimente *allein*, sondern *auch* um etwas wie psychische Vorgänge, die in pseudochemischer Sprache ausgedrückt werden" (emphasis mine); Principe and Newman, "Some Problems with the Historiography of Alchemy," pp. 401-402: "We are called upon to deal, not with chemical experimentations as such, but with something resembling psychic processes expressed in pseudo-chemical language."

and not their greed for gold, that kept them labouring at the apparently hopeless opus, for which they sacrificed their money, their goods and their life.[52]

As for those adepts whom Jung believed were more or less aware of the psychological dimensions of their work, and whose numbers increased following the sixteenth century 'fission' he stipulates, there is no indication in Jung's work that he "wrote laboratory experimentation out of the picture" when considering such individuals.[53] Thus Jung describes Paracelsus as *both* the father of modern pharmacology *and* 'a pioneer of empirical psychology and psychotherapy', and makes mention of the post-Paracelsus emergence of a 'fantastic species of literature' to which the works of Count Michael Maier belong – fantastic because they are neither wholly unconscious projections upon a 'chemical research', nor are they purely speculative alchemical tracts of the ilk of the theosopher Boehme.[54]

Whilst Jung's portrayal of medieval and antique alchemy as 'a great timeless unit' is indeed problematic, there remains no justification for the assertion of Principe and Newman that Jung believed any alchemical text that could be decoded into modern chemical language must thereby be excluded from the realms of a 'good' or 'genuine' alchemy.[55] In light of this fact, the insistence of these authors that the strange symbols utilised by the alchemists are "the products of a skilled use of traditional techniques of deception that extend back many centuries in the literature of alchemy" in no way contradicts the Jungian interpretation of alchemy.[56] Indeed, in the early twentieth century it was widely understood that alchemical symbolism was a secret vocabulary of *Decknamen* for chemical substances, and Jung cited the definitive works of Ruska on this very matter approvingly.[57] Ruska

---

52 Jung, Carl Gustav. "Mysterium Coniunctionis." *The Collected Works of C. G. Jung.* Vol. 14. Trans. R. F. C. Hull. Princeton: Princeton University Press, 1976, p. 521; Jung, Carl Gustav. *Mysterium Coniunctionis.* Vol. 2. Düsseldorf: Walter Verlag, 1995, p. 298: "Ganz gewiß haben die meisten Alchemisten ihre nigredo in der Retort behandelt, ohne zu ahnen, was sie handhabten. Aber ebenso gewiß ist es, daß Adepten wie Morienus, Dorneus, Michael Maier und andere in ihrer Art wußten, worum es ging. Aus diesem Wissen und nicht etwa aus Goldgier entsprang bei ihnen die Nötigung zu dem anscheinend hoffnungslosen opus, dem sie Geld, Gut und Leben opferten."

53 Principe and Newman, "Some Problems with the Historiography of Alchemy," p. 402.

54 See above, n. 11.

55 Jung's assertion that there are "good and bad authors in alchemical literature" refers merely to the existence of charlatanism in the alchemical corpus; the fact that the texts of such charlatans are recognisable, in Jung's view, by their 'studied mystification', clearly reveals that Jung was not referring to texts that were decodable into modern chemical language; see Jung, "Psychology and Alchemy," p. 316.

56 Newman, "*Decknamen* or Pseudochemical Language?," p. 188.

57 See, for example, Jung's *Mysterium Coniunctionis*: "Die 'Chelidonia' kommt als Geheimname vor in jener Fassung der *Turba*, die vom Text, den Ruska gibt, nicht

testified to the wide acceptance of this fact in his formulation of the theory of *Decknamen*:

> It is well known that the Greeks, Syrians, Persians, Arabians, Latinists, in short all nations that concerned themselves with alchemy in the course of two thousand years, gave codenames to the substances utilised in their secret craft, in order to protect the Art against the ignorant masses. The names are taken in part from the characteristics of the bodies concerned, so that quicksilver was known as the "volatile slave," tin the "gnasher," copper "the green" because of the colour of verdigris and the colour of its flame, or ammonia was given the names of various birds. Often they are connected with mystical and religious conceptions, as when the metals are defined with the names of the planets or their assigned Gods. Sometimes the names are also arbitrarily invented.[58]

The central flaw in Principe and Newmans' exposition of the theory of *Decknamen* as it relates to the Jungian hermeneutic lies in their use of a simplistic either-or logic – *either* the symbols of alchemy are products of the unconscious psyche, *or* they are secret code-names for chemical substances. This leads them to the following completely untenable position:

> ...if the images used in alchemical texts are in fact irruptions of the unconscious, then there would be no possibility of "working backwards" from them to decipher such images into actual, valid laboratory practice.[59]

Of course, the notion that a symbol may possess more than one significance is as integral to psychoanalysis as it was to seventeenth century alchemy. As Ruska states, certain symbols in the history of alchemy have borne explicit religious or mystical significance alongside their narrowly chemical meaning; thus we shall soon explore the import of the lead-Saturn-melancholy correspondence in the work of Maier, and his pietistic interpretation of the relationship between gold, the sun and the human heart. As for those symbols which Ruska describes as being of 'arbitrary invention', Principe and Newman explain them away simply by stating that the physical appearance of chemicals in the vessel is sometimes 'evocative'.[60] Whilst the latest neurophysiological research on the nature of religious experience has lent

---

unerheblich abweicht. 'Quidam Philosophi nominaverunt aurum Chelidoniam, Karnech, Geldum' usw. Geldum erklärt Ruska als Chelidonium maius L." Jung, *Mysterium Coniunctionis*, p. 252, n. 81. Throughout his works Jung cites Ruska and his translations as authoritative.

[58] Ruska, Julius and E. Wiedemann. "Alchemistische Decknamen," *Beiträge zur Geschichte der Naturwissenschaften*, Vol. 67, 1924, pp. 17-36; verdigris is a green or greenish blue poisonous pigment resulting from the action of acetic acid on copper.

[59] Principe and Newman, "Some Problems with the Historiography of Alchemy," p. 406.

[60] *Ibid.*, p. 407.

some credence to Jung's ideas,[61] one need not adhere to the Jungian theory of a phylogenetically determined collective unconscious to see that Principe and Newmans' 'explanation' is no explanation at all. When Theobald de Hoghelande describes "the wonderful variety of figures that appear in the course of the work... just as we sometimes imagine in the clouds or in the fire strange shapes of animals, reptiles or trees," there can be no doubt that the 'arbitrary' symbols of alchemy are evoked from the psyche of the individual alchemist as much as from the physical processes in the vessel.[62] The psychoanalyst, of course, admits of no 'arbitrary invention' of the psyche – there is a hidden cause behind every product of consciousness, and each symbol thrown up by imaginative association betrays an unconscious complex of ideas. That the processes in the alchemical vessel were guided by a recognised chemical logic in no way precludes the possibility that another purely subjective logic came into play through the assignment of *Decknamen* to those processes by such association (a phenomenon known as *pareidolia* to the contemporary psychiatrist).[63]

Be this as it may, the following study will have no recourse to psychoanalytic ideas, be they Freudian or Jungian; my purpose here is to reconstruct the worldview of Count Michael Maier via an 'empirical' approach to the study of Western esotericism similar to that recently outlined by Wouter Hanegraaff, and wherever possible to rely upon the alchemists' own testimony concerning the nature of their work.[64] But it is necessary to establish from the outset that an art which variously promises unlimited abundance of worldly wealth, freedom from disease, ancient wisdom and eternal life could not fail to bear a deep psychological significance for its practitioners, and that the substances in the alchemical vessel carried the weight of the adept's hopes and imaginings. In the work of Maier (as Jung correctly surmised) that psychological dimension of the *opus* is consciously

---

[61] See Newberg, Andrew and Eugene D'Aquili. *Why God Won't Go Away: Brain Science and the Biology of Belief.* New York: Ballantine Books, 2001, pp. 75-76 *et passim.*

[62] Cited in Jung, "Psychology and Alchemy," pp. 238-239.

[63] Whilst the objection may be raised that the majority of alchemists dealt only with an established symbolic topology rather than their own imaginative inventions, it is difficult to deny that symbols as burdened with psychological import as the Passion of Christ or as rich in traditional cultural associations as Saturn would continue to constitute a repository for imaginary factors within the practitioner.

[64] On the distinction between 'religionist', 'reductionist' and 'empiricist' approaches to esotericism, and the necessity of recognising the historicity of religious phenomena whilst maintaining a methodological agnosticism concerning meta-empirical claims in the data at hand, see Hanegraaff, Wouter. "Empirical Method in the Study of Eso-tericism," *Method and Theory in the Study of Religion*, Vol. 1, No. 2, 1995, pp. 99-129; see also Hanegraaff, Wouter. "Beyond the Yates Paradigm: The Study of Western Esotericism between Counterculture and New Complexity," *Aries*, Vol. 1, No. 1, 2001, pp. 5-37.

recognised and expressed, and there is no need to draw on reductionist assumptions from modern psychoanalysis to identify or explain it. On the contrary, the origins of Rosicrucianism and the emergence of primarily Germanic 'spiritual' alchemies from heterodox Protestant sources casts a revealing light on the place of Jung's own psychological theories in the history of ideas.

This point leads us back to the criticism voiced by Pagel, Dobbs, Halleux, Obrist, Principe and Newman alike, namely the ahistorical nature of the Jungian approach. By consciously eschewing an historical analysis of alchemical literature, and treating its symbolism as a mythology of timeless origin in the collective psyche, Jung failed to give an adequate account of the cultural matrix from which his own ideas emerged, and consequently failed to recognise the bewildering diversity of endeavours that – for better or worse – have been gathered together under the rubric of the term 'alchemy'. Thus we would not expect alchemists such as the Paracelsian Gerhard Dorn or the traditionalist Michael Maier to be motivated by greed for gold – as Jung suggests in the passage we have cited – because their primary interest lay in *iatrochemia*[65] and the production of the Universal Medicine. Furthermore, Maier understood his relentless *peregrinatio* in search of patronage as a macrocosmic image of the operations within the alchemical vessel, a process of spiritual purification that was indeed integrally linked to his struggle for worldly wealth. And without a detailed understanding of the ultimate goal of Maier's laboratory experiments – a 'medicine of piety' that would cure diseases and impious urges alike by restoring the balance of humours in the body – it is not possible to understand the intimate connection of the 'chemical' and psychological dimensions of his alchemy. Despite the fact that the alchemical canon is littered with pseudonymous and anonymous tracts that are difficult to date, and despite the paucity of biographical data pertaining to many known alchemists, in the case of Count Michael Maier we are presented with a wealth of explicit autobiographical allusions that offer self-avowed insight into the psychological wellsprings of his alchemy.

There are a number of key elements in Maier's alchemy – a distinctively Protestant and individualistic spiritual quest, a paradoxical conjunction of spiritual and material factors, a confluence of pagan and Christian sentiments, an esoteric 'tradition' stemming from antiquity, a nascent German nationalism, solar mysticism, and Rosicrucianism itself – which

---

[65] Although most frequently used in reference to Paracelsian practice, *iatrochemia* in the more general sense of the manufacturing of medicines from inorganic material existed prior to Paracelsus, e.g. in the work of Johannes de Rupescissa in the fourteenth century (see Haage, Bernhard Dietrich. *Alchemie im Mittelalter*. Düsseldorf: Artemis und Winkler, 2000, p. 195). As Maier was not a Paracelsian, the term *iatrochemia* will be used in this broader sense in the following pages.

confirm Obrist's contention that Jung's views have their origins in precisely the type of 'alchemy' propagated by Maier. However, this fact mitigates against Obrist's statement that Jung is dealing with worldviews that are fundamentally 'other' when it comes to early modern alchemy. For all its very tangential relation to the course of modern psychology, Jung's 'analytical psychology' clearly possesses the four fundamental characteristics of modern esotericism set forth by Faivre,[66] i.e. a doctrine of correspondences and sympathies;[67] a belief in a living and revelatory Nature;[68] an emphasis on imagination as the means to revelation;[69] and the practical objective of personal 'transmutation' through such revelation.[70] When we also consider Jung's tendencies towards solar mysticism,[71] his rather unflattering entanglement with a mystical German nationalism,[72] and his explicitly prophetic utterances concerning the imminence (i.e. at some time between 1997 and 2012) of an astrologically determinable catastrophe leading to a New Age in which pagan and Christian doctrines will be united,[73] we are no

---

[66] See Faivre, *Access to Western Esotericism*, pp. 10 ff.; also Faivre, Antoine and Karen-Claire Voss. "Western Esotericism and the Science of Religions," *Numen*, Vol. 42, 1995, pp. 60 ff.

[67] E.g. the concept of 'synchronistic' events arising as the result of acausal correspondences in the universe, c.f. Jung, Carl Gustav. "Synchronicity: An Acausal Connecting Principle." In *The Collected Works of C. G. Jung*, Vol. 8. Trans. R. F. C. Hull. Princeton: Princeton University Press, 1972, pp. 417-531.

[68] E.g. the ultimate indivisibility of psyche and matter, c.f. Jung, Carl Gustav. "On the Nature of the Psyche." In *The Collected Works of C. G. Jung*, Vol. 8. Trans. R. F. C. Hull. Princeton: Princeton University Press, 1972, pp. 159-234, and the existence of archetypes in Nature as expressions of a 'meaningful orderedness', c.f. Jung, "Synchronicity."

[69] E.g. the use of 'active imagination' as a means of uncovering the archetypal layers of the psyche, c.f. Jung, Carl Gustav. "The Concept of the Collective Unconscious." In *The Collected Works of C. G. Jung*, Vol. 9, Part 1. Trans. R. F. C. Hull. Princeton: Princeton University Press, 1968, pp. 42-53.

[70] E.g. the process of 'individuation' towards the Self through the encounter with the archetypal realm, c.f. Jung, Carl Gustav. "On the Psychology of the Unconscious." In *The Collected Works of C. G. Jung*, Vol. 7. Trans. R. F. C. Hull. Princeton: Princeton University Press, 1966, pp. 1-119.

[71] C.f. Jung, Carl Gustav. "Symbols of Transformation." *The Collected Works of C. G. Jung*. Vol. 5. Trans. R. F. C. Hull. Princeton: Princeton University Press, 1967, *passim*.

[72] C.f. "Wotan." In *The Collected Works of C. G. Jung*. Vol. 10. Trans. R. F. C. Hull. Princeton: Princeton University Press, 1970, pp. 179-193.

[73] C.f. Jung, Carl Gustav. "Aion – Researches into the Phenomenology of the Self." *The Collected Works of C. G. Jung*. Vol. 9, Part 2. Trans. R. F. C. Hull. London: Routledge, 1991, pp. 86, 94, *et passim*.; also Jung, Carl Gustav. "A Psychological Approach to the Trinity." In *The Collected Works of C. G. Jung*, Vol. 11. Trans. R. F. C. Hull. Princeton: Princeton University Press, 1969, pp. 107-200; for Jung's last prophetic utterances, see Whitney, Mark (dir.). *Matter of Heart*. Los Angeles: C. G. Jung Institute, 1983.

longer dealing with a doctrine that stands in the realms of science as it is
known today; rather, we are hearing the distant but distinct echoes of
seventeenth century esotericism and a syncretic Protestant millennialism that
once found expression in the Rosicrucian phenomenon.

4. The origins of Jung's alchemy and the work of Richard Noll

Rather than taking their cue from Jung's explicit claim that the 'historical
nexus' of his work lies in the Freemasonic and Rosicrucian traditions,
Principe and Newman follow Richard Noll in emphasising certain nineteenth
century occultists as the predecessors of Jung's interpretation of alchemy (we
might more simply state 'the predecessors of Jung's alchemy', if we follow
Eco in characterising alchemy primarily as a hermeneutic tradition).[74] On this
count Principe and Newman ascribe the origins of Jung's views to the
English occultist Arthur Edward Waite (1857-1942); the rather insubstantial
basis for their assertion is Noll's observation that Waite's works were
circulating amongst members of Jung's Zurich Psychological Club in the
1910's.[75] Principe and Newman point to the supposed influence of Waite in
order to support their central historiographic thesis that the conception of
alchemy as a process of personal transmutation from a base, earthly state into
"a more noble, more spiritual, more moral, or more divine state"– a
conception which we shall follow Principe and Newman[76] in describing as
'spiritual alchemy' – has its origins in the nineteenth century:

Although it was in fact a commonplace of the early modern period to build extended
religious conceits on alchemical processes and to draw theological parallels therefrom – an
aspect of alchemical writing Luther praised in passing – the occultists of the nineteenth
century went much further to claim that alchemy itself was an art of internal meditation
rather than an external manipulation of apparatus and chemicals... The similarity of Jung's
psychologising view to the 'spiritual evolution' system of A. E. Waite's *Azoth* is clear, and
what we now know of Jung's juvenile interest in the occult and the currency of Victorian
esoterica in Jung's early circles supports this observable similarity... we therefore come to
the rather surprising conclusion that the residues of Victorian occultism have deeply colored
the historical study of the discipline. It seems unlikely that many historians would continue

---

[74]   On the history of alchemy as the history of the interpretation of alchemy, see Eco,
       Umberto. *The Limits of Interpretation*. Bloomington, Ind.: Indiana University Press,
       1990, pp. 18-20.

[75]   Principe and Newman, "Some Problems with the Historiography of Alchemy," p. 402;
       Noll, Richard. *The Aryan Christ: The Secret Life of Carl Jung*. New York: Random
       House, 1997, pp. 229-230.

[76]   Principe and Newman, "Some Problems with the Historiography of Alchemy," p. 388.

to engage in the blithe generalizations criticized in this chapter if they realized their dubious origins.[77]

We shall soon contest the crypto-positivist notion that early modern alchemists merely built 'extended religious conceits' on purely 'chemical' processes, and the assertion of Principe and Newman that the 'yoking' of natural magic and astrology to alchemy was "consummated only during the final years of the *ancien régime* in France."[78] For now it will suffice to mention that, even if we accept the unsubstantiated theory of Waite's role in the formation of Jung's views, the Englishman did not disregard laboratory experiment in his portrayal of the history of alchemy, nor did he believe in the possibility of gold-making, as Principe and Newman claim; rather, he adopted the position that the alchemists advanced a 'theory of universal development' with equal application to metals and human beings, and that 'a few of the Hermetic symbolists' focused on 'man' as the subject of their work.[79] Furthermore, Jung's approach has little in common with Waite's argument in the *Azoth, or the Star in the East* (1893) that "all alchemists were mystics and alchemy a mystic work."[80] Rather, his historiography more closely parallels Waite's work of 1926, *The Secret Tradition in Alchemy*, in which Waite revises his earlier opinion and traces the origins of 'spiritual alchemy' to the age of Luther – the time of the 'fission' which Jung believed to herald the widespread emergence of a conscious recognition of the psychological aspects of the alchemical work.[81]

In any case, we find no mention of Waite's theories on alchemy in Jung's works. On this count it must be said that Principe and Newman rely too heavily on the partisan diatribes of Noll, an ex-Jungian who has sought to expose his former mentor as a dangerous right-wing cultist and charlatan. Considerable controversy was aroused in 1994 by the publication of Noll's *The Jung Cult: Origins of a Charismatic Movement*, in which Jung's analytical psychology was depicted as an attempt to fuse Freudian psychoanalysis with neo-pagan sun worship. Employing loosely Weberian conceptions, Noll portrays Jung as a prophet of the *völkisch* movement emergent in German Europe at the *fin-de-siècle*, and a founder of the

---

[77] *Ibid.*, pp. 388, 418.

[78] *Ibid.*, pp. 387-388.

[79] *Ibid.*, p. 394; Waite, Arthur Edward. *Lives of the Alchemystical Philosophers*. London: George Redway, 1888, p. 33: "...though it be impossible for the metal, it is true for the man."

[80] Waite, Arthur Edward. *Azoth, or the Star in the East*. London: Theosophical Publishing, 1893, p. 54.

[81] Waite, Arthur Edward. *The Secret Tradition in Alchemy*. New York: Alfred Knopf, 1926, p. 366.

charismatic cult that is contemporary Jungianism.[82] At the time of his book's publication a strange polemic of Noll's featured in the editorial pages of *The New York Times* entitled *The Rose, the Cross and the Analyst*. Rather than legitimately drawing attention to Jung's place within the history of esotericism, as his title would naturally suggest, Noll oddly had nothing to say concerning Rosicrucianism. Rather, he argued that Jung was a cult leader and 'new Christ' of the same ilk as Luc Jouret of the Order of the Solar Temple, whose followers had been led to their deaths by "the same potent mixture of sun worship, alchemy and spiritual rebirth" espoused by Jung. Noll also took the opportunity to affiliate Jung with David Koresh of the Branch Davidians and Jim Jones of the People's Temple – and given the violent and tragic history of these groups, such inaccurate associations understandably provoked a chorus of protest from Jungian psychotherapists and sympathisers.[83] Whatever genuinely religious foundations analytical psychology may possess, a comparison of Jungian psychotherapy to the millennialist cults in question was simply inaccurate and misleading from the perspective of the academic study of religion,[84] and merely demonstrated Noll's well-established predilection for sensationalism.[85]

There was an unacknowledged personal subtext to the inaccuracies of Noll's work: a clinical psychiatrist by training, he had earlier published a number of articles in which he garnered experimental evidence to support Jung's conceptions of the archetype, psychological projection, and a transpersonal and atemporal 'collective unconscious'.[86] The uncritical naïveté

---

[82] Noll, Richard. *The Jung Cult – Origins of a Charismatic Movement*. Princeton: Princeton University Press, 1994.

[83] Noll, Richard. "The Rose, the Cross and the Analyst," *The New York Times*, October 15, 1994, p. 19. Two days prior to the publication of this article, Luc Jouret had led 52 of his followers in a mass murder/suicide in Switzerland and Canada; according to Noll, both Jung and Jouret were charismatic Swiss occultists posing as 'new Christs'. For the Jungian response to these outlandish claims, see Kirsch, Thomas B. "The Rose, the Cross and the Analyst," *Anima*, vol. 21, 1994, pp. 67-69.

[84] For scholarly critiques of Noll's thesis, see Segal, Robert. "Critical Notice," *Journal of Analytical Psychology*, vol. 40, 1995, pp. 597-608; Shamdasani, Sonu. *Cult Fictions: C. G. Jung and the Founding of Analytical Psychology*. London: Routledge, 1998.

[85] Consider, for example, Noll's *Bizarre Diseases of the Mind* – a book which demonstrates an entirely exploitative attitude towards its 'real-life' subject matter that is strongly reminiscent of contemporary American television culture. A small sampling of the chapter contents should suffice to demonstrate this point: 'True Tales of Lycan-thropy' ("Werewolves? In the twentieth century? You bet there are!"), 'Vampires!' ("these are rare instances – but they do happen. Be certain of that...") and 'Deathly Horrors: Mummification and Necrophilia' ("Morbid? Yes. But many cases have been documented..."); Noll, Richard. *Bizarre Diseases of the Mind*. Berkeley: Berkeley Publishing Group, 1990, pp. 88, 109, 165.

[86] Noll, Richard. "Multiple Personality, Dissociation, and C. G. Jung's Complex Theory," *Journal of Analytical Psychology*, Vol 34, No. 4, October 1989, pp. 353-370; Noll,

Noll exhibited in his earlier writings appears to be inversely proportional to the antagonism expressed towards Jung following his break with the Aion Society and the C. G. Jung Center of Philadelphia in 1993, a fact that leads one to suspect he was less than objective on both counts.[87] Through a repeated emphasis on certain doctrinal commonalities between analytical psychology and Nazi ideology – commonalities that have stronger, older roots in German esoteric tradition than racialist *fin-de-siècle* occultism – *The Jung Cult* utilised a guilt-by-association methodology that played on lingering anti-German sentiments in the English-speaking West. For example, Noll presented Jung's 'Gnostic' myth, the *Septem Sermones ad Mortuos* (1916) as central evidence that Jung was involved in "a *völkisch* intellectual and spiritual elite, an underground 'secret Germany'" that would revitalise the German peoples by means of an Aryan 'inner sun'.[88] It is more pertinent to note that the hero of Jung's adolescence, Johann Wolfgang von Goethe, composed a similar 'Gnostic' tract amidst his own existential crisis, a work inspired by the alchemical and gnostic conceptions he had received from the Pietist Moravian Brethren.[89] As Goethe before him, Jung stood within an esoteric tradition emphasising the unity of pagan and Christian truths. Nevertheless, the one-sidedness of Noll's anti-Germanic caricature in *The Jung Cult* was counterbalanced somewhat in his *The Aryan Christ: The Secret Life of Carl Jung* (1997) – a work which, whilst still advocating the erroneous thesis that Jung believed himself to be an 'Aryan Jesus',[90] dealt at greater length with Pietist and Rosicrucian currents as the ideological source of Jung's thought.[91]

Richard. "C. G. Jung and J. B. Rhine: Two Complementary Approaches to the Phenomenology of the Paranormal." In Shapin, Betty and Lisette Coly (eds). *Parapsychology and Human Nature*. New York: Parapsychology Foundation, 1989.

[87] Hence Noll's introduction to the *Encyclopedia of Schizophrenia and the Psychotic Disorders*, where he speaks with adulation of Jung as a 'giant' on whose shoulders he has stood, and thanks the deceased psychoanalyst "for the tremendous impact his life and work have had on my life, both personally and professionally." Noll, Richard (ed.). *Encyclopedia of Schizophrenia and the Psychotic Disorders*. New York: Facts on File, 2000.

[88] Noll, *The Jung Cult*, pp. 244-246.

[89] Goethe, Johann Wolfgang von. *Poetry and Truth*. Vol. 1. Trans. Minna Smith. London: G. Bell & Sons Ltd., 1911, p. 313.

[90] In the very same lecture that Jung deals with his vision of self-transformation into the Mithraic/Gnostic *leontocephalus*, he clearly states that anyone who succumbs to the temptation of personally identifying with such an image 'would become a crank or a fool', a statement in keeping with his 'phenomenological' approach; Segal, "Critical Notice," p. 605; Noll, *The Jung Cult*, p. 211.

[91] Noll, *The Aryan Christ*, pp. 3-21.

5. 'Secret threads': the seventeenth century 'Carl Jung of Mainz' and Count Michael Maier

However, rather than following the unreliable work of Noll, or looking for Jung's influences on the basis of perceived doctrinal similarities – insignificant as they might be in the case of Waite – we should first look to Jung's own testimony on the matter when considering the genesis of his spiritual alchemy. In the winter of 1955-1956, following the death of his wife, Jung was decorating the tower-house he had constructed on the shores of Lake Zurich at Bollingen. Whilst chiselling the names of his paternal ancestors on three stone tablets for the courtyard of his tower, Jung tells us he became aware of certain 'fateful links' with his forebears:

> I feel very strongly that I am under the influence of things or questions which were left incomplete and unanswered by my parents and grandparents and more distant ancestors... It has always seemed to me that I had to answer questions which fate had posed to my forefathers, and which had not yet been answered, or as if I had to complete, or perhaps continue, things which previous ages had left unfinished.[92]

In accordance with this sense of evolving family destiny, Jung painted the ceiling of his tower with the heraldic arms formulated by his grandfather and namesake, a Grand Master of the Swiss Lodge of Freemasons. Jung's antipathy for his father, a Calvinist preacher, and for the 'lifeless' orthodoxy he represented had led to his strong identification with Carl Gustav Jung senior – a famous Basel physician and Romantic who, family rumour had it, was the illegitimate son of Goethe.[93] The arms of his grandfather apparently

---

[92] Jung, Carl Gustav. *Memories Dreams Reflections*. Trans. R. and C. Winston. New York: Vintage Books, 1973, p. 233; Jung, Carl Gustav. *Erinnerungen Träume Gedanken*. Stuttgart: Rascher Verlag, 1962, p. 237: "Ich habe sehr stark das Gefühl, daß ich unter dem Einfluß von Dingen oder Fragen stehe, die von meinen Eltern und Großeltern und den weiteren Ahnen unvollendet und unbeantwortet gelassen wurden... So schien es mir immer, als ob auch ich Fragen zu beantworten hätte, die bei meinen Ahnen schon schicksalsmäßig aufgeworfen, aber noch nicht beantwortet worden sind, oder als ob ich Dinge vollenden oder auch nur fortsetzen müsse, welche die Vorzeit unerledigt gelassen hat."

[93] *Ibid.*, pp. 41. Whilst Jung described the story of his descent from Goethe as an "annoying tradition," a student friend recalled Jung's pride in recounting the tale – according to Gustav Steiner, "it was not the legend that perplexed me, but the fact that he told us about it;" Ellenberger, Henri. *The Discovery of the Unconscious*. New York: Basic Books, 1970, p. 665. Jung makes no attempt in his autobiography to clarify the question of his ancestry for his readers; the editor of *Erinnerungen Träume Gedanken*, Aniela Jaffé, mentions in an appendix the improbability of Goethe's siring a son by Jung's great-grandmother, but she also recalls Jung's sense of gratification as he recollected the legend: Jung, *Erinnerungen*, p. 399.

depicted a blue cross in the upper right of the shield, separated by a blue bar from blue grapes in a field of gold in the lower left. The symbolism, according to Jung, was 'Masonic or Rosicrucian' – just as the Rosicrucian motif of the cross and red rose represents opposing Christian and pagan forces, so the blue cross and grapes symbolise "the heavenly and the chthonic (i.e. earthly) spirit."[94] In the midst of the separating blue bar is a golden star, which Jung referred to as the *aurum philosophorum* ('philosophers' gold') or symbol for the unity of opposites. For the ageing psychologist, this esoteric symbolism represented "the historical nexus of my thinking and life."[95]

Crucially, in his autobiography Jung goes on to trace the roots of his destiny as the founder of analytical psychology beyond his grandfather. Although his train of thought is typically obscure on this point, Jung suggests he is descended from a Dr. Carl Jung of Mainz (d.1645), whom he portrays as a follower of none other than Count Michael Maier, a 'founder' of Rosicrucianism. As a 'Paracelsian' this supposed ancestor was purportedly acquainted with Gerhard Dorn, a man whom Jung believed to have "grappled with the process of individuation" more than any other alchemist. Jung goes on to comment suggestively that "all this is not without a certain interest" in light of his own concern with alchemical symbolism and the *coniunctio oppositorum* ('conjunction of opposites').[96] In this way Jung intimates that the unanswered questions he felt driven to resolve through his lifelong intellectual and therapeutic work stretch back to the Rosicrucianism of Count Michael Maier and the alchemy of the Paracelsians.

My concern here is not to cast judgment upon Jung's imaginings. Rather, it is to demonstrate that Jung considered the esoteric traditions of Freemasonry and Rosicrucianism as his own spiritual heritage, and that there are good reasons for accepting his claim. Indeed, if we wish to look to citations of theory rather than Jung's autobiographical musing when tracing the origins of his hermeneutic, then our starting point is provided by Herbert Silberer (1882-1923), the man whom Jung followed in proclaiming the *coniunctio oppositorum* to be the central idea of alchemical procedure.[97] Silberer was a Freemason and pupil of Freud who toyed with Jung's theory of archetypes and the progressive nature of the unconscious prior to his suicide in 1923.[98] In the work Silberer dedicated to alchemy, *Probleme*

---

[94] Jung, *Erinnerungen*, p. 236.

[95] *Ibid.*

[96] *Ibid.*, pp. 236-237.

[97] Jung, *Mysterium Coniunctionis*, p. 228; as its title suggests, the *coniunctio oppositorum* is the central problem tackled by Jung in this work.

[98] Apparently Silberer also experimented with sleep deprivation in his quest to unlock the secrets of the 'hypnogogic' and 'hypnopompic' states between waking and sleeping; as he poignantly remarked when discussing the Jungian term 'introversion', "Die Intro-

der Mystik und ihrer Symbolik (1914), we find the fundamental tenets of Jung's alchemy in embryonic form. These include Silberer's comparison of alchemical symbolism with dream motifs and his conception that the "elementary types" of the unconscious had "insinuated themselves into the body of the alchemical hieroglyphics" as the alchemists struggled with the "riddles of physico-chemical facts."[99] Here we have the theory of a projection of psychic contents of a supra-individual nature onto the alchemical work of the laboratory, formulated more than twenty years prior to Jung's first public utterances on the subject. In his autobiographical *Erinnerungen Träume Gedanken* ('Memories, Dreams, Reflections,' 1961) Jung appears (somewhat characteristically) to downplay Silberer's role in the genesis of his own thought by stating that he had 'completely forgotten' the psychoanalyst's work prior to his own 'discovery' of the psychological import of alchemical symbolism in 1928.[100] Nevertheless, in the foreword and conclusion of the work he considered to be his *opus magnum*, the *Mysterium Coniunctionis* (1956), Jung pays homage to Silberer as the 'first' researcher to uncover the psychological significance of alchemy, with the proviso that his predecessor was still constrained by the 'primitive' state of psychological knowledge in 1914 – an allusion to Silberer's dependence on Freudian theory and the undeveloped state of Jung's own ideas at that time:

Herbert Silberer, who unfortunately died too early, has the merit of being the first to discover the secret threads that lead from alchemy to the psychology of the unconscious. The state of

---

version ist kein Kinderspiel. Sie führt zu Abgründen hin, von denen man verschlungen werden kann, rettungslos. Wer sich der Introversion unterzieht, gelangt an einen Punkt, wo sich zwei Wege trennen; und dort muß er eine Entscheidung treffen..."; Silberer, Herbert. *Probleme der Mystik und ihrer Symbolik*. Vienna: Hugo Deller & Co., 1914, p. 171.

99 *Ibid.*, p. 206: "Die viel besprochnen Elementartypen haben sich also bei der Gelegenheit in das Corpus der alchemistischen Hieroglyphik eingeschlichen, als die Menschheit, den chemisch-physikalischen Tatsachen als Rätseln gegenüberstehend, mit dem Ausdruck rang zu ihrer gedanklichen Bewältigung..."

100 "Merkwürdigerweise hatte ich ganz vergessen, was Herbert Silberer über Alchemie geschrieben hatte. Zur Zeit, als sein Buch erschien, kam mir die Alchemie als etwas Abseitiges und Skurriles vor, so sehr ich auch Silberers anagogischen, d. h. konstruktiven Gesichtspunkt zu schätzen wußte. Ich stand damals in Korrespondenz mit ihm und habe ihm meine Zustimmung ausgedrückt. Wie sein tragisches Ende zeigt, war jedoch seine *Ansicht* von keiner *Einsicht* gefolgt... Erst durch den Text der „Goldene Blüte", der zur Chinesischen Alchemie gehört, und den ich 1928 von Richard Wilhelm erhalten hatte, ist mir das Wesen der Alchemie näher gekommen." Jung, *Erinnerungen*, pp. 207-208. On this matter also see Jung's letter to Erich Neumann dated the 22nd of December, 1935, in Jung, Carl Gustav. *Letters*. Adler, Gerhard and Aniela Jaffé (eds.). Vol. 1. Princeton: Princeton University Press, 1973, p. 206 ff.; and Martin, Luther H. "A History of the Psychological Interpretation of Alchemy," *Ambix*, Vol. 22, No. 1, 1975, pp. 10-20.

psychological knowledge at that time was still too primitive and still too much wrapped up in personalistic assumptions for the whole problem of alchemy to be understood psychologically.[101]

Jung's intellectual hubris notwithstanding, it is clear that the confluence of alchemical and psychoanalytic doctrine to be found in the works of Silberer and Jung alike marks a qualitatively new phase in the history of alchemical interpretation. However, if Silberer and Jung are to be evaluated from a broader perspective in the history of ideas as the purveyors of a 'spiritual alchemy', as Principe and Newman suggest, then we must follow those 'secret threads' of which Jung speaks and trace the sources of their (non-exclusive) conception of alchemy as a process of self-transformation within the alchemist.

In his *Probleme der Mystik und ihrer Symbolik*, Silberer attributes the 'rediscovery' of the psychological content of alchemy to the 'profound' Ethan Allen Hitchcock (1798-1870); throughout his work Silberer states that he is indebted to Hitchcock when he argues that the central subject of the Hermetic Art is humankind – i.e. its subject is *das Subjekt*.[102] Hitchcock was a Union general and military adviser to Abraham Lincoln who, like Silberer, was influenced by Freemasonic doctrine: indeed, his father Samuel was a prominent Freemason who incorporated the society's motifs into the seal of the state of Vermont.[103] Hitchcock's thesis as set forward in his *Remarks*

---

[101] Jung, "Mysterium Coniunctionis" (English edition), p. 555; Jung, *Mysterium Coniunctionis* (German edition), p. 334: "Dem leider zu früh verstorbenen Herbert Silberer kommt das Verdienst zu, der erste gewesen zu sein, die geheimen Fäden, die von der Alchemie zur Psychologie des Unbewußten laufen, entdeckt zu haben. Allerdings war der Zustand der damaligen psychologischen Erkenntnis noch zu primitiv und zu sehr in personalistischen Voraussetzungen befangen, als daß das Gesamtproblem der Alchemie psychologisch hätte erfaßt werden können."

[102] Silberer, *Probleme der Mystik*, pp. 211, 97: "Das Verdienst, den über das Chemische und Physikalische hinausgehenden Gehalt der Alchemie wiedergefunden zu haben, gebührt wohl dem Amerikaner Ethan Allen Hitchcock, der seine Ansichten über die Alchemisten in dem Buch "Remarks upon Alchemy and the Alchemists" niederlegte, das 1857 in Boston erschien... Die Entdeckungen, zu welchen der tiefsinnige Hitchcock gelangte, sind für unsere Analyse so wichtig, daß ihre ausführliche Entwickelung nicht umgangen werden kann... Hitchcock liefert uns in einem einzigen Wort den Schlüssel zum Verständnis der hermetischen Meister, wenn er sagt: Das Subjectum ist – der Mensch. Man kann sich auch eines Wortspiels bedienen und sagen: das Subjectum ist das Subjekt."

[103] See Smith, Henry Perry. *History of Addison County Vermont*. Syracuse, N.Y.: D. Mason & Co., 1886, p. 143; also Thomas, John D. "The Engine of Enlightenment: Samuel Hitchcock and the Creation of the University of Vermont Seal." Unpublished paper, an abstract of which is to be found in *The Center for Research on Vermont Newsletter*, Vol. 24, No. 1, April 1999. Although I am loath to further propagate unsubstantiated myths and fabrications concerning the history of esotericism, it has been alleged that Ethan Allen Hitchcock belonged to a certain 'Council of Three' in the Freemasonic 'Order of

upon Alchemy and the Alchemists (1857) is that the alchemists were
concerned with the procurement of a spiritual 'new birth' through the casting
out of the 'superfluity' of evil.[104] Thus he declares that "the *subject* of
Alchemy was Man, while the *object* was the perfection of Man," but as true
'Reformers' of the Church the alchemists were compelled to obscure their
properly religious purpose in a pseudo-chemical language.[105] Silberer did not
adopt as untenable a position on the question of *Decknamen* and laboratory
experimentation as his predecessor, but rather dealt at length in *Probleme der
Mystik und ihrer Symbolik* with "the problem of multiple interpretation."[106]
His research led him to propose three simultaneous significations of
alchemical symbolism: a regressive significance "leading to the depths of the
impulsive life;" an 'anagogic' or progressive significance leading to "high
religious ideals;" and a chemical significance pertaining to the realms of
science and natural philosophy.[107] If we dispense with the 'regressive
significance' drawn from Freud, we have the broad outlines of the dual
interpretation proposed by Jung – on the one hand alchemical symbolism
reflects laboratory experiment, and on the other it reflects 'individuating'
tendencies towards the realisation of the 'Self', to translate Silberer's terms
into those of Jung's spiritual alchemy.

As we cannot accept Jung's claim that he had 'forgotten' Silberer's work,
replete as it is with Jung's own theories applied to the subject of alchemy,
then we must recognise *Probleme der Mystik und ihrer Symbolik* as Jung's
first documented and most formative encounter with alchemy, and it behoves
us to examine more closely the origins of the ideas advanced by Silberer.
Both Silberer and his predecessor Hitchcock drew their spiritual alchemy in
large part from conceptions expressed in the higher degrees of Freemasonry,
which have as their goal the progressive transformation of the human
personality from a state of primitivity and darkness to a higher level of
human consciousness. Indeed, since the late eighteenth century various
Freemasonic Lodges have incorporated spiritual alchemical conceptions into
their higher degrees, a fact which has led many authors in the last two
centuries to trace the origins of modern Freemasonry to Rosicrucian

---

the Lily', which claimed its descent from Rosicrucianism by charter of the Supreme
Grand Lodge of France; Hitchcock supposedly took his place in this 'Council' alongside
Abraham Lincoln and the occultist P. B. Randolph (1825-1875). These assertions have
been discredited in the article "Abraham Lincoln was not a Freemason," *Lincoln Lore*,
No.1595, January 1971.

[104] Hitchcock, Ethan Allen. *Remarks upon Alchemy and the Alchemists*. Boston: Crosby,
Nichols, and Co., 1857, pp. 226-227.

[105] *Ibid.*, pp. viii-ix, 22.

[106] Silberer, *Probleme der Mystik*, pp. 133-146.

[107] *Ibid.*, pp. 138, 145-146.

Hermeticism.[108] The relation of Rosicrucianism to Freemasonry remains a contested issue, both within academic and Freemasonic circles. The origins of the controversy may be traced to Buhle's *Ueber den Ursprung und die vornehmsten Schicksale der Orden der Rosenkreuzer und Freymaurer* (1804), in which the author argued that speculative masonry or Freemasonry arose in England between 1629 and 1635 through the work of Robert Fludd (1574-1637), who had been introduced to the Rosicrucian mysteries by Count Michael Maier (an erroneous lineage recently exposed by Figala and Neumann).[109] Buhle's conception that Freemasonry had its origins in the mania of early Rosicrucianism rather than the guilds of the medieval masons or the Egyptian and Greek mysteries (as Masonic lore claimed) was seconded

---

[108] Alchemical symbolism may be found to this day in the Ancient and Accepted Scottish Rite of Masonry, particularly in the Knight of the Sun/Prince Adept 28th degree; kind information of M. Evans.

[109] Buhle, Johann Gottlieb. *Ueber den Ursprung und die vornehmsten Schicksale der Orden der Rosenkreuzer und Freymaurer. Eine Historisch-kritische Untersuchung.* Göttingen: Johann Friedrich Röwer, 1804, pp 245-246.: "Michael Maier, der persönlich nach England reiste, und sich eine Zeitlang dort aufhielt, fand nicht nur die günstigste Aufnahme; sondern Robert Fludd u. a. schlossen auch mit ihm die innigste Freundschaft, laborirten mit ihm gemeinschaftlich, und, nachdem Maier nach Deutschland zurückgekehrt war, theilten sie ihm noch die Resultate ihrer Forschungen und Experimente in einer vertrauten Correspondenz mit... Wahrscheinlich empfiengen Fludd und seine Genossen die erste Nachricht von der in der Fama und Confessio bekant gemachten Rosenkreuzergesellchaft durch ihren Freund Maier." Unfortunately, Buhle offers us no evidence concerning the existence of correspondence between Fludd and Maier. The contention that Maier brought Rosicrucianism to England via Fludd, who changed its name to 'Freemasonry' due to the disrepute into which the 'Fraternity of the Rose Cross' had fallen, was also set forward by Ferdinand Katsch in his *Die Entstehung und der wahre Endzweck der Freimaurerei*. Berlin: E. S. Mittler und Sohn, 1897. The conception of Fludd's 'friendship' with Maier seems to have arisen on the basis that there is no direct evidence to the contrary; for repetitions of the myth, see Craven, J. B. *Count Michael Maier, Doctor of Philosophy and of Medicine, Alchemist, Rosicrucian, Mystic: Life and Writings*. Kirkwall: William Pearce and Son, 1910, p. 6; Yates, Frances. *The Rosicrucian Enlightenment*. London: Routledge and Kegan Paul, 1972, p. 81; Hubicki, W. "Maier, Michael." In *The Dictionary of Scientific Biography*. Vol. 9. New York: Scribner, 1974, p. 23; Edighoffer, Roland. *Die Rosenkreuzer*. München: C. H. Beck, 1995, p. 13; Åkerman, Susanna. *Rose Cross over the Baltic: The Spread of Rosicrucianism in Northern Europe*. Leiden: Brill, 1998, p. 90. The concept of a 'meeting' or 'friendship' was first cast into doubt by Waite in his *Brotherhood of the Rosy Cross*. London: Rider and Sons, 1924, pp. 314 ff.; convincing evidence against the myth is to be found in Figala, Karin and Ulrich Neumann. "Michael Maier (1569-1622): New Bio-Bibliographical Material." In Martels, Z. R. W. M. von (ed.). *Alchemy Revisited: Proceedings of the International Conference on the History of Alchemy at the University of Groningen, 17-19 April 1989*. Leiden: E. J. Brill, 1990, p. 45, and Moran, Bruce T. *The Alchemical World of the German Court: Occult Philosophy and Chemical Medicine in the Circle of Moritz of Hessen (1572-1632)*. Stuttgart: Franz Steiner Verlag, 1991, pp. 107-108.

in *Über den Wahren Ursprung der Rosenkreuzer und des Freymaurerordens* of Christoph Gottlieb von Murr, who – amongst other things – pointed to certain motifs in Maier's *Septimana Philosophica* as evidence of Freemasonry's true doctrinal heritage.[110] Later in the nineteenth century Sandys further emphasised the role of Elias Ashmole (1617-1692), the noted English enthusiast of Rosicrucian and alchemical lore and one of the earliest known Freemasons, as the chief conduit of Rosicrucian influence on Freemasonry.[111] In this century the Maier-Fludd-Ashmole lineage has been promoted by Masonic writers, notably Lennhof and Naudon.[112] Amongst academic writers Frances Yates advanced a similar theory, postulating both Rosicrucian and courtly Hermetic influences on the rise of Freemasonry in seventeenth century England;[113] Schick argued for the existence of embryonic traces of the Freemasonic grade system in the work of Maier;[114] whilst Stevenson has recently argued for an early and definitive Rosicrucian influence on Freemasonry in Scotland – the land which produced the first hint of a connection between Rosicrucianism and Freemasonry in a verse of the early 1630's:

---

[110] Murr, Christoph Gottlieb von. *Über den Wahren Ursprung der Rosenkreuzer und des Freymaurerordens*. Sulzbach: Johann Esaias Seidel, 1803, pp. 75-76; von Murr's allusion is to the dialogue between Solomon, the Queen of Sheba and Hiram that forms the structure of the *Septimana Philosophica*, and which is drawn from the dialogue concerning the building of the temple in *2 Chronicles* 2; according to von Murr, the dialogue's participants are represented on Maier's title page with certain 'Rosicrucians' (von Murr's term) sitting behind them (see figure 5). Von Murr had seen Buhle's forthcoming work advertised in the *Göttingischen Gelehrten Anzeigen* just as he himself had 'intended to go to the printers', and it seems he beat Buhle to the printing press with his monograph.

[111] In *Encyclopaedia Metropolitana*, Vol. 22, 1845, pp. 11-23; quoted in Gould, Robert Freke. *The History of Freemasonry: Its Antiquities, Symbols, Constitutions, Customs, etc. Embracing an Investigation of the records of the Organisations of the Fraternity in England, Scotland, Ireland, British Colonies, France, Germany, and the United States*. Vol. 2. Edinburgh: T.C. & E.C. Jack, Grange Publishing Works, 1885, p. 115. The Freemason Gould provides us with a thoughtful dissenting view on the Rosicrucian thesis advanced by Buhle and his successors.

[112] Lennhoff, Eugen. *Die Freimaurer*. Nachdruck der Ausgabe von 1929. Wien: Löcker Verlag, 1981, p. 63; Naudon, Paul. *Les Origines de la Franc-Maçonnerie: Le métier et le sacré*. Nouvelle édition entièrement refondue des *Origines Religieuses et Corporatives de la Franc-Maçonnerie* (1953). N. p.: Dervy, 1991, p. 271.

[113] Yates, Frances. *Giordano Bruno and the Hermetic Tradition*. Chicago: University of Chicago Press, 1991, p. 415.

[114] Schick, Hans. *Das Ältere Rosenkreuzertum: Ein Beitrag zur Entstehungsgeschichte der Freimaurerei*. Quellen und Darstellungen zur Freimaurerfrage, Vol. 1. Berlin: Nordland Verlag, 1942, p. 252.

> For we be brethren of the Rosie Cross;
> We have the Mason's Word and second sight.[115]

However, the arguments proposed by these various authors suffer from a paucity of hard evidence, as one might expect of any ventures into Freemasonic history, which was once described as "the happiest of all hunting grounds for the light-headed, the fanciful, the altogether unscholarly and the lunatic fringe of the British Museum Reading Room."[116]

Less fanciful than any supposed early Rosicrucian influence on Free-masonry is the fact that the eighteenth century inheritor of the Rosicrucian mantle, the *Gold- und Rosenkreutz* Order, infiltrated Freemasonic Lodges on the continent in the later eighteenth century and directly inspired the alchemical conceptions of the higher Freemasonic grades. The central work appearing from the circle of the *Gold- und Rosenkreutz* was Jolyfief's *Der Compaß der Weisen* (1779), which placed Rosicrucian alchemical concep-tions in the context of the Freemasonic doctrine of personal moral advancement.[117] We may note that the nineteenth century *Societas Rosi-cruciana in Anglia* was grafted onto regular Freemasonry in a similar fashion to its predecessor and included higher degrees inspired by those of the *Gold-und Rosenkreutz*; and we may also remark in passing that the *Gold- und Rosenkreutz* grades and laws formed the basis for Waite's quasi-Masonic Hermetic Order of the Golden Dawn.[118] In any event, it seems that Silberer wrote his *Probleme der Mystik und ihrer Symbolik* in his capacity as a Freemason as much as that of a psychoanalyst, as he devotes an entire chapter of his work to the subject of Rosicrucian alchemy and its survival in the higher Freemasonic grades of his time (although he adheres to the theory of a seventeenth century Rosicrucian influence on the Lodges).[119] These are the 'secret threads' running from alchemy to the psychology of the unconscious of which Jung speaks, and we may surmise that they were less a 'discovery' of Jung's than of Silberer's.

---

[115] From the *Muses' Threnodie*; cited in Stevenson, David. *The Origins of Freemasonry: Scotland's Century, 1590-1710.* Cambridge: Cambridge University Press, 1988, p. 102.

[116] *Ibid.*, p. 3.

[117] Jolyfief, Augustin Anton Pocquières de. *Der Compaß der Weisen, von einem Mitverwandten der innern Verfassung der ächten und rechten Freymäurerey.* Leipzig: Christian Ulrich Ringmacher, 1779, also published in Berlin by Friedrich Maurer, 1782; Beyer, Bernhard. *Das Lehrsystem des Ordens der Gold- und Rosenkreuzer.* Leipzig: Pansophie-Verlag, 1925, p. 21.

[118] Faivre, *Access to Western Esotericism*, pp. 90-91.

[119] Silberer, *Probleme der Mystik*, pp. 110-133.

6. Spiritual alchemy, Rosicrucianism and the work of Count Michael Maier

Can these 'secret threads', i.e. the conception of a spiritual alchemy present in the work of Silberer and Jung, be traced further back in history than the late eighteenth century *Gold- und Rosenkreutz*? Silberer's entire analysis of alchemy in the *Probleme der Mystik und ihrer Symbolik* was derived from a single primary source, a certain *Parabola* included in the late eighteenth century Rosicrucian compilation, the *Geheime Figuren der Rosenkreuzer aus dem 16ten und 17ten Jahrhundert*.[120] The editor of this compilation states that it had been collated from a number of "old manuscripts" that had been "brought to light" for the first time,[121] whilst Silberer guessed that the *Parabola* was either a work of "the ☉ R. C. ✠" (i.e. the work of the editor as a member of the eighteenth century *Gold- und Rosenkreutz*) or "an older Hermetic philosopher, Fr. R. C" (i.e. an early Rosicrucian text dating to the seventeenth century).[122] Both men were wrong on this count, as the *Parabola* is in fact a portion of the *Güldener Tractat vom Philosophischen Steine* of Johannes Grasshoff appearing in the *Dyas Chymica Tripartita* of 1625.[123] Grasshoff was a laboratory practitioner of alchemy who described himself as a *frater aureae crucis*, a term that demonstrates the author's loose affiliation with the early Rosicrucian phenomenon.[124] Indeed, contrary to the myth of an early seventeenth century origin for the *Gold- und Rosenkreutz* order (to be discussed in our fourth chapter), the late seventeenth century Italian 'Gold and Rosy Cross' and its eighteenth century German namesake may well derive their appellation from the conflation of distinct early seventeenth century tracts written under the 'Rose Cross' and 'Gold Cross' appellations.[125]

---

[120] Grasshoff, Johannes. "Ein güldener Tractat vom Philosophischen Steine." In *Geheime Figuren der Rosenkreuzer aus dem 16ten und 17ten Jahrhundert*. Vol. 2. Altona: n. p., c.1785-1790; in attempting to distance himself from Silberer's work in his memoirs, Jung remarks: "Silberer hatte hauptsächlich spätes Material benutzt, mit dem ich nicht viel anfangen konnte. Die späten alchemistischen Texte sind phantastisch und barock; nur wenn man die Deutung weiß, erkennt man, daß auch in ihnen viel Wertvolles steckt."; Jung, *Erinnerungen*, p. 208.

[121] *Geheime Figuren*, titlepage.

[122] Silberer, *Probleme der Mystik*, p. 134.

[123] Grasshoff, Johannes. "Ein güldener Tractat vom Philosophischen Steine." In *Dyas Chymica Tripartita*. Frankfurt am Main: Lucas Jennis, 1625, pp. 55-66.

[124] On this point see pp. 124-125 below.

[125] Thus the 1656 Italian manuscript 'La Bugia' of the Marquise Massimiliano Palombara, in which mention is made of "una compagnia intitolata della Rosea Croce o come altri dicono dell'Aurea Croce;" Gabrielle, Mino. *Giardino di Hermes: Massimiliano Palombara alchimista e rosacroce nella Roma del Seicento; con la prima edizione del codice*

The *Güldener Tractat* demonstrates the influence of Count Michael Maier, as Grasshoff restates the Renaissance doctrine of the *prisca sapientia* or 'pristine wisdom' with reference to the sages of the twelve nations given in Maier's *Symbola Aureae Mensae Duodecim Nationum* (1617).[126] The whole is a treatise on alchemical natural philosophy drawn primarily from medieval sources, which Grasshoff concludes with the allegorical *Parabola* in much the same manner that the *Allegoria Bella* is presented as the summation of Maier's *Symbola Aureae Mensae*. As in Maier's allegory, Grasshoff begins his *Parabola* with a melancholic proclamation of the wretchedness of earthly life before setting off on a quest for the Philosophers' Stone – in this case symbolised by the Lion rather than Maier's phoenix.[127] The alchemical allegory was much in vogue in the early modern period; authors of that time drew their inspiration from medieval alchemical allegories such as those of Duenech, Maria Prophetissa and Merlin, or mimicked the late antique dream-revelations of the Greco-Egyptian alchemist Zosimos and the Hermetic *Poimandres*.[128] Most early modern allegories demonstrate a similar intent to that of their medieval and ancient counterparts, being mere tropes for natural philosophical conceptions and laboratory procedure rather than consciously constructed allusions to self-transformation.[129] Such may also be said for

---

autografo della Bugia. Rome: Editrice Ianua, 1986, p. 90; the manuscript in question is in the Vatican Library, MS Reginensis Latini 1521. Research is also said to be pending on certain 'statutes and articles' dating to 1678 and relating to an Italian 'Gold and Rosy Cross'; kind information of Susanna Åkerman.

[126] Grasshoff, "Güldener Tractat," p. 17; Maier, Michael. *Symbola Aureae Mensae Duodecim Nationum*. Frankfurt am Main: Lucas Jennis, 1617.

[127] Grasshoff, "Güldener Tractat," p. 55.

[128] For the Duenech allegory, see the *Theatrum Chemicum*. Vol. 3. Ursel: Zetzner, 1602, pp. 756-757; for the allegory of Maria, see "Practica Mariae Prophetissae in Artem Alchimicam." In *Artis Auriferae*. Vol. 1. Basel: Conrad Waldkirch, 1593, pp. 319-324; also "The Practice of Mary the Prophetess in the Alchemical Art." British Library MS Sloane 3641, 17th century, pp. 1-8; for the allegory of Merlin, see "Merlini Allegoria Profundissimum Philosophici Lapidis Arcanum Perfecte Continens." In *Artis Auriferae*. Vol. 1. Basel: Conrad Waldkirch, 1593, pp. 392-396; also "The Allegory of Merlin." British Library MS Sloane 3506, 17th century, pp. 74-75; for an English translation of the *Visions of Zosimos*, see Taylor, F. Sherwood. "The Visions of Zosimos," *Ambix*, Vol. 1, No. 1, May 1937, pp. 88-92; for an example of the reception of the *Poimandres* amongst early modern alchemists, see Khunrath, Heinrich. *Amphitheatrum Sapientiae Aeternae. The Amphitheatre Engravings of Heinrich Khunrath*. Trans. Patricia Tahil. Edinburgh: Magnum Opus Hermetic Sourceworks, 1981.

[129] See, for example, Hinricus Madathanus (Adrian von Mynsicht). "Aureum Seculum Redivivum." In *Dyas Chymica Tripartita, das ist: Sechs Herzliche Teutsche Philosophische Tractätlein*. Frankfurt am Main: Lucas Jennis, 1625, pp. 74-87; Greverus, Iodocus. "Secretum Nobilissimum et Verissimum." In *Theatrum Chemicum*. Ursel: Zetzner, 1602, pp. 783-810; also the "Physica Naturali Rotunda" in *Aperta Arca Arcani Artificiosissimi*. Frankfurt am Main: Johan Carl Unckel, 1617, pp. 117 ff. These allegories follow the dream-vision formula of Zosimos and the *Poimandres*.

Grasshoff's *Parabola*, which was no doubt interpreted as a tale of spiritual initiation amongst the adherents of the later *Gold- und Rosenkreutz* and their Freemasonic brethren.

Nevertheless, we would be mistaken if we were to imagine that the origins of spiritual alchemy can only be traced to the late eighteenth century, or to the work of nineteenth century occultists as Principe and Newman suggest. If we were to do so, we would not have reckoned with the work of Maier, a laboratory worker who played an influential role in the early Rosicrucian milieu and who has been described as "the boldest and most consistent of the alchemists of the German Renaissance."[130] Of particular importance in this regard is his *Allegoria Bella*, which after its initial appearance in 1617 was reprinted in Latin in 1678 and 1749, and in English in Waite's translation of 1893.[131] Whilst Principe and Newman have – with some justification – characterised Waite's translations of alchemical texts as "adulterated by the addition of occultist elements and slants completely alien to the originals," it must be said that Waite's version of Maier's allegory compares favourably with the Latin original, being a slightly abridged but thematically accurate depiction of a work that reveals the essentials of Maier's spiritual alchemy. Needless to say, when dealing with Maier's works in the following treatise there will be no recourse to the translations of other writers, adulterated or otherwise; indeed, analyses of certain of Maier's works appear here in print for the first time. The second document of central importance to the issue of Maier's spiritual alchemy is his autobiography, which constitutes the first chapter of the *De Medicina Regia* (1609) recently uncovered by Figala and Neumann at the Royal Library in Copenhagen.[132] As Maier's alchemy is intimately bound up with his biography, and with the pilgrimage that he considered his earthly life to be, the autobiographical elements of the *Medicina Regia* and other contemporary biographical sources will provide the organisational structure for the following exploration of Maier's alchemy. This juxtaposition of biography and doctrine not only enables us to build an accurate account of the evolution of Maier's thought over time, but also provides a depiction of Maier's alchemy of which he himself would have

---

[130] Figala, Karin. "Die Exakte Alchemie von Isaac Newton." In *Verhandlungen der Naturforschenden Gesellschaft in Basel*. Vol. 94. Basel: Birkhäuser Verlag, 1983, p. 190.

[131] Maier, *Symbola Aureae Mensae*, pp. 561-607; reprinted as "Subtilis Allegoria super Secreta Chymiae." In *Museum Hermeticum Reformatum et Amplificatum*. Frankfurt am Main: Sande, 1678, pp. 701-740; *idem.*, in *Museum Hermeticum Reformatum et Amplificatum*. Frankfurt am Main: Sande, 1749, pp. 701-740; "A Subtle Allegory concerning the Secrets of Alchemy." In *The Hermetic Museum, Restored and Enlarged*. Trans. Arthur Edward Waite. London: J. Elliott and Co., 1893, pp. 199-233.

[132] Maier, Michael. *De Medicina Regia et vere heroica, Coelidonia*. Copenhagen, Royal Library, 12,-159, 4°. Published in Prague, 1609.

approved – for the testimony of Maier's own writings show that, in an important sense, his life *was* his work.

In summary, the aim of the following work is to reconstruct the worldview of Maier through a sensitive, non-reductionist approach to the historical data, and to avoid violating the texts at hand by projecting contemporary categories into another time and place. On this count, it must be said that the hermeneutic paradigm utilised by Principe and Newman in their 'translation' of alchemical symbolism into contemporary chemical process is alien to the spirit of the early modern perspective.[133] Although these authors correctly state that the theosophical alchemy of Jacob Boehme – who was not personally concerned with laboratory process – is of 'a different order' to the experimental outlook of an author such as Basil Valentine, Principe and Newman anachronistically sequester religious and magical elements from their portrait of the worldview of the early modern laboratory worker:

> Although the works of many alchemical writers contain (often extensive) expressions of period piety, imprecations to God, exhortations to morality, and even the occasional appearance of an angelic or spiritual messenger, we find no indication that the vast majority of alchemists were working on anything other than material substances towards material goals... This is not to say that there was nothing whatsoever in the broad spectrum of historical alchemy which was akin to a 'spiritual alchemy'... But Boehme's use of alchemical language and imagery – as extensive as it is – remains clearly of a different order than, for example, the practical and theoretical antimonial exercises of Basil Valentine, Alexander von Suchten, Eirenaeus Philalethes and others, or the rigorous Scholastic alchemy of "Geber," Albert the Great, Petrus Bonus, or Gaston Duclo.[134]

Whilst Principe and Newman make brief mention of the fact that the thought of Heinrich Khunrath and 'the Rosicrucian enthusiast', Robert Fludd, persisted amongst 'secret societies', the developmental continuity of Western esotericism is summarily dismissed on the grounds that, in the hands of such societies, "alchemical works deliberately written to be obscure and secretive in their own age sometimes became meaningless in the next."[135] Of course, the historian of esotericism cannot accept that the use of alchemical symbolism within Rosicrucian or Freemasonic circles was 'meaningless'; rather, it was drawn directly from the work of early modern alchemists such as Count Michael Maier – who did in fact replicate the 'antimonial exercises' of Basil Valentine in his laboratory practice. Spiritual alchemy is a natural extension of the theory of microcosmic-macrocosmic correspondence, and the notion of a vital spirit animating humans, animals, vegetables and

---

[133] See in particular Newman, "*Decknamen* or Pseudochemical Language?," pp. 175-185.

[134] Principe and Newman, "Some Problems with the Historiography of Alchemy," pp. 397-399.

[135] *Ibid.*, p. 387.

minerals alike – regardless if such vitalism is the defining feature of alchemy, as Metzger believed. When considering the worldview of the early modern laboratory worker – and even such influential figures in the development of modern chemistry as Newton and Boerhaave, who both retained vitalistic conceptions alongside their mechanistic innovations – nothing has been said when we assert that most early modern alchemists worked on "material substances towards material goals." Such an assertion merely begs the question as to the nature of matter itself in the early modern worldview, and displays precisely the presentism and positivism Principe and Newman claim to disown, by which contemporary notions of matter are unconsciously elevated to the realm of the definitive. It is surely more pertinent to inquire into the nature of materiality and the scope of chemical law in the eyes of the early modern alchemist, rather than counterposing a narrowly 'chemical' hermeneutic with a psychological model such as that proposed by Jung.

In our conclusion we shall return to the questions of methodology, historiography and nomenclature we have dealt with here. For now, let us immerse ourselves in the world and natural magic of Count Michael Maier, an influential writer on the nature of alchemical *Decknamen* and a purveyor of spiritual alchemy, Rosicrucianism and pseudo-Egyptianism to later esoteric thinkers. In so doing we will uncover the four key elements of his alchemy: a doctrine of solar and astral influence; a 'chemical' interpretation of Greek and Egyptian mythology; a 'medicine of piety'; and a Hermetic theory of correspondence, in which the alchemist's spiritual life mirrors laboratory process.

II. Maier's formative years

1. The context of Maier's life and thought

Count Michael Maier, one-time physician to Emperor Rudolf II, was born in the summer of 1569 in the vicinity of Kiel in staunchly Lutheran Holstein, which at that time was an ethnically German province of Denmark on the northern border of the Holy Roman Empire or *Deutsches Reich*.[1] The greater part of his life spans an uneasy lull in the extensive religious and political hostilities engendered in the heart of Europe by the Reformation; it is against this broad historical background that his life and thought should be understood. The freedoms granted by the Peace of Augsburg (1555) had not been extended to the followers of Calvin and Zwingli, and the formation of the Union for the Defence of Protestant Religion in 1608 by the German Calvinist princes and their allies amongst the Lutheran states set the stage for the fratricidal maelstrom of the Thirty Years War (1618-1648). The interests of Rudolf II lay more in uncovering arcana than attending to affairs of state, and under his relatively tolerant reign humanist scholars such as Maier, be they Protestant or Catholic, still formed "a single body of cosmopolitan scholars" at the imperial court in Prague.[2] Nevertheless, amidst the climate of growing religious antagonism following the fall of Rudolf in 1612 Maier gravitated towards the patronage of the Calvinist princes of Germany. On the eve of war he gained a position at the court of Moritz 'the Learned' of Hessen-Kassel, a close ally of the Calvinist Elector of the Rhineland Palatinate, Friedrich V, and a supporter of his plans to wrest the imperial throne from the Spanish-Austrian house of Habsburg.

Moritz was the leading patron of the occult arts in the German states, and a formidable humanist scholar; his promotion of experimental sciences such

---

[1]   Prior to Figala and Neumann's discovery of the *De Medicina Regia*, to which we will soon refer, Maier's date of birth was given as 1568, on the authority of Matthew Merian's copperplate illustration printed in Maier's *Symbola Aureae Mensae* (1617) and *Atalanta Fugiens* (1617). See Figala, Karin and Neumann, Ulrich. "'Author cui Nomen Hermes Malavici': New Light on the Bio-Bibliography of Michael Maier (1569-1622)." In Rattansi, Piyo and Antonio Clericuzio (eds.). *Alchemy and Chemistry in the 16th and 17th Centuries*. Dordrecht: Kluwer Academic Publishers, 1994, pp. 124, 141 n.20.

[2]   Evans, R. J. W. *Rudolf II and his World: A Study in Intellectual History, 1576-1612*. Oxford: Oxford University Press, 1973, p. 3.

as alchemy was not only an important means of displaying the prestige and power of his court, but also reflected the hope of making technological advances that might grant him the upper hand in his struggle against the Habsburgs and the Catholic states of the fragmented empire.[3] Alchemy in particular promised the development of new techniques for the manipulation of metals (the debasement of coinage through alloying practices caused severe inflation in Hessen-Kassel prior to the war), and the procurement of new medicines by courtiers such as Maier might bolster the health of the aristocracy, if not the state as a whole. Furthermore, within the Calvinist aegis in Germany the Hermetic arts formed something of an intellectual counterculture to the Scholasticism propagated by the Jesuits – a counterculture focussed on an ostensible secret society, the Brotherhood of the Rosy Cross, and the literature of its supporters, amongst whom Maier figured prominently. Whilst orthodox Lutheran and Calvinist theologians railed against the occult sciences, which had as their goal the harnessing of secret and divine powers in Nature, early Rosicrucianism offered a potent mixture of heterodox Protestantism, Paracelsianism, and the millennialist dream of a new age in which the sciences would be perfected and 'papism' would be banished from the empire.

The rise of Rosicrucianism in Protestant Germany reflected a nascent German nationalism and indigenous 'German' preoccupations in culture; thus we find the oft-repeated parallel drawn in the Rosicrucian literature between Luther, the reformer of theology, and Paracelsus, the liberator of medicine from its corrupted Scholastic or 'papal' state. From the twin sources of Protestantism and Paracelsianism there emerged in sixteenth century Germany a striving for a new synthesis in science and religion, a wisdom derived from both divine revelation and the Light of Nature.[4] This synthesis was expressed on the one hand by early theosophers such as Valentin Weigel (1533-1588) and Jacob Boehme (1575-1624), and on the other by laboratory-bound alchemists such as Heinrich Khunrath (c.1560-1605) and Oswald Croll (c.1560-1608, a man who considered Weigel to be "the true successor of Paracelsus"); as the first Rosicrucian manifesto, the *Fama Fraternitatis* (c.1610), stated, "it should not be said that something is true according to

---

[3]   Moran, *Alchemical World of the German Court*, pp. 171, 174-175.

[4]   The 'Light of Nature' is a term utilised by Paracelsus to refer to a principle that both constitutes and penetrates Nature, or a principle standing 'behind Nature' whereby the constitution of humans and things in the world is made meaningful; alongside this principle Croll placed the 'Light of Grace', or the principle of divine illumination: Pagel, Walter. *Paracelsus: An Introduction to Philosophical Medicine in the Era of the Renaissance*. Basel: Karger, 1982, pp. 356-357; Gilly, Carlos. *Cimelia Rhodostaurotica: Die Rosenkreuzer im Spiegel der zwischen 1610 und 1660 entstandenen Handschriften und Drucke*. Ausstellung der Bibliotheca Philosophica Hermetica Amsterdam und der Herzog August Bibliothek Wolfenbüttel. Amsterdam: In de Pelikaan, 1995, p. 17.

philosophy, but false according to theology."[5] Alchemists and theosophers
alike sought to demonstrate the complementarity of the Bible and the 'Book
of Nature', and differed only in their emphasis on the one or the other.

Whilst Maier once spoke nationalistically of Germany as a 'new Egypt',
in deference to the land he believed to be the ultimate source of the
pristine knowledge inherited by the Germanic peoples,[6] it is to the Italian
Renaissance that we must look for the doctrinal roots of the amalgamation of
Neoplatonic, Hermetic and gnostic ideas in the German late Renaissance –
and in particular to the work of Marsilio Ficino (1433-1499).[7] A central
figure in the Florentine revival of Platonism and Hermeticism, Ficino
translated the recently discovered *Corpus Hermeticum* into Latin, and revived
the Greek conception of 'Egyptian Hermes' as the great sage of the Egyptians
and contemporary of Moses.[8] Revered by alchemists as the founder of their
Art, Hermes Trismegistus or 'thrice-great Hermes' was the Greco-Egyptian
incarnation of Thoth, the Egyptian god of science and the inventor of the
hieroglyphs.[9] Following certain of the Church Fathers, Italian humanists such
as Ficino saw the foreshadowing of Christianity in the texts attributed to
Hermes, and identified therein the presence of a *philosophia perennis* (the
'perennial philosophy') or *prisca sapientia* granted directly by God to the
ancients.[10] Through Ficino's misdating of the Hermetic treatises and their
Neoplatonic contents, Hermes Trismegistus also came to be seen as the
primeval source of Platonism.[11]

Maier was the chief exponent of the *prisca sapientia* doctrine amongst
the early modern German alchemists; his work also draws from Italian
Renaissance conceptions of *magia naturalis* or natural magic, which Ficino
defined as the "implanting of heavenly things in earthly objects" by the
philosopher, "who we are wont rightly to call a magician."[12] On this subject

---

[5]   Gilly, *Cimelia Rhodostaurotica*, p. 17; Faivre, *Access to Western Esotericism*, pp. 24-25,
      65-66.
[6]   Maier, Michael. *Verum Inventum, hoc est, Munera Germaniae*... Frankfurt am Main:
      Lucas Jennis, 1619, p. 214: "Si quid igitur utilitatis ex Chymiatria et Paracelsicis
      remediis ad Rempubl. perveniat, id veluti VERUM INVENTUM Germaniae acceptum
      referatur, quae, ut olim Aegyptus, artium est inventrix et ingeniorum mater."
[7]   Pagel, *Paracelsus*, pp. 35 ff.
[8]   Iversen, Erik. *The Myth of Egypt and its Hieroglyphs in European Tradition*. Princeton:
      Princeton University Press, 1993, p. 42.
[9]   *Ibid.*; a reference to Hermes on the Rosetta Stone (195 BCE), the inscription that allowed
      the eventual discovery in the early nineteenth century of the true import of hieroglyphs,
      applies to him the epithet 'Great, Great, Great'.
[10] Faivre, *Access to Western Esotericism*, p. 58.
[11] Schmitt, Charles B. (ed.). *The Cambridge History of Renaissance Philosophy*. Cam-
      bridge: Cambridge University Press, 1992, p. 275.
[12] *Ibid.*, p. 274.

Maier drew directly from his older contemporary, Giambattista della Porta (1535-1615), who developed the threefold division of magic as either diabolic, natural or divine. To a good Lutheran such as Maier, natural magic was simply the application of a deep knowledge of the occult sympathies present in Nature; thus he once described the legendary *Liber M.* of the Rosicrucian Fraternity as "the book of the world (*liber mundi*), or the book of natural magic."[13] The theory of sympathies and correspondences existing between the sub-lunary earth and the celestial spheres was central to Maier's quest for the Universal Medicine, and like his Italian Renaissance predecessors, astrology and the manipulation of astral influences played an integral role in his work.

The antique doctrine of macrocosmic-microcosmic correspondence, drawn from medieval alchemical works such as the *Tabula Smaragdina* of Hermes Trismegistus and mediated by Renaissance Neoplatonism, forms the foundation of Maier's spiritual alchemy, in which the life of the soul is understood to correspond to the processes in the alchemical vessel by virtue of universal 'chemical' laws or patterns. These laws are the 'signatures' in Nature pointing towards her divine origins, or as Maier puts it, the *insignia impressa*.[14] The integral relation Maier perceived between his own life and the *magnum opus* he strove to complete may be discerned from the tale of a certain augury of fortune appearing at the time of his birth, which we shall now proceed to relate.

2. Auguries of fortune: Maier's childhood and parentage

Michael Maier's father was a *Goldsticker* (gold embroiderer) by the name of Peter who served the Danish royalty and nobility, including King Friedrich II of Denmark (1559-1588) and the governor of all Schleswig-Holstein, Heinrich Rantzau (1526-1598; see figure 3).[15] A powerful noble and patron

---

13   Maier, *Symbola Aureae Mensae*, p. 294: "Per librum M librum mundi seu rerum in mundo existentium, earumque proprietatum, aut Magiae naturalis, intelligo."

14   Maier, Michael. *Silentium post Clamores*. Frankfurt am Main: Lucas Jennis, 1617, p. 18.

15   The King of Denmark is mentioned as a patron of Peter Meier (an alternative form of the family name utilised by Maier prior to 1611) in the dedication of Maier's *Cantilenae Intellectuales* (1622), which is directed to the grandson of King Friedrich II, Duke Friedrich III of Schleswig-Holstein-Gottorf: "Meos autem, qui qualesque fuerint, non solum tota Nobilitas Holsata, sed et parens tuus, avusque Divae memoriae, quibus illi, quoad vixerunt, servitio fidelissimo astricti fuerunt, optime noverunt." That this is a reference to the maternal rather than paternal grandfather of Friedrich is suggested by Maier's visit to the 'royal court' at the age of 17 (see n. 75 below); on Duke Friedrich III see the *Neue Deutsche Biographie*. Vol. 5. Berlin: Duncker und Humblot, 1961, pp. 583-584. According to Figala and Neumann, "it is very likely that Peter Meier may be

of the arts, it seems Rantzau entrusted Peter Maier with the brocade-work on the dresses of his daughters, upon whom he lavished precious gifts of gold and silver.[16] Peter Maier's professional concern with gold – the most noble of metals, and a symbol of divine and kingly power – was a portent of things to come for his son. However, he was not content that Michael should learn his own handicraft, which although it had proved lucrative for his family, was nevertheless a manual labour and lacked the prestige of an educated scientific or scholarly profession (which could provide opportunities for social advancement into the nobility).[17] In order to prepare his son for a higher calling, Peter had him educated in the literary arts from the tender age of five.[18] The trajectory Maier's life took at this early stage was to reach its zenith in his appointment as personal physician to the Holy Roman Emperor, and his entrance into the ranks of the hereditary peerage as a Count Palatine or *Pfalzgraf*. However, his was by no means an easy passage to success – and as we shall see in the following pages, it was a success that was to be somewhat transient.

In the course of his work Maier makes a number of autobiographical references that display a degree of reflection on his familial background and career, and offer a glimpse into the foundations of his identity. The most important of these references occur in the *De Medicina Regia* ('On the Royal Medicine,' 1609).[19] The first chapter of this document appears to constitute,

---

identified with one *Peter Perlsticker*, whose widow Anna in 1587 owned a house in the Kehdenstraße in Kiel;" Figala and Neumann, "Author cui Nomen Hermes Malavici," p. 124.

[16] Steinmetz, Wiebke. *Heinrich Rantzau (1526-1598): Ein Vertreter des Humanismus in Nordeuropa und seine Wirkungen als Förderer der Künste.* Frankfurt am Main: Peter Lang, 1991, pp. 274-275.

[17] Beck, Wolfgang. *Michael Maiers Examen Fucorum Pseudo-chymicorum – Eine Schrift wider die falschen Alchemisten.* Doctoral thesis, Zentralinstitut für Geschichte der Technik der Technischen Universität München, 1992, p. 3.

[18] Hubicki's assertion that Maier's studies were financed by Severin Goebel (1530-1612), a well-known physician of Gdansk and Königsberg, are at odds with Maier's own testimony in the *De Medicina Regia*, and seem to derive from a confusion between two different Michael Maiers; see Hubicki, "Maier, Michael," p. 23; Figala and Neumann, "Author cui Nomen Hermes Malavici," p. 125. Indeed, the number of errors in Hubicki's account of Maier's life – even if they are derived from the only sources available to him at the time – must cast a shadow over all his assertions. We need only mention Hubicki's employment of the perennial myth of Maier's association with Robert Fludd, which was refuted as early as 1924 by Arthur Waite (see above, chapter I, n. 109), or his unsubstantiated suggestion that Maier 'had a hand' in the publication of the *Fama Fraternitatis* (which, contrary to Hubicki, was first published in 1614). Consequently I have proceeded with caution with Hubicki's testimony in the current work, and have used the well-documented and up-to-date findings of Figala and Neumann as my major secondary source.

[19] See above, chapter I, n. 132.

in effect, a petition for the Emperor's service in the form of a *curriculum vitae* – for Maier was well-versed in the art of tailoring his publications to suit the predilections of potential patrons, and it seems unlikely that its appearance in Prague in a limited print-run was coincidental to his entrance into the Emperor's service some short months later. In the *De Medicina Regia* Maier makes mention of a certain augury presaging his birth – an augury that draws an intriguing parallel between his life and the alchemical process. After demonstrating his acquaintance with the production of the Mercury of the Philosophers – an indication he had reached the 'white' phase of the work[20] – Maier goes on to describe the strange experience of his mother when she was heavy with child:

Indeed, from the reports of my mother I suspect some sign of augury once came to pass, if faith can be held in this kind of prophesying; because I was told that three days before I was born, my mother was sojourning for the sake of her peace of mind with another relative of mine in the countryside during the summer. As the relative went away for some time, my mother sat down in the grass, whereupon a dove flew into her lap, I know not why or by which instinct; and she, marvelling at its beauty and tameness, tried to catch it, at which point it withdrew and flew away. Although this event may have come to pass by chance, to many it appeared to be a good omen. As for me, I feel indifferently about it – unless I will be provided a better destiny by God, to whom alone is due honour to all eternity.[21]

The dove is a standard alchemical motif, relating the Christian symbolism of a divine power linking heaven and earth to the *spiritus* ascending and descending within the vessel during the cyclical, purifying process of distillation – hence Maier precedes the tale of his augury with a description of the preparation of the Philosophical Mercury, which entails repeatedly "taking a bird from its nest and placing it back again."[22] The medieval alchemists had drawn this motif from the traditional representation of the Holy Spirit as a dove, most commonly depicted in medieval iconology at the baptism of Christ or the impregnation of Mary by the divine seminal

---

20 See below, p. 66.

21 *Ibid.*, p. Ci, *verso*: "Tum demum augurii de me olim concepti ex relatione materna, signum aliquod suspexi, si quid eiusmodi conjecturis, fidei adhibendum sit: Nam triduo antequam in lucem editus dicar, mater in aestate una cum parente meo animi gratia rus expaciatur, cumque ille longius secederet, haec in gramine consedit: En nescio unde aut quo instinctu, turtur matri sedenti in gremium advolat, cuius pulchritudinem ac cicuritatem dum admiraretur, eamque compraehendere tentaret, iterum se fuga subtraxit: Quae res etsi fortituito evenisse potuit, apud multos tamen locum praesagii non infelicis suppleret: Apud me indifferens fuerit, donec Deus de meliori forte prospiciat, cui soli erit laus in aeternum."

22 *Ibid.*: "Aves quoque EX NIDO sumpsi atque iterum in nidum posui, ut philosophi dicunt; hoc est, Sulfur philosophorum longe aliud, quam prius existimaram, ut vidi, agnovi, ut et Mercurium seu aquam mineralem, et ex his duobus, Mercurium Philosophorum."

principle. Here is an indication that Maier, although rarely commenting explicitly on this matter, believed himself to possess a special relationship with the subject of his alchemical work; furthermore, his employment of alchemical symbolism indicates a mode of thought at variance with the purely didactic use of Christian imagery in medieval alchemy described by Obrist. For in juxtaposing his strange tale of augury with an account of the operation of the transmuting or seminal principle, he likens the alchemical vessel to his own mother's womb, and hints at a correspondence between the alchemical process, his own life, and the myth of Christ.

On the point of his 'indifference' concerning the augury, we might expect Maier to dissemble in this manner after making such a seemingly extravagant claim, which may well have been employed as a strategy for finding favour in the eyes of the esoterically inclined Emperor. Nevertheless, there is every reason to believe that Maier was quite sincere in his personal convictions concerning his 'destiny', which, as he suggests in disclaiming the augury, was in need of some improvement at the leisure of God (by which we may also understand the leisure of the Emperor and his divine right). Maier's was without doubt a melancholic temperament, even if he was well aware whilst composing his *De Medicina Regia* that the greatest living exemplar of melancholy was the Emperor himself. The central expression of this temperament in Maier's works is his identification of worldly suffering with the *nigredo* or putrefactive phase of the alchemical process, upheld as indispensable to the Work by the medieval alchemists. In the *Allegoria Bella* ('Pleasant Allegory') appending his *Symbola Aureae Mensae*, Maier writes:

There is in our chemistry a splendid substance, which is passed from master to master, in the beginning of which there is misery with vinegar, but in the end of which there is truly joy with gladness. And so I imagined it would eventuate with me, that in the beginning I might taste much bitterness and endure much frustration, sadness and weariness, but at length I might find ease and happiness.[23]

What exactly was this 'splendid substance' of which Maier speaks? One day Maier would confide to his patron, Moritz of Hessen-Kassel, that the *materia* of the Art from which gold is born is 'Tusalmat'; a *Deckname* or code-name which, when deciphered with the cryptographic key divulged by Borelli in 1656, yields the term 'Saturnus'.[24] Saturn is the point of departure for both

---

[23] Maier, *Symbola Aureae Mensae*, p. 568: "Esse in Chemia nobile aliquod corpus, quod de domino ad dominum movetur, in cuius initio sit miseria cum aceto, in fine vero gaudium cum laeticia, ita et mihi eventurum praesupposui, ut primo multa aspera, amara, tristia, taediosa gustarem, perferrem et experirer, tandem omnia laetiora et faciliora visurus essem."

[24] Kassel, Gesamthochschul-Bibliothek, 2° MS Chem. 19, 1, p. 284 *recto*; Borelli, Petro. *Bibliotheca Chimica*. Heidelberg: Samuel Broun, 1656, p. 254.

the laboratory and spiritual aspects of Maier's alchemy, and as we shall see, it is Saturn which binds these two aspects together as an indivisible whole. The Arabic alchemists and their successors, following Harranian tradition, believed that the planet or 'star' Saturn governs the metal lead.[25] Thus in his *Atalanta Fugiens* (1617) Maier quotes the Arabic author 'Rhazes' (Abu Bakr Muhammad ibn Zakarīyā al-Rāzī, c.865-c.925) when he states that "the gates of knowledge are opened by Saturn," and that "lead is the father of all gentiles or those who love gold, and is the first gate of the arcana."[26] But in the humanist worldview of the early modern period Saturn was bound up with a wealth of associations and correspondences beyond the narrowly chemical. These associations, accrued over two millennia, cast some light on the significance for Maier of this 'gate of knowledge'. Since antiquity Saturn was considered to be the planet of old age, which on account of its slow revolution and its position as the furthest planet beneath the fixed stars had been associated by the Greeks with the deity Chronos – that is to say, Time.[27] From these earliest origins Chronos-Saturn had taken on a contradictory aspect, being both the father of gods and men and the devourer of his children, on the one hand 'a ruler of the nether gods' exiled beneath the earth, and on the other the ruler of the Golden Age and a god of fertility.[28] His representation with a scythe led to the medieval association of Saturn with Death as the Reaper.[29] But the correspondence that is most significant for an understanding of the overarching spirit governing Maier's alchemy is the ninth century Arabic association of the planet, on account of its dark colour, with the melancholy temperament.[30] On this account Ficino once wrote that

---

[25] According to that tradition, stemming from at least the sixth century BCE, Saturn governs lead; Jupiter, tin; Mars, iron; Venus, copper; Mercury, mercury; the Moon, silver; and the Sun, gold; Haage, *Alchemie im Mittelalter*, pp. 27, 203 n. 67.

[26] Maier, Michael. *Atalanta Fugiens, hoc est, Emblemata nova de secretis naturae chymica*. Oppenheim: Johann Theodor de Bry, 1617, discourse 22: "Saturnus omnium gentilium aut potius aureolorum pater est, et prima porta arcanorum: Cum hoc, inquit Rhasis in epist. aperiuntur portae scientiarum." The conception that lead is the 'father of all metals' can be traced to Greek authors in the first century CE; see Lippman, E. O. von. *Entstehung und Ausbreitung der Alchemie*. Hildesheim: G. Olms, 1978, p. 59.

[27] Klibansky, Raymond et. al. *Saturn and Melancholy: Studies in the History of Natural Philosophy, Religion and Art*. Nelson: London, 1964, pp. 136-137.

[28] According to Klibansky, the Roman association of Saturn – their god of agriculture – with Chronos confirmed a contradiction already inherent in the Greek deity; *ibid.*, pp. 134-135.

[29] *Ibid.*, pp. 185-186.

[30] *Ibid.*, p. 127. In Klibansky's words, "the polarity of the notion of Kronos led to two opposing basic attitudes... The Saturn to whom the lethargic and vulgar belonged was at the same time venerated as the planet of high contemplation, the star of anchorets and philosophers. Nevertheless, the nature and destiny of the man born under Saturn, even when, within the limits of his condition, his lot was the most fortunate, still retained a

Saturn "seldom denotes ordinary characters and destinies, but rather people set apart from the rest, divine or bestial, blissful, or bowed down by the deepest sorrow."[31]

The melancholic attitude was pervasive – one might even say fashionable – in the early modern period. In ideological terms, this popularity was derived from the humanist appropriation of the classics; for the pseudo-Aristotelian *Problema* XXX.1 (a tract probably written by Theophrast, a pupil of Aristotle) had associated the melancholic disposition with spiritual exaltation and divine genius, and not only tragic heroes but poets, philosophers and statesmen were believed to derive their greatness from melancholy.[32] With the conjunction of humanist learning and alchemical lore in the Renaissance, alchemists too were considered to hold a special relationship to melancholy: as the sixteenth century Italian alchemist Flavio Girolamo once asked, "why is it said that the age of Saturn was the age of gold, unless it is because gold is not procured except by melancholy and Saturnine contemplatives?"[33] The centrality of Saturn's place in Maier's alchemy was adopted by Newton, who similarly considered lead to be 'the mother of all metals'; but in his thought the term is largely divested of its psychological sense, which is to the fore in Maier's work. Maier depicts Saturn in the emblem from the *Symbola Aureae Mensae* that accompanied his *Allegoria Bella* in its later re-prints; there the alchemist demonstrates the metamorphosis of Saturn (lead), who tends to trees with flowers of gold and silver (figure 2).

If a certain aspect of Maier's life was in some way equivalent to alchemical putrefaction or the unpurified leaden state of the alchemical subject – as our quotation from the *Allegoria Bella* explicitly states – what exactly were the sources of the 'bitterness, frustration, sadness and weariness' that he alludes to in his writings? In the course of this work those sources will become evident as we consider the progress of Maier's career, and we will discover that his life was governed by a spirit of paradox in keeping with that central motif of the alchemical opus, the *coniunctio oppositorum*. For it was precisely his life-long toil to procure the Universal Medicine that formed the *nigredo* phase of Maier's spiritual alchemy.

---

basis of the sinister; and it is on the idea of a contrast, born of darkness, between the greatest possibilities of good and evil, that the most profound analogy between Saturn and melancholy was founded... Like melancholy, Saturn menaced those in his power, illustrious though they might be, with depression, or even madness." *Ibid.*, pp. 158-159.

31 *Ibid.*, p. 159.

32 *Ibid.*, pp. 15 ff.

33 Quoted in Brann, Noel. "Alchemy and Melancholy in Medieval and Renaissance Thought: A Query into the Mystical Basis of their Relationship," *Ambix*, Vol. 32, No. 3, 1985, p. 128.

In the pages of the *De Medicina Regia* Maier relates to the reader a number of hardships he has endured, all of which stem from his struggles to establish a career.[34] "The ascent is not easy, for those who seek the steep ways" – according to the verses that Maier quotes when introducing his educational qualifications in the *De Medicina Regia*, one must spend sleepless nights in toil (the Latin translates literally as "working oneself to death") in order to find eventual success.[35] It was this insomniac lifestyle that would later lead Maier to adopt the owl as the symbol of the alchemist and the true Rosicrucian, a fact which we shall explore further in our fourth chapter. Nevertheless, Maier tells us that he was filled with such ardour for learning as a child, that when his father sometimes threatened to dispatch him to 'another kind of profession' – i.e. the career of an artisan – he would burst into tears.[36] It was just this threat of sliding back towards the ranks of the uneducated masses – a threat that was ever-present in Maier's tenuous academic and professional existence – that played such a great role in generating the elitist occult mentality of Maier.

The young Maier's love of learning was such that he studied not only the usual Trivium at the district school (grammar, rhetoric and logic) but also music and the art of poetry.[37] He would later integrate these pursuits closely with his alchemical work; from the fugues of the *Atalanta Fugiens* to the triad verses of the *Cantilenae Intellectuales*, music and poetry would become a vehicle for Maier to express the universal harmony or 'chemical' order of the cosmos he perceived. Following the death of his father when Maier was only thirteen years of age, his mother took over the expenses of his education, and he spent two years at a 'more famous school', where he further cultivated his skills in Latin poetry.[38] Concerning the four years he spent from February of 1587 at the University of Rostock, where he studied physics, mathematics, logic and astronomy under Heinrich Bruchaeus,[39] Maier tells us that he

---

[34] Maier, *De Medicina Regia*, p. Ai *recto*.

[35] *Ibid.*, p. Ai *verso*: "Non levis ascensus, si quis petat ardua, sudor/ Plurimus hunc tollit, nocturnae insomnis olivae/ Immoritur, delet, quod mox lauda verat in se."

[36] *Ibid.*, p. Ai *recto*: "Postquam a quinto pueritiae anno cura paterna literis semel addicatus fuissem, tantum voluptatis etiam in primis earum radicibus, quae alias juventuti amarae sunt, hausi, ut si quando pater minitaretur, sese ad aliud officii genus me consecraturum, in lachrymas statim irrumperem."

[37] *Ibid.*

[38] *Ibid.*: "Anno aetatis 16 ad aliam Scholam celebriorem perrexi, in qua sumptibus maternis (nam pater ante biennium obierat) duos annos moratus, praeter alia, poesin uberius excolere caepi."

[39] Bruchaeus (1530-1593) was a professor of medicine and mathematics at the University of Rostock from 1567; he was 'the most significant personality' in the medical faculty there, and was wont to combine medical, astronomical, philosophical and physical theories in his works. That he was in all likelihood Maier's teacher is borne out by the

prefers not to relate the injuries inflicted upon him there by his harsh fortune. We are only told that he pushed himself through his course by means of his mental strength for as long as he was able.[40] These difficulties seem to have had some bearing on the fact that he returned home without a degree in 1591, a failure that Neumann and Figala suggest was occasioned by financial difficulties; for in a letter to Heinrich Rantzau dated the 18th of June, 1590, we find Maier recommending himself as a client for the patronage of his father's benefactor.

3. The influence of Governor Heinrich Rantzau

It is not clear whether Maier's bid for patronage was successful. His letter to Rantzau was written from his study-room at Rostock University, "in ward G of the College of Philosophy," more than six months prior to his undistinguished departure – a fact that indicates financial aid was forthcoming from some source.[41] We may also note that he had sufficient financial means to enter the University of Frankfurt an der Oder in 1592. Whatever the case may have been, it was the humanist climate fostered by Heinrich Rantzau that was decisive for the intellectual development of Maier, as Beck has asserted.[42] Indeed, regardless of the love Maier may have felt for his father, there is no doubt that Rantzau was his principle role model from an early age, being at once the power behind his father's wealth and an exemplar of the Lutheran humanist nobility to which Maier aspired. Rantzau had studied at the University of Wittenberg, boarding there at Luther's very house; he was both a patron of the arts and the author of numerous treatises on such diverse subjects as astrology, astronomy, medicine and economics, as well as the history and art of war.[43] Amongst those scholars whose careers he

---

fact that his *Institutiones spherae* (1584) is cited by Maier in the course of his *Septimana Philosophica*; Bruchaeus also taught at Rostock until the time of his death in 1593. See Krabbe, Otto. *Die Universität Rostock im Fünfzehnten und Sechzehnten Jahrhundert.* Vol. 1. Rostock: Adlers Erben, 1854, pp. 708-711; *Biographisches Lexikon der Hervorragenden Ärzte aller Zeiten und Völker.* Vol. 1. Berlin: Urban & Schwarzenberg, 1962, p. 727; *Biographie Universelle,* Vol. 6. Paris: L. G. Michaud, 1820, p. 70; Maier, Michael. *Septimana Philosophica.* Frankfurt am Main: Lucas Jennis, 1620, p. 8.

40 *Ibid.,* pp. Ai *recto*-Ai *verso*: "Deinde ad Academiam me conferens, bonas artes, quoad potui legendo, scribendo, exercendo, disputando, tracta vi per quadriennium: Quas interim fortunae novercantis injurias passus sim, satius erit, hoc loco silere, quam referre: Nam tum carminis illius, quod nunquam non in ore habui, veritatem experiebar."

41 *Ibid.,* p. 328.

42 Beck, *Michael Maiers Examen Fucorum Pseudo-chymicorum,* p. 3.

43 Hansen, Reimer. "Der Friedensplan Heinrich Rantzaus und die Irenik in der Zweiten Reformation." In Schilling, Heinz (ed.). *Die reformierte Konfessionalisierung in*

sustained was the famous Danish astronomer Tycho Brahe (1546-1601), a founder of the geo-heliocentric cosmology utilised by Maier.[44] The Rantzau family was closely associated with the Danish royal family; Heinrich's father Johann was a general of King Christian III (r.1536-1559), who gained the Danish throne with the benefit of Johann's military successes and established Lutheranism as the official state religion in 1536.[45] In subsequent decades the might of the Danish court and the relative stability of the lands under its power led to a steady growth in literary and scientific activity, a development in which Heinrich took up a central role.[46]

Maier's letter to Heinrich Rantzau, written in verse form and replete with classical allusions employed to extol the glory of his father's patron, reflects not only this impressive efflorescence of late Renaissance humanism in Danish Holstein, but constitutes the earliest example of Maier's deft hand with the courting of patrons. Drawing from Cicero and Ovid, Maier deals at length with the themes of fame and mortality:

...why should we undertake such labour in the course of life, which is so brief and insignificant? Certainly our mind, if it anticipates nothing of the future and keeps all thoughts within the boundaries with which the length of life is circumscribed, neither weakens itself with great distress nor lets itself be tormented by so much sleeplessness and trouble, nor struggles against life itself. But there lives within the best people a certain virtue, which drives on the mind day and night with the spur of fame, and warns that the memory of our name should not pass away with the end of life, but should be kept alive for all posterity.[47]

Although derived from a classical source and addressed to Rantzau, these words reflect something of Maier's own mindset, particularly in their pre-occupation with the subjects of hardship, restlessness and death; for the

---

Deutschland – Das Problem der "Zweiten Reformation". Gütersloh: Gerd Mohn, 1986, pp. 360-361.

[44]   The first edition of Brahe's *Astronomiae Instauratae Mechanica* (1598) was issued from Rantzau's castle in Wandsbek; see Hannaway, Owen. "Laboratory Design and the Aim of Science: Andreas Libavius versus Tycho Brahe," *Isis*, Vol. 77, 1986, p. 589.

[45]   Steinmetz, *Heinrich Rantzau*, pp. 24-25.

[46]   *Ibid.*, p. 17; Hansen, "Der Friedensplan Heinrich Rantzaus," p. 362.

[47]   Figala, Karin and Ulrich Neumann. "Ein Früher Brief Michael Maiers (1569-1622) an Heinrich Rantzau (1526-1598): Einführung, Lateinischer Originaltext und Deutsche Übersetzung," *Archives Internationales d'Histoire des Sciences*, Vol. 35, No. 114, 1985, p. 320: "...quid est quod in hoc tam exiguo vitae curriculo et tam brevi, tantis nos in laboribus exerceamus? Certe si nihil animus praesentiret in posterum, et si, quibus regionibus vitae spacium circumscriptum est, eisdem omnes cogitationes terminaret suas, nec tantis se laboribus frangeret neque tot curis vigiliisque angeretur, nec toties de vita ipsa dimicaret. Nunc insidet quaedam in optimo quoque virtus, quae noctes et dies animum gloriae stimulis concitat atque admonet, non cum vitae tempore esse dimit-tendam commemorationem nominis nostri, sed cum omni posteritate adaequandam." Drawn from Cicero, *Pro Archia*: see Figala and Neumann, *idem*.

vestiges of Maier's life and work repeatedly affirm that he too believed a nobler spirit must struggle with earthly existence. Maier again draws on Cicero when he states that fame is the highest reward for virtue, providing us with consolation in the face of death.[48] Those men who reach the heights of fame are, as it were, ascending into heaven; and it is Heinrich Rantzau, whose repute is like "a victory wreath stretching from the mountains of Crete to the Libyan Sea," who has ascended such heights that barely any man could climb higher.[49] Having flattered his would-be benefactor thus, Maier reminds Rantzau of the high regard he once held for his parents, and of the day he led the solemn funeral procession that carried his father Peter on his last journey through the city.[50] After such eloquent and undoubtedly heart-felt words, Rantzau would have found the brief plea for patronage which ends Maier's letter difficult to refuse, particularly given his own love for Latin verse composition.

In the course of his letter Maier also discloses the early sources of his fascination with Egypt, which would later be expressed in the strange Egyptology of his *Arcana Arcanissima*, and in his definitive binding of pseudo-Egyptian lore to early Rosicrucianism. In another adulatory passage, Maier states that Rantzau's love for his Fatherland is such that he has erected 'heaven-high' pyramids and obelisks to the greater glory of the state of Holstein.[51] This is a reference to Rantzau's penchant for the construction of 'Egyptian' monuments; for Rantzau partook in the Renaissance fascination with the religion of Egypt and its cult of the sun, however imperfectly they were known prior to the deciphering of hieroglyphics in the early nineteenth century. In 1578 he completed the construction of a pyramid on a hill in Nordroe, and in 1588 another was built in Segeberg, the administrative and geographical centre of Holstein where Peter Maier had been employed. These buildings not only symbolised the power and eternal fame of the Danish monarchy, but also gave expression to Rantzau's astrological pre-occupation with the nature of the sun's course.[52] Despite the 'Egyptomania' that swept

---

[48] *Ibid.*

[49] *Ibid.*, p. 322; the city of Gortis on Crete was the capital of the Roman province of Libya.

[50] *Ibid.*, p. 326: "Imprimis enim patrem meum, Petrum Meierum, phrygionem, civem chiloniensem filiarum tuarum vestibus acu pingendis Segebergae praefecisti, ubi etiam eo in opere vita defunctum, ipse funus ex oppido, solenni ritu una deduxisti et honorificentissime per subditos tuos Chilonium transvehi curasti."

[51] *Ibid.*, p. 322: "Incredibilem tuum erga patriam amorem declarant tot monumenta ad eius ornatum erecta, tot tantaeque pyramides caelo eductae, tot obelisci, tot tamque variae structurae, tot aedificia in Holsatiae urbibus splendidissime extructa."

[52] Steinmetz, *Heinrich Rantzau*, pp. 251 ff.; on one side of his pyramid at Nordroe, constructed in 1578, Rantzau placed a sun-dial in order to test the theory that the course of the sun might alter over many years; on the other side of the pyramid were the letters D·T·ET·U·S (Deo trino et uni sacrum).

Europe in the Renaissance and early modern period, such monuments were rare in the German-speaking lands of the sixteenth century, and they must have left a lasting impression on the young Michael Maier.[53] Significantly, Maier makes another appeal to Rantzau's Egyptological interests when he mentions in his letter that the Egyptians constructed a two-faced statue of 'Mercury', which depicted on one side a young man in his prime, and on the other a venerable man of ripe old age; according to Maier, their intention was to demonstrate that the bravery and energy of the *puer* must be joined with the wisdom of the *senex*, qualities that are indeed united in the person of Rantzau.[54] Here we have Maier's earliest reference to Mercury, and to the *coniunctio oppositorum* that would become a central element of his alchemical imagination.

4. Galenism and Maier's studies at Frankfurt an der Oder

Further sources of Maier's alchemical worldview – both ideological and experiential – are to be found in the records relating to his university education. The library of the Strahov monastery in Prague houses a copy of the *Theses Summam Doctrinae de Temperamentis Corporis Humani* Maier defended for his Master of Arts at Frankfurt an der Oder on June the 17th, 1592.[55] These theses concern the four temperaments and are purely Aristotelian and Galenic in character.[56] Although it was the custom in

---

[53] *Ibid.*

[54] Figala and Neumann, "Ein Früher Brief," pp. 322, 323 n. 22: Maier's reference is in fact to a Greco-Egyptian depiction of Hermes (Roman 'Mercury'), appropriated by the Romans in their depictions of the deity Janus.

[55] Fersius, Johannes. *Theses Summam doctrinae de Temperamentis Corporis humani breviter complexae, ad disputandum publice; Propositae a M. Iohanne Fersio Strelensis, de quibus iuvante Deo respondebit Michael Meierus Holsatus.* Frankfurt am Main: Sciurianis, 1592. These theses were independently uncovered by Figala and Neumann at around the same time as my own discovery of them, and formed the subject of a seminar by their student Bernhard Zagler at the Deutsches Museum, München, 14th of July 2000.

[56] Galen (130-199 CE), the personal physician to Emperor Marcus Aurelius, drew above all from the natural philosophy of Aristotle and the pre-Socratics in the construction of his physiology. In the course of its development from antiquity Galenism was modified many times, most significantly by the Arabic philosophers Avicenna and Averroes, who had a substantial influence on the Scholastic Galenism that dominated the medieval universities. Jean Fernel (1497-1558) systematised these various developments in his *Universa Medicina* (1544); in his work the complicated dualistic Galenic hierarchy of the rational, eternal soul and its subordinate organs, humours and elements continued to mirror the hierarchy of the medieval cosmos with its divine and angelic powers. In Maier's time Galenism was still a highly influential physiological system, despite the

Maier's time for students to give an oral defence and elaboration of the theses of their professor rather than to write an original work, this short tract reveals the basic natural philosophical conceptions underlying Maier's alchemy. The theses themselves are the work of Johannes Fersius (?-1611), a Catholic doctor of philosophy, theology and medicine.[57] Frankfurt an der Oder had been Lutheran since 1539, and in the late sixteenth century the university there was a well-known centre for German humanism,[58] with an attendant spirit of cross-confessional tolerance – a fact demonstrated by Fersius' authorship of a conciliatory tract commending the early Czech reformer Jan Huss.[59] Despite the fact that Maier's sympathies would undergo something of a transformation in the antagonistic religious climate leading up to the Thirty Years War, and that he would one day issue sharp invectives against the corrupt 'papal medicine', it seems that Fersius was an important early contributor to the overwhelmingly Aristotelian-Galenic elements of his medical theory.

The foundation of the Aristotelian-Galenic system is expressed in the first thesis of the *Theses Summam Doctrinae*, in which it is stated that the human body is composed of the four elements – earth, water, air and fire – and is subject to 'natural mutation'.[60] This is a reference to the fact that the human body partakes in the mutability of the elements, which according to the Aristotelian system are interchangeable by virtue of their common properties, earth being 'cold' and 'dry', water 'cold' and 'moist', air 'hot' and 'moist' and fire 'hot' and 'dry'.[61] Whilst the body is constructed 'artfully and methodically' from the elements by the work of Nature, the first thesis goes on to state that the body's gender and individuality are evidence of the "judgment of a most wise Architect" – an intimation that Nature is the

---

inroads made against Scholasticism by Paracelsus and his followers. For an account of these developments, see Fuchs, Thomas. *Die Mechanisierung des Herzens*. Frankfurt am Main: Suhrkamp, 1992, pp. 29-39.

[57] Jöcher, Christian Gottlieb. *Allgemeines Gelehrten-Lexicon*. Vol. 2. Leipzig: Gleditsch, 1750, p. 587.

[58] Figala and Neumann, "Michael Maier," p. 37.

[59] Fersius, Johannes. *Commendatio Martyrii Beatorum Martyrum Ioannis Hussi et Hieronymi Pragensis*. Wittemberg: Johannes Cratonis, 1586.

[60] Thesis I: "Corporis humani compages mutationibus naturalibus obnoxia, naturae opificio e quatuor simplicissimorum corporum substantiis ea arte ac ratione constructa est, quae et huic generi, et singulis eius individuis sapientissimi Architecti iudicio convenire visa est, secundum quam vires illorum primordiorum permixtas varios efficaciae suae gradus obtinere, partim iudicio assequimur, partim sensu ipso experimur."

[61] The cyclical transmutation of elements is described in detail by Aristotle in his *De Generatione et Corruptione*, which formed the foundation of medieval alchemical laboratory practice: Aristotle, *De Generatione et Corruptione*, II 3-4. For a discussion of Aristotle's schema as it relates to alchemy, see Holmyard, E. J. *Alchemy*. Harmondsworth: Penguin Books, 1957, pp. 19-22.

assistant or 'handmaiden' of God, a pervasive conception in the alchemical
corpus which Maier was to study. The four fluids or 'humours' circulating in
the human body correspond to the four elements – cold and dry 'black bile',
cold and moist phlegm, hot and moist blood, and hot, dry 'yellow bile'.[62]
According to the third thesis, states of health (temperance) and disease
(intemperance) correspond to a balance and imbalance of humours in the
human body; for example, the melancholic fever or quartan which would
afflict Maier in his later life was the result of the dominance of black bile.[63]
In their turn, the four elements and their properties correspond to various
other phenomena in the stratified cosmos, such as the seasons, geographical
locations and stages of life, which also hold sway on the temperance or
intemperance of the human body. The traditional medieval system of
correspondences,[64] although admitting to some variations, may be illustrated
in the following way:

element	air	fire	earth	water
properties	warm, moist	warm, dry	cold, dry	cold, moist
colour	red	yellow	black	white
humour	blood	yellow bile	black bile	phlegm
temperament	sanguine	choleric	melancholic	phlegmatic
stage of life	childhood	prime	decline	old age
season	spring	summer	autumn	winter
region	south	east	north	west

Fersius' work differs from these correspondences in minor respects. Thus
the theses suggest that childhood is dominated by the sanguine humour,
blood, and is the 'spring' of life; youth is dominated by yellow bile, being
predisposed to anger; middle age is a temperate or balanced time; and old
age is cold and dry, corresponding to black bile or melancholy.[65] Although
certain regions of the earth may possess particular properties, the east is
generally warm and dry, the west is cold and moist, the south is warm and

---

62 The key text on this matter is Galen's *De Naturalibus Facultatibus*; see Fuchs, *Die
    Mechanisierung des Herzens*, p. 217.

63 Thesis III: "Proinde cum excessus et defectus medii cuiusdam respectu dicantur: duae
    erunt temperamentorum species: Temperatum et Intemperatum. Temperatum quidem, in
    quo qualitatum primarum omnium par est robur, nec ulla aliam superat: Intemperatum
    vero, in quo quaedam superant, quaedam superantur."

64 For a detailed discussion of this system of correspondences and its development in the
    classical and medieval periods, see Klibansky, *Saturn and Melancholy*.

65 Thesis IX: "Aetas puerorum et adolescentum calida et humida est: florida aetas, calida et
    sicca: matura, temperata: senectus, frigida et sicca." On this variation in the age
    apportioned to melancholy, see Klibansky, *ibid.*, p. 10.

moist, the north is cold and dry.[66] We are told that such factors of location, age and season must be taken into account in the course of diagnosis, which is to be carried out by means of the senses through the temperate doctor's touch, as well as through a more exacting judgment and reasoning.[67] The wording of the sixth thesis suggests that Maier was required to expound at length on this use of judgment, and to supply case examples supporting his assertions.[68]

There are a number of specific points in the theses that bear upon Maier's later alchemical practice. Most noteworthy is their mention of the influence on the human body of the fixed stars, and of the 'moving stars' or planets, which by virtue of their rays and position in the Zodiac preserve particular qualities in the sensitive body of the child at the moment of birth.[69] Astrology played a significant role in Maier's laboratory experiments, as he believed that certain operations must be carried out at propitious times, in order to utilise the influence of the planets' virtue-imparting rays on the alchemical subject. We may note that the theory of astral influence, although commonplace in medieval and early modern natural philosophy, lay in opposition to the thought of Maier's teacher at Rostock – for Bruchaeus resolutely rejected the idea on the grounds that it negated free will, making human beings into slaves of the heavens and unanswerable for their conduct.[70]

Another basic component of Maier's medical worldview mentioned in the theses is the influence of food and drink on human temperament, which together with the seasons, geographical location and air temperature are the major non-constitutional factors impinging on the development of the human body. According to the nineteenth thesis, the liver 'cooks' incoming substances "in order that warm food may beget warmer blood, and cold food

---

66 Thesis XIII: "Regionum autem, praeterquam quod quaelibet peculiares quasdam obtinet proprietates, Orientalis, calida sicca, Occidentalis frigida humida, meridionalis calida humida, septentrionalis frigida sicca censetur."

67 Thesis V: "Earum vero temperatura iudicio potius, compositionem ipsarum considerante, quam tactu deprehenditur. E contrario autem de totius corporis temperamento tactus manus hominis temperati facile decernit: iudicium vero ratiocinando non prorsus aeque facile."

68 Thesis VI: "Argumenta huiusmodi ratiocinationis suppeditant caussae, effectus, et quaedam adiuncta."

69 Thesis VIII: "Universalis est motus coelestis, vel astrorum positus ad momentum nativitatis. Etenim Luminare utrumque, eorumque et Horoscopi signum, et his radio partili addicti Planetae qualitatum primarum virtutem obtinent, quas in tenello infantuli corpusculo excitant."

70 Heidorn, Günter. *Geschichte der Universität Rostock 1419-1969: Festschrift zur Fünfhundertfünfzig-Jahr-Feier der Universität*. Vol. I. Berlin: Deutscher Verlag der Wissenschaften, 1969, p. 41.

colder blood."[71] In the Galenic system it is the *calor innatus* ('innate heat') indwelling in the body that allows first the stomach and then the liver to 'cook' the elemental properties of food and drink in this way, so transforming them into the *spiritus vegetalis* carried by venous blood, which then courses from the liver to the corporeal peripheries.[72] In like manner the heart produces the subtler *spiritus vitalis*, spreading warmth and vitality to the body via the arterial system; and the brain produces the most subtle *spiritus animalis*, which streams through the nerves (considered by the Galenists to be hollow) and imparts sensitivity and motion to the sense organs and muscles.[73] The fundamental driving force in this vitalistic schema remains the *calor innatus*, and its seat is the heart, which is the central organ of the human body; to the extent that it is the source of human vitality, the heart corresponds to the cosmic seat of warmth and life, the sun.[74] As we shall discover when considering Maier's *De Circulo Physico, Quadrato* (1616), these ancient conceptions of innate heat and the influence of food and drink on temperament, when coupled with the alchemical conception of the sun's special relation to gold, would form the theoretical foundations of Maier's 'mercurial medicine' – the temperance-imparting medicine *par excellence*.

In the *De Medicina Regia*, Maier tells us that during the year following the receipt of his Masters degree at Frankfurt an der Oder, he "entered the royal court (*aulam Caesareum*)," which appears to be a reference to the court of Christian IV (r.1588-1648), King of Denmark. This can be deduced from the fact that Maier tells us he had visited this same court at the age of seventeen, which would have been during the last years of the reign of Christian's father Friedrich II (r.1559-1588) – a patron of Maier's father.[75] It also seems likely that the connections Maier made during this second visit to the royal court bore some important fruit.[76] Following this visit he underwent practical

---

[71] Thesis XIX: "Etsi enim humores suam a cibo et potu sortiuntur temperaturam: tamen epatis coquentis calore variantur, ita, ut ex eodem cibo calidus calidiorem sanguinem, frigidus frigidiorem generet."

[72] Thus the Galenic model depicted a centrifugal motion of blood; it was the discovery of the circulation of blood by Harvey in 1628 which was a central factor in the downfall of the Aristotelian-Galenic paradigm. Fuchs, *Die Mechanisierung des Herzens*, p. 37.

[73] *Ibid.*, p. 36.

[74] The centrality of the heart as the *arche* of the body and its relation in the macrocosm to the sun is a conception stemming from Aristotle which was later taken up by the Stoics; see Pagel, *William Harvey's Biological Ideas*, pp. 25, 81.

[75] Maier, *De Medicina Regia*, p. Ai *verso*: "In qua cum ex amicorum suasu, Anno aetatis 24. Magisterii gradum recepissem, publiceque aliquoties disputassem, post annum domum ad officium aliquod subeundum redii: Prius tamen in aulam Caesaream, ubi tum ante sexennium quoque fuissem, commigravi..."

[76] Such is suggested by the fact that the 'period of service' Maier undertook on his return from Frankfurt an der Oder to which he refers in his *De Medicina Regia* took place after his 'entrance' into the *aulam caesaream*; see previous note.

medical training with Matthias Carnarius (?-1620), who since 1591 had been a personal physician to Duke Johann Adolf of Schleswig-Holstein-Gottorf, a son of King Friedrich II who also had connections with Maier's family.[77] This period of training was of three years duration, commencing when Maier was twenty-three years of age. Although Figala and Neumann suggest that Carnarius took "a fatherly interest" in his trainee,[78] Maier would later describe Carnarius as his most intimate friend, being bound to him by 'soul, study, and Fatherland': terms of endearment that suggest Carnarius, although some ten years his senior, enjoyed a less formal and more confiding relationship with Maier.[79] By all accounts Carnarius was a very successful man, who bequeathed to his heirs not only a large library of medical works but also a considerable sum of money. His true family name was de Vleeschouwer; his father Johannes was from Gent, the centre of early Calvinism in Europe, and had also attended the duke of Schleswig-Holstein-Gottorf as personal physician after serving as a Professor of Medicine at Padua University.[80]

During this period of training under Carnarius, Maier tells us he could not resist carrying out certain chemical experiments, including the hardening of mercury with 'smoke of lead', and a failed attempt to 'yellow' silver with a tincture.[81] At the universities of Rostock and Frankfurt an der Oder he had heard and read much concerning such matters. But when it came to the 'dark and profound' Art of *chemia* – i.e. the quest for the Philosophers' Stone rather than simple metallurgical operations or the procurement of basic pharmaceutical remedies – he remarks that he had initially been unwilling to spend his money on such a dubious pursuit:

---

[77] Achelis, Thomas Otto. *Die Ärzte im Herzogtum Schleswig bis zum Jahre 1804*. Kiel: Schleswig-Holsteinische Gesellschaft für Familienforschung und Wappenkunde e.V. Kiel, 1966, pp. 25, 43.

[78] Figala and Neumann, "Michael Maier," p. 37.

[79] The terms are used in Maier's dedication of his Basel doctoral theses to Carnarius: "Clarissimo et optimo viro Dn. D. Matthiae Carnario, illustrissimi Principis Holsatiae Archiatro dignissimo, amico, qua animo, qua studio, qua patria, meo, ter conjunctissimo;" a transcription of these theses is to be found in Stiehle, Hans. *Michael Maierus Holsatus (1569-1622): Ein Beitrag zur naturphilosophischen Medizin in seinen Schriften und zu seinem wissenschaftlichen Qualifikationsprofil*. Doctoral thesis, Zentralinstitut für Geschichte der Technik der Technischen Universität München, 1991.

[80] Hirsch, August (ed.). *Biographisches Lexikon der hervorragenden Ärzte aller Zeiten und Völker*. Vol. 5. München: Urban und Schwarzenberg, 1962, p. 779; Jöcher, *Allgemeines Gelehrten-Lexicon*, Vol. 1, p. 1679.

[81] Maier, *De Medicina Regia*, p. Aii *recto*: "Nihilominus cum domum, ut dictum, ad officium venissem, non intermittere potui, quin unum aut alterum experimentum tentarem, quorum unum erat, Mercurii induratio per fumum plumbi, quod successit; alterum Lunae citrinatio per aquam gradualem seu tinctoriam, quod fefellit."

...I was not willing to squander expenses set aside for more certain studies on doubtful matters, particularly as I saw from the writings of a number of physicians how anxiously they searched for so dark and profound a thing by way of imploring letters to their colleagues. Thus, thinking about the matter myself, I concluded that if a man substantially learned in philosophy and medicine is not able to obtain the chemical Art, so much the less am I; and if he will have obtained it, he will end the quest by writing a book, and meanwhile I would be making the first steps into the inquiry of this Art. Because of this syllogism, I abstained for a total of six years from any serious treatment of chemical matters.[82]

Carnarius' strong family ties with the University of Padua must have had some influence on the direction of the 'more certain' studies Maier undertook, for in the spring of 1595 he decided to travel to that institution, which was one of the most important centres of Galenic medicine in Europe. Indeed, Carnarius had also attended Rostock university in 1578, moving on to Padua in 1586 and Basel in 1589,[83] and it must have seemed quite logical for the younger man to follow in his mentor's footsteps. Nevertheless, on Carnarius' advice Maier delayed his entrance into Padua for a semester and set off on a grand *peregrinatio academica* – as Maier says, "lest I should become weary with leisure or remaining in one place."[84]

5. 'First love and grief': Maier's *peregrinatio academica*

According to the humanist ethos prevailing in Maier's time, travel was considered to be an indispensable means of education, and enrolment at foreign universities offered the possibility of a long journey – an opportunity that Maier did not let pass.[85] Indeed, the theme of travel was popular in the

---

82 *Ibid.*, p. Ai *verso*: "Hoc toto studiorum meorum ac peregrinationis tempore in multis locis multa de Chemicis experimentis audivi, legi et contuli: Verum, ut fatear, illa me religio hactenus tenuit, ut extra patriam in re dubia, sumptus studiis certioribus mancipatos, nollem profundere, praesertim cum viderem ex scriptis nonnullorum medicorum, quam anxie illi ipsi rem adeo obscuram et profundam, emendicatis per Epistolas aliorum responsis, quaererent; hoc modo mecum ratiocinando concludens: Si ille vir tam solide doctus in philosophia et medicina Chemicum artificium non adipiscatur, multo minus tu: Cum vero ille habuerit, scribendi finem faciet; tum tu ejus artis inquirendae initium statues: Hoc syllogismo me totum sexennium a seria Chemicarum rerum tractatione abstinui."

83 Achelis, *Die Ärzte im Herzogtum Schleswig*, p. 25.

84 Maier, *De Medicina Regia*, p. Aii *recto*: "Interim, ne otio aut situ languerem, navigio praecipuas Balthici littoris urbes adire constitui, ut Galeni exemplo, peregrinando simplicium uberiorem noticiam haurire, nec non populorum mores et naturas cognoscere possem."

85 Trunz, Erich. "Der deutsche Späthumanismus um 1600 als Standeskultur." In Alewyn, Richard (ed.). *Deutsche Barockforschung: Dokumentation einer Epoche*. Köln: Kiepen-

humanist literature of Maier's time; Governor Rantzau himself had composed a work, the *Methodus Apodemica*, which set forth a systematic list of subjects to be pursued by the observant traveller.[86] Whether Maier ever read this tract, we cannot say. But Maier does tell us that in the course of his voyage by land and sea Galen himself served as his exemplar; for the young Greek physician, after deciding to take up a career in medicine, had travelled widely from his native Pergamom in search of medical knowledge, and had come at length to Alexandria, the home of the Great Library and the centre of medical learning in the Roman empire.[87] Thus Maier imagined he was following in the footsteps of a great predecessor, for his mission was not only to learn of the peoples and customs in the regions he visited, but above all to gain a better knowledge of their simples – that is to say, uncompounded medicaments derived directly from plants and animals. And even if Maier's was a more northerly itinerary – stretching from the eastern borders of the Swedish empire to Rome – it would also take him to the seat of medical learning in his day.

Sailing through the islands of the Baltic sea, in spring of 1595 Maier travelled through Swedish-controlled Kurland, Livland and Estland (comprising the modern states of Latvia, Lithuania and Estonia) to the Russian city of Ivangorod,[88] before returning to Lübeck and heading for Italy. This journey of Maier's set a precedent for a life of roaming, although in the future his unsettled existence was to be motivated as much by a search for patronage as by a noble desire to read the 'great book of the world'. Despite the fact that Maier's last work was devoted to the figure of Ulysses as the embodiment of human wisdom, Figala and Neumann have argued that Maier's life-long travels lay "well within the bounds of the *peregrinatio academica* normal for the educated man of his time."[89] As Trunz states, the rise of humanism in Germany witnessed the first large-scale migration of the educated middle and upper classes beyond the borders of the Fatherland, and the *peregrinatio academica* created both an important avenue of scholarly communication and a sense of kinship amongst the learned of Europe.[90] Nevertheless, it must be said that the full significance of the *peregrinatio* for

---

heuer und Witsch, 1966, p. 162. According to Trunz, in the years between 1590 and 1609 some 3145 German students visited Padua.

[86] Evans, R. J. W. "Rantzau and Welser: Aspects of Later German Humanism," *History of European Ideas*, Vol. 5., No. 3, 1984, p. 259.

[87] Maier, *De Medicina Regia*, p. Aii *recto*.

[88] Ivangorod had been recaptured by Russia from the Swedes in 1592; the Peace of Teusina signed between the two powers in the year of Maier's departure must have enabled this journey beyond the borders of Swedish territory.

[89] Figala and Neumann, "Michael Maier," p. 48.

[90] Trunz, "Der deutsche Späthumanismus," p. 162.

Maier's worldview seems to have been missed by Figala and Neumann; for Maier regarded his entire earthly existence as a spiritual journey, akin in some sense to a Christian pilgrimage, and a reflected image of the alchemical process itself. Maier's clearest remarks on this matter are given in the aforementioned *Allegoria Bella*, in which he makes a mythical peregrination through the four known continents (each representing a part of the human body) to the 'heart' of the world, Egypt. He justifies this great journey with reference to a divinely instituted natural order:

For we are all strangers in this world, indeed even in our own native land: from which place we migrate at length to those aethereal, most resplendent heavenly homes, to which our Saviour who has gone before invites and leads us. I might look to the swallow, the messenger of spring, to the crane, the stork, and many other birds, and see how every year at fixed times they travel by instinct and set patterns through the air to unknown regions of Nature; for in this way they set an example and model of peregrination through the regions of the world to man, lest he should grow old amidst the smoke and dung of the house altar. To the birds the entire sublunary region of the air lies open, and to man it is the terrestrial globe. I might look to the sky itself, and to the great wayfarer, the sun, and see how it rejoices in continual motion and warms, illuminates and governs all the creatures of the earth and heavens. Likewise I will direct my mind to the human breast, and to the heart itself, and see how it is driven by this perpetual motion for as long as life remains; for life ends when the motion is taken away, damaged or hindered. It is natural therefore for man to move from place to place, from region to region, until he can see into himself, above himself and around himself.[91]

For Maier the *peregrinatio* that is our earthly existence has been prefigured in the life of Christ, and is the complement of the heavenly existence to come; therefore we should travel onwards through the regions of the earth, following the cyclical processes of Nature, which accomplish something of a spiritual transformation in the pilgrim and enable the final homeward return. In his allegory Maier describes the goal of this spiritual 'pilgrimage' as the phoenix, the feathers of which constitute a cure for 'anger and grief'; that is

---

[91] Maier, *Symbola Aureae Mensae*, p. 569: "Peregrini enim nos omnes sumus in hoc mundo, etiam in propria, nempe terrestri patria: Unde ad aetherias illas clarissimas domus, quo Salvator noster, qui praecessit, nos vocat et attrahit, migraturi tandem sumus: Respiciam hirundinem veris nunciam, gruem, ciconiam, multasque alias aves, quomodo annuatim statis temporibus peregrinentur per aera in ignotas regiones naturae instinctu et documento; ut homini specimen et exemplar edant peregrinationis per mundi partes instituendae, ne semper fumo et fimo larium insenesceret: Avibus aer sublunaris universus patet, et homini globus terrestris: Respiciam coelum ipsum, ipsiusque magnum viatorem, Solem, quomodo motu continuo gaudeat et omnia soli et poli creaturas illustret et illuminet, calefaciat et gubernet: Imo in proprium sinum pectoris, ad cor ipsum, mentem dirigam, quomodo hoc motu agatur perpetuo, dum vita manet, quod vitam ut metitur motione illaesa, sic [sic] sublata, laesa, vel impedita, finit: Naturale itaque homini est, moveri de loco ad locum, de regione in regionem, dum in se, supra se et circum se respiciat."

to say, the Universal Medicine, in the beginning of which lies the bitterness of suffering, but in its end a heavenly joy.[92] Behind these sentiments we may detect a certain event in Maier's *peregrinatio academica*, which seems to have been an experiential prototype for the journey described in his *Allegoria Bella*. For something of the impetus driving Maier's alchemical quest, and a source of his specific reference to the problem of anger, may be found in the details of his sojourn in Padua, which he reached in the autumn of 1595.

In the *De Medicina Regia* Maier tells us very little about his time in Padua – only that he received the 'laurel wreath' (i.e. the prestigious title of Poet Laureate), which was obtained 'by custom' after his first experience of 'love and grief'.[93] At this time Maier was writing Latin poetry under the pseudonym Hermes Malavici, an anagram of Michael Maierus. This appellation not only suggests the mercurial, ambiguous nature of the Greek deity, but also implies that the author had somehow "triumphed over misfortune;" indeed, records of an intriguing episode have recently been uncovered by Figala and Neumann which augment the testimony of the *De Medicina Regia*, and suggest that Maier went through more than the 'customary' grief at the University of Padua.[94] In July of 1596 the twenty-seven year old academic attacked and seriously wounded a fellow scholar, Heino Lambechius, following a series of verbal disputes. As a result of this reportedly 'savage act', Maier was put on trial before the elders of the 'German Nation' at Padua, i.e. the administrative body for German scholars residing there. The details of the quarrel that prompted Maier's outburst of aggression are unknown, nor is it clear whether a weapon was used, such as the rapier apparent in the copperplate portrait of the author (figure 1). In any event, the annals of the German Nation record that Maier was adjudged the guilty party in the dispute, ordered to pay expenses and compelled to deliver the following plea for forgiveness before the elders:

I am most grieved by the fact that the glorious Nation was injured by me, when, although I had agreed to terms of peace with Heino in the presence of the Senate, I did not observe this, but dealt him an injury in his own chambers. I seek pardon for this my crime; I worship

---

[92] *Ibid.*, p. 562.

[93] Maier, *De Medicina Regia*, p. Aii *recto*: "Ab hoc itinere sub autumnum reversus, Italiam recta contendi, inibique Patavii aliquamdiu degens medicam meam rem omnibus nervis promovere studui: quin et Lauream frondem ibi primitus amare et mordere, ut moris, cepi."

[94] Favaro, A. (ed.). *Atti della Nazione Germanica Artista nello Studio di Padova*. Vol. 2. Padua: Antenore, 1967, pp. 81-82; I am indebted to Prof. Wouter Hanegraaff of the University of Amsterdam for bringing my attention to the significance of Maier's anagram.

the Nation, I revere it and obey it, and I will be sedulously careful that no such thing shall happen again.[95]

However, the very next day Maier fled in secret from Padua when his adversary declined monetary compensation for injuries sustained in the attack. The response of the elders to this scandalous behaviour was emphatic:

Let others judge how his honour and reputation stand thereon. There is no-one who can persuade himself that these actions will go unpunished.[96]

In the year following this incident, Maier travelled to Bologna, Florence, Sienna, Rome, Loreto, Ancona, and other of "the most splendid cities of the world," before re-crossing the Alps to Basel.[97] However, when Maier entered Basel University to complete his doctorate, a 'warrant-like' letter was sent by the German Nation to the Professor of the Faculty of Medicine there, demanding that Maier not be permitted to graduate, and insisting that he be held until the Nation and Lambechius had attained satisfaction.[98] For the young physician, who had once cried as a child when faced with the possibility of taking up an uneducated profession, and whose university studies had already met once with failure, knowledge of this 'arrest warrant' was probably rather disturbing. Furthermore, he must have wondered how these events would appear in the eyes of his benefactor, Matthias Carnarius, whose father had held an important position within the German Nation at Padua.[99]

Happily for Maier, the Nation's efforts to foil his escape came to nought, as he successfully defended his doctoral theses and graduated on November the 4th, 1596.[100] As the time between his arrival in Basel and his graduation

---

[95] *Ibid.*, p. 82: "Laesam Nationem inclytam a me, dum pacem quam pactus sum cum Heinone coram Senatu non servavi, ipsique in aedibus suis vulnus dedi, est quod plurimum doleam. Hanc meam culpam nunc deprecor, Nationem colo, revereor et observo, ac ne tale quid imposterum fiat sedulo caveo. Michael Meierus Cymber."

[96] *Ibid.*: "Quo honore nominisque existimatione iudicent alii; impune hoc ipsum habiturum nemo qui sibi persuadeat."

[97] Maier, *De Medicina Regia*, p. Aii *recto*.

[98] Favaro, *Atti della Nazione Germanica*, p. 100: "Augusti Domino Heinoni Lambachio Hamburgensi Basileam petenti bina testimonia Nationis nomine dedimus, unum quidem in caussa cum Michaele Meiero Cimbro, qui dictum Heinonem illicito plane modo vulneraverat et contra datam fidem clam Natione aufugerat ad Magistratum quemcunque politicum: alterum vero commendatitium quod professoribus Apollineis exibere posset. Horum exempla in Epistolarum libro reperientur..."; Stiehle, *Michael Maierus Holsatus*, p. 18.

[99] Jöcher, *Allgemeines Gelehrten-Lexicon*, Vol. 1, p. 1679: Johannes Carnarius had held the position of librarian in the German Nation concurrently with his professorship.

[100] Stiehle, *Michael Maierus Holsatus*, p. 19.

amounted to little more than two months, it seems the theses he presented there were the fruits of his learning at the University of Padua – where as a Protestant he was debarred from graduating by papal decree.[101] Nevertheless, as a result of uncontrollable anger, Maier had been forced to abandon his hard-won position at a prestigious university in disgrace – and quite possibly in fear, given that his adversary may have preferred blood to money as compensation. Although student brawls and even duelling were relatively commonplace in Maier's time – to the point that lecturers were sometimes driven to demand that their students leave their weapons outside the classroom – the annals speak of this event as 'unprecedented'.[102] When this mark against Maier's character and threat to his academic future is placed in the context of his lifelong and sometimes inglorious struggle to attract patronage, the impetus behind Maier's quest for an alchemical 'medicine of piety' becomes more clear. These are the beginnings of the Philosophers' Stone, which lie in 'misery and vinegar'; the collision of earthly passions with the unyielding demands of socialisation and economic survival, which marks the first stage of the begetting of an 'alchemical' wisdom.

6. The theses on epilepsy

Despite the emotional turmoil of this period Maier's academic endeavours had borne fruit, a feat that he admits had required the application of all his energies;[103] indeed, the experience of such tribulations so far from home may have overcome lesser men. The *Theses de Epilepsia* produced by Maier for his medical doctorate at Basel, dated the 16th of October, 1596, demonstrate the extensive knowledge of the Aristotelian-Galenic physiological system their author had accrued on his travels, and express above all his knowledge of the employment of simples and the 'composites' derived therefrom. After dedicating his theses to Carnarius (whose reaction to the Paduan incident we cannot gauge), Maier launches into a discussion of the many names given to epilepsy, such as the 'divine sickness', and then goes on to deal with its symptomatology and the points distinguishing it from other similar maladies.[104] He then discusses the aetiology of the disease, which in accordance with the principles laid out in the *Theses Summam Doctrinae* is arranged according to internal and external sources. Thus the principal

---

[101] *Ibid.*

[102] Favaro, *Atti della Nazione Germanica*, p. 82.

[103] See n. 93 above.

[104] UniversitätsBibliothek Basel, *Disputationum Medicarum Basiliensium*, Vol. 3, No. 92; Stiehle, *Michael Maierus Holsatus*, p. 100.

internal cause of epilepsy is the sudden permeation of the brain ventricle by
either thick phlegm, black bile, or poisoned blood, which makes the way too
narrow for the *spiritus animalis* to flow on its proper course through the
nerves into the sense organs. In this way the *facultas animalis* governing
sense and motion is disrupted, causing the dramatic seizures to be observed in
sufferers.[105] Amongst the external causes are the intake of cold and moist
foods, or an over-indulgence in lettuce, cabbage and beetroot. Maier advises
epileptics to avoid the cooked liver of a he-goat,[106] and the smell of bitumen
or jet; moonshine, the south wind and strolling without a hat in cold, moist
weather are also proscribed.[107]

With regard to treatment, Maier mentions trepanning with a drill via the
sutura coronalis, but he follows Galen in reminding the reader of the
considerable dangers of this operation, which is only to be carried out by the
most experienced surgeons.[108] Indeed, his recommendations are directed on
the whole towards diet and herbal remedies rather than surgery; for example,
in order to dilute the cold, thick phlegm that inhibits the flow of the *spiritus
animalis*, Maier would prescribe a warm infusion of hissop, marjoram,
betony, melissa leaves, sage, primrose, peony roots and cat's paw.[109]

Over the years, a great number of writers on Maier have described him as
an ardent follower of Paracelsus, the man whose emphasis on experimental
observation and whose vehement opposition to the Galenic medicine of the
Scholastics laid the foundations for modern pharmacology.[110] However, in
his study of Maier's theses on epilepsy, Hans Stiehle has recently offered an
important corrective to this notion, and has demonstrated in detail the
overwhelmingly Galenic orientation of Maier's medical practice. Indeed,
Maier's teacher at Rostock, Bruchaeus, was a prominent critic of Paracelsus,
whom he regarded as an empiricist, i.e. one who relies on experimental
observation and sense data to the exclusion of the wisdom of the traditional

---

[105] Thesis 23: "Humor *a.* crassus et lentus, pituitosus, *b.* melancholicus *c.* aut sanguis, vel
vapor copiosus ac venenatus, repente *d.* in cerebri ventriculos illabens, ac animali spiritui
in sensuum organa influenti vias angustiores reddens;" Stiehle, *Michael Maierus
Holsatus*, p. 106: these notions are taken directly from Galen's *De Locis Affectis* and *De
Differentiis Symptomatum*.

[106] It seems this remark is related to Bonatti's association of the melancholic humour with
the smell of the goat; see Klibansky, *Saturn and Melancholy*, p. 147.

[107] Theses 75, 76, 77; Stiehle, *Michael Maierus Holsatus*, p. 118.

[108] Also mentioned amongst invasive procedures is blood-letting via the *vena basilica* or
vena saphena.

[109] Thesis 130; Stiehle, *Michael Maierus Holsatus*, p. 136: "Deinde, si frigidus, lentus ac
crassus peccat humor, concoquatur decoctis calidis, incidentibus et attenuantibus ex
hyssopo, sampsucho, betonica, melyssophillo, salvia, primula veris, rad. poeoniae,
stoechade et similibus partem affectam respicentibus..."

[110] For example, Evans, *Rudolf II and his World*, p. 205; Hubicki, "Maier, Michael," p. 23.

medical corpus.[111] Maier's works also contain numerous polemics against empiricists, whom he criticises above all for their lack of a university education. Nevertheless, in his *Themis Aurea* (1617) he would describe Paracelsus as a man who, although vain in character and irreverent in polemic, possessed "an eminent and admirable knowledge of medicine;" in that work Maier also states that both the chemical remedies of Paracelsus and the simples of Galen have their appropriate applications.[112] Likewise, in the *Symbola Aureae Mensae* Maier states that Paracelsus often accomplished alchemical projection before his apprentice, and although he led the life of a libertine he cured illnesses that were previously incurable.[113] Contrary to Stiehle, this syncretic attitude is not merely an opportunistic concession to potential patrons. In certain places Maier lauds Paracelsus as the equivalent of Luther in the field of iatrochemistry, and the defender of an indigenous German medicine against the corrupt Italian or 'papal medicine'; such diatribes of Maier's are overtly political in character, and reflect the increasing interdependence of his religious, political and medical sympathies that developed during the course of his life. They are also, no doubt, the source of the depiction of Maier as an avid Paracelsian.

7. Contact with the arcana

Following the completion of his university studies it seems that Maier revised his earlier opinions on alchemy and undertook an investigation into that 'dark and profound' subject. His first significant contact with alchemical arcana appears to have taken place in Königsberg in Lutheran East Prussia, where he set up a medical practice in 1599.[114] The landlord of his dwelling in that city

---

[111] Krabbe, *Die Universität Rostock*, p. 709; Heidorn, *Geschichte der Universität Rostock*, p. 41.

[112] Maier, Michael. *Themis Aurea, hoc est, de Legibus Fraternitatis R. C. Tractatus.* Frankfurt am Main: Lucas Jennis, 1624, p. 168: "Quod ad medicamenta mere Chymica vel Paracelsica attinet, ea quatenus bona sunt, laudamus, sed ita, ne Galenica et dogmatica vituperemus: His et illis alternatim utendum erit, innullius praeiudicium at contemptum." Similar calls to reconcile Paracelsian and Galenic medicine were made by other physicians who would join Maier at the court of Moritz the Learned, namely Heinrich Noll and Joseph Duchesne; Moran, *Alchemical World of the German Court*, p. 122.

[113] Maier, *Symbola Aureae Mensae*, pp. 284, 286. The reference is probably to Paracelsus' successful use of mercury in the cure of dropsy; it seems he also had some success with the treatment of gout; Pagel, *Paracelsus*, p. 201.

[114] Maier, *De Medicina Regia*, p. Aii *verso*: "Verum ad meos poste rediens, fortunam non minus variam nusquam non offendi: Post duos deinde annos ad celebre illud Emporium, littori Balthico adjacens, ubi ante biennium fueram, iterum me contuli, multis aegris

was skilled in the art of assaying by cupellation,[115] and earned a livelihood by determining the proportion of precious metals to base metals in alloys. Although Maier tells us he learnt much concerning metallurgy from this man, he was not versed in the 'universal work'; that is to say, the production of the Philosophers' Stone according to universal chemical laws.[116] Nevertheless, whilst amongst friends of his landlord who were more closely acquainted with the alchemical Art, Maier's medical curiosity was aroused by the miraculous healing of a chronically ill man through the application of a bright yellow powder that had been obtained in England.[117] The origins of this medicine may well have inspired Maier's later travels to England, where he would immerse himself in the works of the English alchemists.

After witnessing the remarkable results of the English iatrochemical cure, Maier began to seek out alchemical literature. Good luck – or destiny – was to provide some assistance in his endeavour. At some time in 1601 he took up a patient who had been dismissed by other doctors as a hypochondriac, but who happened to be well-educated and most sympathetic towards 'matters chemical'. Impressed by Maier's caring manner, the patient paid him a certain sum of money in order that they should travel together to his country estate outside of Königsberg – a fortunate turn of events, as the city was gripped by a serious outbreak of the bubonic plague at that time.[118] What is

---

ibidem medicam meam opellam per aliquot annos navans." Maier tells us that he had visited this "famous trading centre at the Baltic Sea" during his *peregrinatio academica*, which would suggest that it was Danzig, the free city in Polish-controlled Royal Prussia. Nevertheless, in their work Neumann and Figala give Königsberg as the likely identity of the city, although Maier does not mention it as a destination on his *peregrinatio*; but by the testimony of Hubicki Maier was in Danzig in December of 1601, a fact which tallies with the suggestion of the *De Medicina Regia* that he returned to Holstein at around this time – i.e. in all likelihood he returned via Danzig, some 120 kilometres to the west of Königsberg.

[115] That is to say, the application of heat to alloys placed in a small porous cupel, by which means metals such as lead, copper and tin are oxidized and separated from gold or silver.

[116] *Ibid.*: "Interea temporis hospitem nactus sum, qui artificium probandi et examinandi metalla per cupellam profitebatur: Inde cum multis chemiae deditis familiaritatem inii: Verum nullus ex iis universale opus seu Lapidem, callere visus est. Quidam adtulit argenti massas cupro permixtas, aliquot vicibus, menstruo spacio interposito, easque per cineritium testae depurari voluit: Alius mixturam, quam habuit, aliquot drachmis auri puri cum mercurio loto amalgamatis conjungi et quasi incorporari, deinde mense abacto, per testam examinari, postulavit: Unde ex tribus drachmis auri Mercurio impositis, octo habere se jactavit, idque aliquoties repetiit."

[117] *Ibid.*, Hii *verso*.

[118] *Ibid.*, Aiii *recto*- Aiii *verso*: "Interim quidam gravi per multos annos vexatus morbo, quem medici hypochondriacum indigetant, cum ab aliis plus damni, quam levaminis, sensisset, meae diligentiae exempla passim obvia cernens, certa me pecuniae summa conduxit, ut relicta urbe secum, praesertim peste jam graviter in vulgum saeviente, in suburbanum praedium migrarem, ibique apud se per aestatem manerem."

more, at his patient's house Maier found an excellent library of alchemical works, which he was able to peruse at his leisure.

Maier's reading list included works by the medieval European authors Geber (pseudo-Jabir or Geber Latinus), pseudo-Arnoldus de Villanova and Hortulanus Anglicus, as well as the influential Arabic text, the *Turba Philosophorum*– a fictional dialogue in which nine pre-Socratic philosophers engage in thoughtful discussion on the paths to perfecting the Philosophers' Stone. These are the only details given in Maier's *De Medicina Regia* of the thirty or so writers represented in the library. However, in the course of his reading Maier would have found corrupted pre-Socratic notions concerning the *prima materia* or first matter underlying all elements, and protracted conjectures stemming from Galenic medicine and the Aristotelian sulphur-mercury theory of metallic generation, according to which metals grow in the womb of the earth through the warmth of the sun and the interacting principles of dry sulphur and moist mercury.[119] Medieval alchemical literature is distinguished above all by its vitalism, a doctrine advocating the existence of a living spirit in Nature in which animals, plants and metals alike are thought to possess the power of increase.[120] But the path to the discovery of the 'living' Stone of the Philosophers, which brings temperance to the human body just as it imparts to metals their perfect proportion, is veiled under a thousand words, as pseudo-Arnoldus warns:

Our Stone is cold, moist, dry and hot; it is a Stone and no Stone, and is found by everybody in the air, fields, on the mountains, and in the water; and it is called Albida, herein all physicians agree, for they say that Albida is called Rebio. Thus they name it in hidden and secret words, because they perfectly understand the *materia*; some say it is blood, others say it is a man's hair, others say it is an egg, which has made many fools – who understand no more than the letter, and the mere sound of words – seek this Art in blood, in eggs, and in hair... they have found nothing, for they did not rightly understand the sayings of the natural masters, who spake their words in hidden language. Should they have spoken out plainly,

---

[119] The Latin text of the *Turba Philosophorum* gives the participants of the discussion as Iximidrus, Exumdrus, Anaxagoras, Pandulfus, Arisleus, Lucas, Locustor, Pitagoras and Eximenes; in 1931 Julius Ruska established the text was of Arabic origin, and in 1954 Martin Plessner transcribed the rather confusing names back into Arabic characters, revealing the participants as Anaximander, Anaximenes, Anaxagoras, Empedocles, Archelaus, Leucippus, Ecphantus, Pythagoras and Xenophanes. The work also features guest appearances from Moses (Musa) and the Greco-Egyptian alchemist Zosimos (Zimus). See Holmyard, *Alchemy*, pp. 80-84; on the pre-Socratics' relation to alchemy, see Sheppard, H. J. "The Ouroboros and the Unity of Matter in Alchemy: A Study in Origins," *Ambix*, Vol. 10, No. 2, 1962, pp. 94-95.

[120] Although recent studies by Newman have identified a corpuscularian tradition within medieval alchemy (see chapter I, n. 35 above), my own wide-ranging survey of medieval texts suggest vitalistic conceptions were of paramount importance, and corpuscularianism remained the exception to the rule, or was integrated into a broad vitalistic schema.

they would have done very ill, for all men would have used this Art and the whole world would have been spoiled.[121]

Having noted the confusing diversity of *Decknamen* employed by the different authors in his patient's library, Maier went about comparing and collating them with the aim of creating a concordance; and in so doing he must surely have been aware of the warning, repeated often enough in the alchemical corpus, that by seeking to uncover the true significance of alchemical symbolism "a man may lose his time, goods and substance, and at last his health, and miserably rob himself of life."[122] Nevertheless, Maier tells us that he had never read anything of such subtlety, and he studied his patient's books with such zeal and ardour that he found it difficult to sleep at night:

Indeed, if I am able to understand the circles of Mercury and the motions, distances and magnitudes of the planets and fixed stars, or indeed master music as much in theory as in practice, or the entire art of poetry, and the rest of the most subtle theorems of mathematics, why should I not grasp this chemistry? For if the alchemists use the figures of words or the similitudes of things, the stories of poets or the memorials of history, the axioms of physics, astronomy, medicine and metaphysics, then they do not deceive me, but somehow I may be able to see the truth shining in the light.[123]

These words indicate that Maier's approach to alchemical symbolism from the earliest stage was directed towards the unveiling of universal processes: hence his suggestion that chemistry might be akin to astronomy, music and poetry, and that all are governed by 'mathematical' theorems – a sentiment dating to the time of Pythagoras, for whom 'all things' were number. For Maier laboratory experiment promised much more than the simple operations performed by his landlord in Königsberg: in the young man's eyes, it was a means of discovering the harmony of the spheres and laying bare the microcosm which is the human individual.

---

[121] "A Chymicall treatise of the Ancient and highly illuminated Philosopher, Devine and Physitian, Arnoldus de Nova Villa." Bodleian Library, MS Ashmole 1415, p. 130; c.f. the words of Morienus in Stavenhagen, Lee (ed., trans.). *A Testament of Alchemy.* Hanover: University Press of New England, 1974, p. 45.

[122] *Ibid.*, p. 137.

[123] Maier, *De Medicina Regia*, p. Aiii *verso*: "Quippe, inquam, si Mercurii orbes, motus, distantias et magnitudines planetarum et stellarum fixarum, imo Musicam tam theoricam, quam practicam, poeticam omnem et reliqua subtilissima mathematicorum theoremata capere potero, quid ni haec chemica? Nam si figuris verborum vel similitudinibus rerum, si fabulis poetarum, aut monumentis hystoriarum, si axiomatibus physicae, astronomiae, medicinae, aut metaphysicae utentur Chemici, non subterfugient, quin aliquam veritatis luce scintillare visurus sim."

8. Maier's first alchemical experiment

Having spent his time in relative peace whilst the bubonic plague "ravaged the masses" in Königsberg, it seems that Maier may have been inspired to take up a more salubrious career with which to pursue his intellectual interests. A few short months after his sojourn in the countryside, he entered his name on the rolls of the University of Königsberg, an act which Figala and Neumann, following Hubicki, interpret as an attempt to start a university career.[124] Nevertheless, he evidently failed to obtain the status of professor or *extraneus* at the university, and in late 1601 he returned to Holstein by way of Danzig – where, according to the testimony of Hubicki, he was to be found in December of that year prescribing dried frogs in vinegar to patients at the White Horse Inn.[125] The employment of such remedies was certainly a part of Maier's medical repertoire – thus in his *Civitas Corporis Humani* (1621) he recommends frogs' legs wrapped in deer or vulture skin for the cure of gout.[126] But if Hubicki's report is correct, it indicates that the fortunes of Maier, who was now in his 32nd year, were far removed from those he once envisaged.

Maier had nevertheless been inspired by his studies in Königsberg, and he went in search of certain minerals necessary to begin his own laboratory experiments; we are told he visited Hungary, where the minerals were particularly potent due to the superior influence of solar radiation there.[127] When all the requisite materials had been brought together and the furnace prepared in his hometown in Holstein, he tells us he began work in 1604 at the time of Epiphany, i.e. the celebration of the coming of the Magi to Christ's birthplace.[128] In medieval alchemy astrological influences were often taken into account in the timing of the various operations of the Hermetic Art; in Maier's work these astrological factors are combined with a consideration of the dates in the calendar associated with the life of Christ. After months of often dangerous procedures, the work was completed at Easter, by which time Maier had observed the crucial sequence of phases in the alchemical process – the raven, or black phase; the peacock, or multi-

---

[124] Figala and Neumann, "Ein Früher Brief," pp. 307-308; Hubicki, "Maier, Michael," p. 23.

[125] Hubicki, "Maier, Michael," p. 23.

[126] Tortoise feet are also useful in this regard, the left one being bound to the patient's left leg, the right one to the right. Maier, Michael. *Civitas Corporis Humani, a Tyrannide arthritica vindicata*. Frankfurt am Main: Lucas Jennis, 1621, p. 158: "*Podagram sanant pedes ranae ligati in* [1] corio cervi, et super podagrici pedes positi. [2] *Ad idem* crus et corium cavillae vulturis pedibus aegris adalligantur. [3] *Pes item* testudinis dexter supra aegri pedem dextrum, et sinister super sinistrum applicatur."

[127] Maier, *De Medicina Regia*, p. Ci *recto*.

[128] *Ibid.*

coloured phase; the dove, or white phase; the phoenix, or yellow phase; and the pelican, or red phase.[129]

Since the medieval period the basic colours of the alchemical process were conceived as black, white, yellow and red; they correspond to the four elements earth, water, fire and air, and to the melancholic, phlegmatic, choleric and sanguine temperaments of the Galenic system we have discussed. A progression through black, white, yellow and red forms can be observed during the heating of an amalgam of copper and mercury, which process may first have inspired the alchemists' reliance on this sequence.[130] Maier's schema of black, multi-coloured, white, yellow, red is a typical variation, the multi-coloured peacock phase serving as a transition between black and white. Whilst it is difficult to translate the processes of Maier's experiment into the terminology of modern chemistry due to his silence on the matter of input materials, the black phase traditionally involved 'calcination' (oxidisation) or pulverisation by fire of the alchemical subject in the vessel, followed by solution in caustic fluids and 'putrefaction' in warm dung or water; this was carried out in order to reduce the subject to the chaotic *prima materia*, or alternatively to the mercurial and sulphuric principles that underlie all metals in varying proportions. The white phase indicated the freeing of the mercurial principle – or the 'spirit' contained in matter – through this process, and was often represented in the medieval texts by the upward flight of doves. The subsequent yellow phase marked the return of the volatile mercurial spirit to its 'nest'; that is to say, to the subject at the bottom of the vessel through a process of 'reduction'. Redness typically appeared during 'sublimation', as the alchemical subject was raised to a higher, more sublime level of composition through the re-entry of the mercurial principle.[131] Both the yellow and the red phases of the work point towards a subsequent 'fixation': the containment of the volatile, feminine mercurial spirit in a fixed and useful form through the operation of the stable, masculine sulphuric principle (this process being the marriage of contraries or *coniunctio oppositorum*).

The phoenix and pelican which Maier uses to represent the yellow and red phases were drawn by the alchemists from medieval Christian iconology, in

---

[129] *Ibid.*, p. Ci *verso*: "Aves deinde quinque vidi, quarum quaedam volatiles, quaedam explumes sunt, ut Corvus, Pavo, Columba, Phænix et Pelicanus, hoc est, colores omnes ordine, a philosophis tradito, notavi..."; Basil Valentine, a sixteenth century author from whom Maier quotes approvingly, gives a similar enumeration of the colours with reference to birds: the black crow, the white swan, the multi-coloured peacock and the red Phoenix; Read, John. *Prelude to Chemistry*. London: G. Bell and Sons, 1936, p. 146.

[130] Haage, *Alchemie im Mittelalter*, pp. 15-16; the sulphur-mercury theory itself seems to be derived from the properties of cinnabar (mercuric sulphide), which separates into its component elements through heating.

[131] *Ibid.*, pp. 16-17.

which they served as symbols for Christ – the former on account of its miraculous powers of self-renewal through a fiery death, the latter because of its reputed habit of feeding its young with its own blood. Indeed, alchemical allegory since the medieval period had linked the black phase of the alchemical process to the passion of Christ on the cross, the white phase to the release of his spirit at death, and the perfection of the red phase to the spirit's re-incorporation into a pure and sinless body at resurrection. Thus the early sixteenth century *Rosarium Philosophorum*, a favourite text of Maier's, depicts the completion of the alchemical work with an emblem showing the emergence of Christ from his tomb, and a caption that reads: "after my many sufferings and great martyrdom, I rise again transfigured, free of all blemish."

With the advent of the Reformation the synthesis of Christian mythology and alchemical lore became a prominent component of Protestant alchemy; thus Maier speaks in his *Cantilenae Intellectuales* (1622) of the manner in which the Creator planned by means of 'a great mystery' to free humankind from the death proceeding from original sin:

Thus Omnipotent God became man, and crushed the head of the cunning serpent, and took from him all his power; He was born of a Virgin free from sin, and underwent a terrible death by the cross, shedding His blood. And so these sacred mysteries are also to be found in this mystical Art, having been hidden under obscure images... He who understands the manner in which Christ has saved us from everlasting death, is also able to understand the goal of this arcane Art, and the manner in which worthless and impure metals are perfected.[132]

Here Maier refers to a life-imparting power of transformation and renewal, manifested not only in the Passion, death and resurrection of Christ, but also in the lives of those saved by Christ. Intimations of a parallel between Christ and the Philosophers' Stone stretch back to the earliest Greco-Egyptian texts, in which the Stone is linked with the divine spark in matter and the *anthropos* myth of the Gnostics.[133] The relation of Christ to the Philosophers' Stone in Maier's work is one of sympathetic correspondence rather than identity, and is not dissimilar to the conception of his older contemporary, the Lutheran alchemist Heinrich Khunrath, although that writer utilises the Paracelsian tripartite elemental division of sulphur, mercury and salt rather than the

---

[132] Maier, Michael. *Cantilenae Intellectuales, in Triadas 9. distinctae, De Phoenice Redivivo*. Rostock: Mauritii Saxonis, 1622, verse 7 *media*: "Sic Deus potens homo/ Factus est qui subdolo/ Daemoni caput terit,/ Omne robur et rapit:/ Nascitur dum Virgine/ Labis expers et cruce/ Horridam mortem subit,/ Et cruentus interit./ Sic in arte mystica/ Sunt et haec umbris sacra/ Tecta... Qui modum perceperit/ CHRISTUS ut salvaverit/ Nos ab aeterna nece,/ Hic potest et noscere/ Artis arcanae scopum,/ Quoque tingantur, modum,/ Quae metalla vilibus/ Sunt repleta faecibus."

[133] E.g. Taylor, "The Visions of Zosimos."

Aristotelian schema we have discussed. Furthermore, gnostic Paracelsian elements are to the fore in the work of Khunrath, who thought of the Philosophers' Stone as a "universal spark of the world soul."[134] Nevertheless, Maier's attitude towards salvation could be described as being broadly gnostic in character, as the sufferings of the world mirror the black phase of the alchemical process as a necessary, cathartic means of the spirit's release from bondage.[135]

Having beheld the correct colour sequence in his experiment, and having witnessed the appearance of the 'pelican' at Easter, Maier deemed that the writings of the medieval alchemical masters he had consulted at Königsberg were fully in accord with the laws of Nature. Significantly, he also felt that the experiment had clarified the meaning of his mother's strange experience of augury prior to his birth[136] – another avowal that the alchemical processes he observed in the laboratory were inextricably linked with his own destiny on earth. As we read the closing section of the autobiographical portion of Maier's *De Medicina Regia*, we may begin to gather what that destiny would be. For although we are told by Maier that his experiment had produced a powerful medicament – indeed, a substance he could confidently name the Mercury of the Philosophers, containing sulphuric and mercuric principles in equal part[137] – he had nevertheless failed to complete his experiment due to certain adversities.[138] The promise of future success would form the basis of his supplication to the Emperor, as well as to later patrons, for continued finance of a work that could never be completed.

---

[134] Khunrath, Heinrich. "A Naturall Chymicall Symbolum, or a Short Confession of Henry Kunwrath of Lipsicke, Doctor of Phisick." Bodleian Library, MS Ashmole 1459, II, p. 100.

[135] Although the gnostic attitude is marked by a world-denying anti-materialism, as Quispel remarks, corporeal existence often plays an indispensable role as a catharsis for the spirit in gnostic traditions. See Quispel, Gilles. "Gnosis and Culture." In Barnaby, Karin and Pellegrino D'Acierno (eds.). *C. G. Jung and the Humanities*. Princeton: Princeton University Press, 1990, p. 27.

[136] See above, n. 21.

[137] On the theory of a twofold mercury, see below, chapter V, n. 28.

[138] Maier, *De Medicina Regia*, p. Ci *verso*.

III. Bohemia and England

1. Maier at the court of Emperor Rudolf II

At some point in 1608 Maier moved to Prague, the capital of Bohemia and the empire, which had become a centre of research for alchemy and the occult sciences under the reign of Rudolf II (figure 4). The reasons for this move were not only financial, as we are told in the *De Medicina Regia* that Maier had suffered from the negative attentions of locals in his hometown in Holstein.[1] Persecution by locals was an endemic problem for practising alchemists, and not only on account of charges of diabolic activity; indeed, the Englishman George Ripley (?-c.1490) was once hounded by villagers because of the foul and poisonous fumes emanating from his laboratory.[2] Maier does not elaborate on the content of the "jibes and wicked accusations" directed towards him, beyond stating that some of his persecutors wished that he would surrender the precious fruits of his labours. He goes on to add that winter, spring and summer are finished for him, and that he has reached a melancholic 'autumn' on account of the calumny and injuries which he has endured on a daily basis from his neighbours. But in a defiant aside, he then states that it is just these 'four seasons' which constitute the alchemical work.[3]

---

[1] Maier, *De Medicina Regia*, p. Ci *verso*.

[2] Holmyard, *Alchemy*, p. 183.

[3] Maier, *De Medicina Regia*, pp. Ci *verso*- Cii *recto*: "...verum eo usque me hominum malevolorum dicteria et calumniae redegerunt, ut operi omnino supersedere, prosterisque meis reliquam absolvendam portionem una cum fructibus, qui sperandi sint, relinquere constituerim: Testor igitur hoc meo libro, hactenus omnia quae legi, quae vidi, cum authoribus omnibus et singulis (de veris, non ficticiis loquor) si non verbis, at rebus optime convenire, et a me hyemem, ver et aestatem, anni tempora absoluta, autumnum vero propter calumnias vicinorum et injurias, quas quotidie passus sum, non attigisse: Quamvis autem haec quarta pars sit opus mulierum et ludus puerorum, ac merito requies a philosophis dicatur, respectu praecedentium laborum, in quibus manibus et oculis, Gebro teste, opus est." The reference to "women's work and child's play" is a standard medieval alchemical allusion to the processes of 'cooking' and 'washing' by which the alchemical subject is purified. The phrase is attributed to Geber in the *Rosarium Philosophorum*, but appears in the seventeenth dictum of the *Turba Philosophorum* from the mouth of 'Socrates'; see also the third and twenty-second emblems of Maier's *Atalanta Fugiens*.

Although we might have expected a winter to have followed his autumn, in Prague Maier's fortune was to take a positive turn. Having read the *De Medicina Regia* (as it seems) the Emperor was duly impressed not only by Maier's command of alchemical theory, but also by his tale of hardship. For some two months following its publication, as we have noted, Maier was admitted into the imperial court as a personal physician to the Emperor and, shortly thereafter, raised to the rank of Imperial Count Palatine. Rudolf has been characterised as a 'wizard Emperor', who "trod the paths of secret knowledge with an obsession bordering on madness," and who ended his reign as a self-imposed prisoner in his own castle.[4] He surrounded himself with a host of physicians, who tended to both his melancholic illness and his fascination with alchemy; yet it was the belief of many observers that the latter was the cause of the former, for such was Rudolf's fascination with the occult sciences – from astrology and Kabbalah to necromancy – that he felt himself to be 'bewitched'.[5] Be this as it may, his sickness was certainly associated with an apocalyptically-tinged paranoia, and saw his gradual withdrawal from the practical affairs of State into a magical, narcissistic realm of his own creation.[6] This was a happy circumstance for occultists such as Maier, as the Emperor delighted "in hearing secrets about things both natural and artificial;" according to one observer, "whoever is able to deal in such matters will always find the ear of the Emperor ready."[7]

In pursuit of his obsession, Rudolf assembled at his court a remarkable group of alchemists, Kabbalists, magicians and astronomers, as well as poets and artists from across Europe; amongst his entourage at various times were to be counted the astronomers Tycho Brahe and Johannes Kepler, and the alchemists Oswald Croll and Martin Ruland, whilst occasional visitors included such luminaries of occult science as John Dee and Giordano Bruno. Rudolf himself had a good humanist education, and he welcomed learned Catholics, Lutherans and Calvinists alike to his court, where a spirit of cross-confessional tolerance reigned.[8] His goal was to encourage the pursuit of a great synthesis of the various spheres of knowledge, a *pansophia* or science of the universe. Central to this pursuit was the investigation of the links connecting the microcosm with the macrocosm through the deciphering of divine 'signatures' or 'hieroglyphs' imprinted in Nature.

Interestingly, Will-Erich Peuckert, an important writer on the subject of *pansophia* in the esoteric traditions, once argued that Maier did not share in the pansophic spirit that reigned at the court of Rudolf II; rather, he stated

---

4   Evans, *Rudolf II and his World*, p. 2.
5   *Ibid.*, pp. 89, 198.
6   *Ibid.*, p. 90.
7   *Ibid.*, p. 196.
8   *Ibid.*, p. 85.

that Maier espoused "a philosophy of the laboratory" that leads away from pansophic approaches to Nature and towards the experimental tradition exemplified by Newton.[9] Unfortunately, Peuckert's views on this matter seem to have been based on the testimony of Maier's Rosicrucian writings alone, which on first inspection seem to depict the Rosicrucian brethren as nothing more than hard-working researchers into a Nature divested of divine aspect. Although Maier's pansophic sentiments are not always made explicit, Peuckert was unaware of the scope of the alchemical Art in Maier's eyes.

2. The *Hymnosophia*

That scope is well illustrated in the little-known *Hymnosophia* ('Hymn to Wisdom'), a work written by Maier whilst in Prague.[10] Although there is no date given on the title page (suggesting it underwent a limited print run in the same manner as the *De Medicina Regia*), after Maier's name we find the title 'P. C. Caesar', i.e. *Comes Palatinus* or Count Palatine – from which fact we may understand that the work was composed after the 29th of September, 1609, the date of the conferral of Maier's peerage. Under the author's name on the title page stands the verse, "I have nothing to say against worldly things, when they concern the heavenly; the heavens shine, my matter is granted to me by light."[11] The last phrase of the verse, *res mea luce mihi*, is an anagram of the author's name, and appears to refer to the Light of Nature.

The *Hymnosophia* presents forty hymns praising God, who exists in a co-eternal Trinity, for the 'mystical medicine' that is His gift; their central theme is the correspondence of things heavenly to earthly, and the divine chain linking the two. In form this work could be said to prefigure the *Cantilenae Intellectuales* written in the last year of Maier's life, a more polished tract in which we again find the macrocosmic mysteries of God's Creation and the microcosmic Universal Medicine paralleled in alternating verses. Thus in the twelfth hymn of the *Hymnosophia* Maier writes of the macrocosm as a war of the four opposing elements, by which heavier bodies become lighter and lighter bodies heavier; likewise, the human being is a "smaller copy of the. universe," being composed of the four contrary humours, from the interaction

---

9   Peuckert, Will-Erich. *Pansophie*. Stuttgart: Kohlhammer, 1936, pp. 105-107.

10 Maier, Michael. *Hymnosophia, seu Meditatio Laudis Divinae, pro Coelidonia, Medicina mystica, voarchadumica etc.* Prague: n.p., n.d. I am indebted to Dr. Ulrich Neumann for sharing his copy of this work with me.

11 *Ibid.*: "Nil Mundana moror, cum sint coelestia curae, fulgeat Aetheria res mea luce mihi."

of which are produced the various *spiritus*.[12] This correspondence is based on a view of both body and universe as the sites of a process of distillation,[13] and is explicated in greater detail in Maier's *Septimana Philosophica* (1620), where we are told that the heart produces the *spiritus vitalis* from the blood by its 'natural fire' or *calor innatus*, which travels to the brain and is there transformed into the *spiritus animalis*. Likewise, the sun as the homologue of the heart constructs 'subtle essences' from the purest air (the homologue of blood), and these essences inhere in the light, heat and 'virtue' that are transmitted to the wandering and fixed stars, thus imparting motion to the universe.[14] The twelfth hymn of the *Hymnosophia* goes on to explain that the universe and the human being are mirrored in their turn by the Hermetic medicine, as it is composed in the alchemical vessel through the alternating motions of rarefaction and condensation – activities which proceed "in one marvellously interconnected chain."[15] In this way Maier offers us a picture of the universe, the body and the alchemical vessel as inter-related networks of cosmic sympathy and antipathy, in which ever-finer and subtler *spiritus* are distilled.

Correlations between laboratory process and cosmos are found throughout Maier's work. Thus the six days of God's Creation are suggestively portrayed in the preface of the *Hymnosophia* as a process of separation and refinement in which darkness is separated from light, earth from water, and the stars are gathered together as fires in the heavenly palace.[16] This is the *septimana philosophica*, the 'philosophical week' in which the universe is the Hermetic

---

12 *Ibid.*, p. Cii *recto*- Cii *verso*: "Sic compegit opus caelo septemplice cinctum/ Mundanas Deus arte plagas, contraria ut omni/ Corpora parte sibi discordia bella moverent;/ Hac Elementa vocant, quorum calet ignis, at unda/ Friget, humus siccat, mollit penetrabilis aer:/ Quae tamen unanimi miscentur foedere, ne quid/ Ante diem fugiat, gravibus leviora tenentur/ Fixa solo, levibus gravioraque pondere certant./ Mundus in exemplo minor est, Homo, possidet ille/ Terreno hospitio flammas statusque tenellos/ Cum variis mixtos humoribus, hos regit una/ Mens animae sedes, et motibus incitat artus."

13 The conception of the universe as a site of distillation dates to the pre-Socratic philosophers, and in particular to the theory of condensation and rarefaction proposed by Anaximenes.

14 Maier, *Septimana Philosophica*, p. 7: "Et si bene rem introspiciamus, penitiusque consideremus, Sol in coelo, ut cor in humano corpore procedit in suis operationibus. Cor ex sanguine puriore fabricat spiritus tenues, aerios, sed igneae naturae, calidos et siccos, motu contractionis et dilatationis, quos deinde mittit per arterias carotidas in cerebrum, ut ibi frigiditate et humiditate cerebrim retiformi complexu temperentur et fiant spiritus animales sensibus omnibus et motibus causandis in corpore aptis: ita Sol sive ex puriore aere, sive alias, fabricat essentias subtilissimas, quibus insunt Lumen, Calor, et Virtus, antea dicta, easque transmittit ad stellas omnes circumcirca in coelo sitas, hoc est, errantes et fixas."

15 Maier, *Hymnosophia*, p. Cii *verso*.

16 *Ibid.*, p. Aii *verso*.

vessel writ large, and God – that most "admirable Artificer" – appears as the supreme alchemist (figure 5).[17] For the alchemists of the medieval and early modern periods, the most important source of this conception was the enigmatic *Tabula Smaragdina* of Hermes Trismegistus: and although this text has been described as "cryptic" and "virtually incomprehensible,"[18] we can see that it makes a great deal of sense when understood in terms of the vitalistic Hermetic cosmology held by an alchemist such as Maier:

> That which is beneath is like that which is above: and that which is above, is like that which is beneath, to worke the miracles of one thing. And as all things have proceeded from one, by the meditation of one, so all things have sprung from this one thing by adaptation. His father is the sun, his mother is the moone, the wind bore it in her belly. The earth is his nurse. The father of all the perfection of this world is here. His force and power is perfect, if it be turned into earth. Thou shalt separate the earth from the fire, the thinne from the thicke, and that gently with great discretion. It ascendeth from the Earth into Heaven: and againe it descendeth into the earth, and receiveth the power of the superiours and inferiours: so shalt thou have the glorie of the whole worlde. All obscuritie therefore shall flie away from thee. This is the mightie power of all power, for it shall overcome every subtile thing, and pearce through every solide thing. So was the worlde created.[19]

There exists in the alchemical corpus no more succinct expression of the correspondence of the alchemical work to the cosmogony, or of the place of the divine life force in both. That the wind should bear this power 'in her belly' is an allusion to the Stoic notion of the *logos spermatikos* borne by the air or ether; that it should be 'turned into earth' is a clear reference to the 'fixation' of the volatile mercurial spirit, the *coniunctio oppositorum* which constitutes an act of creation.

In accordance with the unity of the divine power expressed by the *Tabula Smaragdina*, in the thirteenth hymn of his *Hymnosophia* Maier tells us that the Triune God has established "a venerable pattern" on earth, as the Universal Medicine has emerged from a unity, and after many changes

---

[17] The parallels of the alchemical opus with God's work of Creation were elaborated upon at length by the followers of Paracelsus; see, for example, Gerhard Dorn's commentary on the 'Physica' of 'Abbot Trithemius' in *Theatrum Chemicum*, Vol. 1. Strasbourg: Zetzner, 1656, pp. 388-399; an English manuscript translation resides at the British Library: "A Treatise of John Tritheme concerning the Spagirick Artifice exposed & interpreted by Gerhard Dorn." British Library, MS Sloane 632, pp. 6-10. On the subject of the Paracelsian appropriation of the Christian creation myth, see Debus, Allen G. *The English Paracelsians*. London: Oldbourne, 1965, pp. 24-26.

[18] Dobbs, Betty Jo Teeter. "Newton's Commentary on the Emerald Tablet of Hermes Trismegistus: its Scientific and Theological Significance." In Merkel, Ingrid and Allen G. Debus (eds.). *Hermeticism and the Renaissance: Intellectual History and the Occult in Early Modern Europe*. Cranbury: Associated University Presses, 1988, p. 184.

[19] Cited in Roger Bacon's *The Mirror of Alchimy*. London: Richard Olive, 1597, pp. 15-16; Maier, *Hymnosophia*, p. Ciii *recto*.

returns to that unity.[20] Yet the medicine is simultaneously threefold in its nature, a fact to which Hermes Trismegistus has testified.[21] This is a reference to the fifth chapter of the medieval *Tractatus Aureus Hermetis Trismegisti*, in which Hermes asserts that in all Nature there exists three things, a beginning, a middle, and an end – a statement Maier repeats in his thirteenth hymn.[22] These three things are encompassed by God just as the medicine contains the chaotic *prima materia*, the process of purification, and the final perfection within itself. The conception of the Philosophers' Stone as an all-encompassing entity is pervasive in the literature, stretching back to the early Greco-Egyptian texts; witness, for example, the tail-eating *ouroboros* (figure 6), or the "temple of one stone" having "neither beginning nor end in its building" mentioned by Zosimos.[23] Maier's specific references to the Trinity in his thirteenth hymn may also be an allusion to the traditional Christian division of Creation into three eras: the beginning under God, the middle under Christ, and the end under the Holy Spirit (a theme taken up by the Joachimite heretics). Furthermore, in the same passage of the *Tractatus Aureus* to which Maier refers, Hermes asserts that between Heaven and Earth there must be a third, that is to say, a Mediator.[24] Thus Maier again draws a parallel between the Philosophers' Stone and Christ as the incarnate God and redeemer of matter, which he explores further in the thirtieth hymn of the *Hymnosophia*.[25]

The sixteenth hymn – entitled "The sun of the heavens, the sun of the earth: the locus of the medicine" – confirms the many planes of alchemy's significance in its suggestion that the earth, in which metals grow and are perfected through the power of the sun, is also the homologue of the alchemist's vessel:

There is a cave stretching to the centre of the earth, surrounded on all sides by mountains, which holds the hidden seeds of the sun, and which imparts the gift of divine power, and conceals the most golden of treasures. If there are lovers of piety, God the Almighty will make them heirs to the richest gifts. O Lord, if only You would graciously choose me, one in a thousand men, to be a guest at Your banquet. Alas! how am I to repay so great a present

---

[20]   *Ibid.*, pp. Cii *verso*- Ciii *recto*.

[21]   *Ibid.*, p. Ciii *recto*.

[22]   Hermes Trismegistus. "Tractatus Aureus de Lapidis physici secreto." In *Theatrum Chemicum*. Vol. 4. Straßburg: Zetzner, 1613, pp. 672-797; an English translation is to be found in Salmon, William. *Medicina Practica*. London: J. Harris at the Harrow in the Poultrey, 1692, pp. 178-258.

[23]   Berthelot, Marcellin Pierre Eugene (ed., trans.). *Collection des Anciens Alchimistes Grecs*. London: Holland Press, 1963, p. 120: "...un temple monolithe, semblable à la céruse, a l'albâtre, n'ayant ni commencement ni fin dans sa construction."

[24]   Salmon, *Medicina Practica*, verse 5.vii.

[25]   Maier, *Hymnosophia*, pp. Fiv *verso*- Gi *verso*.

with my heart? I possess nothing without You, I am indebted to You for this body and soul, and all the good which You have given to me; these things shall be Yours when I leave [my earthly existence] and are but a ransom to Your kingdom, in order that I may attend You as a servile slave close-at-hand to the celebrated Master and Father.[26]

It must be said that the devotional language utilised in this and other passages of the *Hymnosophia* are unusually florid, and constitute an exception in the corpus of Maier's work; and we might also surmise that the indebtedness Maier felt at this time was as much to his benefactor the Emperor, whom he no doubt attended diligently, if not as a 'servile slave'. Nevertheless, this passage demonstrates well the solar mysticism that is a dominating theme of Maier's work, and the *Tractatus Aureus* may again have been an important source for Maier when formulating these ideas.[27] The central conception here is the 'seed of the sun', by which plants and the "mass submersed in the caverns" are animated.[28] Likewise, we are told that the stars too receive the "pleasing warmth" of this "divine power," which is at its height when they change their aspect to face the radiance of the sun. Although there is nothing of theological speculation in the *Hymnosophia*, Maier strays far enough from an orthodox Lutheran position to represent the sun and God in a language that blurs their distinction.[29]

---

[26] *Ibid.*, p. Di *verso*: "Proximus a centro terrarum tractus habetur/ Undique vallatis conclusum montibus antrum,/ Semina quod Solis tenet abdita, quodque favorem/ Numinis insinuat, thesaurorumque recondit/ Flavissas, si qui fuerint pietatis amantes,/ His beat, haeredesque facit tam divitis arrae/ Largitor Omnipotens: o si me ex millibus unum/ Gratuito talis convivam ad fercula mensae/ Legeris, heu quantas expendam pectore grates,/ Aut referam tanto munuscula munere digna?/ Nil ego possideo sine te, tibi debeo corpus/ Hancque animam, bonaque omnia, quae mihi tute dedisti,/ Haec habeas, mihi me rapiens lytron ad tua regna,/ Ut tibi mancipii servilis sedulus instar/ Cominus assistam, Dominumque Patremque celebrem."

[27] Although these conceptions are common in the medieval alchemical literature, we cannot fail to notice the close resemblance of Maier's sixteenth hymn to the words of Hermes in the *Tractatus Aureus*: "This hidden Secret which is the Venerable Stone, splendid in Color, a Sublime Spirit, an Open Sea, is hid in the Caverns of the Metals: Behold I have exposed it to you; and give thanks to the Almighty God, who teaches you this knowledge: If you be grateful, he will return you the Tribute of your Love"; "...such Gold in Bodies is like the Sun among the Stars, most Light and Splendid. And as by the Power of God, every Vegetable, and all the Fruits of the Earth are perfected; so by the same Power, the Gold, and the Seed thereof which contains all these seven Bodies, makes them to spring to be ripened, and brought to perfection, and without which this Work can in no wise be performed." Salmon, *Medicina Practica*, verses 2.vi, 12.ii.

[28] Maier, *Hymnosophia*, p. Di *recto*: "Sic et humo plantas, nec non submersa cavernis/ Pondera saepe decet vigilante reponere sensu,/ Omnipotensque rudi sub mole requirere Numen."

[29] *Ibid.*: "Sol oculus caeli dum circum voluitur axe/ Fert gyrante diem, radiisque nitentibus umbras/ Discutit, astra super Clarissime justicia SOL/ Tu Deus effulges, solemque solumque refraenas/ Imperio, stet ut hoc perpes, moveatur ut ille."

Did Maier believe at this time that he possessed the '*coelidonia*' or 'gift of heaven' containing the power of the sun? Despite his supplications to God in the *Hymnosophia* to bestow this gift upon him, the evidence of Maier's first experiments described above suggests that he already possessed an iatrochemical remedy that, if not the Universal Medicine itself, was at least something approaching it in virtue and efficacy. Furthermore, according to a letter from Maier to Prince August of Anhalt-Plötzkau cited by Figala and Neumann, the Emperor "graciously condescended to accept a portion of Maier's Universal Medicine."[30] Whether or not the Emperor bravely condescended to ingest this substance, the nature of Maier's principal cure is confirmed in the *Hymnosophia* by the hymn concerning "the resurrection of the dead."[31] In this place, and in the *Civitas Corporis Humani* to be discussed in our fifth chapter, we may gather that Maier's iatrochemical physic was concerned first and foremost with the employment of drastic purgatives. Having told us that the phoenix is not only to be found in Egypt but also in Europe, provided that we "look around with the little eye of the soul," Maier goes on in his hymn to liken that bird's recovery of youth with the treatment of dropsy (œdema).[32] Although this parallel may appear incongruous – as do many of the parallels Maier draws – his reference here is to a process of rejuvenation through catharsis. Thus dropsical limbs are drained of their excess fluid by 'perforation', and the patient is "three times washed by water, three times purged by the flames given by God." The standard treatment for dropsy in the sixteenth and seventeenth centuries was the administration of purgatives, though it seems that Maier may have had some special remedy awaiting his patients beyond the mercuric oxide or sulphur commonly applied.[33]

Despite the successes Maier may have had with this remedy, in the *Hymnosophia* he discusses the four seasons and their parallels to the Great Work, and in the course of the twenty-sixth hymn on autumn we are told that "the ripe fruit does not yet adhere to the tree." This is because such fruit cannot be had "by force of ploughing," i.e. the cycle of Nature must be allowed to take its course, and no premature stoking of the furnace fires will hasten the ripening of the solar seed. This having been said, Maier again

---

[30] Figala and Neumann, "Author cui Nomen Hermes Malavici," p. 130.

[31] Maier, *Hymnosophia*, pp. Civ *recto*- Civ *verso*.

[32] *Ibid.*: "Hoc etenim purae Medicamen amabile Glaurae,/ Innuitur, cui dirus hydrops inflaverat artus:/ Traditur hinc lentae per multa pericula curae,/ Omnis aquae rivis qua per paracenthesin haustis/ Gurgitis a nimio fuit exanimata dolore:/ Tum lymphis ter lota, ter expurgataque flammis,/ Dante Deo, Coelis animam, velut ante recepit,/ Purior et nulla juvenis jam labe perennis."

[33] Kiple, K. F. (ed.). *The Cambridge World History of Disease*. Cambridge: Cambridge University Press, 1993, p. 212.

adopts his melancholic tone when he says that "the hope of succeeding consoles the heart," and he offers up a prayer to God for his future success. Interestingly, this prayer refers to his acquisition of the poet's laurels in Padua: it simply states, "I am he, who was crowned with the laurel wreath in the city of Padua; not because I speak in verses of the frivolous things of this world, but because I speak of the great things of God."[34]

3. The reversal of fortune

Maier was 40 years old when he gained his place in the hereditary peerage on the 29th of September, 1609. The record of the emperor's bestowal of the title of *Pfalzgraf* or Imperial Count Palatine residing in the Allgemeines Verwaltungsarchiv in Vienna lists the privileges associated with Maier's new position; amongst them are the power to grant the right to bear arms,[35] and the power to bestow the title of Doctor, Magister, Baccalaureate and Poet Laureate at the universities of the empire and the Venetian Republic.[36] The university of Padua is mentioned by name, which must have seemed a pleasant reversal of fortune for Maier considering his violent history at that institution, and the efforts of the German Nation there to deny him his own doctoral degree.

In the *Deutsches Reich* the bestowal of a hereditary peerage was accompanied by the ceremonial receipt of heraldic insignia from the Emperor; and in an official manuscript reply to his appointment as Imperial Count Palatine (figure 7), Maier makes a request to the Emperor for a particular symbol to adorn his coat of arms:

Most Merciful Emperor, that true Hermetic Philosopher Avicenna once said in his *Porta Elementorum*, "the magistery is an eagle which flies through the air, and a toad which creeps on the earth." Thereby he understood the eagle to be the volatile part of Mercury, and by the creeping toad he understood the fixed part of the earth, from both of which together arises

---

34 Maier, *Hymnosophia*, p. Fi *verso*: "Arbore fructus adhuc nondum maturus inhaeret,/ Caerea nulla fluunt nec citria, Arantia ve hortis/ Sponte cadunt, nam causa subest, quod frigore duro/ Haec loca pressa diu lento sua semina fotu/ Produxere, calor Solis dum justus abesset:/ Spes sed enim bona successu solatur amico/ Pectora passa graves jam longo tempore curas./ O si detur et hos animo superare labores,/ Et bene speratis in rebus cernere finem,/ Vota tibi Supreme Deus solennibus aris/ Mente lubens faciam, sitque haec inscriptio VOTI:/ ILLE EGO, QUEM PATAVA LAURUS CIRCUMDEDIT URBE/ IAMPRIDEM, STATUO, QUOD NON HAEC FRIVOLA MUNDI/ CARMINIBUS, SED MIRA DEI MAGNALIA DICAM."

35 Vienna, Allgemeines Verwaltungsarchiv: Palatinat, Prag 29. IX. 1609, (R) u. (WB II, 114), p. 11 *verso*.

36 *Ibid.*, pp. 10 *verso*-11 *recto*.

the Hermetic Medicine and Tincture of the Wise, as I will hereafter explain to Your Majesty at length with the greatest pleasure... it is my most humble wish that Your Majesty would recognise me and give me a hereditary double helmet for such a philosophical symbol, like the double helmet that is often to be found on the shields borne by the nobility in Austria...[37]

Evidently the Emperor obliged, as this is a reference to Maier's heraldic insignia (see figure 1), which show a toad and an eagle linked by a golden chain – a representation of the alchemical *coniunctio oppositorum*. The golden chain (*aurea catena*) is a medieval alchemical symbol, mentioned by pseudo-Jean de Meung in the *Remonstrance of Nature* as the means of "reconciling opposites and calming their discord."[38] Just why it should be a golden chain that binds the opposing mercuric and sulphuric principles in the alchemical work may be gleaned from the ultimate source of the *aurea catena* motif in alchemy, Homer's *Iliad*. There Zeus issues a challenge to those who would oppose his will:

...come, try it, gods – then all of you will know. Hang a golden chain down from heaven, and all you gods and goddesses take hold of it: but you could not pull Zeus, the counsellor most high, down from heaven to the ground, however long and hard you laboured... By so much am I above gods and above men.[39]

Clearly, then, the *aurea catena* forms a link between the supreme power of heaven and the mass of the world below; it is the 'marvellously interconnected chain' that Maier speaks of in the *Hymnosophia*, linking the heart with gold, gold with the sun, and the sun with God.[40] From the time of

---

[37] *Ibid.* p. 24r: "Allergnädigster Kayser, Es sagt Avicenna der/ warhafte Hermetisch Philosophus in seiner Porta Elementorum,/ Ein Adler, welcher fleucht durch die Luft, und eine Kröte,/ welcher krigt auf der erde, sey die Meisterschafft; da vorsthet er durch den adtler das fluchtige theil des/ gemeinen Argenti vivi, durch die erdische krichende Kröte,/ das fixe theil der erden, von diessen beiten ist zusamen gefuget die Hermetisch Medicin und Tinctur/ der weissen, wie ich hernach Eur. May: mit grossem Lust weitleuftig zu erkleren habe... so ist mein untertänigste bitte, Ihr May: wolle mir beuelen, solchem philosophischem symbolo einen geduppelten helm erblichen verleihen und mit theilen; wie dan dergeleichen / zwei helme auf einem schilde die vom adel/ meistes theiles zu österreich..."

[38] See the *Musaeum Hermeticum Reformatum et Amplificatum*. Frankfurt am Main: Sande, 1678, p. 165.

[39] Homer. *The Iliad*. Trans. Martin Hammond. Harmondsworth: Penguin Books, 1987, p. 118.

[40] In his *Atalanta Fugiens* Maier mentions a contemporary English report that a toad with a golden chain was found inside a quarry stone: "William of Newberry, an English writer, saith (how truly let others judge) that in a certain quarry in the diocese of Vintonia, a great stone being split, there was a living Toad found in it, with a golden chain, and it was by the Bishop's command, hidden in the same place and buried in perpetual darkness, lest it might bear an ill omen with it." Maier goes on to jestingly question why a toad should require golden jewellery, "lest by chance he should meet the beetle in the

the earliest extant alchemical literature, alchemy was concerned with the powers that link heaven and earth; following the apocryphal *Book of Enoch*, the Greco-Egyptian alchemist Zosimos of Panopolis claimed that the alchemical secrets were taught to humanity by fallen angels, who wrote the primeval books of alchemy.[41] In accordance with that first encounter, alchemists through the millennia toiled to manifest divine power in the world.

Maier's request for the 'symbol of Avicenna' is testament to the great currency held by Hermetic and emblematic symbolism in Rudolfine Prague. Through his archivist, Octavio de Strada, Rudolf had commissioned the collection of a vast registry of symbols and heraldic insignia; these were brought together in a tome known as the *Symbola Divina et Humana*, in which each symbol was illustrated with a copperplate emblem and set together with a motto and short discourse – in similar style to Maier's exclusively alchemical emblem book, the *Atalanta Fugiens*.[42] The emblem gained popularity in the sixteenth century as a pictorial allegory, often accompanied by a short motto, designed to intuitively convey a message of moral significance to the reader.[43] Its origin can be traced largely to the Renaissance understanding of hieroglyphs, and in particular to the discovery in 1419 of the *Hieroglyphics of Horapollo*, a Hellenistic-Egyptian work of the fourth century CE in which the original significance of the priestly script had already been obscured by the Neoplatonic understanding of hieroglyphs as intuitive representations of archetypal truths.[44] Following its reappearance

---

twilight;" and he explains that "it is in the Stone of the subterranean caverns that the Philosophical Toad is really found, not in the quarry (as that fabulous author asserts)." Maier, Michael. "The Flying Atalanta, Or Philosophical Emblems of the Secrets of Nature." British Library, MS Sloane 3645, 17th century, discourse 4.

[41]   *The Book of Enoch*, 8.1-2: "And Azazel taught men to make swords, and knives, and shields, and breastplates, and made known to them the metals of the earth and the art of working them, and bracelets, and ornaments, and the use of antimony, and the beautifying of the eyelids, and all kinds of costly stones, and all colouring tinctures. And there arose much godlessness..."; on this subject, see Mertens, Michèle. "Sur la Trace des Anges Rebelles dans les Traditions Ésotériques du Début de notre Ère jusqu'au XVIIe Siècle." In Ries, Julien and Henri Limet (eds.). *Anges et Démons: Actes du Colloque de Liège et de Louvain-la-Neuve, 25-26 Novembre 1987*. Louvain-la-Neuve: Centre D'Histoire des Religions, 1989, pp. 383-389.

[42]   Trunz, Erich. "Späthumanismus und Manierismus im Kreise Kaiser Rudolfs II." In *Prag um 1600: Kunst und Kultur am Hofe Rudolfs II*. Freren: Luca-Verlag, 1988, p. 58; on de Strada's collection, see Volkmann, Ludwig. *Bilder-Schriften der Renaissance: Hieroglyphik und Emblematik in ihren Beziehungen und Fortwirkungen*. Leipzig: Karl W. Hiersemann, 1923, pp. 58-59.

[43]   Praz, Mario. *Studies in Seventeenth-Century Imagery*. Vol. 1. London: The Warburg Institute, 1939, pp. 12, 19 ff.

[44]   Iversen, *The Myth of Egypt*, pp. 40 ff., 65: "In the Platonic and postsocratic philosophies the Egyptian myths were always considered in the way in which the Greeks had become accustomed to consider their own, which means that the relationship between myth and

in the Renaissance, Horapollo's work gave rise to the idea that hieroglyphs could constitute a universal language without letters, a purely pictorial means of representation embodying the pristine power of words granted to Adam.[45]

4. The most secret of secrets

It is in the context of the search at the imperial court for the *prisca sapientia*, and the pansophic concern with divine signatures in Nature, that we should understand Maier's *Arcana Arcanissima* ('The Most Secret of Secrets,' 1614; see figure 8).[46] In this work the hieroglyphs and myths of ancient Egypt and Greece are interpreted as representations of universal alchemical processes, and constitute the 'pristine language' gleaned directly from the Creator. The *Arcana Arcanissima* was composed during Maier's time at the court of Rudolf, or at least shortly thereafter, as we may gather from the manuscript of Maier's residing at the library of the university of Leipzig entitled *De Theosophia Aegyptiorum* ('On the Theosophy of the Egyptians').[47] Although Christoph Gottlieb von Murr, following Morhof, described the *De Theosophia Aegyptiorum* as a "thorough revision of the *Arcana Arcanissima*" which was never published,[48] there are three facts mitigating against this assertion. Firstly, the contents are largely identical with the *Arcana Arcanissima*, and therefore contain very little to justify a reprint.[49]

---

reality was considered as being of a symbolic and allegorical nature. But the establishment of this symbolic relationship was a fundamental misinterpretation of the very basis of Egyptian thought, and substituted the mythical truth of the Egyptians, with its indissoluble magical identification of myth and matter, by an utterly un-Egyptian interpretation created by Greek philosophy and poetry."

[45] On this subject see Coudert, Allison P. (ed.). *The Language of Adam/ Die Sprache Adams.* Wiesbaden: Harrassowitz, 1999.

[46] Maier, Michael. *Arcana Arcanissima, hoc est, Hieroglyphica Aegyptio-Graeca.* London: Creede, c. 1614.

[47] Maier, Michael. *De Theosophia Aegyptiorum.* Leipzig, Universitätsbibliothek, MS 0396.

[48] von Murr, *Über den Wahren Ursprung der Rosenkreuzer*, p. 45; Morhof, Daniel Georg. *Polyhistor Literarius Philosophicus et Practicus.* Lübeck: Peter Böchmann, 1714, p. 169, n. l: "Qui et idem Argumentum, diversa licet Methodo, denuo pertractavit, in Tr. de Theosophia Aegyptiorum ut antiquissima, sic abdita et Sacra, cuius MStum αυτοχαφου in Bibliothec. Acad. Lips. Paulina superesse, Actorum Orbis Eruditi Lipsiensium Collectores, plura de eodem referentes, M. Jul. A. 1687 p.393, 394 nos edocuerunt, Editionem etiam, Morhofii hortatu, uti ipsemet mihi retulit, moliti."

[49] Thus chapter 1 of the *Arcana Arcanissima* on Egyptian gods and hieroglyphics = *De Theosophia Aegyptiorum*, pp. 8 *recto* ff.; chapter 2 on Jason and Atalanta = pp. 36 *verso* ff.; chapter 3 on the genealogies of the gods = pp. 59 *recto* ff.; chapter 4 on the ancient festivals = pp. 21 *verso* ff.; chapter 5 on the labours of Hercules = pp. 24 *verso* ff.; chapter 6 on the Trojan expedition = pp. 49 *recto* ff.

Secondly, there appear to be certain references in note form to the *De Theosophia Aegyptiorum* on the back page of a manuscript of Maier's dating from early in 1611.[50] Thirdly, on the title page of the *De Theosophia Aegyptiorum* Maier writes "authore Michaele Meyero," an earlier variation of his family name that does not occur in Maier's printed or manuscript works after 1610. This surname is struck out by the same hand (that of the author), and replaced first with 'Maiero', which is struck out again and replaced with 'Maÿero' – the variation Maier decided upon when publishing his *Hymnosophia*, which as we have seen dates from after September 1609 but before Maier's departure from the court of Rudolf II some time prior to the 4th of August 1610.[51] It is not clear whether these revisions indicate some indecision on Maier's behalf concerning the best way to present his name in a printed work; in any case, the *Arcana Arcanissima* appeared under the name 'Maier', as did all his subsequent publications. It is also pertinent to note that after leaving the imperial court Maier spent a period of months in the Saxon town of Torgau, which may explain why the manuscript of the *De Theosophia Aegyptiorum* was to be found at the Paulaner Bibliothek in neighbouring Leipzig as early as 1687, according to the testimony of Morhof.[52] In any case, it would seem that the work is in fact a rough draft for the *Arcana Arcanissima* rather than a 'thorough revision' of that work.

The principal variation in the arguments presented by the *Theosophia Aegyptiorum* and the *Arcana Arcanissima* lies in the question of origins; for according to Maier's draft work, it was Adam himself who was granted knowledge of the Art of alchemy, which was passed on to Egypt by the Jewish patriarchs – in accordance with Ficino's belief – and then on to Greece via the travels of Pythagoras in Egypt.[53] In the *Arcana Arcanissima* Maier only gives Egypt as his starting point, the country from which all art, religion and science are derived.[54] Nevertheless, in his major work on the lineage of alchemical wisdom, the *Symbola Aureae Mensae* (1616), Maier would reiterate his belief that Hermes Trismegistus – the most ancient of Egyptian philosophers – had derived his knowledge from the patriarch Abraham, who had received the *prisca sapientia* in turn from Seth, the son of Adam.[55] Despite the omission of this lineage in the *Arcana Arcanissima*,

---

[50]   Kassel, Gesamthochschul-Bibliothek, 2° MS Chem. 11, 1, p. 64 *verso*.

[51]   We may also mention the consonance of the subtitle of the *De Theosophia Aegyptiorum* – *De Circulo Artium, Coelidonia, Medicina mystica, etc.* – with Maier's other two works of this period: *De Medicina Regia et vere Heroica, Coelidonia*, and the *Hymnosophia, seu Meditatio Laudis Divinae, pro Coelidonia, Medicina mystica, voarchadumica etc.*

[52]   Morhof, *Polyhistor*, p. 169.

[53]   Maier, *De Theosophia Aegyptiorum*, pp. 4-5.

[54]   Maier, *Arcana Arcanissima*, pp. 47-48.

[55]   Maier, *Symbola Aureae Mensae*, pp. 6-8.

both the *De Theosophia Aegyptiorum* and the *Arcana Arcanissima* are in agreement on the nature of that pristine wisdom, which concerned a miraculous medicine for both body and soul:

In order that I might establish the foundation of Egyptian doctrine, I have explored innumerable pieces of evidence showing that there was practised in Egypt – particularly amongst the philosophers, priests and most ancient kings – a certain science, teaching the most secret work of Nature, or a golden medicine, not produced from gold, but a thousand times more precious than gold. In order that this science could be passed on to the wise for posterity, and remain unknown to the common people, certain occult signs drawn from animals were used instead of writing, later called by the Greeks hieroglyphs.[56]

One of the "innumerable pieces of evidence" Maier perused before coming to his conclusions may have been the *Thesaurus Hieroglyphicorum* (c.1607) of Herwarth von Hohenburg, a contemporary collection of hieroglyphic inscriptions (figure 9); another source was certainly the *Hieroglyphics* of Horapollo, who is named as an authority on the first page of the *Arcana Arcanissima*. Maier's theme of secrecy and ciphers is reflected in a verse offered to the reader in the introduction of the *Arcana Arcanissima*, the first and last lines of which are anagrams of his own name:

> (Michael Maierus Doctor, Comes Palatinus.)
> In Christo spes illa deo mea, amo cruciatum.
> Auri ne teneat me malesuadus amor.
> Aurea dos placeat reliquis et lumina pascat.
> Laurus, amo omen sic, dos mihi recta placet.

The middle two lines of the verse also appear to be anagrams, although their solution evades the present author. The whole translates roughly as:

> My hope lies in Christ the God, I love the crucified one.
> Lest the seductive love of gold possess me.
> The golden gift may satisfy others and it does nourish the lights.
> I love and pride myself on the laurel wreath, a just gift and an omen.[57]

In the course of his introduction Maier understandably tackles the question most pressing to his readers: why should a good Christian follow the

---

[56] Maier, *Arcana Arcanissima*, p. 2: "Nos ut fundamentum Aegyptiae doctrinae statuamus, ex innumeris indiciis exploratum habemus, in Aegypto scientiam quandam arcanissima naturae opera docentem, sive MEDICINAM AUREAM, non ex auro, sed auro millies preciosiorem, in usu extitisse, praesertim apud Philosophos, Sacerdotes, et Reges antiquissimos; quae ut posteris sapientioribus tradi posset, vulgo autem ignota maneret, pro scriptione occultas ab animalibus desumptas notas a Graecis postea Hieroglyphicas dictas..."

[57] Maier, *Arcana Arcanissima*, p. Aiv *recto*.

teachings of the pagans? What is there amongst this multitude of gods that concerns those instructed by the true Word of God? In Maier's view, the true significance of myth and hieroglyph were stored beyond writing in the memory of the philosophers, for which reason very few signs still exist concerning their true origin, and the stories of the ancients now appear before us like a treasure lying in "the most secret chest" for over three thousand years.[58] Nevertheless, there still exist works from which their true meaning can be gleaned. On this count Maier names Iamblichus (c.250-c.330 CE), the Syrian Neoplatonist whose *De Mysteriis Aegyptiorum* ('On the Mysteries of the Egyptians') was influential for the Hermeticists of the Italian Renaissance through Ficino's translation of 1497. Unfortunately, Neoplatonists such as Iamblichus had already perpetrated "a fundamental misinterpretation of the very basis of Egyptian thought."[59] Although Maier does not mention the *De Mysteriis Aegyptiorum* by name, it seems likely that this is the work he is referring to, as its ninth chapter deals with the significance of the hieroglyphs – a fact all the more surprising given that Iamblichus' chief concern therein is theurgy, i.e. the magical invocation of the deities.[60] However, Iamblichus followed Plotinus and Plato in stating that all the gods are in reality only One – and it is to this belief that Maier refers when arguing for the compatibility of the ancient writers with Christian teaching:

...it is not likely that the ancient poets attributed so much adultery, homicide, incest and crimes to their gods out of some innate wickedness or gratuitous mockery, nor that they might make sport with gods or men, nor indeed that they might themselves propagate enormous crimes of that kind by the example of the gods (for in that case everyone would have been licentious); but rather in order that they might show these gods to be fictitious and imaginary, and symbols and emblems of an occult Art, hidden to the common people but known to themselves; the one referring to the eye, the other to the mind. Lest moreover they might appear to publicly produce empty names for worthless riddles, each fictitious god was given a quasi-divine function and power of Nature. They ascribed diverse parents to these gods, but notwithstanding they professed One God in all of them.[61]

---

58   *Ibid.*, p. Ai *verso*.

59   C.f. n. 44 above.

60   See Iamblichus. *Iamblichus on the Mysteries of the Egyptians, Chaldaeans, and Assyrians*. London: Stuart and Watkins, 1968.

61   Maier, *Arcana Arcanissima*, p. 59: "...non est verisimile, antiquos illos Poetas ex innata malitia, aut irrisionis gratia tot adulteria, homicidia, incaestus et scelera suis Diis attribuisse, ut vel Deos, vel homines luderent, aut vitia ejusmodi enormia Deorum exemplis propagarent, (tum enim omnium bipedum nequissimi fuissent) sed potius ut demonstrarent Deos illos non esse nisi ficticios, imaginarios et artis occultae vulgo, sed sibi notae, symbola et Emblemata aliud ad oculum, aliud ad mentem referentia: Ne autem inania nomina rebus cassa in medium producere viderentur, singulis illis Diis fictitiis singula officia quasi divinia et vires Naturae: genitricis diversas asscripserunt, ac nihilominus Unum Deum in omnibus istis professi sunt." On the following page Maier also cites 'Orpheus': "Omnia sunt unam, sint plurima nomina quamvis./ Pluto,

Here Maier gives voice to the contemporary conception of emblems, which speak not to the corporeal eye but to the mind, or to the intellect and its divine nature. In order to demonstrate that the 'hieroglyphic emblems' of the Egyptians were indeed 'chemical' *Decknamen*, and did not refer either to gods or to historical personages, Maier devotes some space in his *Arcana Arcanissima* to refuting the claim of Diodorus (fl. first century BCE) in his *Bibliotheca Historica* that Isis and Osiris had lived some ten thousand years before Alexander the Great. According to Maier, any Christian with faith in Scripture can see that this is false, for the age of the world itself cannot exceed 5575 years.[62] The genealogies of the gods known to the Egyptians and the Greeks were neither historical nor mythic, but representations of the *aurea catena* – thus Maier explains the birth of the gods from Saturn, the "father of the Golden Age," as ciphers for the processes to be observed in the alchemical vessel.[63]

Throughout his work Maier follows his ancient sources in correlating the Greek gods with those of the Egyptians; so it is that Thoth became known as Hermes, whom Maier seems to distinguish from Hermes Trismegistus, the 'ancient philosopher'. Egyptian Osiris is correlated with Greek Dionysus; and the story of his murder at the hands of his brother Set, who scattered the dismembered parts of his body across Egypt, is related in detail by Maier. Osiris is the *materia artis* from which the golden medicine is composed, or the philosophical sulphur residing in that *materia*; having been placed in his sepulchre – that is to say, the vessel – he is rent to pieces by his brother, Set or Greek Typhon, who represents the "fiery and furious spirit" of the caustic solution preceding putrefaction. His consort Isis is mercury, the feminine principle, who collects the pieces of Osiris and re-unites them – a reference to the portion of the Egyptian myth in which Isis magically re-animates her husband with the help of Thoth and, mounting the body, sires Horus, the avenger of his father's death (figure 10). Whilst Maier does not mention these facts explicitly, he only reminds us that the "growth-imparting pudenda" of Osiris are those "black and useless dregs" which at first are dissolved and consumed by fire, but thereafter are separated from the body and purified into the most fine and virtuous substance.[64]

Persephone, Ceres et Venus alma, et Amores,/ Tritones, Nereus, Tethys, Neptunus et ipse/ Mercurius, Iuno, Vulcanus, Iupiter et Pan,/ Diana et Phoebus jaculator, sunt Deus unus."

[62] *Ibid.*, p. 11. Here Maier refers to a Christian cosmogonic tradition slightly pre-dating the famous declaration of John Lightfoot in 1642 that the world was created on September the 17th, 3928 BCE at 9 o'clock in the morning.

[63] *Ibid.*, pp. 95 ff.

[64] *Ibid.*, pp. 12-13: "Osiris, ut dictum, pro materia artis, ex qua Medicina aurea componatur, absque omni circuitione habetur; Haec suo sepulchro, hoc est, vasi, imposita a Typhone fratre, in multas partes discerpitur; quas post operis absolutionem

This short account should serve as an example of the method Maier applies to a myriad of myths in the course of the *Arcana Arcanissima*, from the labours of Herakles to the perennial favourite of alchemists in the seventeenth and eighteenth centuries, the quest for the Golden Fleece. The fact that Maier speaks of Osiris and Isis as sun and moon deities[65] serves as a reminder to us that the pre-Hellenistic form of Egyptian mythology and magical ritual was almost entirely unknown to Maier's time – as does one of the more peculiar examples of Maier's rationalising approach to myth and hieroglyph given in the *Septimana Philosophica*, in which he does not speak of the ibis as the bird sacred to Thoth, but rather claims it was used by the Egyptians for the procurement of enemas on account of its long hollow beak.[66] Not surprisingly, Maier's faith never allows him to allegorise Christian mythology in a similar fashion; rather, the truths revealed by the Bible are the referent to which pagan teachings ultimately point.[67] Thus Maier refers in the concluding remarks of the *Arcana Arcanissima* to Christ

---

Isis colligit et unit, sulfure combustibili segregato; Atque sic collectio partium Osiridis ab Iside instituta, est eiusdem operis reiteratio, quae eo usque contingit, donec Typhonis virtus extincta sit, et in eius locum Anima Osiridis sat ardens successerit adeo, ut matrem Isidem, seu coniugem, seu sororem amantissimam facilime ad se convertat; quae est ultima perfectio: Typhon quid sit iam ante diximus, nempe spiritus igneus et furiosus, qui mox Osiridem nostrum penetret, et in suum colorem rapiat, instar veneni; quod non in prima, sed ultima coctione fiaeri debet... Pudendum Osiridis membrum est faex illa nigra et inutilis, qua primo quidem incrementum sumpsit, at post solutionem separanda a corpore reliquo mundo et puro."

65   *Ibid.*, p. 2.

66   Maier, *Septimana Philosophica*, p. 173: "Ibis in Aegypto frequentissima est, forma fere ciconiae, quae serpentes et venenosos vermes ibidem absumit, ideoque inquilinis ut sacra habetur, et honore colitur: Praeterquam enim quod innoxia fit avis, utilitatem quoque hanc mortalibus praestat, ut damna eorum propulset et avertat: Adiectamentum quoque Medicinae contulisse aiunt, dum usum Enematum introduxerit, obstructionem alui seu intestinorum, aqua, rostro posticae inserto, iniecta eluendo tollens."

67   As Matton states, "Maier was not unaware of the danger to which one might subject faith by trying, to quote the words of Mersenne, to 'prove or confirm the mysteries of the Christian religion by the operations of Alchemy'. For the reading may become reversed, in just the same way, leading to an alchemical interpretation of Holy Writ and giving it a 'natural meaning': no longer does the Stone symbolise Christ, but the Christ becomes, like the Phoenix, a simple allegory of the Stone. Thus certain alchemists, vehemently opposed by Maier, did not hesitate to subject Biblical and Christian 'myth' to the same fate as those of Greece and Egypt, propounding, as it were, a sort of 'alchemie libertine' parallel to 'spiritual alchemy'": Matton, Sylvain. "Le Phénix dans l'Oeuvre de Michel Maier et la Littérature Alchimique." In Bailly, J. C. (ed.). *Chansons Intellectuelles sur la Résurréction du Phénix par Michel Maier*. Paris: Gutenberg Reprints, 1984; an English translation of this text was kindly provided to me by Mike Dickman. For Maier's invective against this *alchemie libertine*, see the *Symbola Aureae Mensae*, p. 24: "Quid iam dicemus de iis, qui hoc nostro tempore Creationem mundi, nativitatem, passionem, mortem, resurrectionem et ascensionem Christi, imo fere omnes articulos fide, sacrilege et impiissime ad Chymicam artem transferre conantur?", etc.

as the "doctor of the body and soul" and as "Trismegistus" – an intimation that the Greco-Egyptian title given to Hermes prefigured the doctrine of the Trinity.[68] Christ is the greatest physician, or the transmuting *lapis* which promises eternal life and forms the foundation of the true Church, but which nevertheless was rejected by the vulgar.[69] As such He is the paragon of the true alchemist, who does not seek worldly wealth in the manner of the common *Goldmacher* but devotes his labours to the healing of the sick.

During his time at the imperial court, Maier would have pursued this noble Christian ideal not only by attending his patients, but also through iatrochemical experimentation; for it is likely that he had access to the Emperor's laboratories, which were housed in a building close to the royal castle (Hradschin) and contained a large furnace for smelting ores, a *bain marie* used for maintaining steady low temperatures, and a furnace used in distillation.[70] Nevertheless, Maier's elevated position at the imperial court was to be relatively short-lived, as he had left Prague less than a year following his entrance into the Emperor's service. It is not clear whether this was on account of some failing on Maier's part – the 'Universal Medicine' not being to the Emperor's taste, for example – or whether he saw the writing on the wall for his embattled patron. In any case, by 1610 Rudolf was descending deeper into melancholy; according to Evans, his sickness had been exacerbated by a prophecy – attributed to Tycho Brahe – that he would be intrigued against by members of his own family.[71] Rudolf ended his days as emperor cowering in his palace during the coronation of his usurping brother Matthias, who was to move the imperial capital back to Vienna and reverse the erosion of imperial authority that Rudolf's extravagant narcissism had created.

---

[68] Maier, *Arcana Arcanissima*, p. 285: "Quae omnia cum in nulla alia re, quam MEDICINA ANIMI ET CORPORIS dicta vere aurea conveniant, hanc Summus OPT. MAX: et unice TRISMEGISTUS ille animae et corporis Medicus IHESUS CHRISTUS nobis ad sui nominis gloriam, nostram et proximi utilitatem usurpandam diutissime, et post hanc, Vitam aeternam concedat, qui ut LAPIS ex alto MONTE sine manibus revulsus, et lapis angularis a potiori mundi parte seu gentibus rejectus nobis appropriatus, sit benedictus in secula: AMEN."

[69] See previous note; the reference to the rejected stone is to Psalm 118.22: "The stone which the builders rejected has become the head of the corner;" *Matthew* 21.42: "Jesus said to them, "Have you never read in the scriptures: 'The very stone which the builders rejected has become the head of the corner; this was the Lord's doing, and it is marvellous in our eyes'?"; *1 Peter* 2.4: "Come to him, to that living stone, rejected by men but in God's sight chosen and precious."

[70] Powell, Neil. *Alchemy: the Ancient Science*. London: Aldus Books, 1976, p. 90.

[71] Evans, *Rudolf II and his World*, p. 279.

5. A 'Rosicrucian mission' to England?

Following his departure from Prague Maier gravitated towards the patronage of the Calvinist princes of Germany, and in particular to the court of Moritz the Learned of Hessen-Kassel (figure 11), a close ally of the Calvinist pretender to the imperial throne, the Elector Palatine Prince Friedrich V (figure 12).[72] The court of Moritz was the foremost centre of patronage for the occult sciences in Germany prior to the Thirty Years War, and has been described by Moran as exceeding the court of Rudolf II in regard to "the strength of its focus on the occult arts and the extent of its prince's personal involvement in occult projects."[73] However, the unwavering westward direction of Maier's movements in the year following his departure from Prague – from Leipzig and Torgau in Saxony to Mühlhausen, some 40 miles from Kassel, then on to Bückeburg in Lower Saxony – also seems to indicate a personal ambition to travel to England, the land which was the source of the remarkable medicine that first inspired him to take up alchemical practice. Whilst in England, Maier not only spent his time studying and translating certain English alchemical texts, but he also delivered letters of Christmas greeting to King James I of England and his son Henry, and made the acquaintance of powerful figures at the English court. In light of these facts, Frances Yates propagated the notion amongst many writers that the aim of Maier's journey to England was not only personal, but should be seen in the context of German Calvinist efforts to secure the instalment on the imperial throne of James' son-in-law – Prince Friedrich V. It is in this context that Yates understands Maier's relation to the Rosicrucian phenomenon, and her emphasis on Calvinist intrigue in the empire leads her to cast those writing under the name of the 'Rosicrucians' as the 'true Jesuits' – in accordance with the description given by the early Rosicrucian apologist Adam Haslmayr – playing a role equal and opposite to that of the Society of Jesus in the religious and political affairs of the day.[74]

An analysis of early Rosicrucianism will follow; to determine the truth of Yates' specific conjecture concerning Maier, we must first examine his relation to Moritz the Learned prior to his departure for England late in 1611. From Torgau in March and April of 1611 Maier sent at least two letters and three manuscript treatises demonstrating his alchemical knowledge to Moritz,

---

[72] Electors within the *Deutsches Reich* were powerful princes with the right to cast a vote in the election of the Emperor – Friedrich being the Elector of the lands of the Rheinland-Pfalz or Rhineland Palatinate.

[73] Moran, *The Alchemical World of the German Court*, p. 8.

[74] Yates, *The Rosicrucian Enlightenment*, p. 42 *et passim*.

in a bid to meet the prince and secure his patronage. Figala and Neumann suggest this gesture bore no fruit due to Moritz' focus on the deteriorating political situation in the Empire – which, as we may recall, had recently occasioned the division of the German states into the rival camps of the Catholic League and Protestant Union.[75] There is in fact no evidence of the personal meeting with Moritz Maier hoped for, and as we shall see in our fourth chapter, Maier was not invested with an official position at the court of Moritz until well after his return from England – and that was a relatively minor post outside the inner circle of alchemists at Kassel.

Nevertheless, it seems that Maier had at least established his presence within the courtly circles of Moritz prior to his departure for England, as records exist of a letter sent from Marburg on the 1st of July, 1612 to Maier's friend and former fellow alchemist in Prague, Matthias Borbonius, from Johannes Hartmann (1568-1631) – the iatrochemist appointed by Moritz of Hessen-Kassel to the first professorship for chemical medicine at Marburg, who was an early distributor of the Rosicrucian *Fama Fraternitatis* in manuscript form.[76] In his letter Hartmann states that Maier is already in London with a congratulatory poem for the wedding of Friedrich V and Princess Elizabeth, daughter of James I.[77] However, with regard to the ties Maier made with the court of Friedrich V, it seems likely that these were established after his departure for England. On the 6th of November, 1612 Maier was to be found amongst the 'Elector Palatine's gentlemen' who attended the funeral of Prince Henry of Wales in London.[78] There is also the evidence of the preface to the *Lusus Serius* (1616), a baroque fable of the same order as the *Jocus Severus* (1617) which, in tandem with that tract, was

---

[75]   Figala and Neumann, "Michael Maier," p. 42.

[76]   Gilly, *Cimelia Rhodostaurotica*, p. 29.

[77]   Gellner, G. *Životopis Lékaře Borbonia a Výklad Jeho Deníků*. Prague: Nákladem Česke Akademie Věd a Umění, 1938, pp. 96-97: "V psaní III, daném v Marburku 1/7 (11/7) 1612, oznamuje Hartmann Borboniovi po nové připomínce, že posel pořád ještě není zpět a že nedošla žádaná žlutá antimonová ruda ani návod, jak se z ní extrahuje rtuť, že Michal Meyer je teď v Londýně a že viděl u hraběte hanavského jeho Carmen gratulatorium, připsané králi Velké Britanie Jakubovi I. k chystanému zasnoubení kurfiřta falckého Fridricha V. s Alžbětou Stuartovnou (zasnoubení se slavilo 27/12 1612)." Evans (*Rudolf II and his World*, pp. 206-207) states that "Borbonius seems never to have been a *Leibarzt* [personal physician], though he earned the early favour of Rudolf by producing a poetic-emblematic volume calculated to appeal to his taste for Caesarism mixed with antiquarianism, while he enjoyed the friendship of Maier and a number of the court poets. Borbonius was probably the most sought-after physician in Prague during the first years of the new century... and his alchemical interests emerge from a correspondence with the adept Johann Hartmann."

[78]   Nichols, J. *The Progresses, Processions and Magnificent Festivities of King James the First*. Vol. II. London: Nichols, 1828, p. 485.

rapidly composed on Maier's return to Germany in the summer of 1616.[79] There we find a dedication to Christian Rumphius, physician to the Elector Palatine, and Jacob Mosanus, physician to Moritz the Learned, who are described as "the most sage doctors, expert chemists and my most jocund friends," being bound to Maier by charity, learning and humanity.[80] Although Mosanus was not in England during Maier's sojourn, Rumphius marched with Maier in the funeral procession for Prince Henry in November of 1612; and Maier's description of Rumphius and Mosanus as his 'most jocund friends' suggests that the acquaintance was already of some years' duration at the time of the dedication's composition in September of 1616, rather than the few short months that had elapsed following Maier's return from England. There is also a possibility that Maier walked in the famed garden of the royal palace at Heidelberg, constructed in accordance with Friedrich's penchant for ostentatious displays of his early baroque and occult sensibilities. In the *Jocus Severus* Maier tells us that 'hydraulic organs' simply do not compare with the voice of the nightingale – an indication that he may have heard the rare water-powered instrument erected by Salomon de Caus in the royal garden, and perhaps that he had not been duly impressed by its tone.[81] But the lack of any other evidence for a visit by Maier to Heidelberg suggests he opportunistically attached himself to Friedrich's retinue upon his arrival in England, and not before.

---

[79] Maier, Michael. *Lusus Serius, quo Hermes sive Mercurius rex mundanorum omnium sub homine existentium post longam disceptationem, in consilio octovirali habitam, homine rationali arbitro, judicatus et constitutus est.* Oppenheim: Lucas Jennis, 1616.

[80] *Ibid.*, p. 3: "Dn. Jacobo Mosano Illustriss. Mauritii Hassiae Landgravii, Archiatro digniori. Dn. Christiano Rumphio Electorali Palatino ad Rhenum Med. ordinario circumspecto. Singulis Medicinae Doctoribus sagacissimis, Chymicis expertissimis et amicis meis jucundissimis, tanquam trino Charitum vinculo, doctrinae rarioris scrinio et humanitatis singularis sacello, D. D. D. Michael Majerus Med. D. C. Pal."

[81] Maier, Michael. *Jocus Severus, hoc est, Tribunal aequum, quo noctua regina avium, Phoenice arbitro, post varias disceptationes et querelas volucrum eam infestantium pronunciatur.* Frankfurt am Main: Johann Theodor de Bry, 1617, p. 29: "Nunc altam modulata, imam nunc murmure vocem/ Edit, ut haud aequent Organa hydraula modos./ Ut REsonet MIro FAcilis SOluit LAbra cantu?/ Vox abit ad coelos et nemus omne replet;" which may be roughly translated, without Maier's integration of the *solfege* syllables: "Now he gives forth a high modulation,/ now the lowest voice with a murmur,/ hydraulic organs simply do not compare./ The lips easily open to give out a marvellous song?/ His voice carries to heaven and every grove is filled." Yates (*The Rosicrucian Enlightenment*, p. 12) gives a vivid description of the wondrous garden at Heidelberg; there is also the possibility that this reference to a 'hydraulic organ' refers to the device mentioned in the *Symbola Aureae Mensae* (p. 593), which Maier saw near Florence during his *peregrinatio academica* – although that 'organ' was driven by wind as well as water, and is not referred to as a hydraulic organ. The water organ or *hydraulicus* was first described by Vitruvius in his *De Architectura* (c.20 CE).

Furthermore, if we allow for the possibility that Maier visited the court of Moritz prior to his departure for England in 1611, or even that Maier made the personal meeting he desired with Moritz at that time, there is no evidence of any intelligence role played by Maier whilst in England. And the surviving intelligence report written in Maier's post-1618 capacity as *Chymicus und Medicus von Haus auß* for Moritz – whilst evidence for the polarisation of Maier's own religious and political proclivities – reveals he held no central role in the affairs of his day, let alone that he played a part in a 'Rosicrucian' conspiracy to establish a Calvinist empire or "a state ruled by esoteric wisdom."[82] The existence of a 'Rosicrucian' conspiracy has been proposed not only by Yates but also by Adam McLean, who initially presented his discovery of Maier's Christmas greetings to James I in the Scottish Record Office in Edinburgh as evidence that Maier was "trying to establish links with the highest political authority in Britain" using the symbols of the Rose and Cross.[83] According to McLean and Srigleys' detailed description of the manuscript in question, it presents an eight-petaled rose constructed with letters in red and gold ink, the petals being divided by eight radiating lines of gold letters which read "Long live James, King of Great Britain, hail, may the Rose be joyful under thy protection."[84] McLean interpreted these radiating lines as a 'cross', and argued that the document as a whole indicates Maier was 'an ambassador' for the Elector Palatine on a 'Rosicrucian' mission to Britain to prepare the ground for a political alliance between England and Protestant Germany.[85] However, it is highly unlikely that this document depicts the Rose Cross of the Brethren, not only on the grounds given by Srigley that the lines emanating from the rose are described in the manuscript itself as *interstitia foliorum Rosae*, but also on the grounds of Maier's own admission that he gave scant regard to rumours of a 'Fraternity of the Rose Cross' when he first heard them in England, and only involved himself in the

---

82   McLean, Adam. "A Rosicrucian Manuscript of Michael Maier," *The Hermetic Journal*, 1979, p. 7; Yates, *The Rosicrucian Enlightenment*, pp. 81-82, 89.

83   McLean, "A Rosicrucian Manuscript," pp. 5-6; McLean later revised his position on the 'Rosicrucian' nature of Maier's greetings.

84   "VIVE JACOBE DIU REX MAGNE BRITANNICE SALVE TEGMINE QUO VERE SIT ROSA LAETA SUO;" cited in Srigley, Michael. *Images of Regeneration: A Study of Shakespeare's The Tempest and its Cultural Background*. Uppsala: Acta Universitatis Upsaliensis, 1985, p. 100. Accompanying the rose motif is a fugue in four voices representing the archangels Gabriel, Michael, Raphael and Uriel, to be sung over a repeated *cantus firmus* ascribed to the shepherds Menaleas and Thirsis; a transcription of this example of Maier's musical acumen (or lack thereof) is to be found in Godwin, Joscelyn (ed.). *Atalanta Fugiens: An Edition of the Fugues, Emblems and Epigrams*. Grand Rapids, Mi.: Phanes Press, 1989, pp. 207-208.

85   McLean, "A Rosicrucian Manuscript," p. 7; Godwin also follows the thesis of Yates in "A Context for Michael Maier's *Atalanta Fugiens* (1617)," *The Hermetic Journal*, 1985, p. 5.

affair when he returned to Germany in 1616.[86] Yet Srigley himself describes the rose of Maier's manuscript as the "millenarian Rose of the Protestant Fraternity that Maier wishes James to take under his protection," whilst Åkerman agrees that the rose "certainly indicates a political manoeuvre."[87] Although the marriage of Friedrich V to Princess Elizabeth may certainly be described as such a 'manoeuvre', designed as it was to draw James into alliance with a vulnerable Protestant Union in Germany,[88] a more reasonable assumption is that Maier's manuscript depicts the red rose of England (with the secondary, implied significance of the alchemical rose) and that it is England (and her alchemy) which "may be joyful" under the protection of James I.

6. The seventeenth rung of the alchemical ladder and the art of gold-making

We will return to the question of Maier's relationship with nascent Rosicrucianism in due course; for now let us examine the readily verifiable reasons for his journey to England, rather than supposing that Maier was awarded an official and sensitive diplomatic function on the basis of a single visit to a royal court. Indeed, the evidence of Maier's correspondence with Moritz the Learned in 1611 suggests he had difficulties enough garnering support for the work that was his true passion – the quest for the Universal Medicine.

In the two letters sent by Maier to Moritz from Torgau in March and April of 1611, the recurrent theme is a plea for continued patronage because the perfection of the alchemical Art is within his grasp – a ploy familiar to us from the *Medicina Regia*.[89] Since at least the 4th of August, 1610, Maier had been residing in neighbouring Leipzig, where, according to Figala and Neumann, he had made an unsuccessful bid for a contract with August of Anhalt-Plötzkau, half-brother of the prominent Calvinist intellectual and general, Prince Christian of Anhalt-Bernburg (1568-1630).[90] Having heard that Moritz would be attending a meeting of princes in Torgau, Maier moved to that town on the 10th of March, 1611, in the hope that he might join the

---

[86] On this point see below, chapter IV, p. 114.

[87] Srigley, *Images of Regeneration*, p. 101; Åkerman, *Rose Cross over the Baltic*, p. 133.

[88] Hence the words of a contemporary commentator: "All well-affected people take great pleasure and contentment in this Match, as being a firm foundation and stablishing of religion, which, upon what ground I know not, was before suspected to be *in transitu*: and the Roman Catholics malign it as much, as being the ruin of their hopes." Nichols, *Progresses, Processions and Magnificent Festivities*, pp. 601-602.

[89] Maier, *De Medicina Regia*, p. Ci *verso*.

[90] Figala and Neumann, "Author cui Nomen Hermes Malavici," pp. 130-131.

prince in the 'resting hours' of the meeting and speak in detail concerning his Art.[91] Apparently Maier had already been in contact with Moritz by this time, as he makes reference to a letter he received from Moritz' secretary (presumably after his arrival in Torgau) requesting that he make his way quickly to Kassel *before* the prince's departure for the meeting.[92] On the 16th of March Maier wrote a letter to Moritz from Torgau explaining his dilemma – i.e. whether he should wait in Torgau or make his way to Kassel – and setting forth his plea for the opportunity to demonstrate his knowledge in person.[93] There are many vulgar writers and practitioners, Maier writes, who lie as far from the truth as the earth does from the sky; but if his demonstration to the prince is not in accord with the testimony of Nature and reason, and agreeable with "the hidden nature of mineral essences," then he will demand no remuneration. His only wish is to experience the mercy and liberal grace of His Highness, which he is confident he will receive if he is heard without prejudice.[94] There follows a description of an alchemical 'ladder' with eighteen steps, which Maier is now climbing:

I confess that there are eighteen steps of the ladder to the gold-bearing peak, or to the final perfection of the Art; and the greatest effort is required to move step by step from the lowest to the highest rung. And in truth that ladder has been placed beyond the view of the vulgar writers and practitioners, and thus almost none of them will have reached the first step, much less the second or the third, and still less the higher, since the subsequent steps cannot be overcome without the preceding steps, and the preceding steps without the last of all are of little benefit. Ascending these steps from the lowest to the highest, I have overcome sixteen (God be praised), and standing before the seventeenth or penultimate step I persevere further; not without considerable expense, as Geber testifies, which I have been lacking for two years on account of other misfortunes. And nothing is more difficult than the final or eighteenth step.[95]

---

91   Kassel, Gesamthochschul-Bibliothek, 2° MS Chem. 19, 1, p. 283 *recto.*
92   *Ibid.*: "Utrum igitur mihi agendum, an hic expectandum, an vero ad Celsim. Vam. properandum sit, ut per Secretary Schedulam Significetur, submisse oro."
93   *Ibid.*
94   *Ibid.*, p. 283 *verso*: "Si non vera sint illa sola et maneant, quae demonstraturus sum, nihil posco aut peto praemii: si autem sint, atque ex bis vel decies mille argumentis aut circumstantiis, acclamante rerum mineralium occulta natura, artisque ipsius usu et authorum authenticorum in omnibus reali consensu, pateant, clementiam gratiamque liberalem Cels:is Vae ut experiar, unice exopto."
95   *Ibid.*: "Octodecim, ut fatear, sunt gradus scalae ad aurificam arcem seu artis summam perfectionem; per quos pedetentim ab imo ad supremum contendendum erit; Estque ista scala revera posita extra conspectum vulgarium scribentium aut practiantium; Unde contigit, ut fere nullus eorum primum huius gradum attigerit, nedum secundum, aut tertium; multo minus superiorem; cum posterior absque praecedente superari nequeat, ac praecedentes absque omnium ultimo parvae sint utilitatis. Horum ego graduum (Deo sit laus) ab inferioribus ad superiores ascendendo, sedecim superavi, ac ante decimum septimum seu penultimum, non absque sensibilibus sumptibus, Gebro teste, qui mihi iam

Why Maier should have been lacking the means for alchemical experimentation whilst at the court of Rudolf II is not clear, although certainly his subsequent unsettled existence and his failures to secure patronage would have mitigated against further work. In any case, Maier appended a table to his letter illustrating the eighteen steps of the ladder of which he spoke:

Lapis coagulatus	18. The final operation reaching the ultimate goldenness.
	17. The final operation reaching the ultimate whiteness.
Lapis solutus	16. Of what nature the fire of the solution ought to be.
	15. How the most yellow stone and medicine may be made.
	14. How the stone of moderate yellowness may be made.
Lapis citrinus	13. By which fire the stone tending to yellowness may be made.
	12. How the gold coloured stone, having been perfectly fixed, may be made.
	11. How the stone of moderate goldenness may be made.
Lapis flavus	10. By which fire the stone tending to goldenness may be made.
	9. By which degree of fire the white stone may be made.
	8. By which degree of fire the stone tending to whiteness may be made.
Lapis albus	7. How the black stone – the material to be ground – may be made by a light fire.
	6. The nature of Tusalmat, the material of the Art.
	5. What the material of the Art, Tusalmat, is.
Materia artis	4. What the material of the Art is, from which gold is born.
	3. Of what nature the true aim of the Art is, having been hidden by the philosophers.
	2. That the aim of the Art is agreeable with the nature of gold.
Scopus artis	1. That the aim of the Art is not vulgar.

The second grouping of steps concerning the *materia artis* refers to the nature of Tusalmat, the material from which gold is born, which as we have seen is a code-name for 'Saturnus' or lead.[96] Thereafter the colour series to be observed in the alchemical vessel is black (perhaps a lead oxide), white, gold, yellow, white and gold. This appears to be a slight variation on the first alchemical procedure Maier accomplished in 1604, when he observed the

---

integram biennium, ob alia infortunia, defecerunt, incipiendum et pertexendum, adhuc persisto: ultimus seu decimus octavus, nullius est difficultatis."

[96] In his *Bibliotheca Chimica* (1656) Borelli gives the aenigma on p. 213 of Maier's *Themis Aurea* and its solution under the heading of *Aenigma Majerianum*:

"Clode No Marri in ium dicsit udaoltan plesaritto, Jeait os uperrimit cegmusiemon tus polcopitto, im oc igmon cemslu musalun, im hec musalurou os immusaluron.

Credo me nulli in iam dictis adversum protulisse, Jovis et Apollinis cognationem sat percepisse, in eo ignem contra naturam, in hoc naturalem, et innaturalem."

The simple cryptographic substitutions are revealed as: a = u, b = ?, c = c, d = d, e = o, f = ?, g = g, h = ?, i = i, j = j, k = ?, l = r, m = n, n = m, o = e, p = p, q = ?, r = l, s = t, t = s, u = a; hence Tusalmat = Saturnus, as Newton surmised. Borelli, *Bibliotheca Chimica*, p. 254.

sequence black, multi-coloured, white, yellow and red. Nevertheless, the colour of gold was traditionally distinguished from yellow by the reddish lustre it possesses, and Maier himself speaks of gold as the 'red-yellow metal', so his conception of the anticipated colour of the final 'stone of ultimate goldenness' may not have changed.[97] A very similar table appears in one of the three manuscript treatises Maier sent to Moritz after writing his letter, together with a reiteration of the fact that Maier himself stands at the sixteenth rung of the ladder – having prepared a 'yellow mercurial medicine' – and that only time, labour and money lie between him and ultimate success.[98] The title of this short tract is the *Scala Arcis Philosophicae, Gradibus Octodecim Distincta* ('The Ladder of the Philosophical Peak, having been Divided into Eighteen Steps'), and its burden is to tempt Moritz by partially revealing the nature of the first group of steps on Maier's ladder concerning the 'aim of the Art'. Maier begins his treatise with a poetic analogy for his quest:

A certain philosophical peak of pure shining gold is situated on a lofty and precipitous mountain, carrying the most abundant treasury of all the most precious things. The surrounding region is deserted and rocky, and no fertile trees nor the least twig is to be found across 100 German miles. The concourse to the said peak is filled with people, but as almost all approach without a ladder they stand idly by and are unable to climb; and as often as they strive to overcome the mountain barefoot and unaided they fall on their heads, and break their necks, legs or arms.[99]

Maier makes a similar comparison of the alchemist's quest with the ascent of a mountain in his *Viatorium, hoc est, De Montibus Planetarum Septem seu Metallorum* ('A Guide for the Journey, that is, Concerning the Seven Mountains of the Planets or Metals,' 1618), a treatise focussing on the properties of metals, in which the ascent to the 'philosophical peak' is juxtaposed with the motif of wandering in the labyrinth of Daedalus.[100] Similarly, in the *Examen Fucorum Pseudo-chymicorum* ('The Swarm of Pseudo-chymical Drones,' 1617) Maier employs the symbol of the ascent of

---

[97] Maier, Michael. *De Circulo Physico, Quadrato, hoc est, Auro, eiusque virtute medicinali, sub duro cortice instar nuclei latente.* Oppenheim: Lucas Jennis, 1616, p. 6.

[98] Kassel, Gesamthochschul-Bibliothek, 2° MS Chem. 11, 1, p. 47 *recto*.

[99] *Ibid.*: "Arx quaedam philosophica ex mero et filiis auro splendescens, in quibus copiosissimis omnium rerum preciosissimarum thesauris referta, in ardus et praecipiti monte sita est: Regio Circumquaeque deserta et petrosa, nullis arborisque ac ne minimo ligno per 100. miliaria germanica fertilis; Concursque ad dictam arcem frequentissimus est; verum cum absque scalis fere omnes accedant, stant otiosi ac ascendere nequeunt; Et quotquot eam absque scala nudis pedibus superare nisuntur, in caput decidunt, ac vel collum vel crura aut brachia frangunt."

[100] Maier, Michael. *Viatorium, hoc est, De montibus planetarum septem seu metallorum.* Oppenheim: Johann Theodor de Bry, 1618, pp. 5-10.

Mt. Helicon, home of the Muses and resting-place of the stone devoured by Chronos in place of his son Zeus (figure 13).[101] We can imagine that the imagery of climbing a great edifice or wandering lost in a maze accurately reflects the emotions felt by Maier as he laboured on his never-ending task. The allusion to a ladder in his correspondence to Moritz is drawn from the words of the Arabic alchemist Morienus in the *De Transmutatione Metallica*, who confides to his patron King Khalid:

...whosoever shall seeke any other thinge than this stone for this magistery shall be likened unto a Man that endeavoreth to clyme a Ladder without steppes, which thing he being unable to doe, he falleth to the Earth on his face... this stone is cast in the wayes, it is trodden upon in the dunghills of those wayes, and many men have digged in dunghills in hope to finde it out in them, and herein they have been deceived: but the wise men have known that thinge, and have often used it, which containeth in itself four Elements, and hath Dominion over them.[102]

An illustration of this passage appears in the emblematic depiction of Morienus given in Maier's *Symbola Aureae Mensae* (figure 14); there we see a figure attempting to scale a wall without a ladder, whilst Morienus gestures didactically and the motto warns, *hoc accipe, quod in sterquiliniis suis calcatur: si non, absque scala ascensurus cades in caput* – "accept that it is trampled upon in their dungheap; if not, when climbing without a ladder you will fall on your head."[103] Whilst this saying may appear abstruse, Maier's interpretation of its meaning is to be found in the *Scala Arcis Philosophicae*. On the front page of that treatise there is a rather crudely drawn mountain, with a ladder or staircase leading to a temple on the "peak of pure and shining

---

[101] Maier, Michael. *Examen Fucorum Pseudo-chymicorum detectorum et in gratiam veritatis amantium succincte refutatorum.* Frankfurt am Main: Johann Theodor de Bry, 1617, p. 9; the myth of Chronos/Saturn, who devoured his children but was tricked into eating a stone instead of his son Zeus/Jupiter, is recounted in the twelfth discourse of the *Atalanta Fugiens*; according to antique tradition, many tried to climb Helicon to see the stone with their own eyes, but only a few reached their goal due to the difficult and dangerous ascent. See Beck, *Michael Maiers Examen Fucorum Pseudo-chymicorum*, p. 27.

[102] Morienus Romanus. "Morieni Romani Eremitae Hierosolymitani Sermo." British Library, MS Sloane 3697, 17ᵗʰ century, pp. 52-53; for Maier's source see "Liber de Compositione Alchemiae quem edidit Morienus Romanus." *Artis Auriferae.* Vol. 2. Basel: Conrad Waldkirch, 1593, p. 35; for a modern English translation see Stavenhagen, *A Testament of Alchemy*, p. 27. The original Arabic text is unknown, but a number of identical passages are to be found in an Arabic tract written around 1250 by Abu'l-Qāsim Muhammad ibn Ahmad al-Irāqī; see Stavenhagen, p. 60; also Abu'l-Qāsim Muhammad ibn Ahmad al-Irāqī. *Book of the Knowledge Acquired Concerning the Cultivation of Gold.* Trans. E. J. Holmyard. Paris: Paul Geuthner, 1923.

[103] Maier, *Symbola Aureae Mensae*, p. 141.

gold."[104] On the left side of the mountain a small figure climbs, labelled with the phrase, *ascendere cupiens absque scala* – "he who desires to climb without a ladder." If each step in the alchemical process is the necessary prerequisite for the one that follows, as Maier asserts, then it appears that the first, indispensable step for the Art is recognition of the *materia artis* – Saturnus or lead. For Maier's source on the nature of the Roman rites of Saturn, Macrobius (*Saturnalia*, 1.7.25), gives one of the aspects of the deity as 'Saturnus Sterculius', the god of manure. This is the thing of little value that is "trampled upon in their (i.e. the Philosophers') dungheap," but which nevertheless contains the seeds of gold.

However, we must not overlook the fact that on Maier's 'ladder' there are three steps that precede knowledge of the *materia artis*, which the unlearned for the most part have yet to discover – the true aim of the Art. As we are aware, for Maier this goal was first and foremost the healing of the sick and the procurement of a cure for 'grief and anger'. In another letter to Moritz written on the 29th of April, 1611, Maier declares that he will gladly reveal to the prince the three lower grades of his alchemical 'ladder', although he had already touched upon the matter obliquely in his *Scala Arcis Philosophicae*. The first of these steps consists of the knowledge that the aim of the Art is not a 'vulgar' one, or one of "momentary projection."[105] According to the *Lexicon Alchemiae*, a work of Maier's contemporary Martin Ruland (1569-1611), there are two methods by which the agent of transmutation may be applied to make gold. One is through 'fermentation', whereby the *lapis* is mixed with a molten base metal and 'leavens' it in similar fashion to the yeast in bread, thus mimicking the long duration of the perfection of subterranean metals through the sun's rays; the other is by the 'projection' of the *lapis* upon a base metal, involving a "violent penetration" and instant transmutation.[106]

---

[104] This depiction is reminiscent of the *Visions* of Zosimos, and the seven steps of 'mortification' leading to the 'temple', or the fifteen alchemical steps leading to the altar and the sacrificial priest: "And saying these things, I slept, and I saw a certain sacrificing priest standing before me and over an altar which had the form of a bowl. And that altar had fifteen steps going up to it. Then the priest stood up and I heard from above a voice say to me, 'I have completed the descent of the fifteen steps and the ascent of the steps of light. And it is the sacrificing priest who renews me, casting off the body's coarseness, and, consecrated by necessity, I have become a spirit.'" See Taylor, "The Visions of Zosimos," p. 88.

[105] Kassel, Gesamthochschul-Bibliothek, 2° MS Chem. 19, 1, p. 287 *recto*.

[106] Ruland, Martin. *Lexicon Alchemiae sive Dictionarium Alchemisticum*. Frankfurt am Main: Zachariae Palthenii, 1612, p. 384: "Projectio est per medicinam super re mutanda projectam cum repentino ingressu ex mutatione ex altatio. Convenit cum fermentatione, quod rem intus in substantia mutet; differt autem quod non fiat cum digestione lenta, qua paulatim mistilia alterantur et crasin accipiunt; sed violenta penetratione facta, quasi in momento ingressus, transfiguret;" also p. 211: "Fermentatio est rei in substantia per

Maier considered this latter method to be a sign of charlatanism and one of the extravagant promises of unlearned mountebanks. Indeed, whilst Maier briefly condemns the purveyors of fraudulent alchemical medicines in his *Examen Fucorum Pseudo-chymicorum*, the greater part of that work's invective is aimed towards the self-proclaimed 'gold-makers' and their deceitful practices. In her analysis of the *Atalanta Fugiens* (1617), de Jong has argued that Maier followed Avicenna in denying the possibility of an artificial conversion of species, be that amongst plants, animals or metals.[107] Nevertheless, the fact that Maier included in his communications with Moritz two procedures for the manufacture of gold – one by means of a wet method involving *argenti vivi coagulandi*, and the other by a dry method involving *sulphuris fixi* – demonstrates that gold-making formed part of his early bid for the prince's patronage, even if it was not the main goal of his practice.[108] Although they are characteristically unclear, the main aim of Maier's comments in the *Atalanta Fugiens* is to refute the possibility of artificially converting one metallic species into another "in the short time needed for eating an egg;" the goal of his own quest was to produce an agent possessing the power of transmutation and unlimited increase through fermentation, be that in metals or the human heart.[109]

Another aspect of Maier's appeal to Moritz, who was by all accounts a man of formidable humanist learning, was the promise to reveal the innermost secrets of Nature. Thus in his *Scala Arcis Philosophicae* Maier devotes a great deal of space to the subject of gold as the perfection of Nature, being formed in the likeness of a circle and containing within itself the opposing elements in equal quantity.[110] It was this subject that Maier was to expound at length in the printed work he dedicated to Moritz, *De Circulo Physico Quadrato* ('On the Squaring of the Natural Circle,' 1616), which we

---

admistionem fermenti, qua virtute per spiritum distributa totam penetrat massam, et in suam materiam immutat..."

[107] de Jong, H. M. E. *Michael Maier's Atalanta Fugiens: Sources of an Alchemical Book of Emblems*. Leiden: E.J. Brill, 1969, pp. 17, 155-157.

[108] Kassel, Gesamthochschul-Bibliothek, 4° MS Chem. 39, 12; for a discussion of the contents of this manuscript, see Moran, *The Alchemical World of the German Court*, p. 104.

[109] Maier, *Atalanta Fugiens*, discourse 18: "Quidam ex antimonio vel ejus stellato Regulo cuprum ex cupri odore, eo temporis spacio, quo quis ovum comedat, efficere posse jactant, imo omnia metalla fecisse: verum illis sua sit debita fides, quamvis in hoc mihi non fiat verisimile... Nihilominus Philosophi affirmant, ut in igne ignificandi principium extat, sic in auro aurificandi: verum tinctura quaeritur, cujus medio aurum fiat: Haec indaganda est in suis propriis principiis et generationibus non in alienis: Namsi ignis ignem producat, pyrus pyrum, equus equum tum plumbum plumbum et non argentum, aurum aurum et non tincturam generabit."

[110] Kassel, Gesamthochschul-Bibliothek, 2° MS Chem. 11, 1, pp. 47 *recto*- 64 *verso*, *passim*.

shall shortly examine. In the course of the *Scala Arcis Philosophicae* he likens the vulgar gold-makers' claims of effecting an instant transmutation to the possibility of forming a magic square by a random placement of numerals.[111] Both Paracelsus and Agrippa von Nettesheim had correlated magic squares with the planets and the metals, following Arabic theories concerning the proportion of the four elements within each metal;[112] Maier uses as his example a magic square of the order of 3, which corresponds to lead in the Paracelsian schema:

$$
\begin{array}{ccc}
8 & 1 & 6 \\
3 & 5 & 7 \\
4 & 9 & 2
\end{array}
$$

If the chances of placing the numerals 1 to 9 in this pattern by chance are low, Maier asks how much more difficult it would be to randomly construct higher order magic squares, i.e. those corresponding to the nobler metals.[113] In this way Maier sought to demonstrate to his would-be patron his own knowledge of the harmony and order underlying matter, and thereby distinguish himself from those unlearned practitioners who proceed without a proper understanding of the occult properties inhering in Nature.

The doubts Maier casts on the possibility of an artificial and instant transmutation of metals in his correspondence with Moritz go some way to explaining why he could later find himself in accord with the *Fama Fraternitatis*, the first Rosicrucian manifesto, which rails against "the godless and accursed art of making gold" that has "gotten out of hand in our time," but which goes on to state that gold-making is possible for the true Philosopher, albeit a mere *parergon* or triviality.[114] For Maier, the third step of the alchemical ladder he promised to reveal to Moritz – "the true aim of the Art, having been hidden by the Philosophers" – concerns the medicinal virtues of gold and the production of a 'golden stone' which, like natural gold, contains the opposing sulphuric and mercuric principles in equal part and restores the balance of humours in the intemperate body. If Maier was fortunate enough to meet with Moritz prior to his departure for England, it would have been the allure of this iatrochemical goal that he would have

---

[111] *Ibid.*, p. 50 *recto.*

[112] On this subject, see Karpenko, Vladimír. "Between Magic and Science: Numerical Magical Squares," *Ambix*, Vol. 40, No. 3, November 1993, pp. 121-128; Stapleton, H. E. "The Antiquity of Alchemy," *Ambix*, Vol. 5, No. 1, 1953, pp. 9-15.

[113] *Ibid.*

[114] Kooij, Pleun van der and Carlos Gilly (eds.). *Fama Fraternitatis: Das Urmanifest der Rosenkreuzer Bruderschaft.* Haarlem: Rozekruis Pers, 1998, pp. 98-100.

played upon, and the notion of maintaining health and piety in the body politic – matters close to the heart of a Calvinist prince such as Moritz.

7. A journey to England

Given the content and aim of these communications to Moritz the Learned, it is the pursuit of alchemical knowledge and further patronage for his work that provides the context in which we should understand Maier's journey to England. As the English Freemason and patron of occult learning Elias Ashmole (1617-1692) stated in 1652, Maier "came to live in England, purposely that he might so understand our English Tongue, as to translate Norton's *Ordinall* into Latin verse."[115] Even if Maier did meet with Moritz before setting out for England, it seems that no concrete advantage ensued for him or his work, much less a 'Rosicrucian' diplomatic mission.

On the other hand, Maier was certainly not *persona non grata* following his departure from the environs of Kassel in mid-1611, as he was received at the court of Moritz' brother-in-law, Count Ernst III of Holstein-Schauenburg (1569-1622) in Bückeburg shortly thereafter.[116] There he gave demonstrations of his knowledge to Peter Finxius (1573-1624), personal physician to Ernst and Professor of Medicine at the University of Rinteln, who would later contribute an epigram to the *Symbola Aureae Mensae* (a work which was dedicated by Maier to Count Ernst).[117] At this time Maier also paid a visit to Conrad Hoier, the sub-prior of the monastery at Möllenbeck, some three miles from Rinteln and eight from Bückeburg. Whilst Maier was so impressed by Hoier's literary skills that he conferred upon him the title of Poet Laureate (the only known employment by Maier of the aforementioned privileges adhering to his position as Count Palatine), it seems that Hoier did not immediately reciprocate this stranger's admiration. According to the account of Strieder, the sub-prior found Maier's demeanour somewhat untrustworthy:

In the year 1611 Hoier was crowned Imperial Poet by Michael Maier, Philos. et Med. Doct. et Caes. Maj. Com. Pal.; but he had doubts concerning the authenticity of this Count Palatine, and consequently concerning the authenticity of his own crowning as poet, as shortly before that time there had been a charlatan in the environs of Möllenbeck falsely

---

[115] Ashmole, Elias (ed.). *Theatrum Chemicum Britannicum*. London: J. Grismond, 1652, p. A2.

[116] Figala and Neumann, "Author cui Nomen Hermes Malavici," p. 131.

[117] *Ibid.*; Strieder, Friedrich Wilhelm. *Grundlage zu einer Hessischen Gelehrten und Schriftsteller Geschichte Seit der Reformation bis auf Gegenwärtige Zeiten*. Vol. 6. Kassel: Göttingen: Barmeier, 1786, p. 83.

posing as a Count Palatine. Thus one finds in the front of Hoier's book, *Versus Biblici Antiquiores*, the witnessing stamp of the then Chancellor of Schauenburg, D. Ant. von Wietersheim, in order to corroborate the validity of his laurel wreath.[118]

Whether the talk in Möllenbeck of a roaming impostor had arisen due to some act of Maier's whilst in neighbouring Bückeburg, or due to rumours concerning the man and his Art, we shall never know. But the apparent indifference and distrust Maier inspired in some of his hosts following his departure from Prague certainly cast a revealing light on his persona, and show that wherever he went, he walked a fine line between the status of learned physician and fraud.

From Lower Saxony Maier moved to Rotterdam – his likely port of departure for England.[119] There he met with Pieter Carpentier, the rector of the local grammar school whose natural history collection appears to have been an inspiration for Maier's *Tractatus de Volucri Arborea* ('Concerning the Tree Bird,' 1619) – a compendium of strange tales demonstrating the hieroglyphic significance of those vegetables and animals created contrary to Nature, such as the Tree of Dragon's Blood, the Tartary Lamb and the Lycanthrope.[120] The 'Tree Bird' in question is the barnacle goose, which according to the medieval bestiaries is born from barnacles growing on the underside of driftwood; in Maier's eyes, it had been created thus to mirror the Virgin Birth of Christ.[121]

The next traces of Maier's movements are the manuscript Christmas greetings he offered to James I and his son, Henry Prince of Wales, in

---

[118] Strieder, *Grundlage*, pp. 91-93: "...Hoier sich im J. 1611 vom Michael Maier, Philos. et Med. Doct. et Caes. Maj. Com. Pal. zum kaiserlichen gekrönten Poeten machen lassen; weil er besorgt, man mögte an der Gültigkeit dieses Comitis Palatii, folglich auch an seiner Krönung zum Poeten einen Zweifel tragen, indem sich kurz vorher in dortigen Gegenden ein Betrüger für einen Comitem Palatinum fälschlich ausgegeben; so finde man vor seinem Buche: Versus biblici antiquiores, den Abdruk eines Zeugnisses des damaligen Schauenburgischen Kanzlers D. Ant. von Wietersheim's, um die Richtigkeit seines Lorbeerkranzes zu bestärken."

[119] Figala and Neumann, "Michael Maier," p. 43.

[120] *Ibid.*; Maier, Michael. *Tractatus de Volucri Arborea, absque patre et matre, in insulis Orcadum forma anserculorum proveniente, seu de ortu miraculoso potius quam naturali vegetabilium, animalium, hominum et supranaturalium quorundam.* Frankfurt am Main: Lucas Jennis, 1619, p. 43. In the course of this work Maier corroborates his story of the 'Tree Bird' with reference to communications from a certain 'Doctor of Scotland'. Craven has suggested that this may have been Dr. John Johnston, whose *Thaumatographia Naturalis* (1632) cites the work of the 'most noble' Dr. Maier in turn, and also names Johann Valentin Andreae – the likely progenitor of the Rosicrucian manifestos – as a close friend of the author. Craven, *Count Michael Maier*, pp. 121-122.

[121] It seems that Maier may also have been inspired to create this compendium by the *Kunsthammer* of Emperor Rudolf II, in which many oddities of natural history were to be found: Godwin, "A Context for Michael Maier's *Atalanta Fugiens*," p. 6.

December of 1611. The manuscript given to Henry, recently discovered by Srigley, presents a poem in the form of a pyramid containing anacrostics which was clearly designed to appeal to the prince's interest in Hermeticism.[122] It is executed in red and gold ink and expresses Maier's hopes for the restoration of a Golden Age, in similar fashion to the manuscript destined for James, which mirrors Maier's early letter to Rantzau in its invocation of the pristine wisdom of the 'Egyptian' double-faced Janus.[123] Maier declares in his greetings to Henry that the prince's noble blood is itself a portent of the great deeds he will perform, and he closes with a toast to "the coming new year of good omen, 1612." Unfortunately, however, the stars were not to shine favourably on Henry that year, as evinced by Maier's aforementioned presence amongst the 'Count Palatine's gentlemen' in Henry's funeral procession on Monday the 7th of December, 1612. After 12 days of illness, Henry had capitulated to a certain 'New Disease' or 'corrupt putrid fever', thought by the physicians to have been brought from Hungary.[124] Rumphius, the personal physician of Friedrich V, attended the Prince's dissection with Mayerne, the personal physician of James I, along with "many other Knights and Gentlemen."[125] The funeral procession was some two thousand strong; Maier walked together with Rumphius and others of the German retinue, but at a distance from the Elector Palatine and his closest courtiers, although it seems he was present in Westminster Abbey during the service.[126]

Henry had been rumoured to hold more interventionist views than his father James concerning the religious conflicts in the Empire, and his premature death came as something of a blow to those who hoped for English support of the German Calvinist cause. As a result of his demise, the wedding of Friedrich V to Princess Elizabeth (see figure 15) was postponed by James until Sunday the 14th of February, 1613, lest foreign dignitaries arrive and find the English revelling after the death of his son.[127] It is unclear as to whether Maier was able to personally deliver the 'congratulatory poem' Hartmann speaks of in his letter to Borbonius; nevertheless, it seems likely that Maier at least attended the public nuptial celebrations, which began on the Thursday evening before the wedding. Whilst James, Friedrich, Elizabeth and various English royalty and nobility watched from the galleries and windows of the royal residence at Whitehall, many thousands gathered on the banks of the Thames to witness a splendid fireworks display:

---

[122] Moran, *The Alchemical World of the German Court*, p. 174.

[123] Srigley, *Images of Regeneration*, pp. 101-102.

[124] Nichols, *Progresses, Processions and Magnificent Festivities*, p. 472.

[125] *Ibid.*, p. 485.

[126] *Ibid.*, pp. 496-499.

[127] *Ibid.*, p. 489.

First, for a welcome to the beholders, a peale of ordnance like unto a terrible thunder, ratled in the ayer, and seemed as it were to shake the earth; immediately upon this a rocket of fire burst from the water, and mounted so high into the element, that it dazzled the beholders' eyes to look after it. Secondly, followed a number more of the same fashion, spredding so strangely with sparkling blazes, that the skie seemed to be filled with fire, or that there had been a combate of darting starres fighting in the ayre; and all the time these continued, certaine cannons planted in the fields adjoyning made thundering musick to the great pleasure of the beholders. After this, in a most curious manner, an artificiall Fire-worke with great wonder was seene flying in the ayre, like unto a Dragon, against which another fierie vision appeared, flaming like to St. George on horsebacke, brought in by a burning Inchanter, betweene which was there fought a most strange battell...[128]

That evening and in the following days there were mock battles between 'Turkish' and English ships on the Thames – a spectacular display of anti-Islamic sentiment which included thirty-six galleons, four floating castles with fireworks, and a reconstruction (presumably in miniature) of the town and fort of Algiers at the riverbank. The spectacle cost over £9000, as well as the eyes and limbs of many of the performers, although the royal retinue grew weary of their entertainment after the first night.[129] Given his relatively minor position amongst the courtiers we cannot be sure if Maier attended the various lavish masques and feasts held in honour of the royal couple, and he was certainly not present at the wedding service itself – an honour reserved for "sixteen young men batchelors, being as many as the Bridegroom was years of age; the rest, by the express command of his Majesty, did not enter the Chappel."[130]

8. Francis Anthony and the 'drinkable gold'

In the course of 1613 Maier submitted his *Arcana Arcanissima* to the London printers Crede; like the *De Medicina Regia*, it seems Maier personally circulated the work amongst prominent figures at the royal court in the hope of attracting patronage. One of the courtiers to whom he gave a copy of his work with a hand-written dedication was Lancelot Andrewes (1555-1626), Bishop of Ely, Royal Almoner and one of the king's Privy Councillors, who is said to have "converted many papists" through his "painful preaching"[131]

---

[128] *Ibid.*, p. 537.

[129] *Ibid.*, pp. 525, 539-540, 587.

[130] *Ibid.*, p. 542.

[131] *British Biographical Archive*. Microfiche Edition. München: Sauer, 1984, mf. 26, 407: "painful preaching" here seems to have the meaning of 'careful' or 'painstaking'; a sample follows so that the reader may decide the case: "If this child be Immanuel, God with us, then without this child, this Immanuel, we be without God. "Without Him in

and took up the cause of James' *Defence of the Right of Kings* in the face of Catholic criticism.[132] Another of Maier's dedicatees was Sir Thomas Smith (c.1558-1625), first Governor of the British East India Company and a controversial Treasurer of the Virginia Company from 1609, who was accused by the Virginian colonists of causing famine by favouring the growth of tobacco to the neglect of staple commodities.[133] Maier also dedicated a copy of his *Arcana Arcanissima* to Sir William Paddy (1554-1634), another personal physician of James I, president of the London College of Physicians and close acquaintance of Lancelot Andrewes; Paddy had once gained His Majesty's favour by arguing against the proposition that smoking tobacco is harmful to the health, and was later appointed commissioner of tobacco processing for his efforts.[134]

Yet again, it appears that Maier's efforts to secure patronage came to naught. This much is suggested by the fact that the first dedicatee of the *Lusus Serius* alongside Rumphius and Mosanus is the controversial English alchemist, Francis Anthony (1550-1623). A learned scholar of chemistry from Cambridge University, Anthony had been repeatedly fined and imprisoned by the College of Physicians for peddling his alchemical remedies without a license, and as we shall see, he clearly stood on the outside of the circle of powerful courtiers who Maier had initially wooed. Amongst Anthony's remedies was his famous *aurum potabile* or drinkable gold, a powerful cathartic and emetic, which was said to have miraculously cured certain of his patients, but as often seriously injured or killed them.[135] From the earliest period in the history of chemistry, gold had been held to possess divine properties on account of its seemingly incorruptible and eternal nature; the goal of early modern alchemists such as Anthony was to find a means to dissolve an insoluble substance and make its divine virtues available for human digestion.[136] This was a central problem in Maier's own physic;

---

this world," saith the apostle, and if without Him in this, without Him in the next; and if without Him then, if it be not Immanu-el, it will be Immanu-hell. What with Him? Why if we have Him we need no more; Immanu-el and Immanu-all.' Cited in the *Dictionary of National Biography*. Vol. 1. London: Smith and Elder, 1885, pp. 403-404.

[132] *Dictionary of National Biography*, Vol. 1, p. 404.

[133] *British Biographical Archive*, mf. 1017, 167.

[134] *Dictionary of National Biography*, Vol. 43, p. 35.

[135] *British Biographical Archive*, mf. 31, 215-220.

[136] The noted poet and lutenist, Thomas Campion (1567-1620), who composed a masque for the banquet feast of Friedrich V and Princess Elizabeth, offers a good example of contemporary scepticism regarding the remedy in his epigram *De Auro Potabili*: "Pomponi, tantum vendis medicabilis auri,/ quantum dat fidei credula turba tibi;/ evadunt aliqui, sed non vi futilis auri:/ servantur sola certius ergo fide;" ("Pomponius, the more you vend that medical gold, the more the gullible masses place their trust in you. Some patients are cured, but not by the power of this ineffectual gold: they are

indeed, he tells us that his medicine is similar to the *aurum potabile*, except that it is extracted not from elemental gold but from Philosophical Gold, which, he cryptically remarks, is only conceivable in the imagination.[137] Like the *aurum potabile*, it is also a strong purgative that produces a cathartic reaction in the patient in order to restore the balance of fluids within the body; however, it only affects the sources of sickness, and does not attack the healthy parts of the body.[138] We are told he successfully applied this medicine in both England and Germany; it heals not only epileptics and cripples, but causes grey hairs to regain their pristine colour and teeth to grow back again.[139]

This certainly appears to be an advance on Anthony's medicine, which according to one account caused his patients' teeth to drop out.[140] Nevertheless, Maier's defence of Anthony was emphatic, as we may gather from the introduction he contributed to the Englishman's *Apologia Veritatis Illucescentis* (1616) appearing under the familiar anagram of Hermes Malavici.[141] There Maier commends the sober arguments Anthony has set forth in his work, and defends the 'potable gold' against certain detractors:

Most famous sir, I have read your small treatise concerning the drinkable gold published in your English homeland; the arguments and goal were clearly sound, and whosoever holds another opinion should not be counted amongst good men. I have gratefully examined the sweetest little flowers plucked from the true gardens of *chymia*; and truly when I saw that most venomous pair of spiders alight upon them, making poison out of the nectar and spinning futile and useless webs, I could scarcely contain myself, but that I might blow away those swollen and horrid creatures with one puff, not to say with one fart. But as I have noticed their webs and many little works pleasing so many people, hitherto I have not wished to inflict anything too troublesome on those little animals, lest spiders conspire with hornets. Meanwhile, behold!, I send this sponge imbued with acrid vinegar, with which you can wipe away those nuisances, or the stinking slime carried in by those little beasts; or, if you prefer, totally destroy their unpleasant stains and webs.[142]

---

saved by their trust alone"). See Campion, Thomas. *Thomae Campiani Epigrammatum libri primus*. London: E. Griffin, 1619, Epigram 6.

[137] Stiehle, *Michael Maierus Holsatus*, p. 259; Maier, *De Medicina Regia*, p. 93.

[138] Stiehle, *ibid.*; Maier, *ibid.*

[139] Stiehle, *ibid.*, pp. 258-259; Maier, *ibid.*, p. 84.; c.f. also Maier, *Civitas Corporis Humani*, p. 48; Maier, *Atalanta Fugiens*, discourse 9.

[140] *British Biographical Archive*, mf. 31, 219.

[141] Anthony, Francis. *Apologia Veritatis Illucescentis, pro Auro Potabili: seu Essentia Auri ad medicinalem potabilitatem absque corrosivis reducti; ut fere omnibus humani corporis aegritudinibus, ac praesertim Cordis corroborationi, tanquam Universalis Medicina, utilissime adhiberi possit; una cum rationibus intelligibilibus, testimoniis locupletissimis, et modo convenienti in singulis morbis usurpandi, producta*. London: Johannes Legatt, 1616.

[142] *Ibid.*, p. ¶ 4 *recto*: "Legi vir clarissime tractatulum tuum de Auro potabili apud vos in Anglia editum; argumentum sane et intentio bona; qui aliter aestimet, vix mihi inter

The two 'swollen and horrid' spiders in question were the alchemist Thomas Rawlin and a physician and minor playwright, Matthew Gwinne, who was appointed co-commissioner for the processing of tobacco alongside his friend from the College of Physicians, Sir William Paddy. Gwinne had debunked Anthony's remedy in his *Aurum non Aurum* (1611) as a response to Anthony's first tract on the matter published in 1610,[143] whilst Rawlin's tract – the *Admonitio Pseudo-Chymici* – appeared in 1612 with the aim of exposing Anthony and espousing his own true 'potable gold'.[144] The 'sponge' which Maier offered up to Anthony was a long poem praising the flowers of the 'garden of the Hesperides' which had been sown in England, and which Anthony has plucked.[145] This is a reference to the mythical Greek garden in which golden apples grew and a dragon guarded the Golden Fleece, a motif to which Maier alludes throughout his works as an alchemical hieroglyph. Those who would denigrate Anthony's medicine are likened in Maier's poem to 'Grillus', one of the men of Odysseus who, having been transformed into a pig by the sorceress Circe, preferred the swinish form to his former humanity and so remained thus.[146] When we consider the similarity of Maier's own 'mercurial medicine' to Anthony's *aurum potabile* – both of which act by fortifying the heart's *calor innatus* with the virtues of gold – then we may understand the sympathy he felt for his English friend, and the corresponding vitriol he directed towards Anthony's antagonists. Such was his support for

---

bonos aestimandus. Flosculos tuos dulcissimos ex Chymiae verae hortis delibatos grato animo lustravi; verum cum illis binos areaneos venenosissimos infidere viderem, exque illo nectare venenum sibi haurire et texere futilia et inutilia reticula, vix me continere potui, quin illos turgidos et horridos uno ictu ne dicam flatu dissiparem. At cum animadverterem eorum texturas et opuscula permultis admiranda existere, ideo nihil incommodi illis animalculis hactenus inferre volui, ne scilicet Crabrones cum araneis conspirent. Mitto interim en spongiam Muriaticam, seu muria acri imbutam, qua plagas ab illis bestiolis illatas aut virus infixum elvere, abstergere et sanare possis; aut si mavis, illorum non candidas lituras aut texturas delere et omnino supprimere."

143 Anthony, Francis. *Medicinae Chymicae, et Veri Potabilis Auri Assertio*. Cambridge: Ex officina Cantrelli Legge, 1610.

144 Gwinne, Matthew. *Aurum non Aurum: In assertorem chymicae, sed verae medicinae desertorum, Frac. Anthonivm, Matthaei Gwynn succincta aduersaria*. London: R. Field, 1611; Rawlin, Thomas: *Admonitio Pseudo-chymicis: seu Alphabetarium Philosophicum: omnibus doctrinae filiis, et philosophicae medicinae studiosis, verissime, sincere, et plusquam laconica brevitate conscriptum, et in bonum publicum emissum: in quo D. D. Antonii aurum potabile obiter refutatur, et genuina veri auri potabilis, in omnibus creatis delitescentis, praeparatio proponitur*. London: Allde, 1612.

145 Anthony, *Apologia Veritatis Illucescentis*, pp. ¶ 4 *verso*-¶¶ *recto*.

146 The origins of this tradition are not clear to me, as the tale of 'Grillus' does not appear in Homer's *Odyssey*; however, the German word for a cricket is *die Grille*, and thus the term 'Grillus' may indicate a form of invective.

Anthony that he even took a copy of the *Apologia* back to Germany, with the promise of translating it into his native language.[147]

Given the fact that Anthony's antagonists counted amongst the very courtiers who had been left unimpressed by Maier's advances, then the conspiratorial 'hornets' Maier mentions in the preface to Anthony's *Apologia* may be identified as Sir William Paddy and the London College of Physicians. Thus in his *Prologomena* to the *Theatrum Chemicum Britannicum* Ashmole makes the remark that Maier's entertainment in England "was too coarse for so deserving a scholar."[148] Maier's experiences with unspecified English 'charlatans' inspired his *Examen Fucorum Pseudo-chymicorum*, the more substantial sequel to the earlier 'vinegared sponge' he had presented to Anthony, in which he writes:

When I was in England a few years ago I accrued quite some ill-feeling towards such alchemical frauds, or rather pseudo-chemists, after which time I could not rest until I had seized my pen and made a description of them. I have done this in order that I may give rein to my feelings, and also in order that I might light a torch for all good men, as it were, lest they stumble upon a stone in the gloomy crypt of these frauds, or indeed hit their heads on a beam. That is to say, lest good men be fooled by these leeches and hornets, who not only suck out all blood and life-energy, but also attempt to inflict the greatest pain on the body and soul.[149]

It seems that some of these 'leeches and hornets' were of the ilk of Thomas Rawlin, as Maier devotes some space to the subject of the fraudulent varieties of *aurum potabile* in the course of the *Examen Fucorum Pseudo-chymicorum*. His polemic also draws on testimonies from the works of Heinrich Khunrath and Oswald Croll. In the *Treuhertzige Warnungs-Vermahnung* ('Sincere Warning') cited by Maier, Khunrath relates the story

---

[147] The statement of Maier's intent appears in Maier's letter to the *Stadtarzt* of Frankfurt, Johannes Hartmann Beyer, which will be discussed further in the following chapter: Frankfurt am Main, Stadt- und Universitätsbibliothek, MS Ff. J. H. Beyer A. 161, p. 207 *verso*. It seems that Maier never completed this task, although a Latin edition did appear from the publisher Frobenius in Hamburg in 1618 under the title *Panacea aurea; sive tractatus duo de ipsius auro potabili... nunc primum in Germania ex Londinensi exemplari excusi, oper M.B.F.B.*; thus the possibility remains that this was Maier's translation.

[148] Ashmole, *Theatrum Chemicum Britannicum*, p. A2.

[149] Maier, *Examen Fucorum Pseudo-chymicorum*, p. A2 *verso*: "Cum aliquando in Anglia paucis ab hinc annis nonnihil bilis in eiusmodi fucos alchymicos, aut potius pseudochymicos, collegerim, non potui quiescere, quin eorum delineationem, calamo arrepto, instituerem, tum ut animo meo pro tempore indulgerem, tum ut bonis omnibus hanc quasi facem incenderem, ne facile in tenebricosis illorum cryptis pedem lapidi, aut verticem trabi illiderent, hoc est, se circumveniri ab illis hirudinibus et crabronibus (qui non solum sanguinem, opumque substantiam exugere, sed et dolores acerrimos animo corporique infligere tentant) paterentur."

of the alchemist George Penot, who paid 24 ducats for a suspension of gold filings with camphor, clove and aniseed oil in Prague;[150] whilst Croll recalls meeting a certain 'frivolous Philosopher', who concealed his conniving and snake-like character under the cover of sincerity and Pharisaic piety, and who peddled a sulphurous solution for his own enrichment and the considerable harm of others.[151]

9. The Golden Tripod: "Truth is concealed under the cover of shadows"

Despite his experiences with similar charlatanry in England, Maier held that country in considerable esteem as a centre of alchemical learning, as we may gather from the fruits of his journey contained in the *Tripus Aureus* ('Golden Tripod,' 1618, figure 16).[152] There we find Maier's translation of the *Ordinal of Alchemy* of Thomas Norton (c.1433-1513/14), as well as his transcription of the *Testament* of a certain 'Abbot John Cremer of Westminster' (figure 17). Norton was a citizen of Bristol, a customs agent and purportedly a student of George Ripley. All that is known of the man is an entry in the town records describing a bitter dispute with the mayor, whom he accused of treason; during the trial Norton was denounced for keeping violent retainers and playing tennis on Sunday afternoons, and the whole affair led to his personal humiliation before the king of England.[153] His *Ordinal* is a Middle English poem of 3100 lines, which he intended to write in "playne & comon speche" for "al commyn peple," and to "shew the trouth in few wordis & playne."[154] In the course of the work he sets out the procedures of the

---

[150] *Ibid.*, p. 45; Khunrath's tract is to be found in his *Von Hylealischen, Das ist Pri-Materialischen Catholischen, oder Algemeinem Natürlichen Chaos.* Magdeburg: n.p., 1597; Penotus' original text is given by Beck, *Michael Maiers Examen Fucorum Pseudochymicorum*, p. 54, n. 232.

[151] Maier, *Examen Fucorum Pseudo-chymicorum*, p. 46: "Communicatam ipsum aliquando cuidam Philosopho Corticario sub synceritate et pietate pharisaica, hypocriticum ac colubrinum dexterrime decipientem animum tegenti, qui hunc pulverem (postquam ei sulfuris triti admixtionem, per admonitionem vim percutiendi ademisset) de facie incognitum suis imposturis miscens, cum damno aliorum et suo commodo auri multiplicationem apud plurimos attentavit."

[152] Maier, Michael. *Tripus Aureus, hoc est, Tres tractatus chymici selectissimi.* Frankfurt am Main: Lucas Jennis, 1618.

[153] Norton, Thomas. *Thomas Norton's Ordinal of Alchemy.* Ed. John Reidy. Oxford: Oxford University Press, 1975, pp. xlvi ff.

[154] *Ibid.*, pp. 6-7. As Ashmole once noted, the first syllables of the first lines of each chapter of the *Ordinal* form an anacrostic of the author's name, 'Tomas Norton of Brystow': "To the honour of god oon in persones þree.../ Mastrie ful mervelous & Archymastrie.../

alchemical process "like as the Ordinalle to prestis settith owte the seruyce of the dayes," i.e. in imitation of the order of the Church's liturgies for the year.[155] Maier must have found this manner of ordering the *magnum opus* pleasing, given his own conception of the alchemical significance of Epiphany and Easter; and Norton, like Maier, also brings astrological considerations and celestial virtues to bear in his work.[156] Other aspects of the *Ordinal* which resonate with Maier's worldview are the extensive descriptions it gives of alchemical swindlers – including a certain "monke of Normandie" who attempted to beguile Norton himself – and the insistence on the importance of a knowledge of grammar, rhetoric, arithmetic and music for the practitioner of the Art.[157] However, in the course of his translating work Maier must have felt a little apprehensive when reading the dire warning issued in Norton's introduction not to change a single syllable of his work:

> Now souerayn lord god me gyde and spede,
> For to my maters as now I will procede,
> Prayng al men which this boke shal fynde,
> with deuowte prayers to haue my soule in mynd;
> And that no man for better ne for wors,
> Change my writyng, for drede of goddis curs;
> For where quyck sentence shal seme not to be,
> þere may wise men fynd selcouth priuyte;
> And changing of som oone sillable
> May make this boke vnprofitable.[158]

Normandie norshide a monke now late.../ Tonsile was a laborere in fyre.../ Of þe Grose werk now I will not spare.../ Bryse, when þe change of þe coyne was had.../ Towarde the maters of concordance.../ A Perfite Maister ye may him trowe." In Ashmole's manuscript collection at the Bodleian Library there is a copy of the *Ordinal* transcribed by John Dee (1527-1608), magus resident at the court of Elizabeth I, which may have served as Maier's source; Bodleian Library, MS Ashmole 57, 1577.

[155] Norton, *Ordinal of Alchemy*, p. 8.

[156] Thus Norton speaks of the concord of love "bitwen your werkis & the spere above": "The virtew of ye mover of ye orbe ys formall,/ The virtew of ye viijth spere is here Instrumentall,/ With his signis & figuris et parties aspectuall;/ The planet virtue is propre & speciall;/ The virtew of Elementis is here Materiall,/ The virtew infuside resultith of them all." *Ibid.*, pp. 84, 91.

[157] *Ibid.*, pp. 52-53: "Conioyne your elementis Grammatically/ with alle theire concordis conueniently;.../ Ioyne them also in Rethoricalle gyse/ with naturis ornate in purifiede wyse;.../ Ioyne them to-gedir also Arismetically,/ Bi subtile nombres proporcionally,.../ Ioyne your elementis Musicallye,/ For ij causes: one is for melodye/ whiche theire accordis wil make to your mynde/ The trewe effecte when þat ye shall fynde;/ And al-so for like as Dyapason,/ with diapente & with diatesseron,/ with ypate ypaton & lekanos Mused,/ with accordis which musike be used,/ with theire proporcions cawsen Armonye,/ Moch like proporcions be in Alchymye..."

[158] *Ibid.*, p. 10; 'selcouth privyte' means a 'marvelous secret knowledge' or 'rare secret'.

John Cremer, 'Abbot of Westminster', is a less tangible figure than Norton; indeed, a thorough inspection of the names of abbots and monks given in the obedientiary rolls preserved at Westminster Abbey reveals that no abbot or monk ever went by the name of Cremer at Westminster.[159] Maier's transcription of the *Testament* of Cremer is the earliest record we have of the allegedly medieval author writing under that name; two further manuscript versions of the *Testament* are extant, one in the library of the Wellcome Institute (a French translation dated to around 1675), and the other in Ashmole's collection residing at the Bodleian Library (a copy from Ashmole's own hand).[160] Which manuscript source Maier himself drew upon is unknown, although the work appears to be of sixteenth century origin. Maier himself seems to have had doubts regarding some aspects of the *Testament*, as he introduces the text with the following verse:

> Either the mind of the author, or at any rate his words are deceptive;
> therefore you should be wary, a serpent lies hidden everywhere.
> Do not look down upon this plainly spoken sermon:
> by chance truth is concealed under the cover of shadows.[161]

When Maier says that the mind of the author or his words are deceptive, could he be referring to the identity of Cremer and the strange story of his life recounted in the introduction to the *Testament*? There we learn that the author had been led astray by incomprehensible alchemical authors for some thirty years, but during a journey to Italy Divine Providence brought him into the company of a certain 'Raymund', a man who was as honourable as he was erudite:

I stayed in his company for a long time, and having thus obtained favour in the eyes of this good man, he opened up some part of this great mystery to me. Therefore I made many entreaties to him, and so he came with me to this island and remained with me for two years. During that time I attained the entire work. And afterwards I led this distinguished man into the presence of the most illustrious King Edward, by whom he was welcomed with the

---

[159] Kind information of Christine Reynolds, Assistant Keeper of Muniments at Westminster Abbey.

[160] Bodleian Library, MS Ashmole 1415; Wellcome Institute Library, MS 3557; mention is made of Cremer in Richard Widmore's *An History of the Church of St. Peter Westminster, commonly called Westminster Abbey*. London: J. Fox and C. Tovey, 1751, p. 174, but his account is drawn from Maier's *Tripus Aureus* itself. Nevertheless, Widmore conjectures that 'Cremer' may not be on the abbey records because that is the author's family name rather than the name he took upon entering the monastery, which was customarily derived from the monk's town or region of origin.

[161] Maier, *Tripus Aureus*, p. 184: "Aut mens Authoris, vel certe est littera fallax,/ Inde tibi caveas, anguis ubique latet./ Hunc ne despicias plano sermone locutum,/ Forte sub umbroso tegmine vera tegit."

dignity he deserved and treated very respectfully; and having secured from the King many promises, pacts and conditions, Raymund was content to make the king rich with his Art. The most important conditions were that the king should personally conduct a war against the Turks, the enemies of God, give shelter to the house of the Lord, and least of all make conflict with other Christians by arrogance or war. But (O great sorrow!) this promise was broken by the King, and that pious man was afflicted in his soul and spirit, and he fled across the sea in a miserable state...[162]

These words draw on a tradition that the Catalan theologian and martyr Ramon (Raymund) Lull (c.1235-1316) visited England, a story which derives from the pseudonymous alchemical literature attributed to Lull, as does the erroneous belief that Lull believed in the possibility of the transmutation of metals.[163] Indeed, Cremer's work uses as its literary model the *Testament* of pseudo-Lull, which set the fashion for later alchemical wills and testaments such as Basil Valentine's *Letztes Testament*.[164] Ashmole embellishes Cremer's tale of his dealings with 'Raymund' with a further tradition that King Edward used the riches he gained through Lull's Art to declare war on France, and imprisoned the pious alchemist in the Tower of London, although Lull "made himself a Leaper, by which meanes he gained more liberty."[165] Stories of patrons financing war by means of the spagyric Art are a standard motif in the alchemical corpus; thus Ashmole mentions elsewhere in his

---

[162] *Ibid.*, pp. 185-186: "Et ego huius artis facultatisque veluti sectator studiosus mirandum in modum fui retardatus re obscure mihi in multis variisque codicibus explanata, quos legi exercuique suis per spatium triginta annorum instructionibus ad meum magnum sumptum, detrimentumque laboris mei. Quantoque magis legi, tanto magis erravi, usque dum in Italiam divina providentia me contulerim, ubi Deo optimo maximo visum fuerit, me in sodalitium unius viri non minus dignitate, quam omni genere eruditionis praediti, Raymundi nomine destinare, in cuius sodalitate diu remoratus sum, sicque favorem in conspectu huius boni viri nactus sim quod ille aliquam partem huius tanti mysterii aperuerit, propterea illum multis precibus ita tractavi, quod mecum in hanc insulam veniret, mecumque duos annos manserit. In cuius temporis tractu, sum absolutive totum opus consecutus. Posteaque hunc virum egregium in conspectu inclitissimi Regis Edouardi deduxi, a quo merita dignitate recipitur et omni humanitate tractatur, ibique multis promissis, pactis, conditionibusque a rege inductus, erat contentus Regem promissione divina sua arte divitem facere. Hac solummodo conditione, ut rex in propria persona adversus Turcas, inimicos Dei, bellum gereret impenderetque super domum Domini, minimeque in superbia aut bello gerendo adversus Christianos: sed (proh dolor) hoc promissum erat irritum a rege violatumque, tum ille vir pius in spiritibus penetralibusque cordis sui afflictus hinc trans mare lamentabili miserabilique more aufugit..."

[163] Roberts, Gareth. *The Mirror of Alchemy: Alchemical Ideas and Images in Manuscripts and Books from Antiquity to the Seventeenth Century*. London: The British Library, 1994, pp. 38-40.

[164] *Ibid.*, p. 40; Valentine, Basil. *Letztes Testament und Offenbahrung der Himmlischen und irdischen Gehmeimniß*. Jena: Eyring, 1626.

[165] Ashmole, *Theatrum Chemicum Britannicum*, p. 467.

Theatrum Chemicum Britannicum that George Ripley spent some time on the Isle of Rhodes, and whilst there produced £100 000 worth of gold annually for the Knights of the Order of Saint John in order to aid their struggle against the Muslim Turks.[166]

Nevertheless, whilst there is every reason to doubt the authenticity of Cremer's story and self-professed identity on the basis of his use of such traditional motifs, Maier's historical account in the *Symbola Aureae Mensae* indicates he thought of 'Abbot Cremer' as a true contemporary of Lull who received the secrets of the Art from that man, and he also specifically refutes those who doubt certain aspects of Lull's reported visit to England.[167] This makes Maier's introductory verse to the *Testament* all the more puzzling, and leads us to wonder exactly what it is about the words of this tract or the mind of its author that are deceptive. Like Norton's *Ordinal* – which also draws heavily from the works of pseudo-Lull – Cremer's *Testament* is written in supposedly simple terms, and the author instructs us to ignore any books which deal with an inordinate number of *Decknamen*.[168] Cremer exposes the 'true' meaning of certain of these codenames – thus the 'Black Raven' is oxidised iron ore – although he warns that if any one of his brethren betrays the identity of the central ingredient of the work, 'Red Dragon's Blood', he will have his name erased from the Book of Life.[169] Whether or not the 'true' meanings of certain *Decknamen* supplied by Cremer were themselves codenames, he ends his *Testament* with the supplication that succeeding abbots, priors and seniors make a copy of his work every sixty years, as the written letter is liable to change its form in time.[170] As we will see, the final testament of Maier's life, the *Ulysses*, shows that he failed to find the

---

[166] *Ibid.*, p. 458.

[167] Maier, *Symbola Aureae Mensae*, p. 480: "Hic est ille, qui se Lullium deduxisse in Angliam refert, a quo artem obtinuerit;" the arguments concerning Lull's visit to England are given on pp. 417 ff.

[168] Maier, *Tripus Aureus*, pp. 185, 195.

[169] *Ibid.*, p. 195: "Item iubeo, ut hoc quod vobis revelavi, quod est sanguis draconis rubri, ne cuiquam indicetis, quid id est, nec quantitatem, nec quando in opus nostrum immittatur, neque tempus, neque manifestabitis ulli hominum praeterquam ipsis personis solis supra constitutis: ...quicunque hoc meum mandatum non observaverit, eius nomen e libro vitae abradatur." He also bids his fellow monks not to make use of his Art unless the abbey faces penury or ruin, an 'impossible' circumstance given the treasure he has already bequeathed it: *ibid.*, p. 194.

[170] *Ibid.*, pp. 194-195: "...mandatum vobis do, quod vos, qui in supremo dignitatis gradu in hac domo estis collocati, videlicet Abbas, Prior, gravissimique seniores, ut aliquis vestrum renovet hoc meum opus, exercitiumque rescriptione quotiescunque numerus sexaginta annorum finiatur; Nam illud hoc meum opus conservabit ut quam rectissime possit intelligi: Et quoniam ratio scribendi literas per caracteres varientur, rescriptio de integro est via tutissima conservandi operis nostri, ut integrum et inviolatum successoribus nostris relinquatur."

truth concealed in the shadowy words of Cremer and Norton, and whatever knowledge may once have been held by his English forerunners, something was lost in the translation.

IV. The Rosicrucian 'imposture'

1. Illness and a chance encounter

Maier returned to Germany in the summer of 1616, as we may gather from the preface to the *Jocus Severus* written in Frankfurt am Main in September of that year. He had initially planned to journey once more to Prague, but due to a grave and chronic illness he was waylaid in Frankfurt and could travel no further. In a letter of supplication to Johann Hartmann Beyer (the dedicatee of his *Tripus Aureus*) he identifies this illness as the quartan, the fever of the melancholic, and speaks of the adversities he has faced living in foreign climes whilst suffering "in body and soul."[1] Beyer (1563-1625) was not only the *Stadtarzt* of Frankfurt, but also an important publisher of medical tracts, and the term of address utilised by Maier in the course of his letter ("your Excellency") is an indication of the importance of Beyer's position.[2] Nevertheless, despite Maier's best efforts to secure his patronage, there is no record of any response from Beyer to either the letter or the sample tracts that accompanied it. Furthermore, the fact of Maier's illness (which appears eventually to have led to his demise) must have lent a very personal urgency to his alchemical quest; for Maier's search for the temperance-imparting Universal Medicine was motivated not only by the necessity of securing an income, but also by an increasingly desperate desire to correct the imbalance of humours within his own body. That prolonged exposure to toxic chemicals

---

[1] Frankfurt am Main, Stadt- und Universitätsbibliothek, MS Ff. J. H. Beyer A. 161, p. 207 *verso*: "Non aut em satis fuit: plurimos hic morosos expertum fuisse ab initio, sed praeterea morbus gravissimus et Chronicus, Quartana, invasit, et integrum annum me exercuisse: Durum sane extitit tot mala alienis in omnis peregrino, incognito, adeo afflicto animo et corpore experiri, alias nec satis a fortuna instructo. Quid facerem? Licet iter meum Pragam institueram, hucusque tamen hic praepeditus manere coactus fui. Interea ad Studia mihi recursus, etiamsi vix unum aut alterum penes me librum habuerim, nec amicum ullum ex literatis, a quo mutuo authores paucos acciperim." The letter is dated October 20, 1617.

[2] Beyer was a student of Girolam Fabrici (c.1533-1619), professor of anatomy at the University of Padua; he was also the inventor of a popular 'Frankfurter Pille', made from aloe and gentian for the relief of indigestion. Beyer is not to be confused with Maier's acquaintance Johannes Hartmann (1568-1631), professor of chemical medicine at Marburg.

in the laboratory may well have been the very source of the illness he sought to cure is an ironic circumstance.

More will be said of Maier's downfall in due course; for now it suffices to note that the changes to his travel itinerary occasioned by his illness were to prove fateful for the history of Rosicrucianism. The home of a renowned six monthly book fair, Frankfurt am Main was also a major publishing centre, and Maier now lived in close proximity to the publishers Johann Theodor de Bry and Lucas Jennis, who printed the majority of his publications in the following nine years. Whilst visiting the autumnal book fair of 1616 Maier first became embroiled in the Rosicrucian affair; according to his account in the *Symbola Aureae Mensae*, he had heard rumours during his stay in England concerning the Brethren of the Rosy Cross, but at that time he was occupied solely with the subject of *chemia*[3] and considered the matter to be "obscure and unbelievable gossip." As it had been said that these Brethren were bringing an occult wisdom to Europe via Spain, he had associated them with contemporaneous reports of a certain prophet or 'magician king' named 'Abdela' who had conquered the kingdom of Morocco with the help of occult powers, and he gave the matter no further attention.[4] Nevertheless, during the book fair by "fortunate chance" he came upon the true source of the widespread rumours concerning the Brethren, the anonymous Rosicrucian manifestos. Having read these tracts his opinion was radically altered, and he held it to be a "great and almost unbelievable matter" that had been set in motion by these strange Brethren; and if by "practice itself" the programme of the manifestos might lead to results, he deemed it worthy of being extolled and promoted with every effort.[5] In accordance with this declaration, during

---

3   As Maier utilises the terms *chymia* and *chemia* interchangeably, I have chosen to utilise either the Latin *chemia* or the English 'alchemy' (for reasons elaborated upon in our conclusion) in relation to his work.

4   The tale of the 'magician king' that Maier had heard is related in a contemporary work, *A True Historicall Discourse of Muley Hamets rising to the three Kingdomes of Moruecos, Fes and Sus: the dis-union of the three Kingdomes, by civill warre, kindled amongst his three ambitious Sonnes, Muley Sheck, Muley Boferes, and Muley Sidan.* London: Thomas Purfoot, 1609. In the fifteenth chapter of this tract it is said that in 1608 a certain 'Abdela' had defeated his more powerful brother 'Muley Sidan' in a battle, during which a contingent of 200 English mercenaries with 60 cannons refused to retreat and was routed – the reason, no doubt, for the currency of the rumours Maier heard in England. The role played by occult powers in the conflict seems to have been confused in these rumours, as it was Sidan who eventually wrested control of Morocco back from his brother Abdela some five months after his defeat through the good advice of his soothsayers (see chapter 17 of the *True Historicall Discourse*).

5   Maier, *Symbola Aureae Mensae*, p. 290: "[Fama de Fr. R. C. ad exteros transiit.] FAMA ILLA dictae FRATERNITATIS, quae hic in plurimorum auribus oreque iampridem perstrepuit, adque exteras oras circum circa vagata latissimas regiones pervolavit, mihi quoque tum in Anglia agenti, reique Chymicae unice invigilanti, obscuris quibusdam

the two years that followed the chance encounter at the Frankfurt Book Fair Maier dedicated a number of tracts to the defence of the programme set out in the manifestos, and to the defence of a Brotherhood that remained as elusive as the goals it preached.

On account of his leading role as apologist for this shadowy Order, in time Maier came to be known as a man who squandered his talents not only on the impossible claims of alchemy, but also on the Rosicrucian 'imposture', as Newton would put it when reviewing the manifestos and Maier's defence of them.[6] By the eighteenth century the 'Fraternity of the Rosy Cross' that had inspired the hopes and fears of early seventeenth century Europe was widely condemned alongside alchemy as a malicious fraud, and Maier was depicted as its chief victim, as the *Biographie Universelle* makes clear:

It is difficult to know if the society of the Brothers of the Rosy Cross existed elsewhere than in the imagination of some scoundrels, who used it as a means of extorting money from overly credulous people. The Brothers were believed to possess the power to change metals into gold, or to retain their health over many centuries, and to transport themselves with the rapidity of thought through all the lands of the world. This society commenced with a great deal of noise in Germany at the beginning of the seventeenth century; and Michael Maier was certainly one of its initiates, or rather one of its dupes, since he had the inclination to write up their laws and customs, and took up their defence in his works.[7]

---

rumusculis, incredibilibus, ipsaque veritate longe maioribus insonuit, cui fidem, pro referentis fide, dubiam prima vice adhibui: [A. C. 1613 Barbaria propheticus aut certe magicus rex multa admiranda fecit.] Eodem tempore ex Barbaria innovationes quaedam mirabiles ore referebantur, quomodo prope Marocum et Fessam quidam propheta ex sapientum numero surrexerit, nomine Mullei Om Hamet Ben Abdela, qui plurima occulta signa in se demonstrans, Regem istius regionis, Mullei Sidan, satis magno exercitu instructum, pene inermis, exigua manu aggressus profligavit et vicit, regnique sedem obtinuit. [Prima relatio incerto] Cum vero et hi fratres fama inconstanti ex Barbaria venisse per Hispaniam dicerentur, eiusdem artis et institutionis hi et ille Barbaricus propheta, existimati sunt: [Francf. nundi autumnal: A. 1616] Sed libro ipso de fama et confessione eorum edito, forte fortuna perlustrato, longe aliter de illis ferre iudicium informatus sum. Magna sane res est, quae ab illis agitatur, et pene incredibilis; quam si eventus expresserit, usuque ipso verissimam declaraverit, habebimus satis per vitam, quod miremur, collaudemus et omnibus conatibus promoveamus."

6 Macguire, W. et. al. (eds.) *Alchemy and the Occult: A Catalogue of Books and Manuscripts from the Collection of Paul and Mary Mellon given to Yale University Library.* Vol. 2. New Haven: Yale University Press, 1968, pp. 348-9.

7 *Biographie Universelle*, Vol. 26, p. 232: "C'est encore un problème de savoir si la société des frères de la Rose-Croix a existé ailleurs que dans l'imagination de quelques fourbes, qui en firent un moyen d'extorquer de l'argent à des personnes trop crédules. On leur attribuait le pouvoir de changer les métaux en or, de se conserver pleins de santé pendant plusieurs siècles, et de se transporter avec la rapidité de la pensée dans tous les pays de la terre. Cette société commença à faire du bruit en Allemagne au commencement du 17ᵉ siècle; et Maïer fut certainement un des initiés ou plutôt une des dupes, puisqu'il a eu la bonhomie de rédiger leurs lois, leurs coutumes, et qu'il a pris leur défense dans un de ses ouvrages."

The following chapter will seek to answer one central question concerning Maier's relation to early Rosicrucianism – was he the perpetrator or the victim of an 'imposture', if indeed the manifestos and their programme can be referred to as such? Before considering the evidence of Maier's Rosicrucian writings, some remarks are in order concerning the nature of the Rosicrucian affair that gripped Europe at this time.

2. The origins of Rosicrucianism and the Leipzig Manuscript of Michael Maier

If truth is indeed known by error, as the alchemists have asserted, then we may justly utilise the enigmatic 'Rosicrucian manuscript' of Michael Maier as a means of introducing and defining the Rosicrucian phenomenon with which he was involved. For the literature – both academic and esoteric – concerning the history of Rosicrucianism is so replete with fabrications, intentional and otherwise, that one begins to suspect such deceptions and fantasies form something of the essence of the Rosicrucian phenomenon from its inception to the present day.

That inception was declared across Europe by the publication of the aforesaid anonymous manifestos, the *Fama Fraternitatis* ('Fame of the Fraternity,' 1614) and the *Confessio Fraternitatis* ('Confession of the Fraternity,' 1615).[8] The former was circulating in manuscript form in the cities of Kassel and Marburg, centres of intellectual activity within the Hessian state of Moritz the Learned, from at least July of 1611.[9] It purported to describe the opening of the tomb of Christian Rosenkreutz, the founder of an Order of pious scientist-monks dedicated to the reformation of theology and the sciences; and the discovery of this tomb, and of the books secreted therein, was said to herald the dawn of a new era of the knowledge of God and Nature, in which the proto-sciences of the Golden Age, *Alchemia*, *Cabala* and *Magia*, would be restored:

Seeing as the only wise and merciful God has lately poured out his mercy and goodness so richly to the human race, so that the knowledge of his Son as also that of Nature is continually broadened, we may justly exalt a happy time; because He has allowed us not

---

8   Although the *Fama Fraternitatis* states the manifestos would be propagated in five languages throughout Europe, only German, Latin and Dutch editions are known to us from this early period; an English translation appeared in 1652 under the auspices of Eugenius Philalethes (Thomas Vaughan): *The Fame and Confession of the Fraternity of R: C:, commonly, of the Rosie Cross. With a Praeface annexed thereto, and a short Declaration of their Physicall Work.* London: Giles Calvert, 1652.

9   Gilly, *Cimelia Rhodostaurotica*, p. 70; Kooij and Gilly, *Fama Fraternitatis*, p. 41.

only to discover almost a half part of the unknown and hidden world, and has shown to us many wonderful works and creatures of Nature hitherto never seen, but also He has raised up highly enlightened men of wisdom, who might partly restore the polluted and imperfect arts, in order that Man might finally understand his nobility and splendour, the nature of the Microcosm, and how far his art extends into Nature.[10]

The *Confessio Fraternitatis* states that Christian Rosenkreutz (or 'Father C. R.') was born in 1378 (the commencement of the Great Schism between the popes), and that he lived 106 years (i.e. until shortly after the birth of Martin Luther in late 1483), whilst in the *Fama Fraternitatis* it is said that his tomb was to remain undisturbed for 120 years; which references, considered together, give the date of the opening of the tomb as 1604, the year in which a 'new star' appeared in the constellation of Serpens.[11] The markedly chiliastic *Confessio Fraternitatis* interprets this astronomical event, in tandem with the appearance of a 'new star' in Cygnus in 1600, as a sign and testament to the will of God concerning the coming Reformation of science and religion.[12] Thus, just as the door to the tomb of Father C. R. has been miraculously opened, so soon "a door will open for Europe," as many anticipate with great yearning.[13] The *Fama Fraternitatis* goes on to relate that within the tomb the discoverers found the body of Christian Rosenkreutz, "venerable and undecayed" – evidence of the miraculous properties of his life-prolonging medicine, which, according to the foreword to the reader

---

[10] Kooij and Gilly, *ibid.*, p. 72: "Nachdem der allein weyse und gnädige Gott in den letzten Tagen sein Gnad und Güte so reichlich über das Menschliche Geschlecht außgossen, daß sich die Erkantnuß, beydes seines Sohns und der Natur, je mehr und mehr erweitert, und wir uns billich einer glückseligen Zeit rühmen mögen, daher Er dann nicht allein fast das halbe theil der unbekandten und verborgenen Welt erfunden, viel wunderliche und zuvor nie geschehene Werck und Geschöpff der Natur uns zuführen, und dann hocherleuchte *Ingenia* auffstehen lassen, die zum theil die verunreinigte unvollkommene Kunst wieder zu recht brächten, damit doch endlich der Mensch seinen Adel und Herrlichkeit verstünde, welcher gestalt der Microcosmus, und wie weit sich sein Kunst in der Natur erstrecket."

[11] *Ibid.*, p. 89; Yates, *Rosicrucian Enlightenment*, pp. 255-256; in his *De Stella Nova in Pede Serpentarii* Johannes Kepler describes the star (a supernova known today as SN1604) observed by his assistant on the 27th of September, 1604 of the old calendar as multi-coloured and flickering with astonishing rapidity, which gave it the appearance of a multi-sided adamantine in sunlight. See Kepler, Johannes. *De Stella Nova in Pede Serpentarii.* Prague: Pauli Sessii, 1606, pp. 1-6; the 'new star' in Cygnus (known today as P Cygni) also mentioned by the *Confessio Fraternitatis* was discovered on August the 8th, 1600 by a Dutch astronomer, Willem Blauew – contrary to Yates and other writers on the subject, who speak of the two supernovas appearing in the same year. Kepler's star was visible to the naked eye for 18 months, the supernova in Cygnus for a number of years; neither were as bright as the famous supernova of 1572 analysed by Tycho Brahe.

[12] Peuckert attributes astrological significance to the date of birth of Christian Rosenkreutz; Peuckert, Will-Erich. *Pansophie.* Vol. 3. Berlin: Erich Schmidt Verlag, 1973, p. 74.

[13] Kooij and Gilly, *Fama Fraternitatis*, p. 88.

appended by Thomas Vaughan to the first English edition, takes away all disease, fear, distress and troubles of the soul, just as it transmutes imperfect metals into the finest gold.[14] Clasped within Father C. R.'s hands was the 'Book I.', the most treasured of the Fraternity's texts after the Bible, in which is depicted "a microcosm corresponding in all motions to the macrocosm" – the intellectual fruits of the Father's pilgrimage to Arabia and Africa, where he studied under the wise men of the city of Damcar and the "elemental inhabitants" of Fez.[15]

For all their mythic dimensions, the Rosicrucian manifestos presented to Maier and like-minded Protestants a comprehensive and provocative intellectual agenda, giving expression to a Paracelsian-inspired Hermeticism and a heterodox, humanist Lutheranism with strong millennialist overtones. Nevertheless, they were advertised in the catalogues of the Leipzig and Frankfurt book fairs as "Teutsche Theologische Bücher der Calvinisten,"[16] a classification followed by the chief English Rosicrucian apologist, Robert Fludd.[17] This classification reflects the fact that the first printing of the *Fama Fraternitatis* was made at Kassel with the express consent of Moritz of Hessen-Kassel;[18] despite being far removed from Calvinist theological currents, Rosicrucianism was nurtured above all by Calvinist Germany, that unlikely inheritor of the Renaissance Hermetic tradition, which provided a safe haven for modes of thought inimical to the Counter-Reformation. According to their own testimony, the manifestos were distributed anonymously because the Brethren of the Rosy Cross – their purported authors – faced persecution at the hands of the Jesuits. Thus the *Confessio Fraternitatis* states that, just as the Brethren now openly name the Pope 'Antichrist', so the day will come when they will be able to reveal their true identities to the world.[19] Even if these Brethren did not exist beyond the virtuality of the

---

14   *Ibid.*, p. 93; Vaughan, *Fame and Confession*, p. 42.

15   "Elementarischen Inwohnern;" the 1617 printed edition of the *Fama Fraternitatis* gives the word "Elementaristen;" in MS Nagel they are described with the Latin *Elementarii*; Kooij and Gilly suggest the earth-spirits of Paracelsus may be denoted here; Kooij and Gilly, *Fama Fraternitatis*, pp. 76, 104 n. 35.

16   Gilly, *Cimelia Rhodostaurotica*, p. 41.

17   See Westman, Robert S. "Nature, Art and Psyche: Jung, Pauli and the Kepler-Fludd Polemic." In Vickers, Brian (ed.). *Occult and Scientific Mentalities in the Renaissance.* Cambridge: Cambridge University Press, 1984, p. 179.

18   Gilly, *Cimelia Rhodostaurotica*, p. 70.

19   *Fama Fraternitatis, oder Entdeckung der Bruderschafft deß löblichen Ordens deß Rosen Creutzes/ Beneben der Confession Oder Bekantnuß derselben Fraternitet/ an alle Gelehrte und Haüpter in Europa geschrieben.* Kassel: n.p., 1616, pp. 37-38: "Gleich wie wir aber jetzunder gantz sicher/ frey und ohne einige gefahr den bapst zu Rom/ den Antichrist nennen/... Also wissen wir gewiß/ es werde noch einmal die zeit kommen/ da wir daß jenige/ so jetzunder noch ingeheim gehalten wirdt/ frey offentlich/ mit heller Stimme außruffen/ und vor jederman bekennen werden/..."

mythic manifestos and the literary storm they provoked (a question we shall soon explore in detail), the danger posed to sympathisers of the Rosicrucian programme was very tangible – a fact demonstrated by the fate of Adam Haslmayr, a Catholic Paracelsian from the Tyrol and a distributor of the manuscript *Fama Fraternitatis* from 1610, whose outspoken advocacy of the Fraternity earned him four and a half years in irons on a galley.[20]

The virulent anti-Catholicism of the manifestos went hand-in-hand with their scientific predilections, as those Scholastics who follow "Popery, Galen and Aristotle" are condemned for imagining an "old manuscript" would be equivalent to the "bright, manifest light" of truth.[21] Whilst orthodox theologians of all confessions insisted on the separation of things divine and human in the sciences, the *Fama Fraternitatis* gave expression to the pansophist dream of encapsulating the whole of human knowledge within one overarching schema – a dream epitomised by the words, "it shall not be said, this is true according to philosophy, but false according to theology." The manifestos promoted a humanist resurrection of classical philosophy and upheld its agreement with the teachings of Scripture – together the pagan philosophers and the wisdom of the Bible "form a sphere or globe, whose parts are all removed from the centre by the same distance, which fact should be dealt with further and more elaborately in Christian discourse."[22] As Schick notes, such pansophic sentiments deflected charges of heresy from within the Protestant camp by promising the consummation rather than the dethroning of Christianity; in this sense the Rosicrucian manifestos follow in the syncretic tradition firmly established in Europe by the humanists of the Italian Renaissance.[23]

But what of the identity of these shadowy Protestant Brethren and their founder? One of the most astute esoteric writers on the subject of Rosicrucianism, Arthur Waite, enumerated three different approaches to reading the manifestos: firstly, to regard the story of Christian Rosenkreutz and his founding of the Rosicrucian Fraternity as historically true; secondly, to consider both the society and its founder as purely mythical; and thirdly, to accept the existence of the Rosicrucian Fraternity as a secret society without

---

[20] Gilly, Carlos. *Adam Haslmayr: Der Erste Verkünder der Manifeste der Rosenkreuzer.* Stuttgart: Frommann, 1994, pp. 152-162.

[21] Kooij and Gilly, *Fama Fraternitatis*, p. 72.

[22] *Ibid.*, p. 98: "So soll es nicht heissen: Hoc per Philosophiam verum est, sed per Theologiam falsum, sondern worinnen es Plato, Aristoteles, Pytagoras, und andere getroffen/ wo Enoch/ Abraham/ Moses/ Salomon den Außschlag geben/ besonders wo daß grosse Wunderbuch die Biblia concordiret, daß kömmet zusammen/ und wird eine sphaera oder globus, dessen omnes partes gleiche weit vom Centro stehen/ wie hiervon in Christlicher Collation weiter und außführlich."

[23] Schick, *Das Ältere Rosenkreuzertum*, p. 76.

accepting the historical existence of its supposed founder.[24] We shall soon find Waite's categories wanting; for now it is enough to note that a plethora of traditions have grown up over the centuries amongst those who have devoted their time to uncovering a true secret society lying behind the manifestos. There is no room here to deal with the perennial Rosicrucian – Knights Templar legend, or the myriad other fantasies stretching from Akhenaton's Egypt to the kings of medieval Cambodia. But one of the more pervasive (and persuasive) of these traditions, circulating in academic and esoteric circles alike, purports to derive from a manuscript of Michael Maier residing at the University of Leipzig, in which Maier is alleged to state that the Fraternity of his time was formed in 1570 by followers of Heinrich Cornelius Agrippa von Nettesheim (d.1535), the renowned German natural magician and alchemist whose black dog inspired the appearance of Mephistopheles as a poodle in Goethe's *Faust*.

Although he did not investigate the matter himself, Roland Edighoffer first cast the existence of this "Rosicrucian manuscript" into some doubt in his *Rose-Croix et Société Ideale selon Johann Valentin Andreae* (1982), in which he points to the insubstantial basis of Montgomery's theory of sixteenth century Rosicrucian origins.[25] In his *Cross and Crucible: Johann Valentin Andreae (1586-1654), Phœnix of the Theologians* (1973), John Warwick Montgomery (formerly of the Faculté de Théologie Protestante at the University of Strasbourg) had spoken of 'the claim of the Lutheran alchemist and Rosicrucian Michael Maier that the Rose Cross originated *ca.*1570 through conventicles reflecting the influence of the occultist Heinrich Cornelius Agrippa'.[26] Although Montgomery tells us that he has not verified the manuscript from which this data originates, the idea that Maier ever made such a claim is never brought into question in his work. As Edighoffer correctly states, we may be more sure of Maier's opinion on the matter when consulting his *Silentium post Clamores* (1617), in which he defends the existence of the Fraternity on the grounds that similar secret societies have existed in the past amongst the wise men of many nations, including the Druids of Britain, the Brahmans of India and the priests of Egypt.[27] We shall return to this verifiable testimony of Maier's at a later point; for now, it may be insightful to follow the long and convoluted journey of the 'Rosi-

---

[24] Waite, A. E. *The Real History of the Rosicrucians, founded on their own manifestos, and on facts and documents collected from the writings of initiated brethren.* New York: J. W. Bouton, 1888, pp. 217-218.

[25] Edighoffer, Roland. *Rose-Croix et Société Ideale selon Johann Valentin Andreae.* Paris: Arma Artis, 1982, Vol. 1, pp. 222-223; Vol. 2, pp. 591-592 n. 192.

[26] Montgomery, John Warwick. *Cross and Crucible: Johann Valentin Andreae (1586-1654), Phoenix of the Theologians.* Vol. 1. The Hague: Martinus Nijhoff, 1973, p. 210.

[27] Edighoffer, *Rose-Croix et Société Ideale*, pp. 591-592 n. 192.

crucian' Leipzig manuscript myth through the centuries, as an illustration of the Rosicrucian enigma that continues to lead both diligent and credulous researchers astray.

Montgomery's misleading passage is derived from an article entitled "Historique du Mouvement Rosicrucien" in a French Rosicrucian journal of 1927, *Le Voile d'Isis* ('The Veil of Isis').[28] There the author, a certain Joanny Bricaud, speaks of the "community of mages" organised in France at the beginning of the sixteenth century by Agrippa von Nettesheim. The documentary evidence for the existence of this community is slight; but we shall continue with the story as it stands. Bricaud goes on to state that, upon arriving in London in 1510, Agrippa founded a secret society similar to that which he had organised in France; the members of this society adopted secret signs of *reconnaissance* (presumably *à la* Freemasonry) and thereafter founded corresponding 'chapters' of their society throughout Europe devoted to the study of the occult arts. And – according to the 'Rosicrucian' Leipzig manuscript of Michael Maier – it was this society of Agrippa's that gave rise to the Brethren of the Gold and Rosy Cross around the year 1570:

Si l'on en croit un manuscrit de Michel Maïer conservé dans la bibliothèque de Leipzig, c'est cette communauté qui aurait donné naissance en Allemagne, vers 1570, aux *Frères de la Rose-Croix d'Or*.[29]

Were it to exist, there can be no doubting the significance of such a manuscript of Maier's, as it might provide good reason to push the origins of the Fraternity – as a true secret society rather than a virtual, literary entity – beyond its academically accepted genesis in the imagination of the authors of the *Fama Fraternitatis* and *Confessio Fraternitatis* in the early seventeenth century. The myth of the 'Rosicrucian' Leipzig manuscript has been variously put to work by writers in support of this agenda. Thus Åkerman speaks of Maier's manuscript as evidence for the emergence of the *Gold-und Rosenkreutz* as a "two-tiered Hermetic society" embroiled in sixteenth century French inter-confessional disputes.[30] Likewise, the 'Rosicrucian' Leipzig manuscript myth has taken root in Freemasonic lore – in his *Les Origines de la Franc-Maçonnerie: Le Métier et le Sacré* (1991) Naudon quotes Bricaud *verbatim* as proof of the anteriority of Rosicrucianism (as a forerunner of Freemasonry) to the Rosicrucian manifestos.[31]

---

[28]   Bricaud, Joanny. "Historique du Mouvement Rosicrucien," *Le Voile d'Isis*, Vol. 91, July 1927, pp. 559-574.

[29]   *Ibid.*, p. 561.

[30]   Åkerman, *Rose Cross over the Baltic*, p. 181.

[31]   Naudon, *Les Origines de la Franc-Maçonnerie*, pp. 269-270: "...Une autre société importante dont l'action sur la Maçonnerie, du moins indirectement, est probable, est la

More plausibly, the existence of such a manuscript might also point to a tradition concerning Rosicrucian origins stemming from the early seventeenth century and adhered to by Maier. As related in our third chapter, there is indeed a manuscript of Michael Maier's residing at the library of the University of Leipzig, entitled *De Theosophia Aegyptiorum*.[32] Nevertheless, a thorough perusal of this tract does not reveal the slightest mention of the Rosy Cross, let alone Cornelius Agrippa and his supposed contribution to the foundation of the Order. Nor should such mention be expected, as it would be unusual for Maier to affiliate himself with an Order inspired by a man who was – in Maier's own opinion – an impoverished and fumbling failure in the alchemical Art.[33] Furthermore, we have seen that the *De Theosophia Aegyptiorum* is in fact a rough draft for Maier's *Arcana Arcanissima* (1614), and although Maier was distantly acquainted with the contents of the manuscript manifestos prior to their publication in print, it was only in 1616 that he began to consider the subject worthy of his attention. There is no other manuscript of Maier's to be found at the University of Leipzig; and whilst Åkerman adduces that no manuscript confirming the sixteenth century *Gold- und Rosenkreutz* hypothesis has been found in Leipzig because "no effort has been made to locate it," my own examination of other library catalogues in Leipzig also revealed no trace of a manuscript by Maier.

This absence is hardly surprising, given that at least one element of this curious Rosicrucian tale is derived from the Reverend Craven's work on Count Michael Maier. Writing in 1910, Craven discounts the mention of Maier's Rosicrucian 'Leiden manuscript' made by John Yarker in his *Arcane Schools* (1909) as a mistake; having consulted the librarian of the University of Leiden, Craven was assured that there was no such manuscript residing in

---

Communauté des Mages. Elle fut fondée en 1510 par Henri-Corneille Agrippa, lorsqu'il arriva à Londres, sur le modèle de celle qu'il avait déjà créée en France. La *Communauté des Mages* était une société secrète groupant les maîtres de l'alchimie et de la magie. Les membres usaient de signes particuliers de reconnaissance, de "mots de passe." Ils fondèrent alors, dans divers autres Etats de l'Europe, des associations correspondantes, dénommées *Chapelies*, pour l'étude des sciences "interdites." Si nous en croyons un manuscrit de *Michel Maîer* (1568-1622), conservé à la bibliothèque de Leipzig, ce serait cette *Communauté des Mages* qui aurait donné naissance, en Allemagne, vers 1570, aux *Frères de la Rose-Croix d'or*, antérieurs par conséquent a la *Fama Fraternitatis* de Valentin Andréa." Needless to say, my consultations with French Freemasons and Rosicrucians concerning this passage failed to reveal any further details with respect to the whereabouts and nature of this mysterious manuscript.

[32] See above, pp. 78 ff.

[33] See, for example, Maier, *Examen Fucorum Pseudo-chymicorum*, p. 41: "Cornelius Agrippa testatur alicubi, se potuisse ex auro hunc subtilem spiritum extrahere: Interim qualis vir hic fuerit, ex eius epistolis apparet, nempe egestate obrutus et obaeratus, cui hoc artificium, si id sciverit, nihil profuerit;" also Maier, *Atalanta Fugiens*, discourse 1; de Jong, *Michael Maier's Atalanta Fugiens*, pp. 62-63.

Leiden, and that Yarker had confused 'Leiden' with 'Leipzig'. Evidently the Leiden librarian was aware of the existence of a manuscript of Maier's at Leipzig, whilst not being aware of its contents.[34] Craven believed the document at Leipzig was the only manuscript of Maier's to have "survived the destruction of Magdeburg;" thus the 'Leiden manuscript' became the 'Leipzig manuscript', and this may ultimately be the reason why it appears as such in Bricaud's article – the Leiden librarian's deduction being transmitted to later authors first by Craven and then by Waite.

Yarker's account of a 'Leiden manuscript' in his *Arcane Schools*[35] – which Waite correctly identifies as a "tissue of inextricable reveries," although he follows Craven in referring to an extant 'Leipsic manuscript' with references to the Rose Cross and Agrippa[36] – is based upon the testimony of Hans Heinrich von Ecker und Eckhoffen in his work of 1782, *Der Rosenkreuzer in seiner Blösse (The Rosicrucian in his Nakedness)*.[37] There the author, writing under the name of 'Magister Pianco', makes a disgruntled exposé of the secrets of the "so-called True Freemasons, or Golden Rosicrucians of the Old System," an attack aimed in particular at "Brother Phoebron, General Director of the Supreme Order of the Rosicrucians in Germany" (i.e. Bernhard Joseph Schleiß von Löwenfeld). As we have seen in our introduction, the *Gold- und Rosenkreutz* to which he refers was a Freemasonic offshoot, combining Masonic initiatory grades with alchemical lore and practice. Having been expelled from this group a year prior to his book's publication, and having founded his own rival grouping known as the 'Asiatic Brethren', von Ecker und Eckhoffen attempts to portray the 'Golden Rosicrucians' as puppets of the Jesuits. In the course of his polemic he refers to the manuscript of Michael Maier of Rensburg, "one of the most notorious of the Rosicrucians," to be found at the library of the

---

[34] Craven, *Count Michael Maier*, pp. 4-5.

[35] Yarker, John. *The Arcane Schools; a Review of their Origin and Antiquity; with a General History of Freemasonry, and its Relation to the Theosophic, Scientific, and Philosophic Mysteries*. Belfast: William Tait, 1909, p. 212: "There exists in the library of the University of Leyden a MS. by Michael Maier which sets forth that in 1570 the Society of the old Magical brethren or Wise Men was revived under the name of the Brethren of the Golden Rosy Cross." Amongst other curious 'facts' included in Yarker's account are the ascription of a pre-Reformation date to the *Fama Fraternitatis* and the assertion that Maier "published the *de Vita Morte et Resurectione* of his friend Robert Fludd."

[36] Waite, *Brotherhood of the Rosy Cross*, p. 330.

[37] Ecker und Eckhoffen, Hans Heinrich von (Magister Pianco). *Der Rosenkreuzer in seiner Blösse*. Amsterdam: n.p., 1782. The authorship of this tract is also a matter of dispute; see McIntosh, Christopher. *The Rose Cross and the Age of Reason: Eighteenth-Century Rosicrucianism in Central Europe and its Relation to the Enlightenment*. Leiden: E. J. Brill, 1992, p. 133.

University of Leiden.[38] In this supposed manuscript Maier is purported to describe the reformation of the Rosicrucian Order in 1510, by which the teachings of the Books of Moses and the Book of Revelations were brought into accord with the instructions of the "old Magi." As a sign of their reformation, the Brethren decided to rename themselves "Brethren of the Golden Rose Cross, True Freemasons, and True and Sincere Friends and Kindred of the Golden Rose Cross."[39]

That this history is a fabrication, and does not derive from a true document of Maier's, is confirmed by two important facts. Firstly, whilst Craven was led astray by the good advice of the Leiden librarian, he was correct in stating that no such manuscript exists – or is likely to have existed – at the University of Leiden. The university's manuscript catalogue of the early nineteenth century contains no trace of a manuscript under the names of Michael Maier, Meier or Mayer, either as an acquisition or as a possession, nor have there been any major losses in the collection due to fire, war or other disasters. Nor is such a manuscript held by the library of the Museum Boerhaave in Leiden – the other major seventeenth century collection in that city.[40]

Secondly, the term 'Gold and Rosy Cross' does not appear in the literature until the second half of the seventeenth century, when it is mentioned in certain Italian documents; as a denomination in Germany it is fully established only with the appearance of Samuel Richter's *Die Warhaffte und vollkommene Bereitung des Philosophischen Steins* (1710).[41] There is no mention of a 'Gold and Rosy Cross' in the Rosicrucian apologetic works of Fludd,[42] as Åkerman asserts.[43] Nor does the allusion to "brothers of the

---

[38] Ecker und Eckhoffen, *Der Rosenkreuzer in seiner Blösse*, p. 82.

[39] *Ibid.*, pp. 80-82.

[40] I must thank the current keeper of manuscripts at the University of Leiden, Mr. Anton van der Lem, for his kind investigations into this matter.

[41] Such is affirmed by Peuckert, *Die Rosenkreuzer: zur Geschichte einer Reformation*. Jena: Eugen Diedrichs, 1928, p. 85; see also above, chapter I, n. 125.

[42] Fludd, Robert. *Apologia Compendiaria, Fraternitatem de Rosea Cruce suspicionis et infamiae maculis asspersam [sic], veritatis quasi Fluctibus abluens et abstergens.* Leiden: Gottfried Basson, 1616; Fludd, Robert. *Tractatus Apologeticus Integritatem Societatis de Rosea Cruce defendens. In qua probatur contra D. Libavii et aliorum eiusdem farinae calumnias, quod admirabilia nobis a Fraternitate R. C. oblata, sine improba Magiae impostura, aut Diaboli praestigiis et illusionibus praestari possint.* Leiden: Gottfried Basson, 1617. Both of these works set forth a defence of the Fraternity, natural magic and astrology against Libavius' accusations of necromancy and diabolic magic; in the course of his apologies Fludd uses a number of variations on the 'Bruderschafft des Hochlöblichen Ordens des Rosen Creutzes' and the 'Fraternitet deß R. C.' given in the manuscript Fama Fraternitatis, such as 'Fraternitas de R. Cruce', 'Fratres de Societate R. Crucis', 'Societas de Rosea Cruce', 'Fratres Societatis de Rosea C.' and 'Fraternitas R. C'. I would encourage interested readers not to take my word on

golden cross" made in the *Aureum Seculum Redivivum* (1625) of Adrian von Mynsicht suggest the existence of "a two-tiered Hermetic society" known as the *Gold- und Rosenkreutz*: whilst the term was probably suggested to Mynsicht by the Rosicrucian Order's appellation, he utilises *fratres aureae crucis* as an ornate but general means of addressing those amongst his readers who are affiliated with him by virtue of their alchemical proclivities.[44] Given this fact, the mention made by a certain mid-seventeenth century writer in Italy of "a company entitled the rosy cross, or as others say the golden cross" demonstrates the logic by which the *'Gold- und Rosenkreutz'* term first arose, i.e. from the conflation of tracts written under the *aureae crucis* and *roseae crucis* appellations.[45]

In short, it appears that the 'inextricable reverie' that has grown up around the *De Theosophia Aegyptiorum* is extricated thus: Maier's 'Rosicrucian' Leipzig manuscript is an eighteenth century myth arising within the *Gold- und Rosenkreutz* Freemasonic order, first 'exposed' by 'Magister Pianco', then associated via Yarker with the tale of Agrippa's secret society, and finally conveyed by Craven – quite innocently – as a 'Leipzig' rather than a 'Leiden' manuscript. Assuming that it was not an intentional fabrication, the exact mechanism by which the Leipzig manuscript myth first arose cannot be traced; nevertheless, the subsequent development of the myth shows that the mere proximity in a conversational or textual source of two unrelated

---

this matter, but to read the works for themselves, as reliance on second-hand reports will only further nourish the confused mass of fabulous weeds that have overgrown Rosicrucian history.

[43] Åkerman, *Rose Cross over the Baltic*, p. 181: "[In his *Apologia Compendiaria Fraternitatem de Rosea Cruce*] Fludd then declared that the movement actually draws on two schools, one of "Aureae crucis fratres" dealing with the supercelestial world and one of "Roseae crucis fratres" dealing with the sublunary world; these two schools create divergent theosophical and alchemical traditions for the Golden and Rosy Cross."

[44] Mynsicht, "Aureum Seculum Redivivum," pp. 67-87. Mynsicht addresses his readers as "true brothers of the golden cross" and "exceptional members of the philosophical fellowship in eternal affiliation" in his foreword: "Weil deutlicher und klärlicher hiervon zuschreiben ernstlich und zum allerhöchsten in republica chymica verboten ist: trage aber ganz keinen zweiffel/ es werden all die/ so diß Tractetlein in warer Zuuersicht mit den innerlichen Augen des Gemüths/ so alles vermügen/ recht anschawen/ in denselben fleißig studiren, und darbey für allen dingen Gott inniglichen und von Herzen anruffen/ gleich mir/ die hierin verborgene Philosophische wundersüsse Früchte geniesen/ und derselben nach dem Willen Gottes theilhafftig werden. Und alsdann sein und bleiben sie/ ware Brüder des güldenen Creuzes/ unnd außerlesene Gliedmassen der Philosophischen gemeine in ewiger Verbündnuß." The term is also utilised to describe Mynsicht himself on the frontispiece and in the work's closing paragraphs. The *Aureum Seculum Redivivum* appeared in the *Dyas Chymica Tripartita* edited by Johannes Grasshoff; Grasshoff's own "Güldener Tractat" reiterates the term, possibly in imitation of Mynsicht's work (which follows Grasshoff's tract in the compendium).

[45] Vatican Library, MS Reginensis Latini 1521; see above, chapter I, n. 125.

elements can lead to colourful results in the minds of the credulous. As the *De Theosophia Aegyptiorum* was undoubtedly the most prominent of the surviving manuscripts of Maier, thanks to its mention in the *Polyhistor* of Morhof, it is in fact possible that von Ecker und Eckhoffen himself confused 'Leipzig' with 'Leiden' in the course of his communications with 'Brother Hosmopina Neberus' (on whose authority his story concerning the reformation of the Order in 1510 stands).[46] In any case, the unread manuscript is likely to have formed the focus for considerable conjecture or 'projection', as Jung might have put it. Furthermore, as Arnold points out in his *Histoire des Rose-Croix et les Origines de la Franc-Maçonnerie*, it appears that the *Gold- und Rosenkreutz* of the late eighteenth century was determined to demonstrate its anteriority to the widely discredited Rosicrucianism of the manifestos (although Arnold himself speaks of a "lost Leipzig manuscript").[47]

The history of Rosicrucianism is littered with such spurious traditions, many of which stem from the nineteenth century German occultist Carl Kiesewetter, whom Waite amusingly but accurately describes as Rosicrucianism's *fabulator magnus*. Kiesewetter claimed to be a direct descendant of the last 'Imperator' of the Brethren, and declared himself to be in the possession of priceless manuscripts of the Order dating to the sixteenth century and earlier.[48] He also promulgated a component of the 'Rosicrucian' Leipzig manuscript myth, claiming that Agrippa von Nettesheim had specifically been named as an 'Imperator' of the Order by the seventeenth century English Rosicrucian Thomas Vaughan (who in fact only speaks of Agrippa as "the oracle of Magick" and "the master" of his secretary Wierus).[49] Paul Arnold theorised that Kiesewetter's manuscripts were in fact

---

[46] Ecker und Eckhoffen, *Der Rosenkreuzer in seiner Blösse*, p. 81.

[47] Arnold, Paul. *Histoire des Rose-Croix et les Origines de la Franc-Maçonnerie*. Paris: Mercure de France, 1954, p. 80.

[48] According to Yarker, *Arcane Schools*, pp. 213-214, "Karl Kiesewetter was a grandson of the last Imperator, he holds a manuscript claiming a Rosicrucian society existed in 1622 in The Hague, the members of which wore a black silk cord in their top button hole, having vowed to be strangled with the same sooner than break their silence. Amongst other signs of recognition between members was their wont to leave their houses on festival days by the east door and wave a green flag before sunrise. When two of these brethren met one was compelled to say "Ave Frater!," to which the other would answer "Rosae et Aureae," then the first would say "Crucis," then together "Benedictus Deus Dominus Noster, qui Nobis dedit signum."

[49] Kiesewetter, Carl. Untitled article in *Sphinx: Monatschrift für die Geschichtliche und Experimentale Begründung der Übersinnlichen Weltanschauung auf Monistischer Grundlage*. Leipzig: Vol. 1, January, 1886, pp. 42-54; Vaughan, Thomas (Eugenius Philalethes). *Anima Magica Abscondita*. London: H.B., 1650, pp. iv, 22. Paracelsus is the anonymous author from whom Vaughan claims the Brethren "borrowed most of their instructions;" *ibid.*, p. 37.

fabrications of the eighteenth century *Gold- und Rosenkreutz*,[50] and whilst such fabrications abound, one gets the feeling that Arnold had a little too much faith in the transparency of Kiesewetter's motives. For if the purveyors of Rosicrucianism through the centuries have delighted in providing fellow occultists and academics alike with a veritable school of red herrings, then they are only following in the footsteps of the instigator of the Rosicrucian phenomenon – in all likelihood the Lutheran theologian Johann Valentin Andreae.

3. Johann Valentin Andreae and the nature of the Order

Johann Valentin Andreae (1586-1654) was a student of philosophy and theology at the University of Tübingen; his grandfather had been one of the chief architects of the Formula of Concord, although in the irenicist climate of the early seventeenth century he became an admirer of the Calvinist church order.[51] It seems likely that Andreae wrote the manifestos under the influence of his mentor and colleague at the University of Tübingen, Dr. Tobias Hess – a one-time lawyer, physician, dabbler in alchemy and adept in theology and millennialist prophecy, who was branded by the Medical Guild of Tübingen as "a disciple of that impious Paracelsus."[52] Hess formed the focal point of an "intimate league of friends" in which Andreae spent some years following his premature departure from Tübingen due to an unspecified scandal; such was the influence of Hess on the young Andreae that Gilly has described him as the prototypic theologian-scientist lying behind the figure of Christian Rosenkreutz.[53]

That the manifestos stem from the circle of Hess and Andreae is the majority opinion in the academic study of Rosicrucianism, although Peuckert preferred Tobias Hess to Andreae as the author. Montgomery's is perhaps the most prominent dissenting voice, but his opinion on the matter – that the manifestos stem neither from Andreae nor from his circle, but from the late sixteenth century – not only draws on the myth of the 'Rosicrucian' Leipzig manuscript we have just laid bare, but is also strongly coloured by his own ideological objections to the encroachment of humanism into (contemporary)

---

[50] Arnold, *Histoire des Rose-Croix*, p. 75.
[51] Gilly, *Cimelia Rhodostaurotica*, p. 47; Neumann, Ulrich. "Johann Valentin Andreae." In Figala, Karin and Claus Priesner (eds.). *Alchemie: Lexikon einer hermetischen Wissenschaft*. München: C. H. Beck, 1998, pp. 46-47.
[52] Gilly, *ibid.*, pp. 47-49.
[53] Kooij and Gilly, *Fama Fraternitatis*, pp. 17-19.

Christianity.[54] There is good evidence for Andreae's authorship of the manifestos, not only on stylistic and redactional grounds,[55] but also on the grounds that by 1607 Andreae had already composed his famous alchemical allegory, the *Chymische Hochzeit Christiani Rosenkreutz* ('Chemical Wedding of Christian Rosenkreutz,' 1616) – long before the public appearance of the manifestos.[56] And there is also the testimony of the Pietist Gottfried Arnold, who reports that Andreae confided to a friend, John Arne, that he and his colleagues had first set forth the *Fama Fraternitatis* "in order that under this cover they might learn the judgment of Europe thereon," and to see what "lovers of true wisdom might then come forward."[57]

Furthermore, Gilly has identified a number of passages in Andreae's *Theca Gladii Spiritus* ('Sheath of the Spiritual Sword,' 1616) and in his *Turris Babel, sive Judiciorum de Fraternitate Rosaceae Crucis CHAOS* ('The Tower of Babel, or the Chaos of Judgments concerning the Fraternity of the Rosy Cross,' 1619) that are highly suggestive of Andreae's authorship of the manifestos. In the latter work Andreae states:

More than enough sport has been made with people; at last we may free the binds, we may embolden those who hesitate, we may arouse those who have fallen into error, we may call back those who have gone across, we may heal the diseased. Lo, mortals! There is no need to wait for the Fraternity: the play is finished. The Fama has sanctioned it, and the Fama has ended it. The Fama said yes, now it says no.[58]

---

54   Montgomery, John Warwick. "The World-view of Johann Valentin Andreae." In *Das Erbe des Christian Rosenkreutz*. Amsterdam: In de Pelikaan, 1988, pp. 152-169. In his passage composed under the sub-title of 'The Gospel vs. Hermeticism', Montgomery can surely not be referring to the good Lutheran Maier when he speaks of "the belief of the esoterists that man can become God by way of nature," as Maier quite clearly states that eternal life cannot be gained by means of an elixir, but only by our death and rebirth in Christ. Furthermore, for Andreae to swear by Church and Trinity that "he had always laughed at the Rosicrucian fable and inveighed against the curious little brothers" by no means constitutes a denial of his role in the affair, particularly given the connotation of *fraterculus* as a term of endearment for friends. For a sampling of Montgomery's views on humanism and contemporary Christianity, see *Crisis in Lutheran Theology*. Grand Rapids, Mich.: Baker Book House, 1973.

55   On this point see the comprehensive survey of Schick, *Das Ältere Rosenkreuzertum*, pp. 64-87.

56   Gilly, *Cimelia Rhodostaurotica*, p. 82, gives the probable date of authorship as 1607 on the basis of Carl Widemann's note that he possessed the "alchimistische Hochzeit" by March the 31st of that year, and that it was known to Tobias Hess by that time.

57   Arnold, Gottfried. *Unpartheyische Kirchen- und Ketzer- Historie, Vom Anfang des Neuen Testaments biß auf das Jahr Christi 1688*. Hildesheim: Georg Olms, 1967 (first published 1699), p. 899.

58   Andreae, Johann Valentin. *Turris Babel, sive Judiciorum de Fraternitate Rosaceae Crucis CHAOS*. Strasbourg: Lazarus Zetzner, 1619, p. 69: "Satis superque hominibus illusum est, liberemus tandem constrictos, confirmemus fluctuantes, erigamus lapsos, revocemus transversos, sanemus morbidos. Ehem, Mortales! nihil est, quod Frater-

Gilly asserts that only the author of the *Fama Fraternitatis* would be in a position to speak in such a way.[59] Be this as it may, Andreae's *Turris Babel* presents to us a series of three-way dialogues representing typical respondents to the manifestos, the third respondent representing the views of Andreae himself. In the final chapter, Andreae demonstrates his uneasiness with the unchecked immensity of the furore he has engendered by writing as *Recipiscens*, 'he who has come to his senses'. This mode of self-description not only mirrors the shift in Andreae's thinking away from his 'youthful folly' and towards a more orthodox Lutheran position, but also reflects the danger of being identified as the author of the manifestos. For by the time of the publication of the *Turris Babel* following the outbreak of the Thirty Years War, Andreae's authorship had been uncovered by at least two parties in the Rosicrucian debate, and threatened to become open knowledge.[60]

Is it justified, then, to name the 'intimate league of friends' of Andreae and Hess as the true 'Brethren of the Rosy Cross', as Schick has implied? To answer this question we may turn again to the *Turris Babel*, and to the thirteenth dialogue between *Admirator* (an admirer), *Contemptor* (a despiser) and *Aestimator* (an appraiser according to the intrinsic value of a thing). Andreae as *Aestimator* gives the following revealing assessment of the furore provoked by the Brethren:

The more I inquire into this fraternity, the more ingenious the game appears to me. For it possesses such a sum of human desires, that it inspires the appetite in pre-eminent intellects to obtain those things for which they have long exerted themselves. And truly, by this coming together of intellects, or by this society, if it consisted of the most select and perspicacious men, it would be possible to produce things which surpass our comprehension. That it is indeed such a kind of society, they have not yet persuaded me, because they proffer up too much imprudence, or indeed baseness.[61]

---

nitatem expectetis: fabula peracta est. Fama astruxit: fama destruxit. Fama ajebat: fama negat..."

[59] Gilly, *Cimelia Rhodostaurotica*, p. 79.

[60] *Ibid.*, p. 78; in 1617 the Professor of Rhetoric at the University of Tübingen, Kasper Bucher, alluded to Andreae as author of the manifestos in an anti-Rosicrucian lecture, whilst in 1619 the feared pamphletist Friedrich Grick threatened to expose Andreae as the author of the manifestos. For a discussion of Andreae's reasons for distancing himself from the Rosicrucian affair, see Schick, *Das Ältere Rosenkreuzertum*, p. 72.

[61] Andreae, *Turris Babel*, p. 37: "Quo magis in hanc fraternitatem inquiro, eo mihi lusus videtur artificiosior. Habet enim nescio quam epitomen humanorum desideriorum, quod erectioribus ingeniis salivam moveat ea impetrandi, in quibus jam dudum defudarunt [sic]. Et verisimile est, ingeniorum concursu sive societate, si ea ex selectissimis et perspicacissimis constet, aliquid tale posse exhiberi, quod captum nostrum superet. Talem vero jam esse, nondum mihi persuaserunt, tum quia nimis vel temeraria, vel humilia etiam proferunt."

The crux of this passage is contained in its clear equation of the 'concourse of intellects' brought together by the manifestos with the 'society' itself; for it is clear from Andreae's words that what is ingenious about the 'game' is that a Rosicrucian society of sorts had indeed been constituted by those inspired to the defence of the Fraternity by Andreae's utopian vision – or would have been constituted, if there were not so many vulgar opinions amongst those that flooded the printing presses in response to the manifestos. In this sense the manifestos did not simply constitute an invitation to the learned of Europe to *eventually* build a society akin to that outlined in the manifestos, but also formed a very present and cogent virtual arena for the furtherance of a Hermetic Protestant ideology. In light of this fact, Waite's misleading alternatives of a 'mythic' or a 'real' Fraternity do not hold. This Rosicrucian 'Brotherhood' was not merely a *ludibrium*, i.e. a 'jest' or 'game', as Andreae was later to describe it; to borrow the title of Michael Maier's first 'Rosicrucian' work, the *Jocus Severus*, it was a very 'serious jest'.

That the tale of the opening of the tomb of Christian Rosenkreutz draws from alchemical allegory should have been clear enough to anyone as well versed in the alchemical literature as Maier.[62] We need only mention the fact that the discovery of the sepulchre and the Book I. held to the chest of Christian Rosenkreutz bears a close resemblance to the tale given in the *Tabula Smaragdina*, in which the Emerald Tablet is said to have been found clasped in the hands of Hermes as he lay in state in his tomb.[63] Furthermore, Maier followed the lead of Andreae when composing his *Allegoria Bella*, in which he travels to Egypt and Arabia in search of the phoenix – a journey to the source of the *prisca sapientia* which mirrors the phases of the alchemical work in similar fashion to the journey of Christian Rosenkreutz in Andreae's *Chymische Hochzeit*.[64] Nevertheless, the evidence seems to overwhelmingly contradict the possibility that Maier was aware of the strictly virtual existence of the Brethren: for why did he expend such great energy not only in

---

[62] It is pertinent to note that Rosenkreutz's return journey to Germany follows an important medieval conduit of Arabic science into Europe, i.e. via Fez, the intellectual capital of the Moorish empire, into Spain and beyond. In this sense the *Fama Fraternitatis* presents a parable for the entrance of occult Arabic wisdom into medieval Europe.

[63] The tradition that the discoverer was Alexander the Great is given in a tract ascribed to Albertus Magnus: "Scriptum Alberti super Arborem Aristotelis." In *Theatrum Chemicum*. Vol. 2. Straßburg: Zetzner, 1659, p. 458.

[64] Maier's contemporary, the alchemist Christoffer Rotbard ('Radtichs Brotofferr') issued a work at this time explaining the journey of Christian Rosenkreutz in the *Chymische Hochzeit* in alchemical terms: *Elucidarius Major, Oder Erleuchterunge uber die Reformation der ganzen weiten Welt/ F. C. R. auß ihrer Chymischen Hochzeit- und sonst mit viel andern testimoniis Philosophorum/ sonderlich in appendice/ dermassen verbessert/ daß beydes materia et praeparatio lapidis aurei/ deutlich genug darinn angezeigt werden.* Lüneburg: bey den Sternen Buchf., 1617.

defending the existence of the Fraternity as an organised secret society, but also in promoting the myth of Christian Rosenkreutz as historical fact? In order to understand Maier's relationship to Rosicrucianism, it is necessary to approach his Rosicrucian works in strict chronological order, as they demonstrate the development of his response to the affair from one of initial disinterest, through the issuing of tentative rejoinders to the Rosicrucian programme in his *Jocus Severus* (1616) and *Symbola Aureae Mensae* (1617), to a role as chief apologist for the Order through the publication of his *Silentium post Clamores* (1617) and *Themis Aurea* (1618).

4. The serious jest

Given that anyone assenting in print to the programme of the manifestos or taking up the defence of the Order might be said to belong to this virtual 'Brotherhood', Maier's first genuinely Rosicrucian work is the *Jocus Severus* (1617). There is in fact a record of the *Jocus Severus* in a flyer produced for the Frankfurt Book Fair by Maier's publisher, Johann Theodor de Bry; and whilst the date given at the head of the flyer (1609) might again provide evidence for Maier's earlier acquaintance with the Rosicrucian phenomenon (and indeed for an earlier genesis of Rosicrucianism itself), Maier's work is in fact a later addition by the printer to a list composed in 1609 and used at subsequent fairs.[65] Such are the obstacles that obscure a clear perspective on this subject.

Maier confesses that the *Jocus Severus* was written hurriedly; indeed, he wrote "six or seven chemical treatises" with a "hot quill" whilst lying ill in Frankfurt am Main, which were "inspired more by the small payment which I received for them rather than by the improvement and perfection of the works themselves."[66] Given that all these treatises were either in print or at the printers by October of 1617, then we must count amongst them not only the *Jocus Severus*, but also the *Atalanta Fugiens* (1617), *De Circulo Physico, Quadrato* (1616), *Examen Fucorum Pseudo-chymicorum* (1617), *Lusus Serius* (1616), *Silentium post Clamores* (1617) and *Symbola Aureae Mensae*

---

65 Prof. Karin Figala and Dr. Ulrich Neumann of Technische Universität München brought my attention to this perplexing document.

66 Frankfurt am Main, Stadt- und Universitätsbibliothek, MS Ff. J. H. Beyer A. 161, p. 207 *verso*: "Atque sic aeger plaerumque haerens lecto nonnulla commentatus sum, ad Chymiam spectantia (quorum quaedam proelo subjecta sunt, quaedam subiicienda ab aliis reservantis ad proximas nundinas) lucella, quod inde evenit, magis incitatus, quam maturitate et emendatione ipsorum opusculorum: Tractatus itaque chymicos 6 vel 7 calente calamo deproperavi, sperans me hac via, tantum lucraturum, quo in locum praefixum commode transmearem."

(1617). If we are to take Maier by his word, then this is a remarkable achievement (even if work on some of the texts had been started in England, as Figala and Neumann suggest); moreover, the fact that their publication was specifically intended to raise money for the abandoned journey to Prague gives us some insight into the source of their enduring popularity. In any case, Maier's financial difficulties at this time cast further doubt on Yates' contention that the reference in the *Jocus Severus* to a planned journey to Bohemia is further evidence of Maier's service within a nascent Anglo-German-Bohemian political and military alliance.[67] Rather, it seems more likely that he simply hoped to find a livelihood there with the help of his former colleagues.

There are no explicit references to the Brethren of the Rosy Cross within the main body of the *Jocus Severus*, which fact suggests that the 'Rosicrucian' preface was appended after the encounter with the manifestos at the Frankfurt Book Fair of October 1616 to a work which had been composed before that time.[68] The main text is a rather charming satirical fable in which, according to Trunz, Maier shows himself as "a playful master of Latin verse forms."[69] In its frequent references to the Satires of Juvenalis, and in its recourse to curious zoological data, drawn in large part from Pliny's *Historia Naturalis*, this work shows marked similarities to Maier's *Lusus Serius* (1616), in which Mercury is crowned king of an assembly of animals, plants and minerals beneficial to humanity. The *Jocus Severus* takes the form of a court of judgment upon the bird of wisdom sacred to Pallas Athena, the Owl – in this instance embodying *chemia* as the highest science. The Owl stands accused of a number of misdemeanours by an assembly of squawking and cantankerous birds, who represent the various critics of *chemia*. Counsel for the defence is the Hawk; the judge presiding over the court is the Phoenix, the symbol of the Work's perfection which we shall explore in greater detail in the following chapter. In order to please "both the mind and the ears" of his readers, Maier forms each verse in accordance with the voice of the accusing bird, and the other birds reply in the same 'language', ranging from the Nightingale's graceful and well-spanned Sapphic strophes to the Jackdaw's staccato of five syllables per line. After facing her fellow birds' accusations, the Owl and her Art are eventually vindicated by the Hawk's expert defence, and she is adjudged Queen of the Birds by the Phoenix.

Thus the *Jocus Severus* forms a mythic arena of debate in which the protagonists enact a very real and 'serious' controversy; the Rosicrucian

---

[67] Yates, *The Rosicrucian Enlightenment*, pp. 81, 84.

[68] Maier, *Jocus Severus*, p. 12.

[69] Trunz, Erich. *Wissenschaft und Kunst im Kreise Kaiser Rudolfs II. 1576-1612.* Neumünster: Karl Wachholtz Verlag, 1992, p. 90.

manifestos could also be said to present such a mythic arena to the reader, although there the ambiguous character of the protagonists – the Brethren – blurs the lines between literary symbol and referent. In his foreword to the *Jocus Severus* Maier superimposes the 'Rosicrucian' arena onto that of his own work; in accordance with the emphasis on alchemy given in Maier's reading of the Rosicrucian manifestos, we are told that the symbol of the Owl represents not merely the true chymists of Germany, but specifically the Brethren of the Rosy Cross – who are, to his mind, primarily concerned with the Art of *chemia* and the production of the Universal Medicine. Hence the court of judgment upon the Owl becomes a court of judgment on the Brethren themselves, who are now defined in Maier's exclusively alchemical terms:

I dedicate and bequeath this tract to all lovers of true *chymia* throughout Germany, known and unknown; and amongst them, unless Fame deceives us, to that ORDER OF GERMAN BLOOD, hitherto lying hidden, but manifested by the bringing forth of the *Fama Fraternitatis*, as well as by the admirable and pleasing *Confessio Fraternitatis*.[70]

Maier's reference to deceiving 'Fame' here is to the *Fama Fraternitatis*, and it indicates that although he was unsure of the existence of an organised Fraternity lying behind the manifestos, he proceeded with his apologetics regardless. Given his own predilection for literary conceits and 'serious jests', the possibility that the manifestos were 'deceitful' could not have escaped Maier; but if by 'playing the game' he might promote his own interests, then he was more than willing to do so.

Accordingly, we find a double meaning in Maier's words; for the word *fama* possesses not only the connotation of the English 'fame' with which it has been translated, but also that of 'rumour' or 'common talk' – an ambiguity not lost to the manifesto's creator. In this sense the *Fama* might deceive because truth withers away upon exposure to the vulgar and ignorant masses; thus Maier states that the anonymous members of the Fraternity are themselves like the Owl, because they shun the light of fame to avoid exposing the secrets of the Hermetic arts. And whilst it has been their custom to lead lives of anonymity,[71] as the 'evening of the world' rapidly approaches

---

[70] Maier, *Jocus Severus*, p. 10: "Omnibus Verae Chymiae Amantibus, per Germaniam notis et ignotis, et inter hos, nisi nos Fama fallat, ILLI SANGUINIS GERMANICI ORDINI, adhuc delitescenti, at Fama Fraternitatis et Confessione sua admiranda et probabili, in genere manifestato, asscribo, dico et dedico." It is noteworthy that de Rola omits 'ILLI SANGUINIS GERMANICI ORDINI in his rendering of this passage; de Rola, Stanislas Klossowski. *The Golden Game: Alchemical Engravings of the Seventeenth Century.* New York: George Braziller, Inc., 1988, p. 62.

[71] *Ibid.*: "Cum enim tantus Dei Thesaurus ab iis, quibus oblatus est, nulli prostitui aut manifestari debeat, hinc authores ipsi quasi Deo dicati, mundoque abrogati, Deo sibique viventes rarissime agnosci uni aut alteri, nunquam vero vulgo voluerunt."

the Brethren – like the Owl – emerge from their diurnal concealment to manifest the truth of the coming age:

...Now there arises that profession of divine and human matters, which like a fanfare of trumpets declares the indisputable conviction of truth throughout the whole of Germany, under the name of the Fraternity. This Fraternity, like the Owl, hides itself with good reason from the abduction of rapacious and hostile birds until the evening arrives – which evening is now approaching as the great day of this world comes to its end, and as the truth manifests itself in signs that should not be dismissed. Thus I offer this Owl to the Fraternity, as to others working under the same noble Muse, known and unknown; not for the sake of creating a work of great subtlety (because here you will find none), but (according to our title) for the sake of a SERIOUS JEST.[72]

Here Maier's worldview is revealed to us as deeply millenarian. His reference to the evening of the 'great day of this world' derives from the more chiliastic and prophetic of the two manifestos, the *Confessio Fraternitatis*, which as we have seen was particularly 'admirable and pleasing' to Maier. In that tract the anonymous author speaks of the coming Sabbath of the world:

Whatsoever is published, and made known to everyone, concerning our Fraternity, by the foresaid *Fama*, let no man esteem lightly of it, nor hold it as an idle or invented thing, and much less receive the same, as though it were only a mere conceit of ours. It is the Lord Jehovah (who seeing the Lord's Sabbath is almost at hand, and hastened again, his period or course being finished, to his first beginning) doth turn about the course of Nature...[73]

These words derive in part from the apocryphal fourth book of Ezra;[74] as Gilly notes, Andreae also utilises the passage from 4 Ezra concerning God's 'hastening' in his *Collectanea Mathematica*, in which a table is given

---

[72] *Ibid.*, p. 11: "Ex quatuor igitur hisce, quae inseparabiliter convenire oportet, coniunctis exurgit PROFESSIO illa divinarum humanarumque rerum, quae iam quasi TUBA quadam praecentoria per Germaniam haud dubia veritatis opinione, sub FRATER-NITATIS nomine, insonuit: Haec cum iure suo, Noctuae instar, ab avium rapacium et se infestantium raptu, donec vesper advenerit, occultetur, qui iam inclinante magni huius mundi die instet, ut illa per indicia haud aspernandae se manifestavit, sic ego illi merito hanc NOCTUAM, ut et aliis eiusdem Musae procis, ignotis et notis, asscribo, dico et obfero, non pro magnae subtilitatis (quae hic nulla est) opere, sed (ut inscriptio habet) pro IOCO SEVERO."

[73] Yates, *The Rosicrucian Enlightenment*, p. 251.

[74] *4 Ezra* 4.34-37: "You do not hasten faster than the Most High, for your haste is for yourself, but the Highest hastens on behalf of many. Did not the souls of the righteous in their chambers ask about these matters, saying, 'How long are we to remain here? And when will come the harvest of our reward?' And Jeremiel the archangel answered them and said, 'When the number of those like yourselves is completed; for he has weighed the age in the balance, and measured the times by measure, and numbered the times by number; and he will not move or arouse them until that measure is fulfilled.'"

representing the six millennia of the world, and Luther is portrayed as the herald of the end-time.[75] It may be pertinent to add that the conception of 'the Lord's Sabbath' also hearkens to the medieval and early modern tradition of seven ages of the world corresponding to the seven days of Creation in *Genesis*, derived from the *De Temporum Ratione* of the Venerable Bede (673-735), who in his turn elaborated upon the world chronology of the Church Fathers Isidor of Seville and Augustine.[76] In the worldview of the authors of the Rosicrucian manifestos and their followers, Christian millennialism merges with the Paracelsian prophecy of the coming of Elias Artista and the restoration of the arts and sciences to their pristine state. Thus, in congruence with representations of the alchemical process as the *septimana philosophica*,[77] the Sabbath of the Lord establishes the completion and perfection of God's work through a return to the point of origin. This return brings the recovery of the *prisca sapientia* for which Maier strove, but which he realised in the dying hours of his age must remain "polluted and imperfect," as the *Fama Fraternitatis* would have it.[78]

In the course of his preface to the *Jocus Severus*, Maier makes it clear that he considers himself to be a member of that 'Order of German Blood' which is ushering in the new age. As once the wise men of Athens worked under the figure of the Owl, so in Maier's time the "true investigators of Nature, known and unknown" are denoted by that same hieroglyph;[79] and amongst these true scientists are numbered not only the Brethren of the Rosy Cross, but Maier himself. For the *Jocus Severus* is a game that he plays in the nocturnal hours, in order to "escape the silence of Vulcan's work" and to "obey his soul," rather than for the purpose of publishing his knowledge and exposing it to the common folk.[80] Thus we can envisage Maier patiently sitting before the furnace in the late hours of the night, scratching at a manuscript with his quill pen whilst the chemical processes within the vessel take their course. In defence of such a nocturnal lifestyle, Maier invokes the authority of Avicenna, who writes in his commentary on Aristotle's *De Anima*:

---

[75] Gilly, *Cimelia Rhodostaurotica*, p. 75.
[76] Schmidt-Biggemann, Wilhelm. *Philosophia Perennis: Historische Umrisse abendländ-ischer Spiritualität in Antike, Mittelalter und Früher Neuzeit*. Frankfurt am Main: Suhrkamp Verlag, 1998, pp. 593 ff. The tradition reflects the centrality of the number 7 in *Revelations* – the opening of the seventh seal upon the Day of Judgment, the trumpet-call of the seventh angel announcing the fulfilment of the Mystery of God, etc.
[77] See Roberts, *The Mirror of Alchemy*, p. 56.
[78] Kooij and Gilly, *Fama Fraternitatis*, p. 73.
[79] Maier, *Jocus Severus*, p. 5.
[80] *Ibid.*, p. 3: "En tibi iterum, candide lector, Iocum Severum insinuo, quem aliquando nocturnis horis ad vulcanias operas potius ad fallendum silentii illius moras, animoque obtemperandum meo, lusi, quam, ut vulgo ederetur, perfeci."

I have learnt all this by frequent reading, little sleep, little food and less drinking; and as much money as my colleagues spent during the daytime in order to have wine at night, so much did I spend for oil to stay awake and read; and as much as they have spent in eating by night, I have spent more for the light necessary to stay awake and learn: and unless I do this, I will not have skill in the magistery.[81]

Thus only the pious are afforded the secrets of the Great Work, whilst those who revel in the pleasures of the senses will surely fail. As the Owl might be said to represent Maier's self-understanding as an alchemist – and by association, his understanding of the Fraternity – so those birds arrayed against the Owl in the *Jocus Severus* represent his own detractors. These detractors, who bestow insults upon *chemia* and defame her with clamorous reviling, are divided by Maier into three different classes. The first are the foolish, unlearned and ignorant mob, represented under the names of the Jay, Magpie, Raven, Goose and Swallow; at their head is the quarrelsome Crow, the pre-eminent enemy of the Owl, denoting those "ignoble and unrefined censors" who do not consider the true causes of things, but rather judge *chemia* prejudicially as a vain and frivolous pursuit.[82] Thus the Crow argues before the court that his dispute with the Owl is an ancient one, and as he was born of what he imagines to be a noble seed, that is enough reason for him to follow his forefathers in attacking the Owl. Although he asks the court to excuse his somewhat coarse mode of speech, the sentence of the Phoenix is emphatic:

The words that you have uttered, which fill the air with droning, do not help at all; if you take away the body from the light, the shadow is lost. And if you do not rage with anger about the blind habits that your parents teach you and your offspring, you are being deceived and are in want of reason, courage and fairness. If that is the crime of your forefathers, do not take it up yourself.[83]

---

[81] *Ibid.*, p. 5: "*Ego hoc totum*, inquit, *didici frequenter legendo, et parum dormiendo, et parum comedendo et minus bibendo, et quantum expenderunt socii mei in lumine ad potandum vinum de nocte, tantum ego expendi ad vigilandum et legendum de nocte in oleo, et quantum expendebant in comestione, amplius expendebam ego in lumine ad vigilandum et discendum de nocte: Et nisi hoc facerem, non scirem de magisterio.*"

[82] *Ibid.*, p. 14: "*Sub nomine actoris ex vulgo imperiti, qui causas rerum non attendit, sed ex alterius praeiudicio de Chemia, in qua ne tantillum expertus est, iudicat. Argumentum eius est, Chemiam esse vanam et frivolam, odioque dignam censendam, quia sic iudicarint nostri maiores sapientia longe excellentissimi: Sunt autem cornices, (hoc est eiusmodi illiberales et impoliti censores) noctuae inprimis inimicae, adeo ut sibi invicem ova suffurentur: Inauspicatae quoque sunt garrulitatis.*"

[83] *Ibid.*, p. 17: "*Nil data verba iuvant, quae replent aera bombo,/ Corpora si luci dempseris, umbra perit./ Si nihil irarum furias, quam caeca parentum/ Consuetudo docet te sobolemque tuam:/ Falleris et rationis eges, virtutis et aequi,/ Si quod erit patrium, ne tibi sume, scelus.*"

The judgment having been passed, the little Crow plods away with a slow and gloomy step. In this passage Maier again associates blind emotion, stemming from a want of reason, with the masses – an association that, as we have seen in our second chapter, has a special significance for his own biography. The subject of piety is also uppermost when Maier depicts the third class of the detractors of *chemia*: those men pre-occupied by greed, the depraved in mind who fritter away expenses, signified by the Cuckoo, Jackdaw, Woodpecker and Heron. Whilst possessing means and titles, such men stand at the forefront of the mob on account of their love of sensual pleasure. The Cuckoo represents one such "uncivilised civilian":

Amongst those actors pre-occupied with worldly pleasures, or 'uncivilised civilians', stands the Cuckoo. His argument is that *chemia* makes a man solitary and keeps him from conversation with others, so he entertains himself only by burning up coal, emaciating the body with labour and wakefulness, and vexing the soul with sorrows and fruitless meditation: whereby the Cuckoo rejects the Art and argues vehemently against it, in order that he may return more freely to the revelling and drinking to which he is accustomed, and distinguish himself thus amongst the common people.[84]

According to Maier's curious analogy, drawn in part from the sixth Satire of Juvenalis, the gluttonous Cuckoo is in the habit of breaking the eggs of other birds and sucking out their contents, for which reason it has gained a bad reputation amongst its avian cousins; consequently it lays its eggs in other birds' nests, by which subterfuge its unnoticed chicks escape retribution.[85] Nevertheless, the Owl, being a wise creature, willingly offers up its eggs to this glutton, "in order that they may deliver abstinence, and infuse wisdom, sobriety and the yearning for temperance."[86] The eggs of the Owl in this case denote Maier's medicine itself, which is offered up to his presumably undeserving patients in the most altruistic and Christian manner. For Maier's was a medicine of piety, a cure for intemperance of mind and body stemming from a time in which the diagnosis and treatment of disease was closely intertwined with concepts of morality. As the Cuckoo has inadvertently eaten the temperance-imparting eggs of the Owl, the Phoenix returns no judgment

---

[84] *Ibid.*, p. 24: "Sub nomine actoris, in mundo praeoccupati negociis ad ventrem spectantibus, aut sensuum delitias, sive impoliti Politici. Argumentum eius est, Chemiam hominem solitarium reddere et a conversatione cum aliis revocare, dum ei vacantes solis carbonibus comburendis sese oblectent, corpus laboribus et vigiliis, animum curis et meditationibus in subtilitatibus vanis et inanibus, macerantes: Unde plerique Chemiae valedicunt et prorsus contradicunt, ut ad solitas commessationes et compotationes liberius rederant, frontemque cum vulgo exporrigant."

[85] *Ibid.*

[86] *Ibid.*: "Noctuae ova comesta eam vim habere traduntur (quod scire, ad sequentia intelligenda non inutile) ut abstemium reddant, atque ita quasi sapientiam et sobrietatem, vini sublato desiderio, ea comedenti instillent et inducant."

upon him: although he may be "a brigand worthy of hemlock," the "cure of
the pharmacist" has already rendered the appropriate remedy, and he is told
to leave in order to avoid a harsher fate.[87] Given the unpleasant effects of
Maier's medicine, the double meaning of *pharmacus* as 'pharmacist' and
'poisoner' cannot go unnoticed here.

In describing the second class of the detractors of *chemia* – those who are
learned, but are nevertheless ignorant of the truth of *chemia*, represented by
the Parrot, Nightingale and Crane – Maier seems to make oblique reference
to the Scholastic ethos, which to his mind is founded upon the reiteration of
received wisdom without recourse to empirical data. Thus the Parrot is
"erudite enough in the arts and sciences of other learned men," but argues
that the study of *chemia* distracts the mind from more useful and fruitful
professions such as medicine and law.[88] Similarly, the Nightingale attempts
to beguile the court with harmonious speech alone, as she is the most
eloquent of the birds. In her judgment the Phoenix advises the Nightingale
that those proficient in *chemia* have brought their speech and their hearts into
accord – "as musical harmonies ought to be present in the voice, so also
should they be present in the heart, and no tone is dissonant in the thread of
life itself."[89] It was this pansophic theme that Maier brought to its fullest
expression in his *Atalanta Fugiens*, in which the truths of *chemia* and the
harmony of the spheres are expressed in the form of Maier's (not always
harmonious) fugues.

The words of the *Jocus Severus* and its preface show us precisely the
manner in which Maier approached the Rosicrucian 'furore' that was raging
around him on his return from England. Whilst he found himself in accord
with both the religious and the scientific sentiments of the manifestos, a work
that had been written without the 'Fraternity' in mind immediately became
the means by which he could define the 'Brethren' as men who value *chemia*
as "the most precious good in all the world after the Word of God."[90] Their
labour is his labour: to procure "the most exquisite means of preserving

---

[87] *Ibid.*, p. 28: "Qui non virus atrox ovis, sed pharmaci medelam/ Latro bibisti, dignior
    cicuta:/ Ne crimen regeratur, abi, ne morte praeoccuperis,/ Inferre noli funus innocenti."

[88] *Ibid.*, p. 51: "Sub nomine actoris, viri alias docti et in reliquis artibus et scientiis satis
    eruditi, licet cum vulgo hac parte consentientis. Cuius argumentum est: Quod studium
    Chemiae avocet animum a magis utilibus et frugiferis scientiis, quales sunt Medicina,
    Iurisprudentia aut aliae de pane lucrando. Cum econtra Chemica ars sit sterilis et inanis,
    delitamentis phantasticorum hominum plena, qui eam ad otiosorum ingenia exercenda,
    cupiditatemque magna spe auri proposita explendam, manuum labore et sumptuum
    temporisque interpositione, inventam et introductam voluerunt."

[89] *Ibid.*, p. 35: "Voce concordes ut adesse debent/ Musici, sic sint quoque corde, non est/
    Dissonans ullus tonus ac in ipso Stamine vitae."

[90] *Ibid.*, p. 10.

health and restoring health which is lost."[91] Although the manifestos already possessed an alchemical bent, they became the receptacle for Maier's own anti-social, elitist and secretive alchemical predilections: thus the anonymity maintained by the Brethren is a sign that they are unwilling to 'prostitute' their knowledge of *chemia* to the masses.[92] Maier's interpretation of the programme of the manifestos is less an attempt to narrow its scope, and more to widen the scope of *chemia*, an Art which deals with the "great things of God" once alluded to in the *Hymnosophia*.

5. An invitation to Rosicrucians, wherever they may lie hidden

The second work in which Maier devoted some attention to the Rosicrucian Brotherhood was his *Symbola Aureae Mensae* ('Symbols of the Golden Table,' 1617); the dedication, directed to Count Ernst III of Holstein-Schauenburg, is dated December 1616 at Frankfurt am Main. This lengthy work, sometimes considered to be Maier's *magnum opus*, is a defence and legitimisation of the alchemical tradition with reference to the practitioners of twelve nations – Hermes Trismegistus of the Egyptians, Maria Prophetissa of the Jews, Democritus of the Greeks, Morienus of the Romans, Avicenna of the Arabs, Albertus Magnus of the Germans, Arnoldus de Villanova of the French, Thomas Aquinas of the Italians, Raymond Lull of the Spanish, Roger Bacon of the English, Melchior Cibinensis of the Hungarians, and an anonymous author from Sarmatia, figurehead of the Slavic practitioners. As in the *Jocus Severus*, Maier places his protagonists within an allegorical arena of debate – in this case a banquet held in honour of the Virgin Queen Chemia. The distinguished alchemists preside at a circular banquet table, formed "in the image of the world," and composed of two semi-circles, one red and one snow-white, the colours of the sun (gold) and moon (silver) – a 'hieroglyph' to warn the guests of the legitimacy of the alchemical work in question, and that no "colour-changing chameleon" can possibly imitate the colours of the true alchemical phases.[93] However, also presiding at the table is the troublesome guest Pyrgopolynices, the braggart centurion from the *Miles Gloriosus* of Plautus; in Maier's work he represents Queen Chemia's adversary, whose objections to her laws are at each opportunity refuted

---

[91] *Ibid.*

[92] *Ibid.*

[93] Maier, *Symbola Aureae Mensae*, p. 3: "Erat autem mensa haec instar Orbis rotunda, ex duabus Hemicycliis compacta, quarum una ruberrimi coloris, altera nivei visa est; nullam aliam ob causam, quam ut hoc quasi Hieroglyphico Convivae assidentes admon-erentur, hos inprimis colores esse veros et legitimos, Lunae et Solis proprios, quos Chamaeleon versipellis nullo modo imitari aut exprimere possit."

succinctly by the gathered alchemists. And whilst the phoenix was the chief judge of the avian court in the *Jocus Severus*, in his dedication Maier invites Count Ernst himself to act as arbiter of the dispute.[94]

According to Waite, Maier's *Symbola Aureae Mensae* marks the first usage of the denomination *Collegium Philosophorum Germanorum de R.·.C.·.*, or 'College of German Philosophers R.·.C.·.', which was propagated in the nineteenth century amongst certain esoteric initiatory societies.[95] The passage in the *Symbola Aureae Mensae* concerning the Rosicrucian Brethren occurs in the midst of the sixth chapter, which is dedicated to the German alchemists, and in particular to the great German scientist and theologian Albertus Magnus (c.1200-1280), who is said by Maier to have "produced the phoenix," and was moreover the first to perfect the Art after the Arabs.[96] In the course of this chapter Maier launches into a nineteen-page discourse on the subject of the Brethren, which is placed within the wider context of the transmission of the alchemical Art from the Arabs to the Germans. In so doing he establishes not only alchemy but Rosicrucianism itself as the heir of the wisdom of the great Egyptian sage, Hermes Trismegistus.

Whilst discussing Paracelsus as a compatriot of Albertus, Maier states that the "hitherto unknown" Brethren have given favourable testimony concerning this man – a reference to the *Fama Fraternitatis*, in which it is stated that although he led a free and careless life and preferred to mock rather than peaceably confer with his peers, Paracelsus had nevertheless diligently read the Fraternity's treasured work, the *Liber M.*.[97] Using this reference as a bridge to the topic of Rosicrucianism, Maier describes how the Brethren profess 'occult medicine' and the operation of 'astral properties' – properties to which he, too, has recourse in his work.[98] He goes on to present two of his chief arguments for the Fraternity's reality and legitimacy:

Since indeed we may recall that in ancient times there were instituted diverse and solemn philosophical colleges by experts in the Art of *chymia*, would it not be marvellous if this kind of college should at some time have come to pass in our most populous German nation, which has been divided into so many peoples and regions? For as [these Brethren], being authors of truth, and having obtained the goals of the Art by their own faculty of invention, or alternately by communication, have spoken of and exhibited compassion and philanthropic service to humankind, and pious prayer to God; so it is lawful that they maintain silence and ill-will against the undeserving...[99]

---

[94] *Ibid.*, p. vi.

[95] Waite, *Brotherhood of the Rosy Cross*, p. 324.

[96] Maier, *Symbola Aureae Mensae*, pp. 236, 248.

[97] *Ibid.*, p. 286; Kooij and Gilly, *Fama Fraternitatis*, pp. 79-81.

[98] Maier, *Symbola Aureae Mensae*, p. 288.

[99] *Ibid.*, pp. 288-289: "Cum vero antehac diversorum collegiorum philosophicorum solennitatumque antiquitus ab artis Chymicae gnaris institutarum meminerimus, quid

The first argument implied here, and elaborated upon at length in the *Silentium post Clamores* – that it is not unreasonable to suppose a secret Fraternity exists in Germany, given the existence of similar 'philosophical colleges' in other countries – might seem spurious to the contemporary reader. Nevertheless, Maier makes sporadic mention of such societies throughout the *Symbola Aureae Mensae* and the *Arcana Arcanissima*, which he reiterates succinctly in the fifth chapter of the *Silentium post Clamores*. His aim is to demonstrate the oral transmission of chemical arcana since the time of Hermes Trismegistus, the 'Viceroy' of the Virgin Queen Chemia; and if a direct lineage cannot always be traced, one may in any case account for the congruency of arcane teachings throughout the millennia simply because insight into Nature will always give rise to the same unvarying truths. Thus Maier allows that the Brethren may have perfected the Art either "by their own faculty of invention" or by "communication;" and thus he interprets the *Liber M.* of the Brethren as the *liber mundi*, which having been codified by the Arabs was passed on to Germany, but which nevertheless is universally available to those with eyes to see. In answer to those critics of the *Fama Fraternitatis* who argue that Paracelsus could not have read the *Liber M.*, as the tomb of Christian Rosenkreutz had been sealed some nine years before his birth, Maier goes on to state that it is irrelevant whether Paracelsus had read a particular book of the Brethren, as the *Liber M.* is in fact "the book of the world, or of things existing in the world, and of their properties; or indeed, the book of natural magic."[100]

The second argument set forward in the *Symbola Aureae Mensae* follows a theme of the preface to the *Jocus Severus*: that the silence of the Fraternity is lawful, as their arcana are a gift from God and should not be exposed to the undeserving rabble. Such silence does not imply the non-existence of the Brethren, which was an oft-heard accusation given their failure to answer the many enthusiastic replies and entreaties for admittance provoked by the publication of the manifestos.[101] It might be deduced from these arguments that Maier was convinced of the existence of an organised secret Fraternity lying behind the manifestos, and was thus victim rather than perpetrator of a

---

mirum, si huiusmodi in natione Germanica populosissima, inque tot gentes et regiones divisa olim hunc usque contigerit? Nam ut artifices veri, qui ex propria inventione vel alterius communicatione finem artis consecuti sunt, Deo votum pietatis, hominibus officium humanitatis et commiserationem dicant et praestant, ita licet silentium et invidiam contra indignos obtineant..."

[100] *Ibid.*, pp. 294-295: "Per librum M librum mundi seu rerum in mundo existentium, earumque proprietatum, aut Magiae naturalis, intelligo: Talem librum Arabes habuerunt, qui cum descriptus fuerit in Germaniam allatus est: sive igitur hunc ipsum aut ei similem Paracelsus legerit perinde est, nihilominus constat eum in hoc libro versatissimum extitisse."

[101] *Ibid.*, p. 289.

ludibrium, as later generations of writers were to describe him. Nevertheless, we find certain discrepancies and ambiguities in Maier's account which bring such a judgment into question. The first of these occurs shortly after the passage cited above:

> Lest we the rearguard remain too long unbelieving, we declare: that praiseworthy German society, however many they are and wherever they may lie hidden amongst the living, are invited, called together, and led to this our Table, named Golden because of its golden guests, provided that they will be satisfied with quite simple dishes, which are the only courses we have to offer here (for the cook has been seized during his preparation by a hostile fever, sometimes cold, sometimes hot, and his breathing has been agitated, wherefore he is unable to serve up more splendid and opulent dishes of oxen).[102]

It is clear from his words that Maier considers himself to be amongst a 'rearguard' (*post principia*) of a similar ilk to the Protestant Hermeticists portrayed in the manifestos; by inviting the Fraternity to the Golden Table he is calling upon those of his own persuasion to join together in face of their critics. The words 'too long unbelieving' might indicate Maier was still uncertain concerning the status of the author of the manifestos; nevertheless, it seems that he did not go to any great length to investigate the matter, given that he might have followed the same route that Friedrich Grick had taken to uncover Andreae's identity – the Frankfurt Book Fair. Like other Rosicrucian apologists, Maier constructed his Rosicrucian writings as a rallying point for his own ideas, and a call to realise an already-existing but dispersed and disorganised brotherhood in Christ and Hermes. In this sense the words of the *Symbola Aureae Mensae* are not unlike the invitation that the manifestos themselves form.

It is also evident that Maier's 'invitation' to the Fraternity is an attempt to demarcate the boundaries of true Rosicrucianism in accordance with his own proclivities; for those who would not be satisfied with the dishes served at the Golden Table are those with no interest in the practical labour of alchemy and the production of iatrochemical cures. Thus the puzzling allusion to the feverish cook refers to the labours of the alchemist, and the dishes he serves are the fruits of those labours. This allusion rests in part upon the traditional depiction of the alchemical process as a feverish man, to be found in the medieval *Allegory of Merlin* reprinted seven years prior to the *Symbola*

---

[102] *Ibid.*: "Ne itaque et nos, post principia, nimis diu increduli remaneamus, constituimus LAUDABILEM ILLAM SOCIETATEM GERMANICAM, QUOTQUOT ET UBI LATEANT APUD VIVOS, AD HANC NOSTRAM MENSAM, AUREAM DICTAM OB AURATOS CONVIVAS, invitare, convocare et adducere, si modo vulgaribus sint contenti missibus, (coquus enim certe dum in hac praeparatione tota occupatus fuit, quartano hoste nunc frigidum nunc calidum expirante agitatus lautiores bovis epulas apponere nequit) quos hic solos offerimus."

Aureae Mensae, or the strange tale of the melancholic duke dosed with sudorifics presented by the *Allegory of Duenech* and referred to in the twenty-eighth discourse of Maier's *Atalanta Fugiens*.[103] But Maier also clearly states that he himself is the 'cook' at the Golden Table; for this entire passage appears under the curious marginal heading, "The author has been fighting with the disease for four days (as the guests fought with Pyrgopolynices)."[104] As the 'hostile fever' suffered by the cook is the quartan, there can be no doubt that Maier was sick at the time of writing, a fact that underscores his very personal involvement with his Work. Just what Maier is cooking up at the Golden Table is made evident by omission, when he states that the feverish cook is unable to serve the guests "opulent dishes of oxen." This is not only a warning that those who wish to engage with the pleasures of the senses will not find their appetites satisfied at the Golden Table, but also an oblique reference to the temperance-imparting Universal Medicine, which is the 'only course' on offer.

Nevertheless, in the following pages of the *Symbola Aureae Mensae* Maier playfully reverses notions of piety and desire when he presents ten short enigmas to the Brethren; in a typically obscure allusion, it is said that he offers these enigmas to the Fraternity at the Golden Table just as *philothesia* was offered up to the table guests during the Saturnalia.[105] Although the word *philothesia* is not to be found in any of the major Latin lexicons, from another reference to this term made by Maier in the fourth epigram of the *Atalanta Fugiens* we may identify it as a love potion (figure 18).[106]

---

103 See "The Allegory of Merlin." British Library, MS Sloane 3506, pp. 74-75; also "Merlini Allegoria profundissimum Philosophici Lapidis arcanum perfecte continens." In *Artis Auriferae*. Vol. I. Basel: Conrad Waldkirch, 1610, pp. 252-254. The Duenech allegory is to be found in the *Theatrum Chemicum*. Vol. 3. Ursel: Zetzner, 1602, pp. 756-757; Maier, *Atalanta Fugiens*, discourse 28: "Duenech itaque a Pharut in Laconicum introducitur, ut ibi sudet, et tertiae concoctionis foeces per poros excernat: Est autem hujus regis affectus melancholicus seu atrabilarius, unde omnibus aliis principibus in minori authoritate et precio est habitus, dum Saturni morositate et Martis cholera seu iracundia fuerit taxatus: Ipse igitur aut mori aut curari voluit, si id possibile sit." Maier explains the allegory in terms of the purification of both human and metallic bodies.

104 Maier, *Symbola Aureae Mensae*, p. 289: "Authoris cum morbo (uti convivarum cum Pyrgopolynice, conflictu) quarto quoque die."

105 *Ibid.*, p. 291: "Denique nostri conatus ad Minervae Aenigmata, prout illa in mentem manumque venerint, eidem Collegio Germanico studiose, ceu philothesia in Saturnalibus propinamus hoc est, discumbentes inservientibus pro temporis ratione."

106 Maier, *Atalanta Fugiens*, epigram 4: "Non hominum foret in mundo nunc tanta propago,/ Si fratri conjunx non data prima soror./ Ergo lubens conjunge duos ab utroque parente/ Progenitos ut sint foemina masque toro./ Praebibe nectareo Philothesia pocla liquore/ Utrisque, et foetus spem generabit amor." In the German translation of the epigram in the *Atalanta Fugiens* "der Lieb Becher mit süssem Reben Safft" is given, i.e. "the love goblet with the juice of the vine;" there is the possibility that this is a

According to Maier's letter of Christmas greetings to Prince Henry of England, the Saturnalia was a midwinter Roman festival which marked a brief return to the conditions of the Golden Age;[107] significantly for Maier's reference to 'serving' the Brethren his enigmas, during this festival the roles of master and slave were reversed and moral restrictions were relaxed. Thus Maier appears impishly to question whether the Brethren are in fact masters or servants at the Golden Table. However, it is not simply Maier's penchant for riddles that motivates this strange portrayal of the purveying of love potion to the chaste Brethren, or his depiction of the Golden Table as a feast in honour of Saturn, symbol of old age, decay and the deep materiality of lead. Rather, it is his concern with the *coniunctio oppositorum*, and the paradoxical relationship in his alchemy of corporeality to the divine.

On first inspection the ten enigmas composed by Maier give the impression that their solutions may well have died with their author; and as draughts served up to the Fraternity they would have proved less than potable, even to the author of the enigmatic manifestos. Nevertheless, they furnish us with interesting clues concerning Maier's perspective on the Rosicrucian affair. The first nine enigmas are dedicated to the Muses; and in the ninth enigma dedicated to Urania, the Muse of astronomy, Maier ponders over the number of 'Brethren' brought together by the manifestos and their message:

> As I consider the eternal signs of your house R. C.,
> and ponder the number of our allies united in one troupe,
> a man from the common people passes by.
> He asks eagerly, how many have I counted in my sum total;
> Might it be five times fifty? For seemingly I had so much.
> In reply I declare: that number which I have gathered,
> if just so many is increased by half,
> and this by a sixth part moreover,
> then there would be given just so many as you say.
> But he was unable to deal with this complicated addition.[108]

Deckname for an actual herbal medicament employed by Maier, as *philothesia* may be derived from the Greek θησειον (originally, 'temple of Theseus') denoting a parasitic plant known as the bastard toad-flax, *Thesium linophyllum*.

[107] Srigley, *Images of Regeneration*, p. 101.

[108] Maier, *Symbola Aureae Mensae*, p. 301: "Vestrae signa domus R. C. perennia/ Dum lustro, numerosque ex sociis agens;/ Unito agmine, praeterit/ Quidam de populi grege./ Hic quarens cupida mente, quot egerim/ In summam numeros, anne ea quinquies:/ Quinquaginta referrent?/ Tot namque esse viderier./ Quem contra asservi: Quot numeri mihi:/ Collecti, totidem si fuerint adhuc,/ Atque hoc dimidio auctum, et Sexta hoc parte sit insuper;/ Tunc, quot dicis, erunt hinc numeri dati:/ Extricare sed his plexibus impotens..."

Whilst this enigma may have confounded the common folk of Maier's time, the solution is roughly 142.857; and if we might consider this to be a nonsense, at the end of the enigma we are reminded by Maier that it is not our place to guess the number of those whom God has chosen to bring together. Nevertheless, it would seem from his words that the Fraternity is formed not only by the authors of the manifestos but by all those "German chemical and philosophical authors, unknown and anonymous, lying hidden under the symbol of R. C."[109] In Maier's eyes the letters R. C. form a *Deckname* or hieroglyph under which alchemists across Germany are working; and the significance of that hieroglyph is dealt with in the tenth and final 'twofold enigma', dedicated to Apollo, god of the Sun:

> For me R. refers to the sea,
> In which fish are being hunted at three different times:
> The first when Cancer thrust forth his claws,
> The second under the righteous judgement of Libra,
> The third when Aquarius pours forth wet waves:
> Tell me, of which fish do I speak, and of which waves of the sea?[110]

The reference here to fish in a sea appears to be an allusion to the well-known alchemical allegory concerning "the little round fish in our sea" to be found in the enigmas of the *Visio Arislei*.[111] In the context of this allegory, the sea may be understood as the Mercurial Water, a universal solvent used to extract the 'miraculous power' from the base metals or primary subject (the 'fish') within the alchemical vessel. In the twenty-second discourse of his *Atalanta Fugiens* Maier follows Paracelsus in referring to the alchemical fish as trout, as it was believed that trout hold within themselves traces of the river gold they swallow (and hence, according to Maier's alchemical cosmology, they are a model for the divine power of the Sun, the seed of gold, lying at the heart of all metals).[112] A good emblematic depiction of the alchemical sea and its fish is to be found in Lambsprinck's *De Lapide Philosophico Libellus* (see figure 19), which Maier mentions a little prior to the enigmas in his *Symbola Aureae Mensae*.[113]

---

[109] *Ibid.*, p. 289: "Germani authores Chymici et philosophi, incogniti et anonymi, latentes sub symbolo R. C."

[110] *Ibid.*, p. 302: "R. mihi adest aequor, pisces captantur in illo/ Tempore tres vario, primus cum brachia Cancer/ Exerit, atque alter sub iusto examine Librae,/ Tertius humentes cum fundit Aquarius undas:/ Dicite, quos pisces statuam quas Aequoris undas?"

[111] "Aenigmata ex Visione Arislei Philosophi." In *Artis Auriferae*. Vol. 1. Basel: Petrum Pernam, 1572, p. 162. Reprinted in 1610.

[112] On this subject see de Jong, *Michael Maier's Atalanta Fugiens*, pp. 179-180.

[113] Maier, *Symbola Aureae Mensae*, p. 272. De Jong, *Michael Maier's Atalanta Fugiens*, p. 6, discusses the relationship of Lambsprinck's emblems to those of the *Atalanta Fugiens*.

It follows that the "three different times" at which the fish are hunted represent three different phases of solution in the lengthy alchemical process, as dictated by astrological law; the first when the sun is in Cancer (from June 22), the second in Libra (from September 23) and the third in Aquarius (from January 20). These signs of the Zodiac correspond to summer, autumn and winter, giving spring as the time of the work's completion – and perhaps Easter, in accordance with Maier's first alchemical experiment detailed in the *De Medicina Regia*, although it must be said that the threefold solution given in the enigma does not correspond to any of the disparate procedures alluded to elsewhere by Maier.

Whilst the details of Maier's laboratory practice are impossible to reconstruct, these enigmatic allusions again confirm the importance of practical alchemical work to his Rosicrucian ideal. Peuckert once remarked that Maier's Rosicrucian works do not completely reflect the attitude of the *Fama Fraternitatis* and the *Confessio Fraternitatis*, because "gold is always as valuable as *sophia* to him," and whilst alchemy forms a part of the manifestos' message, "for Maier it was everything."[114] Whilst it is true that Maier's emphasis on alchemy is at variance with that of the manifestos, divine wisdom and laboratory process are not counterposed in his work, as the Hermetic doctrines of sympathy and correspondence stipulate that the divinely instituted laws at operation in the alchemist's vessel are mirrored in the various tiers of the cosmos. Thus it is said in the second half of the tenth 'twin' enigma that C. refers to the "sublime laws of a fortress":

> C. gives you the sublime laws of a fortress; and there is
> No other bird that has more power with threatening wings and eyes
> Than the winged being thought to be yours.
> By that bird's command a nest has been constructed in a tree,
> Which some time ago produced a series of gold-born chicks.[115]

On one hand we may understand the fortress to be the alchemical vessel itself; it is analogous to the nest of the bird of the Rosicrucians, which, from the references given in Maier's fifth enigma, we may identify as his beloved phoenix.[116] From its nest, unassailable in the heights of an oak-tree, new life

---

[114] Peuckert, *Pansophie* (1936 edition), p. 152.

[115] Maier, *Symbola Aureae Mensae*, p. 302: "C. vobis Castri sublimia iura dat, et non/ Inter aves est, quae valeat pernicibus alis/ Aut oculis ante hanc volucrem, quae vestra putatur,/ Et cuius nutu est constructus in arbore nidus,/ Qui pridem Aurigenos produxit in ordine pullos."

[116] The fifth enigma, dedicated to the muse of Tragedy, Melpomene, describes the nest of the Phoenix built high in a gnarled oak where it rears its chicks; the bird is to be found in the remote Arabian forests of Sheba, where it prepares for its long flight through all the world: "Iovis volucris olim/ Quercu plicasset alta/ Nidos, suos penates,/ Pullos ut

is born through a process of fiery destruction (the black phase of the work) and re-creation. On the other hand, the 'nest' and 'fortress' possess a significance beyond the vagaries of laboratory work. They are also a symbol for Protestant Germany, the heart of the spiritual regeneration of Europe, and the womb that has brought forth the generations of the Fraternity, as Maier puts it in his *Themis Aurea*.[117] Thus in Maier's preamble to the enigmas, he tells us that "the defences of the high wall" have been built around the "place of truth" – and although the wall crumbles before those that assail it, nevertheless the 'artisans' within rush forward to build it up again, "in order that, by the command of God, the threats may cease."[118] These words are reminiscent of the famous emblem printed in Daniel Mögling's *Speculum Sophicum Rhodo-Stauroticum* ('Sophical Rosicrucian Mirror,' 1618), in which the dwelling-place of the Fraternity is depicted as a fortress of God's truth prevailing against its detractors – the most pernicious of whom, in the eyes of the Rosicrucian apologists, were the Jesuit calumniators and other agents of the papal yoke.

How far was Maier implicated in the religious strife of his day by his involvement in the Rosicrucian affair? Evidence for the depth of hostilities harboured by the Jesuit camp is to be found in Father François Garasset's *La Doctrine Curieuse des Beaux Esprits de ce Temps, ou Pretendus Tels* (1623), a polemical tract appearing in Catholic France a year after Maier's death – the same year that hysteria was created in Paris with reports of the entrance of the 'invisible' Brethren into that city. In this tract Garasset names Maier as the 'secretary' of the Fraternity, which he portrays as a "pernicious company of sorcerers and magicians" whose doctrine stems from Satan and the "Turks and cannibals" of the Middle East.[119] According to Garasset, Maier's books

---

educaret:/ Rerum feracitate/ Estque apta visa sedes./ Quod cum Sabae remotis/ Sylvis eo propinquans/ Phoenix videret, inquit,/ Hic est quies parata/ Volatuum labori,/ Qui factus est per annos/ Tot, integrum per orbem..." *Ibid.*, p. 299.

[117] Maier, *Themis Aurea* (1624 edition), pp. 123-124: see n. 212 below.

[118] Maier, *Symbola Aureae Mensae*, p. 291: "*Mina muri extant*. Minas extare alti alicuius muri cum ipsis fatemur, ex quarum lapsu concursuros opifices ad eas erigendas, at ita erigent, ut minae esse desinant, ex Dei nutu: Nullus enim timor aut minae apud veritatis amantes locum inveniunt..."

[119] Garasset, François. *La Doctrine Curieuse des Beaux Esprits de ce Temps, ou Pretendus Tels. Contenant Plusieurs Maximes pernicieuses à l'Estat, à la Religion, et aux bonnes Moeurs. Combattue et Renversee par le P. François Garassus de la Compagnie de JESUS.* Paris: Sebastien Chappelet, 1623, pp. 86-87: "Les Freres de la Croix des Roses parlant de ce venerable enluminé leur fondateur, disent deux choses, de ses estudes, 1. Inter Turcas maxime profecit, inde doctrinam suam hausit, il profita grandement en Turquie, c'est de là qu'il apprist les secrets de sa doctrine, et je ne me puis persuader que les fondateurs de cette cabale d'impieté ayent appris les horribles blasphemes qu'ils prononcent insolemment contre Iesus-Christ, que parmi des Turcs ou Cannibales, je

are "as enigmatic as Lycophron,"[120] and he and his fellow conspirators
(Rudolph Goclenius and Adam Haslmayr are mentioned by name) pose a
threat to the church, to the secular state and to good morals. Consequently, he
writes that no torture would be great enough for these men, whom he
condemns as Sodomites and perverters of youth.[121] It seems the Jesuits also
had a theory concerning the true significance of the Fraternity's name.
Garasset relates that a wreath of roses was hung in the German drinking halls,
where the Fraternity's heresies were inspired by "the warmth of the wine;"
and when the *Fama Fraternitatis* states that the Order's founder was from a
poor background, so Garasset concurs, stating that Father C. R. was a barfly
(*moucheron de cabaret*) who found illumination in his beer.[122] Given the
emphasis on temperance to be found in Rosicrucian writings, these passages
are clearly designed to offend Protestant sensibilities (indeed, in his *Verum
Inventum* Maier argues specifically against inspiration through the
consumption of alcohol). It is also clear that the polemical description of
Maier as 'secretary' of the order cannot be taken seriously. Nevertheless,
Garasset's tract reveals that Maier and his writings assumed a central place
within the Rosicrucian controversy, at least from the perspective of the
Fraternity's detractors.

As for Maier's actual commitment to Protestant political or religious
goals, it is important to state that his writings portray the Brethren first and
foremost as good alchemists, opposed by those ignorant in the ways of the
Art. Thus we have seen in the tenth enigma of the *Symbola Aureae Mensae*
that Maier again depicts the enemies of Rosicrucianism as the cantankerous birds of the *Jocus Severus*, assailing the phoenix of the Brethren.
Furthermore, Maier clearly states in the oft-quoted passage from the final
chapter of his *Themis Aurea* that the Brethren do not confess a universal
reformation with the goal of one empire and one religion – an answer on
the one hand to Jesuit accusations that the Rosicrucians sought world

---

dirois, qu'ils les ont appris des Diables, s'ils ne m'enseignoient eux mesmes par les
maximes de leur creance, qu'ils ne croyent ny Dieu ny Diable."

[120] A Greek poet known for the extreme obscurity of his erudite style.

[121] *Ibid.*, pp. 91-92: "Je conclus que si ces Freres de la fraternité de Roses sont coulpables,
meschans et condamnez par arrest en qualité de Sorciers et d'une meschante conjuration
de faquins prejudiciable à la Religion, aux Estats seculiers et à la doctrine des bonnes
moeurs, quoy qu'ils ayent en apparence quelque attrait de pieté, je ne voy point de
supplices assez grands pour nos dogmatisans, qui n'ont en leurs parolles que blasphemes
et impietez, en leurs actions que brutalitez et Sodomies, en leurs escrits que tropheés de
leurs impudicitez, en leur hantise, que corruption de jeunesse, en leur visage
qu'impudence, en leur ame que trahison, en leur corps que les marques de leurs sueurs,
dont ils se vantent eux-mesmes par leurs livres imprimez, a fin que personne n'en
pretende cause d'ignorance."

[122] *Ibid.*, pp. 84, 86.

government through a pact with Islam, and on the other to those "Anabaptists and Enthusiasts" who, acting under the good name of the Fraternity, disturb "all order and law" with their foolish dreams.[123] Maier only concedes that some years in the past a Reformation had indeed been necessary, which has already been effected by Father C. R., as by Erasmus, Luther, Melanchthon, Paracelsus, Copernicus and Tycho Brahe.[124] It is only within God's power to change the hearts of individuals and turn the Papists towards the true Church of God, a task the Brethren do not presume to take on themselves.[125] This having been said, however, Maier immediately launches into a tirade against "the seven-hilled city" which oppresses the "German Eagle," i.e. the *Deutsches Reich* and her princes, from whose labour and blood Rome acquires her glory.[126] Given these sentiments of Maier's, perhaps we may see in the arch-villain of the *Symbola Aureae Mensae*, the Roman centurion Pyrgopolynices (literally, 'tower-town-taker'), an allusion to the Rome of Maier's day and the Protestant-Hermetic 'fortress' standing against it.[127] Thus Maier ends his discourse with the remark that the Fraternity has recently been augmented by ten men; on hearing this fact, Pyrgopolynices "digests the matter with difficulty" before he "bursts forth" with another tirade against the good alchemists seated at the Golden Table.[128] In any case, it seems the cardinals of the Sacred Congregation of the Index in Rome were able to decipher enough of Maier's enigmatic references to inspire their

---

[123] Maier, *Themis Aurea* (1624 edition), p. 233. These sentiments lie in accord with the *Fama Fraternitatis*, which rails against all "enthusiasts, heretics and false Prophets."

[124] Maier, *Themis Aurea*, p. 234.

[125] *Ibid.*, p. 235.

[126] *Ibid.*, p. 234: "Tyrannidem in religione occupatam et tanti temporis praescriptione possessam illi, qui Septicollem falso sibi asscribit urbem, Aquilae Germanicae subjectam, Regum cervices (instar superbissimi illius Sesostridis Aegyptii) calcare solitus et regna ad se transferre verbis, quasi alieno labore et sanguine partam gloriam, ut Thraso apud Comicum, non excepero, sed ut in veram Christi ecclesiam, quae non gladiis sibi regna quaerit aut tuetur, quam primo redeat, relictis mundanis, unice optamus." Sesostris (1878-1841 BCE) was an Egyptian pharoah who according to Herodotus (*Histories* 2.102-110) sacrificed two of his own sons in an act of cowardice, yet set up obelisks across the lands of Egypt to demonstrate his own power (and placed female genitalia upon them to signify the cowardice of those who did not resist his dominion).

[127] According to Frick, in Maier's time the character from Plautus' play had also become a literary symbol for the archetypal braggart; see his introduction to the *Symbola Aureae Mensae Duodecim Nationum*. Graz: Akademische Druck- und Verlagsanstalt, 1972, p. xi.

[128] Maier, *Symbola Aureae Mensae*, p. 306: "Decem probatissimis viris dicitur collegium adhuc auctum. Hostis interim Pyrgopolynices irarum materiam ruminans aegreque concoquens apud sese, ubi silentium fieri animadvertit, in hunc erupit modum. Argumentum Adversarii contra Chemiam..."

wrath, as the *Symbola Aureae Mensae* was banned by papal decree on December the 12th, 1624.[129]

6. Uncovering the true Brethren

Maier's was only one amongst a number of possible interpretations of the manifestos, each of which gave their own emphasis to the broad Protestant and Hermetic contours portrayed there, be it theological, theosophical, alchemical, astrological or chiliastic. Indeed, in the decade following the first publication of the *Fama Fraternitatis* in 1614 over four hundred 'Rosicrucian' apologies and opposing *Kampfschriften* appeared, and many of the former were composed under the name of the Fraternity itself.[130] In the *Symbola Aureae Mensae* Maier gives us some intriguing clues concerning the Rosicrucian literature he had encountered by 1617, and the form of Rosicrucianism he found most pleasing. At the end of his discourse on the Rosicrucians, he sets out a condensed version of the Order's history given in the manifestos.[131] He goes on to depict in list form the membership of the Order through three centuries and generations, each being composed of 8 Brethren; the first two generations (of the fifteenth and sixteenth centuries) are reconstructed in accordance with the members' initials given in the *Fama Fraternitatis* – those given in the main narrative of the text, as well as those inscribed in the parchment book found clasped in the hands of the perfectly preserved corpse of Father Christian Rosenkreutz. It is unlikely that any of these initials refer to historical personages – for example, we are told that Brother I. O., who "cured a young Earl of Norfolk of leprosy," did not live to see the death of Father C. R. in 1484; yet there were no Earls of Norfolk in the fifteenth century, nor were there any cases of leprosy amongst the Mowbray and Howard families who held the duchy of Norfolk during this

---

[129] Moller, Johannis. *Cimbria Literata, sive Scriptorum Ducatus Utriusque Slesvicensis et Holsatici, Quibus et Alii vicini quidam accensentur, Historia Literaria Tripartita.* Vol. 1. Havniae: Orphanotrophius, 1744, p. 378. Apparently the books prohibited by this decree were included as an appendix to the Index of prohibited books originally published at the direction of Pope Clement VIII in 1596.

[130] In the course of his research Carlos Gilly has collated over 700 printed works and manuscripts relating to the Rosicrucian affair appearing in the years 1610-1660; see Gilly, *Cimelia Rhodostaurotica*, p. 76; also Gilly, Carlos. "Iter Rosicrucianum: Auf der Suche nach Unbekannten Quellen der Frühen Rosenkreuzer." In *Das Erbe des Christian Rosenkreutz: Vorträge gehalten anläßlich des Amsterdamer Symposiums 18.-20. November 1986.* Amsterdam: In de Pelikaan, 1988, p. 63.

[131] The bulk of this history is derived from the *Fama Fraternitatis*, with the exception of the dates of the birth and death of Father C. R. (1378-1484), which are taken from the *Confessio Fraternitatis*.

period.[132] Be that as it may, it is the third generation of the Order given by Maier – that of the seventeenth century – that interests us here:

Tertius ordinis et seculi moderni.

1.
2.
3. Tertius in ordine, qui Wetzlariae, A. C. 1615. se fratrem ore est confessus et multis modis demonstravit.
4.
5.
6.
7. B. M. I. qui Haganosae scripsit quaedam impressa, A. C. 1614. Sept. 22.
8. N. N. bonus Architectus; casu aperuit fornicem sepulchri Fr. R. C. A.C. 1604 aut circiter.

Decem probatissimis viris dicitur collegium adhuc auctum.[133]

Mention of the eighth member, Brother N. N., who "by chance opened the vault of the sepulchre of Father C. R. in 1604 or thereabouts," may be found in the account given by the *Fama Fraternitatis*.[134] However, Maier's reference to the third member from Wetzlar (a town in the Calvinist state of Nassau-Dillenburg bordering Hessen-Kassel) is derived from Georg Molther's *Gründtliche Relation von einer frembden Mannsperson, Welche inn jüngst verflossenem M. DC. XV. Jahr durch deß H. Reichs Statt Wetzslar gereißt* ('Thorough Report of a foreign man, who in the recently elapsed year of 1615 travelled through the town Wetzlar of the Holy Roman Empire'). Molther was a court physician to Count Johann of Nassau-Dillenburg, a close ally of Moritz the Learned and Friedrich V of the Palatinate. Whilst biographical records on Molther are exceedingly scanty, the fact that he moved close to the inner circles of Rosicrucianism is made clear by the inclusion of his theses in the *Disputationes Chymico-Medicae* presided over by Johannes Hartmann – the personal physician to Moritz of Hessen-Kassel who, as we have mentioned, was both an acquaintance of Maier and an early distributor of the *Fama Fraternitatis* in manuscript form.[135] The *Gründtliche*

---

[132] Nor have there been any subsequent cases of leprosy in those families – kind information of Dr. John Martin Robinson, Librarian to Major-General His Grace the Duke of Norfolk.

[133] Maier, *Symbola Aureae Mensae*, p. 306.

[134] Kooij and Gilly, *Fama Fraternitatis*, pp. 89 ff.

[135] That Molther was a student of Hartmann's may be gathered from the twelfth disputation concerning "the obstruction of the liver," appearing under the respondent name of Georg Molther of Grünberg in *Disputationes Chymico-Medicae: Pleraeque sub Praesidio Joh. Hartmanni, Med. D. et Chymiatriae in Academia Marpurgensi Professoris Publici, ab aliquot Medicinae Candidatis et Studiosis, ibidem censurae publicae expositae...*

Relation, addressed in the preface to Count Johann, first appeared in a Latin edition of 1616, and was reprinted in German translation as an appendix to the 1617 Frankfurt am Main edition of the *Fama Fraternitatis*.[136] It describes Molther's strange encounter in the town of Wetzlar with a wonder-working naturopath, who not only described himself as a 'brother of the Order of the Rosy Cross', but also demonstrated an astonishingly multi-faceted skill and learning. Although most researchers in the field of early Rosicrucianism have neglected this tract, testimony to its importance was given by Schick when he described Molther as "defender and chief witness for the existence of real Rosicrucians."[137]

According to Molther's 'report', a citizen was tending his hops garden one day in early May of 1615 when he spied a poorly dressed stranger passing by, collecting herbs and roots by the way to put in his sack. Striking up a conversation, the citizen inquired as to the purpose of his activity, to which the stranger replied that he could cure many diseases with these plants and with "the assistance of God."[138] The stranger went on to cure the citizen's wife of a respiratory problem, charging no fee for his services (in accordance with the first law of the Order given in the *Fama Fraternitatis*); whereupon he was taken to a patient of Molther's, who was suffering from breast cancer, and was laid low with pain. Although he could not cure the disease on account of its advanced state, he nevertheless delivered a precise prognosis in accordance with astrological principles – a prognosis that, according to Molther, proved to be entirely accurate.[139]

Marburg: Paul Egenolph, 1614, pp. 301-310. The town of Grünberg lies some 40 kilometres from Wetzlar. For Hartmann as a distributor of the manuscript *Fama Fraternitatis*, see Gilly, *Cimelia Rhodostaurotica*, p. 29; Kooij and Gilly, *Fama Fraternitatis*, pp. 13, 15 n. 6.

[136] Molther, Georg. *De quodam peregrino, qui anno superiore MDCXV imperialem Wetzslariam transiens, non modo se fratrem R. C. confessus fuit verum etiam multiplici rerum scientia, verbis et factis admirabilem se praestitit.* Frankfurt am Main: Johann Bringer, 1616; Molther, Georg. "Von einer frembden Mannsperson/ Welche inn jüngst verflossenem M. DC. XV. Jahr durch deß H. Reichs Statt Wetzslar gereißt/ und sich nicht allein für ein Bruder deß Ordens deß Rosen Creutzes außgegeben/ sondern auch durch vielfältige Geschickligkeit/ unnd allerhand Sachen Wissenschafft/ mit Worten unnd Wercken sich also erzeigt hat/ daß man sich ab ihme verwundern müssen/ Gründtliche Relation." In *Fama Fraternitatis, oder Entdeckung der Bruderschafft deß löblichen Ordens deß Rosen Creutzes... Sampt dem Sendtschreiben Iuliani de Campis, und Georgii Moltheri Med. D. und Ordinarii zu Wetzlar Relation/ von einer diß Ordens gewissen Person.* Frankfurt am Main: Johann Bringer, 1617. Molther also composed a Rosicrucian tract under the title E. D. F. O. C. R. Sen., *Antwort, der Hochwürdigen und Hocherleuchten Brüderschafft deß RosenCreutzes.* N.p: n.p., 1617.

[137] Schick, *Das Ältere Rosenkreuzertum*, p. 69.

[138] Molther, "Von einer frembden Mannsperson," p. 90.

[139] *Ibid.*, pp. 91-92, 98-99.

Word of these miraculous powers spread through Wetzlar, and Molther met the stranger, who confirmed the physician's suspicion that he was indeed a Brother of the Rosy Cross, and (breaking his oath of silence a second time, as we may note) divulged the meeting place of the Fraternity.[140] Being the third admitted into the latest generation of the Order (as Maier faithfully records in his membership list), the Brother stated that there were yet two others from the Order visiting the region. By Molther's reckoning, the Brother was a wretched looking man, with poor farmer's clothes, a medium stature and a cropped beard; and although he confessed to being 81 years old, he had no grey hair or imperfections on his teeth – the tell-tale signs, as we may recall, of the application of a chemical medicine such as that purportedly possessed by Maier.[141] He spoke all the languages of the world, and it is cryptically stated that he accommodated his speech to certain "hieroglyphical figures."[142] His cures were effected not only by means of the influence of the stars, but also through his remarkable knowledge of the Bible, which he was wont to cite whilst administering his herbal remedies; and such was his devout faith that Molther believed no man could possibly accuse him of purveying "an ungodly Black Art."[143] Through his knowledge of astrology he predicted to Molther the coming of a great cold spell at Pentecost, which did indeed fall deleteriously at that time.[144] He was well-versed in alchemical preparations, as well as certain magical procedures – for instance, he knew how to drive mice out of the house with a bull-whip, or drive moles out of a field; how to attract fish from a distance, "that they make their way in great numbers, and are happy to be caught;" and how to fend off lightning bolts by means of laurel leaves, seal fur and eagle skin.[145] Indeed, it seemed to Molther that this man was "blessed by all the counsel of Nature," and that all

---

[140] *Ibid.*, p. 97.

[141] *Ibid.*, pp. 96-97: "Ganz deutlich unnd rundt bekannte er/ daß er der dritte in der Ordnung der Fratrum R. C. were/ und daß noch zweene von der Fraternitet fast in gleichem gradu sich in derselben Gegent auffhielten/ Er were vor Zeiten ein Münch gewesen/ und jetzund ein unnd achtzig Jahr alt/ hette auch keinen Mangel an den Zähnen/ denn er dieselbigen noch alle frisch und vollkommlich hatte/ Item daß er hette sieben Probierjahr und etliche Tage müssen außstehen. Viel andere Sachen dergleichen mehr sagte er/ als den Ort seiner Geburt/ seiner Reise/ unnd ihrer Zusammenkunfft." For the properties of Maier's medicine, see above, chapter III, pp. 103-104.

[142] *Ibid.*, p. 97.

[143] *Ibid.*

[144] *Ibid.*, p. 100.

[145] *Ibid.*, p. 102: "Wie man sonsten erfehret von den Lorberzweigen/ Seehunden/ und Adlershäuten/ daß sie den donnerstrahl verhüten." Apparently the 'Brother' was also wont (rather impiously) to perform mischiefs which would lead to the persecution of Gypsies: "wie man ein Feuwer auff einem Bauschen Stro/ oder anderm/ das gerne brennt/ machen solle/ daß man sonsten meynt/ es geschehe durch deß losen Gesindlins/ der Ziegeuner Zauberey/ unnd es nicht weiter/ als man wil/ vom Feuwer verletzet werde."

the things that occurred in the world were known to him. Nevertheless, the Brother did not allow the details of his remarkable skills to be noted down on paper, and he assured Molther that were he to record his knowledge against his will, the words would thereafter be either unreadable or their sense unintelligible.[146] With this admonition he declared that he would make his way to a "wild forest" to collect more herbs and roots, as he would not suffer to spend more than two nights at the same location for fear of detection.[147]

Writing in 1942, Schick appears to have been undecided as to whether this document is in fact a real report of events "or only the literary form of such a report," although he seemed to favour the former possibility when he described the anonymous Rosicrucian as "der Schwindler von Wetzlar" – i.e. he believed that Molther's story was a genuine relation of fact, but that the account given by the 'wonder-working' naturopath concerning his powers and collegial affiliations was not.[148] Likewise, Waite (an advocate of the existence of an organised secret Fraternity) cites Molther's tract as proof that "impostors were thought and known to be about."[149] Nevertheless, there are good reasons to favour the latter possibility proposed by Schick – that the 'imposture' was Molther's, and not that of a roaming charlatan.

In themselves, the strange powers of the 'Brother' related by Molther may not arouse our suspicions concerning the veracity of his report, as they are not unlike certain of the magical procedures related in the works of Maier. There, too, we may find the medicinal employment of minerals, herbs and various animal parts, amalgamated with theories of astral influence. In his *Themis Aurea* Maier identifies the herb utilised by Molther's brother as bryony, a powerful cathartic and diuretic which causes a very painful death in cases of overdose; he goes on to state that the gathering of medicinal herbs according to the alignment of the constellations of the Zodiac may indeed effect cures for dangerous diseases.[150] It is clear that Maier would have found much in agreement with the stranger of Wetzlar, given his devout Protestant leanings and iatrochemical prowess. Considering his sympathies with the

---

[146] *Ibid.*, pp. 103-104: "Was denckwürdiges er etwa redete/ wolte er nicht leiden/ daß es notirt und inn Schreibtaffeln uffgezeichnet würde: ja er betheurte es/ daß/ wann wir etwas von seinen Sachen wider seinen Willen uffnotiren würden/ wirs entweder nicht lesen/ oder doch nicht würden können verstehen..."

[147] *Ibid.*, p. 104.

[148] Schick, *Das Ältere Rosenkreuzertum*, p. 69.

[149] Waite, *Brotherhood of the Rosy Cross*, p. 236.

[150] Maier, *Themis Aurea* (1624 edition), pp. 183-185; according to this testimony, one source of Maier's knowledge of herbal lore was Bartholomaeus Carrichter, the '*Kräuterdoktor*' resident at the imperial court of Rudolf's predecessor Maximillian II, who described various herbal cures as well as the Zodiac signs under which their healing powers thrive in his *Kräutterbuch des Edelen und Hochgelehrten Herzen Doctoris Bartholomei Carrichters*. Straßburg: Antony Bertram, 1609.

religious and natural philosophical outlook of Molther's 'Brother', there was no reason for Maier to be concerned that he was lending credence to a literary creation in compiling his list. On this count, any observant reader may identify the simple narrative devices Molther employs in the course of his report and the logical inconsistencies they entail; for example, the Rosicrucian Brother divulges to Molther both his membership in the Fraternity and its meeting place, although by Molther's own reckoning they had conversed together for only "one or two hours."[151] Such a divulgence would have raised the suspicion of anyone remotely acquainted with the laws of the Fraternity published in the *Fama Fraternitatis*; and with knowledge of the Fraternity's meeting-place, there would be no reason for Molther to lament the Brother's unfulfilled promise that he would one day renew their acquaintance.[152] The fact that Molther finds it so hard to recall the details of his conversation, as if confirming the mysterious warning of the Brother that it is simply impossible to record the words he utters, is rather difficult to swallow.[153] And finally, Molther protests a little too much when he states that no honourable man could suspect that he would lie to his very own patron, as we can well imagine that Johann of Nassau-Dillenburg was an insider to the entire *jocus severus*.[154] The concluding words of the *Gründtliche Relation* seem to be those of someone who has a stake in promulgating the myth of a Rosicrucian Order:

> In this way there should be some Brethren, just as one would wish them to be, no matter whether they really exist in the world or not; in order that we may know it for sure, everyone should make the greatest efforts and try to find out.[155]

The seventh Rosicrucian Brother given in Maier's list is derived from the *Assertio Fraternitatis R. C.* ('Vindication of the Fraternity R. C.,' 1614), a relatively early Rosicrucian publication written by a certain B. M. I., who

---

[151] Molther, "Von einer frembden Mannsperson," p. 106.

[152] *Ibid.*, p. 105.

[153] *Ibid.*

[154] It is difficult to say if there is any significance in the dating of the dedication to Johann – April 1st. The expression "jemand in den April zu schicken" first occurs in the literature in Germany in 1618, suggesting this sixteenth century custom was well and truly current at the time of Georg Molther's little tract. Nevertheless, it seems likely the custom prevailed primarily in Catholic areas. See *Meyers Lexikon*. Vol. 1. Leipzig: Bibliographisches Institut, 1924, pp. 718-719; also *Meyers Grosses Universal Lexikon*. Vol. 1. Mannheim: Bibliographisches Institut, 1981, p. 502.

[155] Molther, "Von einer frembden Mannsperson," p. 108: "Dergleichen seyn sollen etliche R. C. Fratres, wie es zu wünschen were/ als ob sie in der Welt seyen oder nicht/ damit wirs gewiß erfahren mögen/ soll sich billich ein jeder uffs fleissigste bemühen/ unnd darnach forschen."

claims to be one of the Order.[156] This tract emanated from the same publisher as the *Gründtliche Relation*; Peuckert attributed its authorship to the Reformed theologian and alchemist, Raphael Eglinus, whom Moran suggests played a key role in the promulgation of Rosicrucianism at the court of Moritz of Hessen-Kassel.[157] Whilst the *Assertio Fraternitatis* is a short work and does not contain such exorbitant detail as Molther's *Gründtliche Relation*, it again offers us a picture of the form of Rosicrucianism Maier supported.

The tract is addressed on the title page to "whosoever harbours doubts concerning the Order of the Brothers of the Rosy Cross;" it promises the reader that "the verses having been read through, you will be certain."[158] We are informed that during his third peregrination B. M. I. was held up by the rain at 'Hagenoa' – possibly the monastery town of Haina in Hessen-Kassel – where he decided to pass his time by writing these Latin verses.[159] The clues he gives as to the nature of the Fraternity's dwelling, Father C. R.'s 'House of the Holy Spirit', further embellish those given in the *Fama Fraternitatis*; for whereas the third law given in the manifesto states that the Brethren must assemble there on a certain day of each year, B. M. I. states that their House of the Holy Spirit is a permanently inhabited monastery lying in the midst of Germany, not far from a city of great reputation, amidst woods and fields through which a splendid river runs.[160] Moreover, the building's inhabitants

---

[156] B. M. I. (Raphael Eglinus?). *Assertio Fraternitatis R. C. Quam Roseae Crucis vocant, a quodam Fraternitatis eius Socio Carmine expressa*. Frankfurt am Main: Johann Bringer, 1614. Bringer published a number of Rosicrucian tracts apart from the *Gründtliche Relation* and the *Assertio Fraternitatis*, including the 1615 Frankfurt am Main edition of the *Fama Fraternitatis*.

[157] Peuckert, *Die Rosenkreuzer*, p. 171; Moran, *The Alchemical World of the German Court*, pp. 98ff. Gilly also supplies evidence that Eglinus was privy to the contents of the manuscript *Fama Fraternitatis* from an early stage: Gilly, *Cimelia Rhodostaurotica*, p. 29.

[158] B. M. I., *Assertio Fraternitatis*, title page: "Quisquis de Roseae dubitas Crucis ordine Fratrum:/ Hoc lege, perlecto Carmine certus eris."

[159] *Ibid.*, p. 3 *recto*: "Tertia perficitur mihi nunc Apodemia, meque/ Urbs non incelebris nunc Hagenoa tenet." 'Hagenoa' resembles 'Hagena' or Haina given in Graesse, Johann Georg Theodor. *Orbis Latinus*. Berlin: Schmidt, 1922. Another possibility is 'Haganoa', i.e. the town of Großenhain in Saxony; it must be remarked that the references to events in Austria in the *Assertio Fraternitatis*, and the fact that 'Hagenoa' may refer to 'Hageno' or Gendorf bei Baldramsdorf in Austrian Carinthia, may suggest a more southerly origin of the tract, although the fact that the town is said to be "non incelebris" mitigates against this possibility.

[160] We may wonder if the 'House of the Holy Spirit' has some relation to the monastery of Haina in B. M. I.'s eyes, and that the nearby "town of great reputation" is Marburg lying some 25 miles to the northeast. B. M. I., *Assertio Fraternitatis*, p. 3 *verso*: "Ordo latet noster media Germanide terra.../Arboribus nemorum cum nostris cingimur arvis,/

are well-known to the local people, who daily beat on the monastery doors
and go away loaded with abundant gifts; the Brethren also use their healing
powers to cure illnesses amongst them, for which reason they do not betray
the Fraternity to its enemies.[161] Here the *Assertio Fraternitatis* gives clear
expression to the sectarian sentiments presaging the coming conflagration of
the Thirty Years War: for although the Brethren are currently spared "the
Papist yoke," the Jesuits plot against them and search for their dwelling-
place night and day. In the course of the tract imprecations are made to God
to protect the Fraternity from the jaws of these 'wolves'.[162] But we are
also ominously informed that an army – presumably sympathetic to the
Rosicrucian cause – is encamped near the House of the Holy Spirit, although
"for important reasons" B. M. I. does not betray its position.[163] In similar
fashion to Maier's portrayal of the Protestant-Hermetic 'fortress', the author
of the *Assertio Fraternitatis* is warning that although the Brethren may pray
for divine intervention, they nevertheless have recourse to the very tangible
power of Calvinist Germany and its allies.

The *Assertio Fraternitatis* also inveighs against certain men posing falsely
as Rosicrucians, and seeks thereby to establish the true inheritors of the
Rosicrucian mantle created by the manifestos. This invective is evidence that
various streams of thought and practice had grown up within the Rosicrucian
milieu from an early stage of its development, as the *Assertio Fraternitatis*
was published within the same year as the *Fama Fraternitatis* itself. In his
Themis Aurea Maier also sought to demarcate true Rosicrucianism from false
by identifying certain 'impostors' who write and act in the name of the
Brethren;[164] and just as Maier railed against the charlatanism of the vulgar
gold-makers in his *Examen Fucorum Pseudo-chymicorum*, so the relation in
the *Assertio Fraternitatis* of the sorry fate of a certain 'purse-thief' is
suggestive of alchemical *Betrügerei* and the "gold-making rogues" censured
in the *Fama Fraternitatis*:

Praeterit et tacitis nobile flumen acquis./ Nec procul a nobis urbs inclyta fama
habitatur..."

[161] *Ibid.*, p. 3 *recto*: "Quotidie pulsant tamen ostia nostra rogantes,/ Qui larga semper stipe
onerati abeunt./ Quin etiam duris afflicti in corpore morbis,/ A nobis Medica saepe
levantur ope;/ Unde favet nobis circum vicinia tota,/ Nec quisquam nostras laedere vellet
opes."

[162] *Ibid.*, pp. 4 *verso*- 5 *recto*: "Insidias etiam tendit Jesuitica turba/ Sedibus et nostris nocte,
dieque inhiat./ Ut fauces horum fugiamus et ora luporum/ Multa jubet cautos dissimulare
dies./ Sancte Deus nostrum conserva et protege caetum,/ Si te rite colit, si tibi grata
facit./ Et prohibe saevos furiati pectoris hostes,/ Ne possint ulla parte nocere probis."

[163] *Ibid.*, p. 3 *recto*: "Pene locum dixi, quo nostrum consideat agmen,/ Nomen at ob causas
prodere cesso graves."

[164] Maier, *Themis Aurea* (1624 edition), p. 233.

And nor do I disguise the fact, that certain writings less esteemed by us have been published
in the name of the Brethren. Which writings one will easily recognise, because they are not
in agreement with our *Fama*, as anyone who reads it with an attentive mind will realise.
Maybe there are some who name themselves Brethren, whilst not being at all in harmony
with our choir. Such an impostor some time ago spread the most deceitful rubbish amongst
the peoples of the lands between Innsbruck and Vienna. That purse-thief was exposed, and
paid a bitter price by being suspended on a cross. Another such meddler was similarly caught
in the city of Augsburg, and he lost his earlobes with the lash.[165]

It must be remarked that, authentic or otherwise, any 'Rosicrucians' found
peddling their ideologies or alchemical wares in Austria – at that time a seat
of the Counter-Reformation – could expect short shrift from the authorities.
However, B. M. I. himself gives a clue that the true Fraternity was rather
more virtual than tangible when – in a somewhat cryptic aside – he
admonishes such impostors not to "throw our gaming-board (alveolus) into
confusion."[166] Here we have another allusion to the game or 'serious jest' set
in motion by Andreae.

Given this reference, we may take B. M. I.'s account of life within the
Fraternity as another portrait of the ideal *collegium*, and a Rosicrucian vision
of which Maier approved. Thus the Brethren of the *Assertio Fraternitatis* are
concerned first and foremost with the procurement of iatrochemical remedies;
in accordance with the statement of the *Fama Fraternitatis*, gold-making to
them is a mere *parergon* or ornament. B. M. I. also makes a point of refuting
allegations of Satanic involvement in their Art, levelled at that time not only
by the Jesuits but also by many Protestant theologians:

He who has defamed us lately on account of the magic arts, errs and is ignorant of our way. I
do not deny that we often achieve stupendous things, but they are achieved by the silent
means of nature. That in which we excel in skill is the matter of *chemia*; every day it
employs our furnaces. If somebody imagines this Art is performed by a contract with Satan,
woe to me, how totally wrong he is! For this our chief cure derives from chaste minds and
hands, duly and at the leisure of God. Our whole life is spent in the fear of God, and likewise
in obliging duty to all humanity.[167]

---

[165] B. M. I., *Assertio Fraternitatis*, p. 4 *verso*: "At neque dissimulo, quod fratrum nomine
quaedam/ Vulgantur, nobis scripta probata minus./ Quae facile agnoscet, nostrae quia
dissona famae,/ Attenta quisquis talia mente legit./ Forsitan et Fratrem se quis de nomine
fingit,/ Cum tamen a nostro sit procul ille choro./ Qualis deceptor pridem per Norica
rura,/ Sparserat ad populum plurima vana rudem./ Donec convictus quod fur, quod
manticulator,/ De cruce suspensus triste pependit onus:/ Qualis item ardelio Augustana
prensus in urbe,/ Verberibus caesus perdidit auriculas." *Norica* refers to the region in
Austria between the Wienerwald to the east, the River Inn to the west, the Danube to the
north and the River Drau to the south.

[166] *Ibid.*, p. 4 *verso*: "Alveolos nostros turbare omittite fuci."

[167] *Ibid.*, p. 4 *recto*: "Qui nuper Magicas nos diffamavit ob artes,/ Errat et est nostrae nescius
ille viae./ Non Ego diffiteor, patramus saepe stupenda,/ Naturae tacitis cuncta sed illa

Thus B. M. I. states that the Brethren are guided by the contemplation of Nature, but to the greater glory of God and not of Satan – a reiteration of the distinction between natural and diabolical magic adhered to by Maier and the *magi* of the Italian Renaissance. They tend to the body in accordance with the laws of Nature, "from whence flows good health and long life;" and those to come will wonder at the lofty goals that will be achieved by this means.[168] To this end the Brethren scour the lands of Europe in search of new knowledge – a custom in which the medieval Christian ethic of holy pilgrimage meets the natural philosophy of Paracelsus, who once stated, "he who wishes to explore Nature must tread her books with his feet... one land, one page."[169] Maier's life of wandering suggests this was an ideal that he too held dear.

On account of the Brothers' journeys B. M. I. informs us that "there is nothing that occurs on the soil of Europe that is not noted precisely by our luminaries" – and this includes the publication of learned tracts with which to complement the Fraternity's "abundant library."[170] Indeed, every day at a fixed hour the prefect of the Order calls together the Fraternity, and each Brother has the opportunity to tell what he has "seen, read, meditated and heard."[171] Here B. M. I. is elaborating upon the statement of the *Fama Fraternitatis* that the Brethren travelled widely in order that their *axiomata* could be scrutinised more keenly, and also because "they wished to inform each other if in one land or another some error came to light through observation."[172] According to B. M. I.'s elaboration, each item of knowledge brought back to the House of the Holy Spirit by the Brethren – when

---

modis./ Qualia chemiae sunt quae praestamus ab arte:/ Exercet nostros quotidie illa focos./ Quae si quis Satana fieri putat astipulante,/ Hei mihi quam tot a fallitur ille via!/ Haec etenim nobis est cura potissima, puris/ Mentibus et manibus rite vacante Deo./ Vita agitur nobis Divino plena timore,/ Et simul in cunctos officiosa homines..."

[168] *Ibid.*, p. 4 *recto*: "Corpora curamus naturae convenienter,/ Inde valetudo, vitaque longa fluit..."; p. 4 *verso*: "Grandia molimur, sua quae mirabitur aetas/ Quaeque seipsa probent utilitate sua."

[169] Pagel, *Paracelsus*, p. 56.

[170] B. M. I., *Assertio Fraternitatis*, p. 3. *verso*: "Discendi cupidi sumus, atque ut multa sciamus,/ Venamur tacite quicquid ubique boni./ Sic nihil Europa rerum geritur prope terra,/ Quod non exacte Lumina nostra notent./ Quicquid librorum profertur ubique novorum,/Ad nostras curat Bibliopola manus."

[171] *Ibid.*: "Quotidie certis praesul nos convocat horis,/ Ponereque in medium cognita quemque iubet./ De quibus in partem mox disceptatur utramque,/ Vera probant cuncti, falsaque rejiciunt./ Tunc sibi quid visum, quid lectum, quid meditatum,/ Auditumve refert ordine quisque suo." Note that the term 'prefect' or *praesul* is used here rather than the eighteenth century Rosicrucian denomination of 'commander' or *imperator*.

[172] Kooij and Gilly, *Fama Fraternitatis*, p. 82: "...wie es gleichs anfangs verglichen ward, theileten sie sich in alle Land, damit nicht allein ihre *axiomata* in geheimb von den Gelehrten schärffer examiniret würden, sondern auch sie selbst, da in einem oder anderm Land einige observation ein Irrung brächte, sie einander möchten berichten."

approved as factual – is entered into a special book for the sake of future
generations. Every philosopher, physician and professor of the Holy Scripture
acquainted with the powers of alchemy is being watched by the Fraternity;
and B. M. I. states that if he would make the names of those men known, the
book would become monstrously large.[173] We are also told that the ranks of
the Fraternity have recently been increased with ten "great men skilled in the
Art"[174] – a fact that roused Pyrgopolynices' ire at the Golden Table of the
Symbola Aureae Mensae.[175]

7. Defining Rosicrucianism: the *Silentium post Clamores* and the *Themis Aurea*

The two tracts that Maier devotes exclusively to the defence of the Order, the
Silentium post Clamores ('Silence after the Clamour,' 1617) and the *Themis
Aurea* ('Golden Themis,' 1618), are dedicated generally to the reading public
rather than to patrons or friends of Maier. The *Silentium post Clamores* deals
with the silence of the Fraternity in face of the furore provoked by the
manifestos; it sets itself the task of explaining this lack of response from the
Fraternity, as well as refuting those malevolents who have impersonated or
attacked the Order in print. In his preface to the reader, Maier states that the
Fraternity prefer to bring the slanderers back to repose and a sounder state of
mind, rather than stir up more passion by composing tedious responses – and
true to his medical training, he uses the analogy of a doctor placating a
delirious patient simply by displaying tranquillity.[176] In order to explain why
he does not follow the serene example of the Brethren, Maier justifies his
apology in the following way:

Even if the Brethren have no need of my protection or service – and I do not expect anything
from them, except the goodwill which the virtuous offer to other good people – nevertheless
I could not forbear to cast a white stone[177] on behalf of the truth, lest it might appear that

---

[173] B. M. I., *Assertio Fraternitatis*, p. 5: "Norunt Philosophi, Medici, Sacramque professi/
Scripturam, Chymicas quique tuentur opes./ Quorum proferre in vulgus si nomina
vellem,/ Vah mihi quam grandis cresceret inde liber!"

[174] *Ibid.*, p. 2: "Nuper is est auctus, quem pauci valde tenebant,/ Ingenio et magnis quinque
bis arte viris."

[175] See above, p. 149.

[176] Maier, *Silentium post Clamores*, pp. 4-5: "Sed quia ita mores hominum atque haec aetas
ferunt, maledicos silentio suo potius ad quietem et saniorem mentem (ut Medici
phreneticos) reducere conantur, quam responsionibus longioribus, quas sine dubio
veridicas adferre possent, irritare ad affectum a bile augendum."

[177] The reference here is to stones used in antiquity for voting; a white one was cast for
assent or acquittal, a black for denial or condemnation.

truth is overwhelmed with malice by the censure of ignorant people, rather than freed with righteousness by the fairness of the intelligent. For that censure is undoubtedly very similar to that illiterate commoner, who did not recognise the face of Aristides, the most meritorious of the Athenian republic, and on that account followed the others in condemning him for being too just. But we relegate such people to their ploughs and hoes, not to writing and judgment; and we commend you to God, candid reader, who are not amongst them. Vale.[178]

In considering this address, Arthur Waite proposed two possible ways of reading Maier's words; the first is to consider them as the expression of someone whose "congenital credulity" has led him to an "*a priori* belief in the actuality and honesty of the Order, because its claims are, from his standpoint, without offence to possibility."[179] From this perspective the *Silentium post Clamores* constitutes an open declaration of Maier's desire for admission into the Order, analogous to the many other entreaties that emerged in the wake of the manifestos' publication. The second possible interpretation given by Waite – who, as we may recall, advocated the existence of an organised secret Brotherhood – is that Maier's words constitute "a defence issued from within the occult circle, which – while advancing what it can on its own behalf – is determined to remain anonymous and requires its champions to dissemble."[180] Waite in fact opted for the former of these two readings, although he saw in Maier's subsequent Rosicrucian work, the *Themis Aurea*, evidence for Maier's entry into "the ranks of the Society."

Whilst his remarks concerning Maier's "congenital credulity" may not be so far wide of the mark, the inadequacy of Waite's underlying paradigm is revealed in the elaborate classical allusions that Maier utilises in the course of his preface to the *Silentium post Clamores*. We have seen that Maier refers to Aristides, the just Athenian patriot from the work of Plutarch bearing his name, who was ostracised by the citizens of Athens on account of their envy

---

[178] *Ibid.*, p. 5: "Interim, etsi nostro patrocinio aut officio non indigeant, nec ego quid ab illis, nisi benevolentiam, quam bonis boni ultro offerunt, expectem, tamen intermittere non potui, quin pro veritate calculum non nigellum iacerem, ne illa potius literam quoque Theta scribere ignorantium livore oppressa, quam recte sentientium candore absoluta videretur: Permultos enim esse illi cerdoni, qui Analphabetarius Aristidem optime de Repub. meritum, nec de facie agnitum, una cum caeteris ideo damnavit, quia nimis iustus esset, in hoc censu similes, non est dubium: Sed hos ad ligones et aratra, non ad literas et tribunalia destinatos ut novimus, sic relegamus, ac te, Candide lector, ex eorum numero exemptum Deo commendamus. Vale."

[179] According to Waite, "the will to believe was obviously much too predominant in Michael Maier for him to see that there was another point from which it might be possible to approach the subject, namely, that statements in anonymous documents which offer no evidence and cannot be checked otherwise can at most be left only as open questions and are certainly not justified by the appeal to an alleged possibility of things." Waite, *Brotherhood of the Rosy Cross*, p. 321.

[180] *Ibid.*, p. 320.

of his fame; during the ballot of ostracism a 'clownish' illiterate approached Aristides, and, imagining him to be an ordinary citizen, asked him to write his own name on the ballot-sherd, with which request the disgusted Aristides complied. Here Maier again expresses his occultist elitism, and his disapproval of certain parties writing under the name of the 'just' Fraternity who have impugned true Rosicrucianism by giving forth "calumny and viperous language."[181] Similarly, Maier contends that those who deceitfully write in the Fraternity's name have brought forth monsters in the manner of Ixion, who attempted to mate with Juno, the 'goddess of riches'; according to the Greek myth, Jupiter (Zeus) substituted for his wife an image formed of cloud, by which Ixion begat the Centaurs. The unhappy fate of the would-be adulterer was to be strung to an ever-turning wheel by Jupiter, which might be seen as an appropriate analogy for the seemingly endless dialectic set in motion by Andreae. The allusion Maier makes to the myth of Ixion demonstrates at least a partial awareness of the virtual nature of the Rosicrucian affair, for he tells us that the cloud with which the calumniators have mated is the "cloud of frenzied opinion" that has grown up around the manifestos, leaving the true Fraternity of the manifestos as the "unhappiest of parents."[182] Maier again refers to the Order as the surrogate parent of a vile offspring by comparing the calumniators to Autolycus, the son of Mercury who deceived and robbed his victims by using his inherited ability to transform himself into manifold forms. According to Maier's allusion it is Mt. Parnassus itself, throne of the Philosophers, that the 'Rosicrucian' impostors have sought to assail with the power they have usurped.[183] It is significant that the Fraternity is portrayed here as Mercury, who has lent his shape-changing power to an unworthy child – a suggestion that the Order itself partakes of a mercurial nature. At the very least, the evidence of Maier's preface indicates that his primary interest did not lie in admission to a secret Order; he was less concerned with the existence of a 'real' secret Fraternity, and more concerned to distinguish true Rosicrucianism from false and establish himself as the chief spokesman of the former.

In so doing it is clear that Maier too could be portrayed as an 'Ixion' or an 'Autolycus'; as Schick notes, without personal acquaintance with the Tübinger circle of Andreae, he stood with "sovereign supremacy" above the dispute, as if he was completely privy to the secrets of the Rosicrucians on

---

[181] Maier, *Silentium post Clamores*, p. 3.

[182] *Ibid.*

[183] *Ibid.*: "Hinc tot in eam Calumniae et viperinae linguae exercentur, quibus pro deceptoribus Ixionibus seu monstrorum, dum cum nube insanae opinionis, vice Iunonis, Divitiarum deae, coiverint, parentibus infelicissimis, et Autolycis, qui proxima Parnasso loca furtis infestarint, habentur et proclamantur."

account of his alchemical studies.[184] But Schick also states that Maier adopts a tone in the *Silentium post Clamores* "as if the Order already existed" – for Schick regarded the manifestos principally as a plan and invitation to establish an Order, rather than as a very real focal point for the Hermetic tendency in German Protestantism, which itself formed a Brotherhood in Hermes and Christ.

In the *Silentium post Clamores* Maier again stresses the alchemical aspect of the manifestos, although when he refers to the godliness of the Brethren he is by no means paying mere lip service to contemporary notions of piety, as Principe and Newman might have it. Rather, piety is a fundamental element of his alchemical theory and practice, as the Owl's temperance-imparting eggs in the *Jocus Severus* suggest. In Maier's eyes the chief axioms of the Fraternity are:

To owe to God above all things honour and fear, to procure the advantage of humankind, to turn away harm, to encourage piety and a frugal life, to destroy demonic work or vexation (as in cases of possession), to live satisfied with the least gift of Nature in victuals and clothing, and to shrink back from violent impulses and crimes.[185]

Whilst the Brethren possess the "most excellent Art of gold-making" amongst those gifts granted by the Almighty for the benefit of the human race, it is the Universal Medicine that is the most outstanding of the secrets of their Fraternity. This medicine has been uncovered through an enquiry into the occult powers of Nature – which enquiry is to be distinguished from magic, necromancy and the work of the Devil, because these things display nothing of the 'insignia' or signatures imprinted in Nature.[186] The diabolic sense of 'magic' as it is used here is to be distinguished from 'natural magic', which Maier defended as a deep knowledge of the interconnections of Nature – as we have seen in the *Symbola Aureae Mensae*, in which he describes the

---

[184] Schick, *Das Ältere Rosenkreuzertum*, p. 250.

[185] Maier, *Silentium post Clamores*, p. 41: "Quorum axiomata sunt, se debere Deum super omnia honorare et timere, hominum utilitatem procurare, damnum avertere, ad pietatem et vitae frugalitatem adhortari, daemonum opera seu vexationes (ut in obsessis) tollere, et minimis naturae donis in victu et vestitu contentos vivere, ab affectibus violentis et vitiis abhorere."

[186] *Ibid.*, pp. 17-18: "Arcanorum nomine, ne tamen quis existimet compraehendi cuiusque inventa sive phantasmata, quae nec in natura, nec in Experientia locum inveniunt, nos solum intelligimus occulta potentialis naturae opera, quae in actum naturalibus mediis deduci possunt; a quibus magica, negromantica, diabolica et somnia ab hominibus excogitata, quae nec caput nec caudam habent, hoc est, quae nulla naturae impressa insignia ostendunt, secludimus et relegamus." That Maier understands the *insignia* to be of divine origin is not only demonstrated by their counterposition to the subjects of diabolic magic, but also by the fact they have been 'impressed' or 'imprinted' upon Nature – without doubt by the Creator.

Fraternity's *Liber M.* as "the book of natural magic."[187] This distinction was probably drawn by Maier from his older contemporary, Giambattista della Porta (1535-1615), and follows in the long-established tradition of Renaissance *magi* such as Ficino and Agrippa, who also declared that *magia naturalis* is "the most perfect achievement of natural philosophy."[188] Whilst Maier uses the term *insignia* rather than the *signatura* that is so common in Paracelsian works and the theosophical thought of Boehme, the two words appear to be largely synonymous, as both refer to traces of a divinely instituted order present in Nature – the reading of which constitutes a central concern of Maier's natural magic.

The main argument Maier employs in his *Silentium post Clamores* to explain the Fraternity's silence is that knowledge of this natural or 'chemical' order should not be prostituted to the common people – therefore those who expect the Fraternity to answer all who have called upon them are simply childish, as the Brethren have without doubt decided to share their science with only a very few from that great number.[189] Indeed, Maier tells us that the Brethren follow the same vows of silence concerning their *arcana* as the ancient 'philosophical colleges' that have preceded them. Thus the Egyptians worshiped the god of Silence, Sigalion, "or rather an image of Sigalion," represented with the left hand covering the genitalia and the right suppressing the lips; according to Maier, its position at the altar indicated that the sacred rites performed there were of an occult nature and should not be imparted to non-initiates. Likewise the Romans revered Angerona, the goddess of Death and Silence, whose effigy was depicted with a sealed mouth, and who received sacrificial offerings on January the 13th of each year.[190] True to his alchemical inclinations, Maier seems to suggest that the *arcana* protected by these deities concerned the mysteries of cyclical transformation, as he also mentions the Roman worship of Consus (possibly synonymous with Janus) whose festival marked the end of the solar year. Sigalion – or the Egyptian

---

[187] See above, n. 100.

[188] Schmitt, *Cambridge History of Renaissance Philosophy*, p. 266; that Maier was conversant with della Porta's work is shown by the citations from his *Magia Naturalis* to be found in the *Themis Aurea* (1624 edition), p. 112; Maier, *Atalanta Fugiens*, discourses 18, 29.

[189] Maier, *Silentium post Clamores*, pp. 53-54.

[190] *Ibid.*, p. 58: "Hinc Ethnici Deos silentii produxerunt varios, ut Consum Romani, quasi consiliorum secretorum largitorem, Angeronam deam, quae (teste Plinio lib. 2.) ore obligato, obsignatoque Romae simulachrum habuit, eique sacrificatum fuit ad diem 13. Calend. Ianuarias: Apud Aegyptios Sigalion seu Harpocrates colebatur, aut potius eius simulachrum, quod sinistram verendis tegendis, dextrae, indicem et medium, digitos labris compressis adhiberet, in altaribus ponebatur, ad indicandum, sacra, quae ibi peragerentur, esse occulti sensus et silentio premenda." In his *Historia Naturalis*, 3.5.65 Pliny in fact gives January the 12th as the date of the sacrifice of Angerona.

Heru-pa-khered, the young Horus – was also a god of the newborn sun, although it seems unlikely Maier was aware of this fact, as it was the Greeks who mistakenly associated Sigalion with their own god of Silence, Harpocrates, on account of the Egyptian deity's depiction with a hand covering his mouth.[191] It seems more likely, however, that Maier was aware of the Greek tradition concerning Cupid's gift of a rose to Harpocrates, bestowed in order to ensure his silence concerning the sexual improprieties of Venus. As tradition has it, this myth marks the origins not only of the phrase *sub rosa*, denoting something carried out in secrecy, but also of the European (and purportedly 'Rosicrucian') custom of hanging roses over tavern tables referred to by Father Garasset.[192]

Amongst other 'precursors' of the Rosicrucian Brethren, Maier names the Mauritanians of Fez, the Druids of Britain, the Brahmans of India and the 'Gymnosophists' of Ethiopia – a word deriving from the Greek γυμνοσοφισται or 'naked philosophers', who were in fact the ascetic Brahmanic philosophers known to the Greeks through the reports of the companions of Alexander.[193] Elements of Brahmanic lore are present in Rosicrucianism to this day; and whilst the nineteenth century esotericists pilloried by Principe and Newman laid particular emphasis on a perceived harmony of eastern and western esoteric modes of thought, it is clear from the evidence of the *Silentium post Clamores* that they were only following in a syncretic tradition stemming from the Renaissance and firmly established in Rosicrucian circles by Maier.[194] According to Maier, all the occult traditions of the world are in agreement, and stem from one author: namely, Hermes Trismegistus.[195] Thus it was from the Egyptians that Pythagoras derived his magic and knowledge of the arcana, as well as the doctrine of metempsychosis or the transmigration of the soul through reincarnation.[196] As for the Rosicrucian Brethren, Maier asserts that they follow the custom of

---

[191] According to another tradition, Harpocrates was a Greek philosopher who enjoined silence concerning the nature of the gods.

[192] See p. 148 above; the Swiss Freemasonic Lodge, the 'Loge sub Rosa', draws on a Rosicrucian significance of the phrase.

[193] Maier, *Silentium post Clamores*, pp. 26 ff.

[194] Principe and Newman, "Some Problems with the Historiography of Alchemy," pp. 388-401.

[195] Maier, *Silentium post Clamores*, pp. 40-41: "Non solum enim ab uno authore, nempe Hermete, videntur omnes hae coloniae dependere et ab una gente ad aliam, quasi per manus, tradita haec arcanorum cognitio progressa, sed quoque in legibus et regulis, vitae moribusque praefixis pro temporum et religionis ratione consentiunt."

[196] *Ibid.*, p. 38: "Pythagoras in Aegypto a sacerdotibus et Babylone a Chaldaeis arcana naturae et magiae una cum Metapsychosi didicit: Eius discipuli facultates omnes in unum conferebant, ut omnibus essent communes: Quinquennium totum silebant, antequam in collegium et ad praeceptorem admitterentur."

the Pythagoreans of Greece and Italy, who maintained a period of five years' silence before being initiated into the higher mysteries of their college. Likewise, the Rosicrucian Brethren conduct an intensive inquiry into the lives of those they are about to select, and admittance into the Order is only allowed after a private ballot cast by the quarter of the Fraternity holding voting rights; then capable members are further tested with *at least* five years' silence before admittance into the higher secrets.[197] Although it is not clear from which source (if any) these details concerning voting derive, Maier's reference to a grade system appears to stem from Georg Molther's *Gründtliche Relation*, in which the wonder-working Brother states that he has almost completed his probationary period of seven years, and that the two other Brethren sojourning in the same region are of the same 'grade' as himself.[198] In any case, Schick saw in the grade system mentioned by Maier the "unmistakeable germs of the organisational units of Freemasonry developed some decades later in England under the influence of Rosicrucian ideas."[199]

The historian of Freemasonry Robert Gould once argued that Maier believed so firmly in the Fraternity of the Rosy Cross that he endeavoured to join it, but finding this impossible decided to found his own order, and in subsequent writings he "spoke of it as already existing, going so far even as to publish its laws."[200] Here he was referring to the *Themis Aurea* (1618), in which Maier sets out and elaborates upon the laws of the Fraternity given in the *Fama Fraternitatis*. However, once the hypothesis of an organised secret society is dispelled, and hence Waite's suggestion that Maier was physically able to "enter into the ranks of the Society," we are left with no other option but to accept Maier's awareness of the virtual nature of the Order when considering his *Themis Aurea*. For there Maier does indeed write as if from the 'inside' of the Order, as Waite asserts. This fact in itself demonstrates a conclusive shift in Maier's thinking *away* from the possibility of the

---

[197] *Ibid.*, pp. 80, 82: "Sed societas illa excusari poterit, quod quemlibet associandum sibi, etiam quo ad doctrinam dignissimum, primum quinquennali silentio (veluti Pythagoras suos discipulos) vel etiam longiori probandum habeant, ut potentia suos affectus et freno linguam domare prius discat, quam tantorum arcanorum particeps fiat"; "Deinde non solummodo doctrinam respici, inde patet, quod et pictores, aliosque sibi adiunxerint, alias morum severitate et silentio probatos: Unde testantur, se longo usu et respectu primum inquirere in vitam illorum, quos electuri sint: Fieri quoque solet eiusmodi electio, ut quarta eius societatis lex habetur, non votis communibus sed uniuscuiusque privatim, quocirca quod a toto sodalitio quis non sit acceptus, id illi imputari non debet, sed ei, a quo gratiam illam accipere potuit et non accepit."

[198] Molther, "Von einer frembden Mannsperson," p. 97.

[199] Schick, *Das Ältere Rosenkreuzertum*, p. 252; on this subject see also Buhle, *Ueber den Ursprung der Orden der Rosenkreuzer*, p. 207.

[200] Gould, *The History of Freemasonry*, p. 92.

existence of an organised secret Order – for if he had still entertained such a possibility, he could only have hoped to provoke the ire of the Fraternity as an outsider usurping their very laws.

Rather than being an attempt to found a secret order or evidence of Maier's membership in such an entity, the *Themis Aurea* is in fact dedicated to defining for the reading public the true alchemist and Rosicrucian brother with recourse to the laws of the Fraternity. In order to facilitate his exploitation of the platform granted him by the appearance of the manifestos, Maier produced both a Latin and a German edition of the work in the course of 1618.[201] The laws of the Fraternity, as set out in the *Fama Fraternitatis*, run as follows:

1. None of the Brothers should exercise any other profession than to cure the sick, and that without charge.
2. None of the Brothers should be obliged by the Fraternity to wear a particular clothing, but should follow the custom of the country they inhabit.
3. Every Brother should present himself once a year upon the day C. at the House of the Holy Spirit, or send a message concerning the cause of their absence.
4. Every Brother should look around for a suitable person who will take his place in the event [it is necessary].
5. The letters R. C. should be their seal, password, and emblem.
6. The Fraternity should remain secret for one hundred years.[202]

Concerning the first law, Maier's burden in the *Themis Aurea* is to demonstrate that the true Rosicrucian is concerned primarily with the art of healing, and not with the production of gold or other self-aggrandising pursuits. This goal is reflected in the title of the work, which is explained in the foreword as Maier relates the myth of Themis, the Greek goddess of law and prophecy known to the Romans as Justitia. According to the first book of Ovid's *Metamorphoses*, after the Deluge Themis was asked by Deucalion and Pyrrha how humankind could again be restored to the earth, to which the goddess replied that they must throw the bones of their mother over

---

[201] Maier, Michael. *Themis Aurea, hoc est, de Legibus Fraternitatis R. C. Tractatus.* Frankfurt am Main: Lucas Jennis, 1618; Maier, Michael. *Themis Aurea, das ist, von den Gesetzen und Ordnungen der löblichen Fraternitet R. C.* Frankfurt am Main: Lucas Jennis, 1618. Here I again cite the Latin edition of 1624.

[202] Kooij and Gilly, *Fama Fraternitatis*, pp. 82-85: "Erstlich: keiner solt sich keiner andern profession außthun, als Krancken zu curiren und diß umbsonst./ Zum Andern: keiner solte genötigt sein, von der Bruderschafft wegen ein gewiß Kleid zu tragen, sondern der Land Arten sich zu gebrauchen./ Zum Dritten: Ein jeder Brüder soll alle Jahre auff C. Tag sich bey *Sancti Spiritus* einstellen oder seines aussenbleibens ursach schicken./ Zum Vierten: ein jeder Brüder soll sich umb ein taugliche Person umbsehen, die ihm auff den fall möchte succediren./ Zum Fünfften: Das Wort R. C. soll ihr Sigill, Losung und Character sein./ Zum Sechsten: Die Bruderschafft soll hundert Jahr verschwiegen bleiben."

their heads. Although Pyrrha understood the injunction literally, Deucalion recognised the words of Themis as a reference to the stones of the earth; and having been thrown, two stones miraculously softened and grew into a man and a woman, by which means the earth was repopulated. Drawing on the hermeneutic first established in the *Arcana Arcanissima*, Maier argues that the true significance of this myth lies in the procurement of the Golden Medicine, which has the power of unlimited increase and is formed by two 'stones', feminine Mercury and masculine Sulphur.[203] It is this Golden Medicine which the Brethren altruistically labour to procure, and through which they can impart not only physical health but piety, justice and truth to those they treat.[204]

In the course of his work Maier defines the ideal Rosicrucian in accordance with his own medical practice; thus the Brethren are neither Scholastics who slavishly follow established opinion without recourse to experimentation, nor are they empiricists who disregard the ancient foundations of medicine in Galen and Hippocrates. Paracelsus was an eminent physician of great learning, but others must decide whether that gave him the right to trample down the ancient medicine and introduce a new one.[205] On this count Maier censures those Paracelsians who follow their master in directing coarse diatribes towards their opponents, whilst exhibiting nothing of substance in their own works. Disease, we are reminded, is the true enemy of the physician.[206] Both chemical and herbal remedies have their place in the physician's armoury, and both draw their power and virtues from the influence of the heavenly bodies.[207]

---

[203] Maier, *Themis Aurea* (1624 edition), p. 103: "Unde prima legum promulgatrix Themis habetur, cuius tamen responsio non de hominibus reparandis a vetustissimis Poetis accepta fuit, at de duobus lapidibus, masculo et foemina, a quibus multiplicatio Medicinae aureae causata est."

[204] *Ibid.*, p. 227: "Denique habent iidem Fratres, nescio quid arcani maximarum virium, quo se posse et velle succurrere uni, si quando opus sit, personae, quo pietas, iustitia et veritas superiorem locum obtineant, nec supprimantur a suis contrariis vitiis."

[205] *Ibid.*, p. 166: "Virum doctissimum et singularem in Medicina eum fuisse non est dubium: An propterea sat causae habuerit, omnem veterem conculcandi et novam his ultimis seculis in mundi senio, introducendi Medicinam, aliorum sit iudicare."

[206] *Ibid.*, p. 168: "Chymici vel Medici, qui Paracelsi doctrinam sequuntur, utinam nec in mores sui magistri degenerarent, et res relictis personalibus tractarent: Multorum hoc seculo eius farinae inveniuntur libri, ex quibus si calumniae et canina eloquentia, in medicos exercita, tollantur, quod reliquum est, tantum doctrinae, quantum inania stramina frugis, continebunt... Personae maneant intactae, communis hostis est morbus, eiusque causa et effectus seu symptoma."

[207] *Ibid.*: "Quod ad medicamenta mere Chymica vel Paracelsica attinet, ea quatenus bona sunt, laudamus, sed ita, ne Galenica et dogmatica vituperemus: His et illis alternatim utendum erit, innullius praeiudicium aut contemptum;" *ibid.*, pp. 132-133, 184-185.

With regard to the second law of the Fraternity, Maier states that the Brethren are merely following the admirable example set by Nature in changing their attire to suit the country of their dwelling; for just as the chameleon changes it colour to suit its surrounds, or the fur of certain hares becomes white in winter (a fact Maier himself observed in Lithuania), so the Brethren are compelled to alter their appearance for the sake of their own safety.[208] Their peregrinations are driven by their desire to read the *liber mundi*, and if sometimes they appear to be uneducated empirics (witness Molther's somewhat rustic 'Brother'), nevertheless their medicine is drawn from the "marrow of the great body" that is the world.[209] When we consider Maier's decidedly folksy analogies and sentiments, it is not altogether surprising that he was once characterised in the Rosicrucian polemics of his time as *der Deutsche Michael*, i.e. as a *Bauerntölpel* or yokel from beyond the northern borders of the empire.[210] Nevertheless, Maier seems to have found some comfort in the image of the Rosicrucian, particularly as it was set forth by Molther: to the genuine Brother of the Rosy Cross – as to the wandering Maier – the world is a place of pilgrimage, and he must remain an oft-reviled stranger and traveller until he reaches his true heavenly home.[211]

---

[208] *Ibid.*, p. 195.

[209] *Ibid.*, p. 129: "At hic mox obstrepent nobis illi, qui omnium cupiunt esse primi, et non sunt, dicentque, Fratres non esse medicos, at forte Empyricos, qui Medicinam exercere satagant: Verum hi manticam in tergo non vident suam, alienam semper habentes in conspectu: Fateor, plerosque fratrum non militasse in eorum castris, ideoque pro commilitonibus haud agnosci: Sed nec id quidem desiderant, cum sub Phoebo, Musis et Charitibus omnibus non solum tyrocinia, sed quoque summa officia merverint et exercuerint: Medicina, quam faciunt, est illis propria Medulla magni corporis, remotis ossibus, nucleus dulcissimae nucis rejectis corticibus."

[210] Thus the meaning of 'Meier' is 'farmhand' or 'dairy farmer'; Wahrig, Gerhard et. al. (eds.). *Brockhaus-Wahrig Deutsches Wörterbuch*. Vol. 4. Stuttgart: Deutsche Verlags-Anstalt, 1982, p. 634; the reference to *der Deutsche Michael* occurs in the *VII. Miracula Naturae* (1619) of Hisaias sub Cruce Ath. (aka. Isaac Habrecht); a vindication of Maier in face of this slander comes from Habrecht's opponent Irenaeus Agnostus (aka. Friedrich Grick) in the *Prodromus Fr. R. C. Das ist: Ein vorgeschmack und beyläuffige Anzeig der grossen außführlichen Apologi εισ φανεραν ομολογησιν, welche baldt folgen sol, gegen und wider den Zanbrecher, und Fabelprediger Hisaiam sub Cruce*. N.p: n.p., 1620, p. C4.

[211] Maier, *Themis Aurea* (1624 edition), pp. 215-216: "Cur vero Fratres R. C. latere non debeant in loco et personis, cum in latibulis non semper haereant, sed maxime per mundum, ut sapientes, quibus omne solum patria est, versentur? Cur non peregrinentur incogniti? An forte, si agnoscerentur, tantum boni expectent, an plus mali? Qui multum et saepe homines et terras obeunt, multa dicuntur hospitia experiri, pauca candoris foedera, varias blanditias, nullas fere amicitias, ita vere dicendas: Si hoc etiam illis, qui ortu, nomine et officio agnosci non refugiunt, contingit, nulla est causa, cur se quis totum aperiat et quantus qualisque sit, omnibus absque discrimine ebuccinetur: Dicunt ne tam sacrae quam prophanae literae, nos omnes in hoc mundo esse peregrinos, ac coelum appeti debere pro patria?"

Concerning the third law of the Fraternity given in the *Fama Fraternitatis*, Maier makes two pronouncements in the course of his *Themis Aurea* that bear upon the nature of the 'meeting place' of the Brethren. Firstly, it is stated that the House of the Holy Spirit is not in Utopia, but in the middle of Germany – for Europe is like unto a virgin (figure 20), and although it is not meet for a virgin to uncover herself, nevertheless she has brought forth the hitherto unknown arts and sciences of the Brethren from that secret place. In this way Maier relates the rise of the occult sciences in Germany to a miraculous virgin birth, an allegorical means of depicting the late Renaissance in Germany. This efflorescence of the *prisca sapientia* will not be violated by its enemies; thus Maier also likens Germany to an alchemical rose garden, where roses and lilies secretly grow "lest wanton hands damage or indeed pluck those little flowers."[212] Here he uses the traditional symbols for the final white and red stages of the work to denote the Brethren or true alchemists of Germany, 'known and unknown'. The second reference to the House of the Holy Spirit given by Maier in the *Themis Aurea* further accentuates his alchemical reading of the manifestos. He tells us that although he cannot divulge the time or place of the Fraternity's meeting, nevertheless he once saw a place he imagined to be the House of the Holy Spirit: Mt. Helicon, home of the philosophers, where Pegasus opened a perpetual spring with his hooves, and Diana bathed herself with Venus as her handmaid and Saturn as her usher.[213] These words are clearly a cipher for processes Maier may have observed in the alchemical vessel late one night; thus Diana as goddess of the moon represents the white phase of the alchemical subject, the 'white lead' which must be purified by 'washing' or solution following the putrefactive black phase. In accordance with the genealogies given in the *Arcana Arcanissima*, Saturn is her grandfather, or

---

[212] *Ibid.*, pp. 123-124: "De Loco huiusce congregationis, aut legum promulgationis ne quoque quis sit nimis curiosus in indagando, videndum erit: Non enim hoc utile est sciri ab omnibus, sed sufficit si a solis confoederatis et electis agnoscatur: in Utopia non est, ut opinor, nec apud Tartaros aut Lappones, sed forte in umbelico Germaniae, cum Europa forma virginem, et Germania in ea ventrem referre dicatur: Non convenit virgineos sinus patefacere vulgo, ne meretrix potius, quam virgo, vidatur: Satis est scire, eam non esse infoecundam, sed in utero suo (ut Themis ex Iove) hanc Eunomiam concepisse, aut hos Palycos fratres, tanquam ignotos et ex terra natos, (ut Thalia ex eodem) protulisse: Venter hic quidem virgineus est, at permultas artes et scientias, ante incognitas, edidit, GERMANIAM dico et intelligo, quae germinat nunc perpetuo ROSIS ET LILIIS, quae nec hyemem nec aestum ignis reformident, et in Philosophicis hortis seu Rosetis conservantur, ne petulca manus tenellos flosculos laedat aut carpat."

[213] *Ibid.*, p. 201: "Vidi aliquando Olympicas domus, non procul a fluviolo et civitate nota, quas S. Spiritus vocari imaginamur: Helicon est, de quo loquor, aut biceps Parnassus, in quo equus Pegasus fontem aperuit perennis aquae adhuc stillantem, in quo Diana se lavat, cui Venus ut pedissequa, et Saturnus ut anteambulo, coniunguntur: Intelligenti nimium, inexperto minimum hoc erit dictum."

the progenitor of all metals; and the 'perpetual spring' is the quintessence or *aqua foetida* used in the solution, a powerful spirit "with the smell of sulphur and the grave" mentioned in the tenth and thirty-seventh discourses of the *Atalanta Fugiens*.[214] Maier states that his words will reveal a great deal to the intelligent, but nothing to the inexperienced:[215] in this way he demonstrates an allegorical understanding not only of Greek myth, but of central elements of the narrative in the *Fama Fraternitatis* itself.

In the discourse on the initials R. C. given in his *Themis Aurea*, Maier states that the Egyptians possessed two scripts, one profane and commonly known, the other holy and understood by the priests alone. These latter were the hieroglyphs, symbols of deep wisdom; and although popular belief holds that the letters R. C. refer to *rosa* and *crux*, they are in fact just such sacred signs serving to cover the mysteries of the Order.[216] Following this statement, Figala and Neumann have suggested an interpretation of the letters as *res chymicae*; but although this interpretation is ingenious and fully in accord with Maier's ethos, it may be futile to attempt to discover one final, definitive phrase to which Maier adhered.[217] Thus we have seen that Maier gave the initials the significance of 'the sea' and 'the sublime laws of a fortress' in the tenth enigma of the *Symbola Aureae Mensae*; likewise the seventh enigma speaks of R. as the 'canine letter', which contains in itself war and the *pugnatrix* (she who fights), whilst the eighth enigma speaks of C. as the waning moon:

> Lo the half moon is resplendent with rays before you!
> Hence it is also consecrated to the C.,
> For just as the horns of Phoebe foretell the demise of dark and shady night,
> Thus also by and by the clouds are put to flight,
> As your public Confession promises.
> Six companions follow, of whom two times two are making a clamour,
> But two give forth harmonious speech:
> This will have been enough to reveal to your judgment.[218]

---

214 Maier, *Atalanta Fugiens*, discourse 10: "Est quoque eadem aqua acetum acerrimum,quae corpus fecit merum spiritum... Est autem haec aqua ex Parnassi petita fonte, quae praeter naturam aliorum fontium in vertice montis existit, ab ungula Pegasi, volatilis equi, factus;" *ibid.*, discourse 37: "Foetida dicitur, quia foetorem sulphureum de se mittit, et odorem sepulchrorum: Haec est illa aqua, quam Pegasus ex Parnasso ungula sua percusso elicuit..."

215 See above, n. 213.

216 Maier, *Themis Aurea* (1624 edition), pp. 209-211.

217 Figala and Neumann, "Author cui Nomen Hermes Malavici," p. 138.

218 Maier, *Symbola Aureae Mensae*, pp. 300-301: "En mediata vobis/ Luna resplendet radiis, hinc quoque C. dicata est,/ Cornua namque Phoebes/ Ceu monent decrescere noctis tenebras opacae,/ Sic quoque mox fugandas/ Esse nubes, publica confessio vestra

Here Maier appears to make another allusion to the processes in the vessel, and the 'washing' of the moon we have just discussed. Nevertheless, the reference is also to the 'promise' of the *Confessio Fraternitatis* that God is "turning about the course of Nature," as the Lord's Sabbath is almost at hand – a cyclical return to the beginning, or a re-establishment of the Golden Age through an apocalyptic purification. In the *Themis Aurea* Maier gives a similar interpretation of the initial C. as 'the moon'; and in accordance with the 'canine' musings of the seventh enigma in the *Symbola Aureae Mensae*, R. is given as 'rabies' or 'madness'.[219] These references to violence and chaos may refer to the fires of the alchemical furnace, by which means the purification of the alchemical subject is ultimately achieved. Thus R. is referred to in a second place in the *Themis Aurea* as 'Pegasus', which struck its hooves against Mt. Helicon (the vessel) and opened up the eternal spring in which Diana bathed. C. in this second allusion is given as 'Julius' – a possible reference to Julius Caesar, who traced his ancestry to the gods via a son of Venus; for if we follow Maier's interpretation of the genealogies of the gods in the *Arcana Arcanissima* as the phases to be observed in the vessel, then Caesar is a representation of the completion of the work in which things heavenly and worldly coalesce.[220]

Tentative as these conclusions are, it would seem that Figala and Neumann were on the right track when they proposed the significance of *res chymicae*; for although a 'chemical' truth may be both manifested and represented in different ways, the letters R. C. (in Maier's view) are indeed ciphers for the all-pervasive alchemical process. In concluding his discourse on the initials of the Order in the *Themis Aurea*, Maier gives expression to his pietist leanings when he says that if the sun mediates between 'rabies' and 'the moon' a heart is formed, which if it is sincere may be an acceptable sacrifice to God.[221] This appears to be a reference to the seal of the Fraternity illustrated in the *Themis Aurea* (figure 21), in which 'S' as *sol* mediates between 'R' and 'C' – a symbol apparently of Maier's own invention which expresses universal, occult laws in a manner similar to John Dee's *monas hieroglyphica*. In relation to this seal Maier offers up the phrase "d. wmml. zii, w. sgqqhka. x.," and challenges us to understand it if we can.[222]

---

spondet:/ Sex comites sequuntur,/ Ex quibus clamant duo bis, sed duo consonantem/ Ore ferunt loquelam:/ Haec satis vestro fuerit iudicio indicasse."

[219] Maier, *Themis Aurea* (1624 edition), p. 214: "Hinc canina illius litterae R. rabies et media illa C. Luna non sunt despicienda Elementa: Si enim Sol illis medius adveniat, cor efficiunt, quod primarium est in humanis visceribus, si synceritatem conjunctam habeat, sacrificium unicum Deo gratum, quo ad voluntatem existens."

[220] *Ibid.*, p. 212.

[221] C.f. n. 219 above.

[222] Maier, *Themis Aurea* (1624 edition), pp. 212-213.

Unfortunately, the meaning of this last riddle seems to have passed away with its author, as even the key divulged by Borelli is of no avail to us here.

8. *Regni Christi frater*: Maier's 'entrance into the Order'

Clearly, then, the riddles of the *Themis Aurea* are not the work of a member of the Rosicrucian Order, at least in the sense of the member of an organised secret society; rather, Maier's efforts to define the virtual entity of Rosicrucianism seem to have borne some fruit, given Garasset's description of him as 'secretary' of the Order, and given the largely alchemical bent of later Rosicrucianism. Furthermore, the fact that Maier chose not to use a pseudonym when publishing his works must have raised his profile in Germany considerably, as we find his tracts are given a good deal of publicity in the subsequent debate concerning the true nature of the Order. In concluding this discussion of Maier's relation to early Rosicrucianism, let us now turn to two Rosicrucian tracts that make mention of Maier, the *Colloquium Rhodo-Stauroticum* ('Rosicrucian Colloquium,' 1621; see figure 22) and its rejoinder, the *Echo Colloquii Rhodo-Staurotici* ('Answer to the Rosicrucian Colloquium,' 1622) – this latter work having been cited alongside Garasset's claim as evidence for Maier's 'entrance into the Fraternity'.

The *Colloquium Rhodo-Stauroticum* was first published in a German edition of 1621 and is, putatively, a lengthy letter delivered from a certain C. V. A. I. B. F. to a certain A. W. B. D. S. F.[223] The latter addresses his foreword to "the theosophical reader," and tells us that he had read a number of works which had been circulating in the name of the "highly illumined Fraternity of the Rosy Cross," but which nevertheless did not agree in their

---

[223] C. V. A. I. B. F. *Colloquium Rhodo-Stauroticum, Das ist: Gespräch dreyer Personen/ von der vor wenig Jahren/ durch die Famam et Confessionem etlicher massen geoffenbarten Fraternitet deß Rosen Creuzes; Darinnen zu sehen/ Was endlich von so vielen unterschiedlichen in ihrem Namen publicirten Schriefften/ und denn auch von der Brüderschafft selbsten zu halten sey. Allen trewherzigen/ und aber durch so vielerhand Schreiben irrgemachten Christlichen Lesern zu lieb in druck gegeben.* N.p.: n.p., 1621. Curiously, the initials C. I. B. F. and A. S. N. B. rather than C. V. A. I. B. F. and A. W. B. D. S. F. are given in the Latin version of the work: *Colloquium Rhodo-Stauroticum trium personarum, per Famam et Confessionem quodammodo revelatum, de Fraternitate Roseae Crucis.* Frankfurt am Main: Lucas Jennis, 1624. I cannot see any good reason for this discrepancy, although a pointless invention on behalf of the translator seems unlikely. It is possible that the variant initials of the Latin edition derive from the Latinisation of the original non-abbreviated forms of these pseudonyms, with which the translator (who as we shall see was none other than Maier's publisher, Lucas Jennis) may have been acquainted.

fundamentals with the original manifestos issued by the Order. Mentioned in particular are the *Tintinabulum Sophorum*, the *Apologia F. R. C.* and the *Prodromus F. R. C.* of Irenaeus Agnostus. It seems that as a result of his reading A. W. B. D. S. F. was in a quandary concerning the true interpretation of the manifestos – and therefore in doubt concerning the nature of the genuine brotherhood. Therefore he wrote to C. V. A. I. B. F., "a trusted friend who can better judge these things than I," and asked for his opinion on the matter. An answer arrived in the form of a 'colloquium' or three-way conversation between the imaginary characters Tyrosophus, Quirinus and Politicus, each participant representing a particular perspective on the nature of the Order and its beliefs – and Tyrosophus representing a true Rosicrucianism in accord with the original manifestos. In this way the *Colloquium Rhodo-Stauroticum* follows the formula set forward by Andreae in the *Turris Babel*. Having found this 'colloquium' pleasing, A. W. B. D. S. F. approached a publisher (who was himself "a denizen of the citadel of wisdom") and with the permission of the author, C. V. A. I. B. F., it was published for the enlightenment of others on that topic. The foreword is dated March 1st, 1621.[224]

Schick has attributed this work to the personal physician of the Calvinist Landgrave Phillip von Hessen-Butzbach, Daniel Mögling. It appears that Mögling wrote as an apologist for the Rosicrucians under the pseudonyms of Theophilus Schweighardt and Florentinus de Valentia in such works as *Pandora Sextae Aetatis* ('Pandora of the Sixth Age,' 1617), *Rosa Florescens* ('Blooming Rose,' 1617) and the *Speculum Sophicum Rhodo-Stauroticum* ('Sophical Rosicrucian Mirror,' 1618). Whilst the *Colloquium Rhodo-Stauroticum* did not appear under the names of either Schweighardt or de Valentia, Schick has attributed its authorship to Mögling on the basis of certain thematic and editorial factors, and on the basis of a communication of 1618 from Landgrave Phillip von Hessen-Butzbach to the Rosicrucian Kabbalist and prophet, Johann Faulhaber, in which Phillip reveals the identity of Schweighardt and de Valentia as that of his own physician.[225] According to Edighoffer, Mögling was a personal acquaintance of Johann Valentin

---

[224] *Ibid.*, 1621, pp. 3-6; the foreword of the 1624 edition, pp. 45-48, gives no date.

[225] Hessisches Staatsarchiv Darmstadt, Hausarchiv, Abteilung 4, Konv. 72, Fasc. 9; see Schick, *Das Ältere Rosenkreuzertum*, p. 185. Schick gives the following reasons for his attribution: firstly, the *Colloquium* appears in part to be the continuation of a polemic against a certain 'Menapius' to be found in Mögling's (i.e. Schweighardt and de Valentias') previous works; secondly, those works display a consonance with the *Colloquium* in the style of their titles; thirdly, whilst the author of the *Colloquium* cites many Rosicrucian authors, including Maier, only the works of Schweighardt and de Valentia are quoted word-for-word. On this latter point we must note that Schick was mistaken, as the *Colloquium* author also cites Maier word-for-word.

Andreae, although I do not know on which authority this claim rests.[226] The matter is thrown into further confusion by Arnold's suggestion that the author writing under the name of de Valentia in the *Rosa Florescens was* in fact Andreae, although again, there are no specific grounds given to support this idea.[227] Yates completes the chaos by quoting Arnold and stating that both Schweighardt and de Valentia "may be Andreae himself."[228] In any case, we will proceed with the working hypothesis that Daniel Mögling was both the author of the *Colloquium* and the true identity behind these pseudonyms, which seems reasonable on the basis of Schick's arguments.

Whilst the story of C. V. A. I. B. F.'s letter to A. W. B. D. S. F. given in the *Colloquium Rhodo-Stauroticum* is clearly a literary invention, the participants of the colloquium represent genuine ideological threads in the tangled web of 'Rosicrucian' apologies and opposing *Kampfschriften* that grew up around the *Fama Fraternitatis* and the *Confessio Fraternitatis*. As the mouthpiece of Mögling himself, the 'Tyrosophus' of the colloquium gives expression to a heterodox Protestantism of a theosophical strain. In the course of the colloquium Tyrosophus presents a list of books he says are highly recommended by the Fraternity itself; first and foremost is the *De Imitatione Christi* of the Rhenish ascetic Thomas à Kempis (*c*.1379-1471), a key work of Christian piety; also named are the *Vier Bücher vom wahren Christentum* (1605-1609) by Johann Arndt, a work influential for later Pietism that was itself inspired by à Kempis and the Rhenish mystic Johann Tauler (c.1300-61); the *Philosophia Mystica*, an important compilation of Paracelsian and Weigelian tracts published in Neustadt in 1618; the *Offenbahrung* of Paul Lautensack; and the *Vom Baum des Wissens Gutes und Böses* of Sebastian Franck (c.1499-c.1542). These latter two authors were once counted amongst the possessors of a "paradoxical and uncommon learning" by Andreae.[229] It seems humility demanded that Mögling place his own tracts, *Rosa Florescens* and *Speculum Sophicum Rhodo-Stauroticum*, towards the end of the list of recommendations.[230]

In the course of his *Colloquium* Mögling also makes repeated and approving mention of the works of Michael Maier; in particular the *Symbola Aureae Mensae*, the *Themis Aurea* and the *Silentium post Clamores*, which he cites as evidence that knowledge of the *lapis philosophorum* has been passed to the Brethren *quasi de ore ad ora* through many

---

[226] Edighoffer, *Die Rosenkreuzer*, p. 14.

[227] Arnold, *Histoire des Rose-Croix*, p. 113.

[228] Yates, *The Rosicrucian Enlightenment*, p. 93.

[229] Gilly, *Cimelia Rhodostaurotica*, p. 8.

[230] C. V. A. I. B. F., *Colloquium Rhodo-Stauroticum* (1621 edition), pp. 110-111: the list is considerably abridged in the Latin edition of 1624, pp. 140-141.

centuries.[231] It is these references which seem to have inspired the peculiar allusions to Maier made in the rejoinder to the *Colloquium Rhodo-Stauroticum*, the *Echo Colloquii Rhodo-Staurotici*. The author of this work is one Benedictus Hilarion – and the 'joviality' implicit in his surname should immediately arouse our suspicions concerning the authenticity of the author's claim that the work was issued "according to the mandate of the superiors" of the Rosicrucian Order, in imitation of certain passages in the *Colloquium*. As Schick writes, 'Brother' Benedictus Hilarion "banters with the author of the *Colloquium* with impish ease, and takes the public for a ride."[232]

The *Echo Colloquii Rhodo-Staurotici* was first published in a German edition in 1622.[233] In the opening paragraphs 'Benedictus Hilarion' addresses the author of the *Colloquium* as "well-known friend Anonymous," and states that the identity of this "well-beloved and highly trusted" man is in fact known to the Order, as is the fact that C. V. A. I. B. F. and A. W. B. D. S. F. are one and the same person. And whilst the members of the "highly gifted Order" had knowledge of the *Colloquium* before it was sent to the press, and thus may have intervened to stop its publication, nevertheless they allowed the author to proceed without hindrance for three reasons:[234]

Firstly, in order that you get some good experience, so that in future times of leisure you might spend your time fruitfully rather than in vain. Secondly, in order that the disputation or rather dissertation of the fictive persons would not only incite some pious men and good

---

231 *Ibid.*, p. 138: "Si enim illa incredulis Ethnicis, qui de Deo, neque eius verbo atque voluntate certi aliquid sciverunt, tali modo largitus est, quod etiam, veluti Dominus Michael Mayerus, in suo Silentio post Clamores, eius rei meminit, integra Collegia huius professionis inter ipsos fuerint, in quibus naturae mysteria summo studio agitata, et multis seculis quasi de ore ad ora, posteris suis, quos ex aliis Philosophis elegerunt, ista reliquerint." On page 93 the author cites Maier to confirm his views on the *lapis philosophorum*: "Intempestivi autem isti judices in Domini Michaelis Mayeri Symbolis aureae Mensae legere deberent, quid videlicet, hoc in puncto, pro et contra possibilitatem Lapidis, inter artis istius assertores, eiusdemque hostes, disputatur, tunc enim, meo quidem pro judicio, praeconceptam suam opinionem mox dimissuri essent."

232 Schick, *Das Ältere Rosenkreuzertum*, p. 189.

233 Benedictus Hilarion. *Echo Colloquii Rhodo-staurotici, Das ist: Wider-Schall/ oder Antwort/ auff das newlicher zeit außgegangene Gespräch Dreyer Persohnen, die Fraternitet vom RosenCreutz betreffendt.* N.p: n.p., 1622.

234 *Ibid.*, pp. 3-4: "Zu wissen sey dir hiemit/ vielgeliebter unnd hochvertrawter Freund Anonyme Wolbekandt/ daß dein selbst gestelletes Colloquium Rhodostauroticum, so zwar das ansehen hat,/ als wann es von einem Christiano Ungenandt/ dir zugeschickt wäre/ nach seiner Datirung/ uns Collegianten/ deß hochbegabten Ordens vom RosenCreutz/ zeitlichen ist zu Händen kommen. Und wir nun wohl/ ehe dann du dasselbige sub praelo geben/ deines Vorhabens dißfalls sehr gute Wissenschafft gehabt/ und demnach solches verbleiben zulassen/ dich gar wol hätten berichten können: So haben wir jedoch/ folgender Ursachen halben/ dich darmit unverhindert groß-günstiglichen fortfahren lassen."

citizens (of whom quite a few are known to us from time to time) to research us and our intentions; but also that they might thereby have reason to behave in their daily life in such a way as to show themselves worthy of acceptance into our Society at the given time. Thirdly, in order to show all the more clearly the white next to the black...[235]

Following this riposte, 'Benedictus Hilarion' goes on to state that the Fraternity has recently admitted a number of good men into its ranks, amongst whom are "P: N. I: A. M: B. I: H. I: B. I: M. I: D: M. I: S. I: D: B. G: A. etc." – a jesting comment on the inordinate number of initials used in the Rosicrucian literature.[236] In the course of the *Echo* Hilarion gives some droll advice to those who might die before the prophesised dawning of the Golden Age in 1624, and speaks of the great "Reformation of grammar" instituted by certain supporters of the Order.[237] He also speaks at length concerning the 'Narrosophus' (fool-philosopher) who passes judgment on the existence of the Philosophers' Stone before he has found it, although Hilarion himself seems to view the "extraordinary mysteries of theosophy and *chemia*" in a favourable light (his work is, after all, an 'echo' of the sentiments set forth in the *Colloquium*).[238] Appending the tract is a poem concerning the forthcoming "eclipse of the entire world,"[239] as well as a list of eleven prophetic and apocalyptic works: and in the copy of the *Echo* residing at the Bibliotheca Philosophica Hermetica in Amsterdam a sarcastic seventeenth century reader has penned in a twelfth work – the 'Tintinabulum' (a bell on a door to summon attendants) of the "highly learned and celebrated" Tilman Eulenspiegel (a semi-mythical medieval jester), dedicated to his dear sons, the Brothers of the Rosy Cross, and containing all their 'Narrosophia' in one short compendium.[240]

---

[235] *Ibid.*, pp. 5-6: "Erstlichen/ dich hierdurch etlicher massen zu uben/ damit du zu andern horis subcesivis, unnd Erquickstunden/ nich vergebens/ sondern fruchtbarlichen die Zeit vertreiben möchtest. Zum Andern/ damit die Disputatio oder vielmehr Dissertatio der fingirten Personen/ möchte noch manchen frommen Menschen und Biderman (derer uns/ hin unnd wieder/ sehr viel bekandt) nicht allein erwecken/ uns und unserer Gelegenheit ferner nachzuforschen: Sondern auch dardurch möchte verursacht seyn/ sich in seinem täglichen Leben/ Thun und Wandel/ dergestalt zuverhalten/ daß Er/ zu seiner zeit/ mag würdig sein in unsere Gesellschafft auff und angenommen zu werden. Zum Dritten/ damit/ also zu reden/ das Weisse/ neben dem Schwartzen/ desto besser/ und viel eher/ mag erkandt werden."

[236] *Ibid.*, pp. 9-10.

[237] *Ibid.*, pp. 19, 31-32.

[238] *Ibid.*, p. 32.

[239] *Ibid.*, pp. 40-45.

[240] *Ibid.*, p. 39: "Des hochgelerten und Weitberümpten Vilosophi, Tilman Eülenspiegels Tintinabulum, seinen lieben sönen, Roseae Crücis Fratribus, dedicieret, darinn alle ihre Narosophia in ein kürtz compendium gebracht ist. Getrücket zu Quinsai, in der grössesten stadt der gantzen Welt."

For all the *Eulenspiegeleien* contained in the *Echo Colloquii Rhodo-Staurotici*, a certain passage within that work was once taken by Waite as evidence for Maier's 'entrance' into the order "ere he died." Whilst addressing the author of the *Colloquium* Hilarion states:

> It is quite accurate that our silence has hitherto made many people crazy, nevertheless only those who cannot wait in patience for the time. However, you should not be counted amongst those people, because you have always been more for than against us, together with some other good-hearted people known to us: as you have shown in many ways with your verbal defence against those who, by their great ignorance, have proved to be full of hatred towards us. Being an educated man, Master Michael Maier also did the same in writing, as he proved in a worthy and reasonable manner in his *Silentium post Clamores, Themis Aurea, Verum Inventum, Symbola Aureae Mensae*, etc. Which writings from him should not have been written in vain.[241]

Unfortunately for Waite's hypothesis, it must be noted that the 1624 Latin translation from which he quotes elaborates a little on the first German edition, stating in tandem with the original that Maier will not have written his defences of the Order in vain, but adding that "we will deservedly reward him before his death, as much with great honours as with communications of singular mystery."[242] That Latin translation was made by Maier's publisher,

---

[241] *Ibid.*, pp. 7-9: "Nicht ohn ist es zwar/ daß unser Silentium oder Stillschweigen bißhero/ viel Leuth irre gemacht/ jedoch nur die jenigen/ so der zeit nicht mit Gedult erwartten können. Unter welche du für deine Person gleichwol nicht solst gezehlet seyn: dieweil du sambt noch etlichen uns wolbekandten feinen guthertzigen/ jederzeit mehr pro als contra nos gewesen. Wie du dann dasselbige mit mündlicher Defendirung/ alleweg bey den jenigen/ so uns/ auß grober Unwissenheit/ gehässig/ sehr wol erwiesen. Deßgleichen dann auch Herr Michael Mayer/ als ein Gelehrter Mann/ solches Schrifftlich verrichtet und gethan hat/ wie dasselbige vernünfftig unnd wol außweisen/ sein Silentium post Clamores, Themis, Verum Inventum, Symbola Aureae Mensae etc. Welche Scripta dann auch von ihme dem Domino Authore nit umbsonst oder vergebens sollen geschrieben seyn."

[242] Benedictus Hilarion. *Echo Colloquii Rhodo-Staurotici, hoc est: Resolutio sive Responsio ad nupero tempore editum trium personarum Colloquium Fraternitatem Roseae Crucis concernens.* Frankfurt am Main: Lucas Jennis, 1624, pp. 167-168: "Equidem non abs re est, quod Silentium nostrum multos hactenus homines in errorem praecipitaverit, illos tamen solummodo, qui tempus patienter expectare minime potuerunt. Inter quos tamen te non numeratum volumus, quod, una cum quibusdam, nobis bene notis piis, benevolis, ab initio, in hodiernum usque diem semper magis pro, quam contra nos extiteris: quemadmodum etiam illud ipsum orali defensione omni tempore apud ipsos, qui, crassa ex ignorantia, nobis infecti sunt, mascule praestitisti. Quemadmodum etiam Dominus Michael Majerus, tamquam vir Clarissimus, illud ipsum scribendo egregie praestitit, veluti ejus rei luculentum praebent testimonium, ipsius Silentium post clamores, Themis aurea, Verum inventum, Symbola aureae mensae, etc: quae scripta etiam a Domino Authore ipso non frustra scripta esse debent, sed illum, haud immerito, ante mortem ipsius, tam ingentibus honorariis, quam non minus singularium mysteriorum communicatione, beabimus."

Lucas Jennis, who included both the *Colloquium Rhodo-Stauroticum* and the *Echo Colloquii Rhodo-Staurotici* with his publication of the dead Maier's *Ulysses*, together with a reprint of the *Silentium post Clamores*. In his foreword to the *Ulysses* Jennis states that he publishes the four tracts together partly out of love for the departed Maier, partly out of Christian duty, partly out of politics, and all for the service of humanity; and whilst the *Echo* may be a "work of vexation," nevertheless it is one which Maier would also have commended.[243] These words seem to indicate that Maier was more closely bound up with the origins of the *Colloquium* and the *Echo* than Jennis reveals: a suspicion which becomes greater when considering Hilarion's strange description of Maier as a person who has defended in writing that which the author of the *Colloquium* has defended 'verbally'.[244] Furthermore, the name 'Tyrosophus' from the *Colloquium* seems to be an allusion to Hiram, the wise king of Tyre who participates in a three-way dialogue with Solomon and the Queen of Sheba in Maier's *Septimana Philosophica*; and the *Colloquium* also makes mention of the 'feather of the phoenix' as the Universal Medicine in the manner of Maier's *Symbola Aureae Mensae*.[245] Nevertheless, these latter facts may only indicate the influence of Maier upon the author; and it must be said that whilst the theosophical bent of the tract does not run counter to Maier's ideals, it is out of character with the alchemical emphasis in the rest of his printed Rosicrucian works, and mitigates against the possibility that Maier himself was the author of the *Colloquium* (or, for that matter, the *Echo* itself).

Whatever the case may be, it would appear that Jennis was paying his own respects to the memory of Maier when he elaborated upon the German original of the *Echo* with his statement that Maier would be 'rewarded' by the

---

243 Maier, Michael. *Tractatus Posthumus, sive Ulysses, hoc est, Sapientia seu intelligentia, tanquam coelestis scintilla beatitudinis, quod si in fortunae et corporis bonis naufragium faciat, ad portum meditationis et patientiae remigio feliciter se expediat. Una cum annexis tractatibus de fraternitate Roseae Crucis.* Frankfurt am Main: Lucas Jennis, 1624, pp. 5-6: "Itaque partim ex amore, erga proximum meum, Christiano, et simul politico, omnibus pro virili inserviendi desiderio (praesertim cum cognoverim, quod etiam externae nationes de fraterna ista societate jam primum majori Studio inquirere incipiant) intermittere nec potui, nec volui, quin res istas hisce simul conjungerem Colloquium Rhodo-Stauroticum (in quo cunctis de rebus Fraternitatem concernentibus tractatur) et ad illud pertinens Echo. Quae cum nulla alia, quam in vernacula (uti quidem recordor) typis impressa viderim, ea propter illa, in tui benevoli Lectoris gratiam, in Romanam linguam transferri curavi. Quo de meo instituto et jam pro lubitu tuo nunc ipse judicare poteris. Pro mea tamen persona commemorata ista opuscula non adeo inconcinna mihi videntur, praesertim autem Echo. An vero a Fraternitate forsitan suam trahat originem, vel saltim figmentum, et scriptum vexatorium sit, quorum similia multa hactenus sunt edita illud ipsum cuiusvis nunc relinquo judicio."

244 See above, n. 241.

245 Maier, *Ulysses*, p. 113; the form *tyros* may also refer to a 'new recruit'.

Fraternity before his death. Perhaps the final word on Maier's relation to Rosicrucianism should be given to Jennis, a man who was in a better position than any of us to understand the true nature of the Rosicrucian Fraternity. In his foreword to the *Ulysses* he appears to refer to his very own fabrication when he asks if the reader would be happy to hear that Maier had been accepted into the Order before his death. He goes on to write that he does not know if this is true, although he knows very well that Maier has been associated with the Order *ad extremum*. Furthermore, it is common knowledge that Maier was "a brother of the kingdom of Christ" (i.e. a *Regni Christi frater*, or 'Brother R. C.').[246]

---

[246] *Ibid.*, pp. 7-8: "Quoniam etiam, peramice Lector, mox ab initio Domini Doctoris Majeri aliquoties mentionem fecimus, forsitan libenter scires, an videlicet ille ipse Doctor Majerus, tanquam dictae Fraternitatis Roseae Crucis Defensor, adhuc ante suum ex mortali hacce vita digressum, in ordinem istum receptus fuerit? Ad hoc me illud nescire, respondeo. Hoc tamen minime ignoro, quomodo videlicet ad extremum cum ipso quodammodo comparatum fuerit. Etiamsi autem in Roseae Crucis Fratrum societatem forsitan non receptus sit, ipsum tamen Religionis Christianae, vel Regni Christi Fratrem fuisse, notum est."

V. The completion of the work

1. The squaring of the natural circle

Having examined the consequences of Maier's fateful encounter with the Rosicrucian manifestos at the Frankfurt Book Fair in 1616, let us return to the course of events in the last five years of his life, and to a consideration of his ongoing quest for alchemical wisdom. In Maier's time Frankfurt am Main was an imperial city; there the edict of *cuius regio, eius religio* established by the Peace of Augsburg did not hold, and political authority was vested in the city council, which did not owe its allegiance to a particular prince or confession.[1] Nevertheless, the city was a predominantly Lutheran centre, with a large population of Calvinist exiles from the Netherlands, and its religious composition must have made it an attractive place for Maier to settle.[2] Whilst living there Maier not only came under the influence of Rosicrucian ideas, but also came still closer to the Calvinist and occult orbit of Moritz the Learned and his court – a fact which is reflected in the overtly political content of some of the works we will shortly consider. Indeed, a major event in the life of Frankfurt in 1617 was the Reformation Jubilee, which had been instigated by Friedrich V during a meeting of the Protestant Union as a means of drawing together Calvinists and Lutherans in the face of the impending conflict with Catholicism.[3] Although Maier spent much of his time attending a wealthy nobleman by the name of von Riedesel in Stockhausen,[4] some forty miles from Frankfurt, it seems likely that he witnessed some of the sermons, fireworks and solemn processions of the Jubilee, and judging by his writings during this period he certainly partook of the intense millennialist expectations they expressed.

Maier's marriage in Frankfurt is an event little remarked, either by Maier himself or by his biographers. The only reference to the fact comes obliquely

---

[1] Po-Chia Hsia, R. *Social Discipline in the Reformation: Central Europe 1550-1750.* London: Routledge, 1989, p. 6; Schilling, Heinz. *Religion, Political Culture and the Emergence of Early Modern Society.* Leiden: E. J. Brill, 1992, pp 171-172.

[2] Schilling, *ibid.*

[3] Po-Chia Hsia, *Social Discipline in the Reformation*, p. 14.

[4] Von Riedesel belonged to a prominent noble family with links to Hessen-Kassel and the court of Moritz; of the four branches of the family, one resided at Hermansburg in the environs of Stockhausen.

in the course of a letter to Moritz the Learned dated the 17th of April, 1618, in which he tells the prince he must break off his stay at Stockhausen with von Riedesel and go directly home, as his wife is heavy with child and will give birth at any moment.[5] In the same letter Maier also asks the leave of Moritz to name the child after His Highness or His consort Juliana, but at no point are we informed of his own wife's name.[6] Nor is there any indication from other sources that the birth went as Maier had hoped. Since there is so little information concerning Maier's own family life, we must satisfy ourselves with the knowledge that Maier held fairly orthodox Lutheran views on the subject of gender, as we may gather from certain comments he makes in the *Symbola Aureae Mensae*. There he states that a republic is liable to become a depraved den of iniquity if it is governed "by that sex which, on account of its inconstant mind and feeble temperament, is born to suffering."[7]

Although his contacts with Moritz prior to his English journey do not seem to have been fruitful, Maier paved the way for his eventual entrance into the court of Moritz by dedicating a book to him in August of 1616 entitled *De Circulo Physico, Quadrato* (*On the Squaring of the Natural Circle*).[8] In this work we find a comprehensive elaboration of the themes

---

5   Kassel, Gesamthochschul-Bibliothek, 2° MS Chem. 19, 1, p. 285 *recto*: "Serenissime, illustrissimeque Princeps, Domine Clementissime, post submissam servitii mei oblationem non possum praeferire, quin ex debito et promisso Celsitudinem Va:m hisce invisam, eamque certiorem hoc proprio tabellario, cum alius ordinarius non occurreret, misso, faciam, me in Stockhausen apud Nobi. Dom: Riedeselium hucusque detineri, eiusque curationi adhuc vacare, quam, ut spero, propediem, Deo dante, nisi aliud quid interveniat, absoluturus, meque Francofurtum, ubi Uxorem gravidam et partui vicinam reliqui, collaturus sum." Around this time Maier also sent a manuscript containing four memoranda concerning chemical matters to Moritz; the third memorandum states that Maier has already divulged to Moritz that which he knows concerning the 'Philosophers R. C.', and that his opinion seems to have been confirmed by reason and experience: Kassel, Gesamthochschul-Bibliothek, 2° MS Chem. 19, 1, p. 280 *verso*: "Quantum mihi cognitum sit de Philosophis R.C. iam ante in aurem Serenituri. V:ae dixi, in qua opinione a ratione et experientia stabilitus et confirmatus videor." It should be noted that Moran, *Alchemical World of the German Court*, pp. 105-106, suggests that this document was amongst the earlier testimonies to Maier's alchemical knowledge sent to Moritz in 1611 – an impossibility given the timeline of Maier's involvement with Rosicrucianism.

6   *Ibid.*, p. 285 *verso*.

7   Maier, *Symbola Aureae Mensae*, p. 578: "Ibi enim mulieres fere viros et hi illas repraesentant; et adulteria sunt adeo frequentia, maritatarumque foeminarum, in secretis lupanaribus se aliis, ex laenarum nutu, prostituentium tanta multitudo impunita, ut incredibile sit auditu: In quibus civitatibus liberi aut potius spurii habentur communes, tanquam in Republ. quadam Platonica, cum fere et uxores communes habeantur: Adhaec indecorum putabant, ut ille sexus, qui propter ingenii imbecillitatem animique inconstantiam ad patiendum sit natus, omnium actiones regeret et gubernaret."

8   Maier, Michael. *De Circulo Physico, Quadrato: Hoc est, AURO, Eiusque virtute medicinali, sub duro cortice instar nuclei latente; An et qualis inde petenda sit, Tractatus haud inutilis.* Oppenheim: Lucas Jennis, 1616.

presented to Moritz in Maier's earlier manuscript communications, and a clear statement of the fundamentals of Maier's mature alchemical ideas. Drawing on neo-Pythagorean speculation and the numerical mysticism of Plato's *Timaeus*, Maier explains to Moritz in his foreword that there are certain hidden bonds which maintain the harmony of the universe, namely those between God, the sun, the human heart and the hidden power of gold, which "correspond to each other in their mutual change."[9] Between God and the sun, we are told, there exists an interval of one octave; between the sun and gold, there are four intervals; and between the human heart and God there are eight.[10] Here Maier takes a leaf from the work of Ficino and the Renaissance Neoplatonists, who closely affiliated the Hermetic doctrine of microcosmic-macrocosmic correspondence with the Pythagorean conception that the universe is an ordered system of interconnected parts bound together "by universally valid numerical principles and harmonic (i.e. proportional, musical) relationships."[11] This Hermetic musical philosophy can be traced through the sixteenth century in the work of Agrippa and Giorgi, and finds its most elaborate baroque expression in the fugues, emblems and discourses of Maier's *Atalanta Fugiens*; indeed, references to the *De Vita Libri Tres* (1489) in the sixth discourse of that work raise the possibility that Maier was directly influenced by Ficino.[12] Maier's theories of universal harmony are not as clearly expounded or sophisticated as those of his contemporary, Robert Fludd (1574-1637); nevertheless, Fludd's major work on the matter, the *Utriusque Cosmi Maioris scilicet et Minoris Metaphysica, Physica, atque Technica Historia* (1617), offers us a graphic illustration of a neo-Pythagorean cosmology very similar to Maier's, with the universe represented as a double octave reaching from earth to heaven and divided by the sun (figure 23).

In Maier's work the sun, gold and the human heart are linked with divinity by virtue of a hidden consonance, which is akin to the striking of an octave. But this relation is also illustrated by Maier with recourse to the cyclical processes in the alchemical vessel; as he writes in the *De Circulo Physico, Quadrato*, the divine virtue or *spiritus* descends to earth and ascends again to heaven through "the rotation of the circle":

---

9   *Ibid.*, p. 6: "Sunt tria, mirificis graduum concordia vinclis/ Harmoniam mundi, quae Monumenta docent:/ Nempe COR humanum, SOL coeli atque AUREA virtus,/ In se dum vicibus convenienter eunt."

10 *Ibid.*, p. 7: "Unius Octavae velut intervalla videntur/ Solem interque Deum, si bene mente notes:/ Quadrupla sic inter solem numerantur, et aurum,/ Corde sed octuplo Numen abest spacio..."

11 Mitchell, Kenneth Stephen. *Musical Conceptions in the Hermetic Philosophy of Robert Fludd: Their Nature and Significance in German Baroque Muscial Thought*. Doctoral thesis, Washington University, 1994, p. 84.

12 *Ibid.*, p. 91; Maier, *Atalanta Fugiens*, discourse 6.

God gives power to the sun, the sun to the gold, this eventually to the human heart, and this through the rotation of the circle looks back to God, so everything that is created mortal stems from God and tends back towards God. This circle fills everything everywhere... As the sun is the image of God, so the heart and gold are the image of the sun, and the gold reveals God with everlasting honour; thus also our heart, constant like gold in the fire, will last forever, when the plague of earthly existence is sloughed off. And what is more, the mind goes on from the sensible world to that which is forever, and to what will be, though not being seen. Those will last, these will pass away; those are hidden, these are signs, and the goodness of God is evident in both.[13]

In Neoplatonic fashion, Maier proclaims that gold is a sign in the material world pointing towards invisible and eternal divinity; it is "the mirror of the whole world" and "the visible proof of the great heavens as an image."[14] And just as gold is incorruptible, so our own heart – as the seat of the soul – is unchanging like gold in the fire, and will continue on after the trials of earthly existence have ended. For Maier the flow and ebb of Creation is a cosmic work of alchemy, in which the human soul descends into the darkness of materiality – the *putrefactio* or black phase of the work – and returns again to its heavenly origins. The 'goodness of God' is evident in things transitory as well as eternal because the present world is a sign pointing to the realm to come, an 'open book' teaching the nature of this life and the next.[15] These ideas are a central element of Maier's spiritual alchemy, and may be broadly characterised as gnostic, echoing as they do the ancient Gnostic descent into *physis* of the divine *scintilla*. Thus in the course of his exposition Maier cryptically remarks that the heart is a "little eye" which possesses "the light of heaven" – an intimation that our own souls possess something of divine perception, by which we may behold the cosmic harmonies instituted by God at the Creation.[16] In the *Hymnosophia* Maier also referred to the "little eye of

---

[13] Maier, *De Circulo Physico, Quadrato*, p. 7: "Utque Deus Soli, Sol auro, hoc denique cordi/ Vim dat, et hoc verso respicit orbe Deum:/ Omnia ab hoc et ad hunc mortalia condita tendunt,/ Circulus hic, quicquid constat ubique, replet.../ Sol, ut imago Dei, sic est cor solis et aurum;/ Utque hoc perpetuo monstrat honore Deum:/ Sic quoque cor nostrum, constans velut ignibus aurum/ Semper erit, terrae cum sit abacta lues./ Quod superest, ex sensibilibus Mens pergat ad illa,/ Quae sunt, et quamvis non videantur, erunt./ Illa manent, abeunt haec, illa abscondita, sunt haec/ Nota, DEI Bonitas hinc ut et inde patet."

[14] *Ibid.*, p. 6: "Subdita nam fulvo sunt haec terrena metallo,/ Hoc speculum mundi totius abdit opes./ Hoc patuli succincta soli compendia praebet,/ Et specimen magni monstrat imago poli."

[15] See also *ibid.*, p. 43: "Quod totus hic mundus apertus liber sit, docens rationales homines in genere, quod et qualis sit DEUS, quod haec vita transitura, aliaque aeternae felicitatis expectanda sit, in quo Aurum, qui paginam esse negat, Elleboro indigeat."

[16] *Ibid.*, p. 6: "Sol equidem supera, ceu Rex, regit Arce Planetas,/ In terram radios insinuatque suos:/ Hinc hominum calido vis vivida corde movetur,/ Hinc invicta AURO

the soul" as the means of perceiving the phoenix, be it in Egypt or in Germany – for the mythical bird is not seen with the corporeal eye, but constitutes a hieroglyph concealing an eternal law of death and resurrection, manifested in both the macrocosm of Creation and the microcosm of the individual.[17]

Maier placed theses notions of correspondence and sympathy in the context of the geo-heliocentric cosmology set forth by Christoph Rothmann (1550-1605), *mathematicus* to Moritz's father, Wilhelm IV of Hessen-Kassel (figure 24). Like his contemporary Tycho Brahe, Rothmann offered up a compromise between the earth-centred Ptolemaic system and the new heliocentrism of Copernicus, although Rothmann's cosmology may be distinguished from Brahe's by the fact that the orbit of Mars does not intersect with the solar orbit.[18] In Maier's work this geo-heliocentric macrocosm corresponds to the microcosm of the human body, or at least to Maier's Galenic conception of the human body, as we have found it described in the *Theses Summam Doctrinae de Temperamentis Corporis Humani*. All light stems from the sun, which as the homologue of the human heart constructs 'subtle essences' from the 'purest air', the homologue of blood which surrounds the celestial bodies in Rothmann's system.[19] These essences inhere in the light, heat and 'virtue' which are transmitted to the planets and fixed stars – the homologues of the organs – thus imparting motion to the universe.[20] The reflected radiance of the planets and fixed stars

---

forma decusque venit./ Hic veluti centrum reliquis et Regula motus/ Cernitur, hic coeli lumen Ocellus habet."

[17] Maier, *Hymnosophia*, p. C4 *verso*: "Ales ab ingenio natus viget ille Sophorum,/ Nec magis Aegypti, quam nostris, visitur arvis,/ Si modo circum nos animi spectemus ocellis."

[18] Rothmann's 'correction' of the Ptolemaic system may be found in *Christophori Rothmanni Bernburgensis Astronomia: in qua hypotheses Ptolemaicae ex hypothesibus Copernici corriguntur et supplentur et inprimis intellectus et usus tabularum Prutenicarum declaratur et demonstratur*. Landesbibliothek und Murhardische Bibliothek der Stadt Kassel, MS Astron. 4° 11; see Barker, Peter and Bernard R. Goldstein, "Realism and Instrumentalism in Sixteenth Century Astronomy: A Reappraisal," *Perspectives on Science*, Vol. 6, No. 3, 1998, p. 241.

[19] On the subject of Rothmann's system and the air-blood correspondence, see Granada, Miguel A. "Christoph Rothmann und die Auflösung der himmlischen Sphären. Die Briefe an den Landgrafen von Hessen-Kassel 1585." In Dick, Wolfgang R. and Jürgen Hamel (eds.). *Beiträge zur Astronomiegeschichte*, Vol. 2. Frankfurt: Deutsch, 1999, pp. 34-57.

[20] Maier, *Septimana Philosophica*, p. 7: "Virtutem, quam similiter circum se superius et inferius diffundit, ad stellas, in primis Planetas, ut per reflexionem quandam ab illis communicetur rebus nascentibus, cum singuli Planetae suas virtutes temperarint et coniunxerint cum solari: ad terram, ubi crescentibus necessaria est omnibus. Et si bene rem introspiciamus, penitiusque consideremus, Sol in coelo, ut cor in humano corpore procedit in suis operationibus. Cor ex sanguine puriore fabricat spiritus tenues, aerios,

contain specific virtues which influence the individual's temperament at the moment of birth, as well as determining the most propitious moment for conducting certain alchemical operations or picking medicinal herbs. In the course of his preface to Moritz in the *De Circulo Physico, Quadrato* Maier further extends the scope of his doctrines of virtue and macrocosmic-microcosmic correspondence by describing the monarch and his court as another bond in the chain of harmonies linking heaven and earth – an idea that his patron-to-be seems to have appreciated. As the sun directs the motion of the planets and warms the metal-bearing womb of the earth with its radiation, so the prince rules his subjects and nurtures his princedom, and so the human heart commands the organs of the body, imparting the vital spirit or innate heat to the veins, "from whence flows the flaming torch of life."[21]

The first half of the *De Physico Circulo, Quadrato* is devoted to a theoretical exposition of the occult qualities of gold. Maier explains that the 'squaring of the circle' is a problem of natural science as much as it is of geometry – by which he refers to the mystery of gold, which like the sun and the soul is formed in the image of the perfect figure, the circle, but nevertheless contains within itself the quaternity of elements in equal proportion. A further paradox Maier refers to is that gold is a homogeneous unity, yet at the same time a trinity, containing within itself volatile mercury, fixed sulphur and the bond that unites the two – a structure that corresponds with the Holy Trinity.[22] Maier also alluded to these 'geometrical' matters in the twenty-first emblem and discourse of the *Atalanta Fugiens* (figure 25), where we find the original source of his speculations – the *Rosarium Philosophorum*, in which 'Aristotle' declares:

Make a circle out of a man and a woman, derive from it a square, and from the square a triangle: make a circle [again] and you will have the Philosophers' Stone.[23]

---

sed igneae naturae, calidos et siccos, motu contractionis et dilatationis, quos deinde mittit per arterias carotidas in cerebrum, ut ibi frigiditate et humiditate cerebrim retiformi complexu temperentur et fiant spiritus animales sensibus omnibus et motibus causandis in corpore aptis: ita Sol sive ex puriore aere, sive alias, fabricat essentias subtilissimas, quibus insunt Lumen, Calor, et Virtus, antea dicta, easque transmittit ad stellas omnes circumcirca in coelo sitas, hoc est, errantes et fixas."

[21] Maier, *De Circulo Physico, Quadrato*, p. 6: "Mobilis hic orbis punctus, stipante corona/ Errantum incedit Duxque caputque Facum./ Sic COR et humani dominatur corporis Aula/ Proque suo nutu subdita membra trahit./ Illud spiritibus venas, vegetoque tepore,/ Unde fluit vitae flammea taeda, beat./ Omnibus, in medio Princeps velut imperat Urbis,/ Artubus hoc vires datque negatque suas."

[22] *Ibid.*, pp. 41-42, 45-46.

[23] Maier, *Atalanta Fugiens*, epigram 21: "Fac de masculo et foemina circulum rotundum, et de eo extrahe quadrangulum, et quadrangulo triangulum; fac circulum rotundum et habebis lapidem philosophorum." From "Rosarium Philosophorum." In *Artis Auriferae*. Vol. 2. Basel: Petrus Pernam, 1572, p. 278.

This puzzling pronouncement ultimately pertains to the secret of Creation, in which the four elements emerge from the 'monad' or unity that is God. In the *Atalanta Fugiens* the square within the circle is again said to correspond to the four elements, whilst the triangle within the square corresponds to "soul, spirit and body." Although de Jong takes this to be a reference to the Paracelsian *tria prima*, there is no mention in Maier's discourse of salt, the third element Paracelsus added to the traditional sulphur-mercury dyad.[24] Indeed, elsewhere Maier clearly states that there are in reality only two primary elements, sulphur and mercury.[25] Rather, this mention of 'soul, spirit and body' is another reference to Aristotle's theory of elemental transmutation: thus according to the *Atalanta Fugiens* the 'body' is the blackness of Saturn or lead, corresponding to earth; the 'spirit' is the white phase of the work corresponding to water; and the 'soul' is the 'yellowness of the air'. The final 'redness' of fire is the "unity and eternal peace" of the Philosophers' Stone (represented in Maier's emblem by the union of man and woman), which marks the perfection of the work through "the return to the Monad."[26] In the *De Circulo Physico, Quadrato* Maier employs the symbols of the trinity and quaternity within the unity to represent gold rather than the Philosophers' Stone, but in both cases he is using an occult geometry to describe a 'spiritual' body that is the image of divine perfection, uniting opposites within itself.

For all Maier's paeans to gold as "the measure of measures" and "the physical image of eternity," was he looking for gold or the Philosophers' Stone as the end-product of his laboratory work, the *lapis coagulatus* of the 'ultimate goldenness'? As we have discovered in our earlier consideration of the *Hymnosophia*, in accordance with Maier's medieval sources the virtue or 'seed' of the sun imparts 'vital sensations' to animals, plants and the metals 'submersed in the caverns of the earth'; by nurturing this solar seed in the

---

24 De Jong, *Michael Maier's Atalanta Fugiens*, p. 169.
25 Maier, *Septimana Philosophica*, p. 74: "Saba: 'Sed alii tria huius subjecti statuunt principia, veluti et rerum omnium, Sal, Sulphur et Mercurium; Quid tu ad haec?' Solomon: 'Sunt sane, qui ex binario binarium deducunt, et unum pro alio accipiunt, binarium materiae, et unitatem formae attribuentes, unde fit Trias compositi ex Monade, vel triangulus ex circulo, idque aptissime et vere, sed hos alii imitantes sinistre interpretantur de principiis, quae proprie bina sunt, nempe materia et forma, seu Mercurius et Sulphur.'"
26 Maier, *Atalanta Fugiens*, discourse 21: "Similiter volunt Philosophi quadrangulum in triangulum ducendum esse, hoc est, in corpus, spiritus et animam, quae tria in trinis coloribus ante rubedinem praeviis apparent, ut pote corpus seu terra in Saturni nigredine, spiritus in lunari albedine, tanquam aqua, anima sive aer in solati citrinitate: Tum Triangulus perfectus erit, sed hic vicissim in circulum mutari debet, hoc est, in rubedinem invariabilem. Qua operatione foemina in masculum conversa et unum quid cum ipso facto est et senarius primus ex perfectis numerus absolutus per unum, duo, cum ad monadem iterum redierit, in quo quies et pax aeterna."

alchemical vessel Maier constructs his 'golden' medicine, which imparts its virtue to the human heart, thus fortifying the *calor innatus* and restoring the balance of the humours. Maier's central concern in the *De Circulo Physico, Quadrato* is to demonstrate that the medical virtue of gold lies hidden under a hard husk in the manner of a kernel.[27] Although the second half of the tract is devoted to the practical question of obtaining this virtue, Maier speaks in very general terms rather than offering the reader specific recipes. We only learn that the virtue of gold, if made digestible as an *aurum potabile*, corrects intemperance in the human body, even if different organs are suffering from different deficits. This is because gold is the temperate metal *par excellence*; its golden bonds unite the 'finest atoms' of the four elements in indivisible harmony, just as they hold the four qualities together and bind volatile mercury and fixed sulphur in equal proportion.[28] Maier likens these three bonds to a "golden castle surrounded by three walls," which remains unconquerable in the face of all enemies – unless someone has received the key from "the master of the castle" (i.e. the Creator) through long meditation and manual labour.[29]

Needless to say, the nature of this 'key' is not divulged to the reader; but we already know that Maier commences his work not with gold but with lead, 'the mother of gold', lying in the alchemical vessel. This is reduced through the black phase of the work to its constituent components – volatile mercury and fixed sulphur – which are then reconstituted and united in a more perfect proportion. Thus Maier writes to Moritz that "a straw house cannot become the marble stone castle of a great prince through the mere rising up of a seed;" rather, one must "tear down the straw house to its foundations and thereafter build the marble castle from the ground up."[30]

---

27 Maier, *De Circulo Physico, Quadrato*, p. 73: "Quod aurum detectum a suo cortice, nucleum medicinalem offerat, sine quo tota compages ejus fere inefficax habeatur."

28 *Ibid.*, pp. 40-42: "Triplex omnino aurei nodi filum est, quo ille connectitur: Primum, Elementorum, terrae, aquae, aeris et ignis illa proportione et mixtionis subtilitate mira complexio et perminimos atomos mutua colligatio... Hinc natura lente festinat in suis mutationibus naturalibus, donec Aquila Bufonem attollat, et bufo aquilam deprimat, hoc est, alterum ab altero inseparabiliter teneatur, et sulfur ex argento vivo generetur, identitate substantiae Mercurialis manente. Secundum filum complexionis aureae est in duplici jam dicta substantia Mercuriali, fixa et volatili, rubea et alba, matura et immatura... Tertium aurei nodi vinculum est aequatio quatuor qualitatum." In this passage Maier utilises the theory of a twofold mercury, developed by pseudo-Arnoldus de Villanova, which postulates the existence of a volatile mercury and a mercury which is fixed by virtue of an internal sulphur; Roberts, *Mirror of Alchemy*, p. 62.

29 *Ibid.*, p. 42: "Hoc triplici muro Castrum aureum circumdatum omnibus Elementorum hostibus insuperabile permanet, nisi quis veram clavem a Domino Castri acceperit diutina animi speculatione, exercitio manuum et labore Chymico."

30 Kassel, Gesamthochschul-Bibliothek, 2° MS Chem. 11, 1; cited in Moran, *Alchemical World of the German Court*, p. 104.

Maier envisaged that the final *lapis coagulatus* 'of the ultimate goldenness' lying in his vessel would not be gold itself, but the miraculous medicinal 'kernel' to be found underneath the impregnable husk of that metal. In this 'tincture' or seed of gold the four contrary elements would be united – the 'squaring of the circle', which would provide the means for producing gold through fermentation, and imparting a like equilibrium to the four humours of the human body.

2. Maier and the Calvinist court of Moritz of Hessen-Kassel

Whilst Maier's dedication of his *De Circulo Physico, Quadrato* to Moritz did not immediately result in his entrance into the princely court, in April of 1618 he sent exemplars of the eleven works he had hitherto published to Moritz, and was accepted as *Medicus und Chymicus von Hauß aus* shortly thereafter.[31] This position was extra-mural, and allowed Maier to continue residing at Frankfurt;[32] according to the letter of service issued by Moritz, he was to be paid 150 rix-dollars (*Reichstaler*) per year and 75 rix-dollars extra to represent the court at each Frankfurt Book Fair, "for as long as the appointment remains":

Through the mercy of God, We Moritz, Prince of Caznelbogen, Diz, Zigenhain and Nidda, do hereby make publicly known that we have adopted by our grace the most learned and faithful Michael Maier as our Doctor and Chymist; and we do this by power of this letter, so that he will be our Doctor and Chymist and will be trusty, obedient and willing to warn us of danger when he resides at Frankfurt or other places; not only to faithfully communicate and consult with us concerning medical and chymical matters, as the opportunity occurs, but also to give all kinds of good intelligence concerning other matters.[33]

It seems that Maier's principal task concerning matters medical and alchemical was to test new medicines at Moritz' monetary expense – and as we might imagine, at the possible physical expense of his patients, unless Maier chose

---

31 Figala and Neumann, "Author cui Nomen Hermes Malavici," p. 135.
32 Moran, *Alchemical World of the German Court*, p. 108.
33 Hessisches Staatsarchiv Marburg, Bestand 4b, Nr. 266: "Von Gottes gnaden Wihr Moriz Landgrave von Hesen, grave zu Caznelbogen, Diz, Zigenhain und Nidda, thun kund hiemit offentlich bekanndt, das wihr den hochgelarte unsern lieben getreuen Michaelem Majerum vor unseren Medicum und Chymicum von hauß auß in gnaden bestelt, uff- und angenommen haben und thun daß hirmit in craft dieses brives derogestalt und also daß er unser Medicus und Chymicus, unß getreu, wolt gehorsamb und gewilig sein, unseren schaden alzeit treulich warnen und hergegen bestes werken, mit unß, wen er etwa zu frankfurt oder derglichen orter einen sich uffhalten wirdet, nicht allein in medicina und chymia nach vorfallender gelegenheit getreulich communiciren, und consuliren, sondern auch in andere wege allerhandt gute nachrichtung geben..."

to follow the example of other physicians at the court of Hessen-Kassel and self-medicate.[34] But the reference in his letter of appointment to further intelligence-gathering duties beyond matters of alchemy has fortified the Rosicrucian thesis of Yates in the eyes of some recent writers, and thus a more thorough examination of Maier's relation to the Calvinist court is called for.

Firstly, it should be noted that German courtiers in the early modern period were generally required to report the details of their movements and experiences whilst residing in foreign lands or states. In Maier's time a universal postage system had recently been established within the Empire, and with war impending the exploitation of all possible intelligence opportunities was paramount.[35] This was particularly true for Moritz, who was amongst the vanguard of the 'Second Reformation' in Germany – an attempt to fully implement Luther and Calvins' 'Reformation of Doctrine' in a comprehensive 'Reformation of Life', which had as its goal the fusion of ecclesiastical and secular power under the prince's absolute authority.[36] Although his humanist education went hand-in-hand with an irenicist approach to intra-Protestant relations, Moritz was the possessor of an "undiplomatic and radical Calvinist spirit" which alarmed his Catholic adversaries; his desire for reform extended beyond the borders of his own lands, and he played a central role in efforts to install the Elector Palatine on the imperial throne.[37]

Whilst his position compelled Moritz to remain well-informed concerning developments in the Empire, the historical record does not support the conjecture of Yates that Maier was a key figure in his intelligence network.[38] During Maier's years in Frankfurt am Main Moritz had at least three other agents operative in that city, including a certain 'Hessian agent' by the name of Hans Breul, a postal administrator by the name of Weigand Uffsteiner, and

---

[34]　*Ibid.*: "...uff unßer costen medicando und sonste, wozu wihr ihne dienlich und geschickt befinden und wißen, gebrauchen laßen..."; on the duties of 'testers' at the court of Moritz, see Moran, *Alchemical World of the German Court*, p. 69.

[35]　Kleinpaul, Johannes. *Das Nachrichtenwesen der deutschen Fürsten im 16. und 17. Jahrhundert*. Leipzig: Adolf Klein, 1930, pp. 138 ff.

[36]　Given the occurence of similar developments in Lutheran and Catholic lands at this time, Schilling prefers the term 'Calvinist confessionalisation' to 'Second Reformation'; Schilling, *Religion, Political Culture and the Emergence of Early Modern Society*, pp. 247 ff.

[37]　Borggrefe, Heiner, Vera Lüpkes and Hans Ottomeyer (eds.). *Moritz der Gelehrte: Ein Renaissancefürst in Europa*. Eurasburg: Edition Minerva, 1997, p. 11; on Moritz' 'Points of Improvement', an irenic attempt to harmonise worship and belief between the Lutherans and Calvinists of his lands, see Menk, Gerhard. "Die 'Zweite Reformation' in Hessen-Kassel." In Schilling, *Die reformierte Konfessionalisierung in Deutschland*, pp. 154-183.

[38]　Yates, *The Rosicrucian Enlightenment*, pp. 81-82, 88.

a postmaster by the name of Johann von den Birghden.[39] Another royal agent in Basel mentions Maier at one point in a letter to Moritz, but only to express a certain displeasure with the acquaintance.[40] And as we have seen, there is no justification for the belief that Maier had a hand in organising an Anglo-Bohemian axis for the Calvinists whilst he was in England: at that time Moritz used a certain Francis Segar to conduct any important political business in London, such as seeking subsidies from James I to counter incursions into the Empire from the Spanish Netherlands.[41]

What was the basis, then, for Moritz' employment of Maier? In his work *The Alchemical World of the German Court*, Moran argues that Moritz' patronage of the occult arts was motivated primarily by "a form of political despair," which in the case of alchemy inspired particular interest in the manipulation and transformation of metals as a possible technological solution for his political problems.[42] Whilst it is certainly true that princely patronage in the early modern period was driven by "practical concerns relating to the demonstration or preservation of political power," it was the medical application of alchemy that took the centre stage in Maier's work and in his appeals for patronage; thus the particular reasons behind Moritz' employment of an iatrochemist such as Maier remain unclarified by Moran, beyond the very general aim of investigating and gaining control over Nature.[43] Given the close connection perceived between physical and moral states in the medical worldview of the day, the iatrochemistry of Maier and other physicians at the princely court offered not only a means of curing diseases but also establishing a pious life amongst subjects through the restoration of the body's natural order – a proposition that would be particularly attractive to a Calvinist prince who held the moral state of his dominion close to his heart. Needless to say, contemporary pharmacology continues to play a central role in the maintenance of social order, with the proviso that its application to the realms of physical and mental health is no longer integrated in the same manner. In his practice and in the theoretical ideas he directed towards Moritz, Maier placed particular emphasis on the establishing of 'temperance' – conceived holistically as a psychosomatic state – in both individual and society through the operation of a divine virtue.

Thus the unified Hermetic worldview propagated by alchemists such as Maier not only offered Moritz "an intellectual balsam for religious and political confusion," as Moran has it, but also promised a very practical

---

39 Kleinpaul, *Das Nachrichtenwesen der deutschen Fürsten*, p. 78.
40 *Ibid.*, p. 80.
41 *Ibid.*, pp. 79-80.
42 Moran, *Alchemical World of the German Court*, pp. 171, 174-175.
43 *Ibid.*, p. 176.

means of imbuing the princedom with "the flaming torch of life."[44] Although they are largely alien to the contemporary scientific worldview, Moritz held firmly to such vitalistic notions.[45] Furthermore, printing provided the state with a powerful ideological tool, and Maier's writings on macrocosmic-microcosmic correspondence communicated to the educated elite an episteme in which the natural and social orders are mirrors of the divine.[46] Humanist intellectuals such as Maier formed an important well of support for the authoritarian programme of the Calvinist monarchs, and although the 'Second Reformation' in Germany had first arisen in the city-states of the Lower Rhine through the congregational pressure of Dutch Calvinist exiles, in states such as Hessen-Kassel Calvinist confessionalisation was imposed by princely autocracy through the collusion of the academic and civic echelons.[47] In both its practical and ideological aspects, then, Maier's work complemented a process of 'social disciplining' that advanced in Calvinist Germany under the rubric of the 'Reformation of Life' – a process by which powerful centralised states were constructed through the promotion of a culture of piety and obedience amongst citizens.[48]

3. Millennialism, nationalism and the descent into war

However, even if Maier's duties as *Medicus und Chymicus von Hauß aus* did not earn him a central role in some 'Rosicrucian' intrigue, or even a place amongst the inner circle of alchemists at the court of Moritz, the surviving manuscript from his intelligence service is a fascinating document which reveals something of Maier's own sensibilities as Europe descended into war around him. On May the 23rd, 1618 – that is, around the time of Maier's entrance into the service of Moritz – Protestant rebels in Prague accused two imperial ministers of violating the Letter of Majesty, the guarantee of religious freedom for Bohemian Hussites, Calvinists and Lutherans issued by

---

[44] *Ibid.*, p. 24; Maier, *De Circulo Physico, Quadrato*, p. 6.

[45] Moran, *Alchemical World of the German Court*, p. 174.

[46] On this point see the much-criticised work by Michel Foucault: *The Order of Things: An Archaeology of the Human Sciences*. London: Tavistock Publications, 1970; for a discussion of the audience of Maier's works, see Figala and Neumann, "Michael Maier," p. 49.

[47] Schilling, *Religion, Political Culture and the Emergence of Early Modern Society*, p. 290; Cameron, Euan. *The European Reformation*. Oxford: Clarendon Press, 1991, pp. 369 ff.; Cohn, Henry J. "The Territorial Princes in Germany's Second Reformation, 1559-1622." In *International Calvinism 1541-1715*. Oxford: Clarendon Press, 1986, p. 141.

[48] Po-Chia Hsia, *Social Discipline in the Reformation*, pp. 35-37, 122 ff.

Emperor Rudolf in 1609. After an improvised trial, the two men were thrown from the windows of the Royal Chancellery in the Hradschin, an event known as the Defenestration of Prague (figure 26).[49] Although the men survived their eighty-foot fall with the help of a dunghill in the castle trench, the event and its expected consequences inspired a full-scale Protestant insurrection in Bohemia; and whilst the ailing and childless Emperor Matthias made some efforts towards conciliation, his nephew and chosen successor as Emperor and King of Bohemia, Archduke Ferdinand of Styria, was known as a zealous defender of Roman Catholic and Habsburg interests in the Empire.[50] Fears concerning the imminent death of Matthias and the accession of Ferdinand to the imperial throne figure prominently in Maier's report to Moritz, which is dated the 18th of January, 1619:

One report says that the Emperor is already dead... others say that he is very weak, and cannot keep any food down, and everything must be expelled from above rather than beneath; it is for this reason that he is said to see dead people coming before him, such as the Empress, Clösel and some others, and is very terrified about it. Clösel is dead, and after his death hung up; the reason for his imprisonment was that he let the Bohemians know that Ferdinand is attempting to weaken the Letter of Majesty in order that it might be completely nullified when he becomes king... As reasonable people here can well imagine, the whole preparation and war armament that the Spanish have undertaken in the last year in Naples, Sicily, Spain and Milan, is in order that they may offer their hand to the Emperor against the Bohemians and the united [Protestant] princes; let Almighty God enlighten our leaders and princes to defend themselves in good time against such mischief. People say that the Venetians have allowed the Spanish to pass freely through their land, though this is not to be believed... It is also announced that a request for access through Your Majesty's land for 10000 men has been made [by the Spanish], as also through the lands of the Earl of Wetterau, with the condition that if such access is not permitted, to make it by force.[51]

---

[49] Schiller, Friedrich. *Der Dreißigjährige Krieg.* München: Kindler, 1975, p. 70.

[50] *Ibid.*, pp. 67-68, 70 ff.

[51] Hessisches Staatsarchiv Marburg, Bestand 4g, Paket 57- 1619, pp. 1-2: "Man sagt alhie, Ihr Kay: May: sey schon todt... Andere sagen, er sey sehr schwach, könne kein essen bey sich behalten, also das alles von oben, und nicht Unten, musse weg gehen, dazu ursach gegeben, das er die keisserinne, Clösel und ezliche andere vorstorbene personen fur sich kommente gesehen, daruber er sehr erschrocken; Dan der Clösel sey gestorben, und nach seinem todt gehencket; die Ursache des Clösels gefengniss sey auch diesse, das er geoffentbaret den behmen, wie der k. ferdinandus habe sich bearbeitet, zufor er zu den kron erhoben, durch der behmen Maiestet brief ein loch zu bringen, oder denselben umbzustossen, damit er, wan er konig geworden, desto fuglicher ihn ghar konte vornichten... Was der Expedition gehgen Behmen und der spannier hulf anlanget, könen Vornunftige alhie wol abmessen, das die ganze zubereitung und kriegesrustung, so der spannier dis Vorgangene Jar zu Neapolis, zu sicilien, spannien und Meylandt bis anhero gehabt, dahin gereichen, das er Ihr Kay: May: die handt biete, gegen die behmen und die voreinigten fursten, Godt der Almechtige wolle unsere haupter und fursten also erleuchten, damit solchem unheil in zeiten gewäret werde. Man sagt, die Venetianer haben deme Spannier den pas durch ihr landt vorgunnet, welches doch nicht gleublig..."

We can be fairly certain that this was not the first Moritz had heard of a threatened Spanish foray through his lands; indeed, Maier himself opens his letter with the self-depreciating admission that he hasn't any good reason to write, but that he knows he is duty-bound to do so.[52] The remainder of Maier's letter deals with articles of hearsay and superstition that would have been of little or no use to Moritz, but which highlight the millennialist anxieties inspired by the deteriorating state of the Empire. The fact that Maier suggests certain of these portents should be heeded shows that he, too, was deeply imbued with the prevalent spirit of foreboding:

That the comet which has recently appeared brings with it changes in many things is believable. The ordinary man says that three stars were to be seen; one was a comet, another was fiery red, the third (although unbelievable) often gave out a noise. However, these last two stars should be understood as the planets Venus and Jupiter, which are unknown to the common man and are seen in unusual parts of the Zodiac. That the star should give forth a noise is not believable. Nevertheless people say that here around the city walls such voices ("Woe! Woe!") were heard at night. People also say that the comet fell into the moat in Nancy, Lotringen, and in case it had reached the town, it would have flattened it. I don't know, however, what to make of these things. Nevertheless I have heard from truthful people that meteors were seen in the sky in Holland, and that people running together were seen, and shooting was heard together with the beating of drums. This one should truthfully report, and also make it publicly known.[53]

The comet of 1618 (figure 27) was widely understood as an omen of impending doom for Europe. In his *Septimana Philosophica* Maier describes comets as "viscous ascending exhalations" which are drawn up from the earth by the sun, and may ascend as high as the superlunary regions; we are told that they do not emit their own light, but like the stars resemble "clear

---

Es werdt auch vormeldt, das durch E. F. G. landen fur 10. tausent man ein pas begeret geworden, wie auch durch der Wetterawischen grafen landen, mit der Condition, woferne solches nicht vorgunnet wurde, durch macht ihn zu suchen..."

52   *Ibid.*, p. 1.

53   *Ibid.*, p. 2: "Das der Comete, so newlig erschienen eine mutationem mit sich bringen werde in vielen sachen, ist glaublig, Der gemeine man saget es sein 3. Sterne gesehen worden, davon der ein Ein comete, der ander sey rodtfeurig gewesen, der dritte habe (obwol ungleublig) oftmahl ein Stimme von sich gegeben, Jedog werden ohn zweifel die 2. leste sterne Von den planeten Venere oder Hespero und Iove vorstanden, so dem gemeinen man unbekandt und an ungewönlichen orteren Zodiaci gesehen seint, Das der Sterne solte ein stimme hören lassen, ist wol ungleublig, Jedog sagt man, das alhie umb den mauern auch solche Stimme (Wehe, Wehe) des nachtes gehöret worden, Man sagt auch der Comeht sey in lotringen zu Nancy in den schlossgraben gefallen, welcher so er die stadt erreichet, sie ertrucket hette, Ich weis aber nicht, was hie von zu halten, Jedog hab ichs von warhaften leuten gehöret, Das auch Chasmata in der luft in hollandt gesehen, da auch die personen zusamen laufende gesehen und das schiessent gehöret, sambt der trummel schlagent, Sol man warhaftig berichten; auch in patenten umbtragen."

crystal" which reflects the sun's rays.[54] That these coagulated vapours contain fine earthy matter is attested to by the fact that such particles also adhere to vapour in the alchemical vessel during distillation.[55] Thus in Maier's alchemical worldview the cosmos is created in the likeness of a great alembic, and the possibility that the *spiritus* or solar virtue reflected from unusual heavenly bodies such as comets might cause momentous transformations in worldly affairs is very plausible.

Mention is also made in his letter of an anonymous verse disseminated on the walls of Rome which read, "The house of the Austrian Emperor perishes: England will smile, Austria will groan, the Pope will grieve, after 60 years the glory of the fifth will cease."[56] Maier goes on to give a lengthy exposition of a 'believable' vision had by a watchman in a town near Frankfurt, in which a ghostly prince was seen on horseback slaughtering his enemies, the words 'Heinrich Friedrich' were heard, and the city of Frankfurt was seen in flames.[57] Maier also appended to his letter a certain prophecy that had come into his possession, now apparently lost; he concludes with a solemn request that Moritz take heed of his humble service and remain his merciful Master.[58]

---

[54] Maier, *Septimana Philosophica*, p. 60: "Quid Cometae sunt? Non sunt stellae, quo ad formam, motum, aut durationem; quamuis, ut stellae, lumen Solis in se recipiant: Qui enim putant, esse Cometas igneos vapores in aere incensos, et ardentes eo usque donec absumantur, falluntur: Sol est, qui Planetis, stellis fixis, et Cometis lumen communicat; Unde patet, quod materia Cometarum sit aeque receptiva Solaris luminis, hoc est, viscosa, et instar crystalli clara, quam stellarum... Saepe in sublunari visuntur aere, sed nec raro supra lunam prope Solis altitudinem, aliquando et Martis; qualis fuit, qui ante 40. annos, aut circiter in Cassiopeia apparuit, quem propterea miraculosam stellam quidam putarunt."

[55] *Ibid.*, p. 35: "Ex vaporibus ascendentibus viscosis fiunt Cometae. Cum vero alicubi rarefactus est aer, Sol attrahit vehementius vapores, et sic nonnunquam quid crassioris materiae cum illis elevat (ut quoque fieri potest perignem vehementem arenae vel cinerum in distillatione aquarum, ut aliquid terrestrioris materiae una cum vaporibus aqueis attrahatur) quae materia crassior in nubibus consistit;" also Maier, *De Circulo Physico, Quadrato*, p. 41: "...si [substantia mercurialis] cruda alba et volatilis per se consideretur, invenitur, quod in eo aqua ita adhaereat terrae, et terra aquae, quod terra cum aqua simul in aera seu alembicum ascendat, quod est alias contra communem naturae institutum." Although his speculations concerning the origin of comets stray from the mark, it is an interesting coincidence that Maier's thoughts on their composition (i.e. water and earthy particles) conforms closely to our contemporary knowledge of these objects.

[56] Hessisches Staatsarchiv Marburg, Bestand 4g, Paket 57- 1619, p. 3: "InteritUs DoMUs aUstrIa Cae:/ Anglia ridebit, gemet Austria, Papa dolebit,/ Post ter viginti cessabit gloria Quinti."

[57] *Ibid.*, pp. 3-4: the words 'Heinrich Friedrich' possibly depict Friedrich V as the avenger of Henry IV of France, the implacable foe of the Habsburgs whose assassination in 1610 by a Roman Catholic fanatic, Ravaillac, dealt a blow to Protestant hopes in both France and the *Deutsches Reich*.

[58] *Ibid.*, p. 4.

The sentiments expressed by Maier in his report are in keeping with the "intense Lutheran eschatology" of the time, in which an apocalyptic conflict with the Antichrist – i.e. the Roman Catholic Church – was thought to be the precursor to the establishment of God's kingdom on earth.[59] However, there are other specifically esoteric millennialist elements to be found in Maier's work, particularly in relation to the 'Rosicrucian brotherhood' and its role in the re-establishment of the Golden Age.[60] In Rosicrucian circles these elements emanated above all from the Paracelsian prophecy of the destruction of a third part of the world and the appearance of 'Elias Artista' – a great artist and scientist identified in certain texts as the chemical agent of transmutation itself.[61] Maier's fellow alchemist and Rosicrucian at the court of Moritz, Raphael Eglinus (1559-1622), believed this apocalyptic event would mark the overthrow of a 'bestial estate', i.e. the rule of humans as unenlightened beings driven by animal desire and lust.[62] Whilst there is nothing of the Elias myth to be found in Maier's work, given his own proclamations concerning the coming Hermetic Golden Age it is possible that he envisaged the divine virtues of his own medicine playing a role in the construction of just such a pious new world.

As we have seen, Maier's attitude towards Paracelsus was somewhat ambiguous; on the one hand, certain fundamentals of his alchemical theory were opposed to the Paracelsian schema, whilst on the other hand he praised the Swiss alchemist as the 'Luther' of chemical medicine. In Maier's time

---

[59]   Po-Chia Hsia, *Social Discipline in the Reformation*, pp. 12-13.

[60]   See above, pp. 133-135.

[61]   Moran, *Alchemical World of the German Court*, pp. 42-43. Elias appears to be an amalgam of the biblical prophet Elijah and certain medieval alchemical figures; an interesting account of the myth is given by 'Tharsander', or Georg Wilhelm Wegner in his *Adeptus Ineptus, Oder Entdeckung der falsch berühmten Kunst ALCHIMIE genannt*. Berlin: Ambrosius Haude, 1744, pp. 38-39: "Basil Valentine and Theophrastus Paracelsus also dreamt much of this Elias Artista. Glauberus, who amongst all the alchemists easily wrote the most, also wrote a tract concerning this Elias, wherein he showed how and what this Elias Artista should reform, namely the true spagyric medicine of the ancient Egyptian philosophers, which was lost for more than 1000 years. However, he declares in the second part of *Miraculi Mundi* that this Elias is in fact the white Sal Artis Mirificum, and highest medicine: and if one changes about the letters of Elias Artista, as Glauberus himself adduces, one receives: 'Et artis Salia'. I leave the alchemists to work out whether this Elias is in fact a real man, or the Philosophers' Stone itself; and only remark, that one of these alchemists gives us to believe that Elias is already at hand. Helvetius, in his tractate *Vitulus Aureus*, believes that in the year 1666 some adept came to him in the Hague, who gave to him a small kernel of stone, half as big as a turnip seed, with which he tinged one and a half pounds of lead into the most beautiful gold, for which reason he took this Adept to be Elias Artista himself."

[62]   Moran, *ibid.*, p. 42; Eglinus predicted 1658 as the date of this second coming, rather roughly following Paracelsus, who stated that Elias would return in the fifty-eighth year following the first fifteen centuries of the Christian era.

such comparisons of Paracelsus and Luther were commonplace, and reflected a striving to establish a pan-Germanic identity amongst a patchwork of states fragmented by politics and religion. Since the time of the Reformation anti-Catholicism in the *Deutsches Reich* had been closely allied to a nascent German nationalism, and humanist Lutheran scholars such as Maier not only sympathised with efforts to wrest control of the empire from the clutches of Papism, but also attempted to establish their own claims to a German 'Renaissance' distinct from its Italian predecessor. Thus Maier speaks of Germany as the 'new Egypt'; and in the *Arcana Arcanissima* we find the rather remarkable assertion that the name of the Teutons derives from the word 'Thoth', whose cult Maier believed was particularly strong amongst his ancient forebears.[63] In this way Maier sought to affirm the legitimacy of German Hermeticism as a unique entity, rather than portraying his knowledge as the derivative of the Italian Renaissance that it truly was.

These contemporary tendencies towards cultural nationalism and *Reichspatriotismus* are most clearly demonstrated in Maier's *Verum Inventum* (*True Inventions of the German Nation*, 1619), a work printed simultaneously in German and Latin editions in which he praises the ingenuity of the German peoples in the fields of warfare, empire-building, theology, medicine and chemistry. The first three chapters of the *Verum Inventum* deal with the history of the German Empire and its prerogatives; Maier's burden is to demonstrate that the first 'true invention' of the Germans was the founding of the *Deutsches Reich* by Karl the Great (Charlemagne) – not as a gift of the Pope, but rather by the "law of war."[64] When German authority was threatened by the Italians and the French after the cessation of the Carolingian line, the empire was maintained for the "Germans alone" through the ingenuity and strength of Otto the Saxon and his successors, an independence which persisted thereafter through divine providence.[65] In the following chapters Maier goes on to enumerate German inventions in the art of war; mention is made of the medieval German monk and alchemist Berthold the Black, who reputedly discovered the cannon in 1380 when a laboratory experiment went horribly wrong.[66] According to Maier, whilst

---

[63] Maier, *Verum Inventum*, pp. 214-215; Maier, *Arcana Arcanissima*, p. 142; comparable efforts to link Egyptian lore with the indigenous inhabitants of Schleswig-Holstein were made by Johannes Goropius Becanus (1518-1572), whilst the Swedes Olaus Magnus and Olaus Rudbeck attempted to demonstrate the kinship of Egyptian hieroglyphs and Nordic runes. See Iversen, *The Myth of Egypt*, pp. 88-89, 159.

[64] *Ibid.*, pp. 10 ff.

[65] *Ibid.*, pp. 36 ff.

[66] *Ibid.*, pp. 90-91: "Quibus omnibus consideratis Bertholdus Schwartz miscuit haec tria simul, nempe carbones eos, ut corpus, sulphur, ut animam, sal petrae, ut spiritum, et posuit invase forti ad ignem fixatis, adhibitis ignis gradibus: Verum quamprimum calor ignis incendium sulphuris causatus est, vas in mille partes dissiliit maximo cum bombo:

Berthold's invention has delivered so many more up to death than have been
freed by medicine, its efficacy is just one of the useful by-products of the
search for the panacea, as it has liberated the Christian world from the
incursion of barbarians such as the Huns and Tartars.[67] A chapter is devoted
to the German 'purification' of theological doctrine through Luther and
Calvin, which although rejected by the ignorant is particularly salutary for the
Christian world.[68] On the subject of medicine Maier argues that the
conglomeration of the fields of chemistry and medicine instituted by Paracelsus has given rise to great advances. This is despite the fact that the Swiss
alchemist's doctrines have been refuted by the 'learned' Erastus (1523-1583)
– the Calvinist theologian who established the doctrine of the Church's total
subjection to the power of the state ('Erastianism'), but who railed against
Paracelsus as a restorer of Gnostic heresy and disciple of the Devil.[69] A
staunch opponent of the Hermetic arts and zealous persecutor of witches,
Erastus had been close to the court of the Rhineland-Palatinate; Maier
diplomatically steps around the problem of his censure by implying that it is
certain unlearned followers of Paracelsus who are most deserving of the
theologian's reproach.[70] In Maier's eyes, Protestants and iatrochemists face
the common enemy of a 'papist medicine'; and just as Luther has "purged the
papist faeces" from German theology, so Paracelsus has undertaken a similar
task in the realm of Medicine.[71]

Ut autem huius effectus causae probe agnoscerentur, est credibile ipsum monachum non
acquievisse in eo, cum vas fractum esset, forte lapideum, sed vas metallicum fortis-
simum accepisse, ex ferro vel aere campanarum confecto, qualia sunt mortaria vel ollae
metallicae, inque hoc disposuisse hanc suam eandem materiam in maiori copia, et
orificium vasis arctissime conclusisse cum metallo eiusdem generis: sed vase ad ignem
posito, quamprimum calor incenderit dictum pulverem, tanta violentia erupit obtura-
mentum vasis, ut omnia, quae attigerit, penetrarit, fregerit et impetu validissimo
prostraverit: Hoc fuit initium fortuitae inventionis Pyrii pulveris."

[67] *Ibid.*, pp. 84, 90: "Ita dum monachus sapientiam quaerit Chymicam, hoc est Medicinam morborum omnium in homine et metallis, reperit Pyrium pulverem, quo tot et
plures tradendi sunt morti, quam inde ea medicina liberandi."; "Secundum VERUM a
Germanis inventum est pulvis tormentarius et machina bellica, qua insignis mutatio facta
est in mundo, tantum habens boni in vero suo usu, quantum mali in abusu; idque
Christianum orbem a barbarorum, ut olim Hunnorum, Tartarorum, et aliorum, incurs-
ionibus liberavit."

[68] *Ibid.*, pp. 143 ff.

[69] Pagel, *Paracelsus*, pp. 311 ff.

[70] Maier, *Verum Inventum*, p. 214: "Etsi vero a doctissimo Thoma Erasto Paracelsica
Medicina examinata sit et refutata in multis, tamen suos adhuc inventi cultores tam inter
doctos, quam indoctos: Et quotidie nova exeunt opera, quae Chymicam cum medicina
coniunctam optimum ei adminiculum esse declarant."

[71] *Ibid.* pp. 210-211, 214: "Haec Medicina corporis non curat verba Sophistarum et
Thrasonum, sed mox ad Examen et probam eius professor vocatur; Papistica illa
medicina animae per Sophistas logomachos et distinctionum subtilium authores, Iesuitas

Not surprisingly, these sentiments earned the *Verum Inventum* a place alongside the *Symbola Aureae Mensae* on the papal Index of banned books.[72] The publication of the *Verum Inventum* at the outbreak of the Thirty Years War and its distribution in the vernacular for the sake of a wider audience were not facts coincidental to its author's purpose. Indeed, the evidence of Maier's own words does not support the view of some esotericists that Maier sought nothing more than a peaceful reformation of the arts and sciences; rather, they show he was inclined in his later life to authoritarianism, anti-Catholicism and a militaristic nationalism.[73] In September of 1618 Maier had already dedicated his *Viatorium* to Prince Christian of Anhalt-Bernburg (1568-1630), the military commander of the German Calvinists and their allies amongst the Lutheran states.[74] The autocratic Erastian programme of Moritz and the German Calvinist princes accorded well with Maier's own elitist attitudes concerning alchemy and its relation to the unwashed masses; thus in his discourse on the subject of alchemical secrecy in the *Silentium post Clamores*, Maier recommends to the reader the work of 'Clapmarius'.[75] Arnold Klapmeier (1574-1604) was a follower of Machiavelli and a professor of history and politics patronised by Moritz of Hessen-Kassel; in the book mentioned by Maier, the *De Arcanis Rerum Publicarum*, he advocates the use of draconian measures for the establishment of religious unity, and reiterates Tacitus' insistence on the necessity of withholding state secrets from the common people.[76]

---

verbo tenus defenditur et sustentatur, veluti mox ruitura domus per columnas... Cum Medicina animae esset a purificatore Saxone a foecibus humanis seu papisticis clarior et syncerior reddita, ita ut quilibet non omnino intellectus oculis privatus, puritatem et salubritatem doctrinae Evangelicae perciperet, En ex montanis Helvetiorum (quos Swiceros vocitant et Cymbrorum reliquias) locis alius prorupit Eremita, qui, quod factum erat in Theologia, similiter in Medicina corporis testare ausus est, et hoc non minore foelicitatis eventu, quam animi magni conatu."

[72] Moller, *Cimbria Literata*, p. 378; the honour was bestowed by special decree of the Congregation of the Index on the 12th of April, 1628.

[73] A view derived from statements in Maier's *Themis Aurea* concerning the necessity of the Reformation; see above, pp. 148-149.

[74] Figala and Neumann, "Michael Maier," p. 130, suggest that Prince Christian may have been a benefactor of Maier's during his time in Prague.

[75] Maier, *Silentium post Clamores*, pp. 57-58: "Nemo autem, qui sanae mentis est, existimabit, non solum in mundo arcana haberi, quae in vulgum proferenda non sint, cum omnes aetates, regiones, personae publicae et privatae, civitates et status sua habeant secreta, in quae inquirendum aut involandum non sit: De secretis Rerum publicarum Clapmarius: De naturae arcanis innumeri scripserunt, non quasi omnia revelaverint, sed quaedam pro Exemplis adduxerint, ex quibus de aliis, quae latent, iudicium ferre liceat."

[76] Oestreich, Gerhard. "Clapmarius." In *Neue Deutsche Biographie*. Vol. 3. Berlin: Duncker & Humblot, 1957, p. 260.

The formation of a German national identity amongst Protestant scholars in the early modern period was particularly influenced by the *Germania* of Tacitus, the ancient account of the German tribes and their invincibility in the face of the might of Rome, which took on a specifically anti-Italian significance through German redactors such as Conrad Celtis.[77] Thus Maier liberally intersperses his *Verum Inventum* and other works with citations from the *Germania*, and takes particular pride in the fact that Tacitus attested to the greatness of the 'Cimbri', who vanquished entire Roman legions with their vast numbers and mighty army. Maier followed his patron Rantzau in signing his name with the appendage 'Cimbri', in order to identify himself to his readers as a member of the indigenous ethnic grouping of Schleswig-Holstein. Following Tacitus, in his *Atalanta Fugiens* Maier proudly recalls that when the Cimbri were denied their land by the Romans, they entered Italy and slew several thousand Roman soldiers together with their consuls. As a people who had also fought through the centuries against the encroachment of the sea on their lands, the problem of *Lebensraum* was very real for the Cimbri; thus the point of Maier's boast is to demonstrate the alchemical truth that whilst the earth as the last repository of things putrefied is most vile, it is also most precious as "the mother of all things."[78] Clearly, it was German earth in particular that Maier held precious, and the nation that had given rise to those occult sciences which are like "roses and lilies" in the alchemical rose garden.

It also seems that Maier planned a more ambitious means of expressing his nationalism – a work in which he would tie these sentiments more closely to his belief in an occult natural order. In his *Grundlage zu einer Hessischen Gelehrten und Schriftsteller Geschichte* (1786), Strieder makes note of a printed document not to be found in other bibliographies entitled the *Aquila Germanica* ('German Eagle'). Now apparently lost, this document consisted of just two pages, and constituted the announcement of a larger work that was to be forthcoming. Indeed, it was amongst the material Maier offered up to the judgment of Johann Hartmann Beyer in his letter of the 20th of October, 1617. There we are told that Maier planned the work whilst in England in order to honour his homeland – an understandable impulse given his bad experiences amongst the English.[79] The text is given by Strieder, and runs as follows:

---

[77] See Muhlack, Ulrich. "Die Germania im deutschen Nationalbewußtsein vor dem 19. Jahrhundert." In *Beiträge zum Verständnis der Germania des Tacitus*. Göttingen: Vandenhoeck & Ruprecht, 1989, pp. 136 ff.; also Schama, Simon. *Landscape and Memory*. New York: Alfred A. Knopf, 1996, pp. 92 ff.

[78] Maier, *Atalanta Fugiens*, discourse 36.

[79] Frankfurt am Main, Stadt- und Universitätsbibliothek, MS Ff. J. H. Beyer A. 161, p. 207 *verso*: "Quod si vero ita vivendum mihi foret, uti absque medica praxi (quam in

The German Eagle; that is, the collective body of the great modern Germans, consisting of head and limbs, or leader and subordinates, with ten organs or classes as well as similar institutions; partly ecclesiastical, with Elector Archbishops, Bishops, Masters of the Orders, Prefects and Abbots, and likewise partly secular, with Elector Archdukes, Princes, Counts, Barons, Nobles, free cities and subjects of other dominions, as well as extraordinary members. Together with the particularities of topography and genealogy, and the history of outstanding places, persons, events and memorable deeds; demonstrated, enumerated and collated from widely dispersed sources into one composition, and arranged in twelve chapters, in order that the duty owed to the nation may be discharged.[80]

The theme of the correspondence of society to body, and of both to the universal order, was touched upon by Maier in the *De Circulo Physico, Quadrato*, and was developed at length in the *Civitas Corporis Humani* we will shortly analyse. Strieder correctly deduces that the plan for the *Aquila Germanica* was printed in 1617, on the grounds that the second page displays the copperplate engraving of Maier with the words "Aetatis suae. 49. Ao. 1617" (see figure 1).

Like Maier's *Aquila Germanica*, the Calvinist project in the empire was to remain incomplete, and the dominion of Catholicism and the House of Habsburg prevailed. In August of 1619 Ferdinand of Styria was crowned Emperor in Frankfurt; shortly thereafter the General Diet in Prague deprived him of the crown of Bohemia, and elected Friedrich V in his stead.[81] So began the short reign of the 'Winter King'; for some Lutheran German states wavered in their support for Friedrich's venture, and even James I refused to commit himself to his son-in-law's perilous bid for the imperial throne. At the Battle of the White Mountain near Prague on November the 8th, 1620, it took a Catholic League army sent by Ferdinand less than an hour to defeat

---

commodiori loco potius eligerem) semper aliquid meditandum ac scribendum esset, opus quoddam hic animo concepi (dum absum a meis) in totius Germaniae, tanquam communis Patriae, honorem et multorum commoditatem concinnandum, quod quale sit et ex quibus partibus constare debeat, in pagellis adiunctis, AQUILAM Germanicam referentibus, patebit, de quo ut iudicium, Excellentiae Tuae candidum et maturum, hoc est, consilium auxiliumque, eo promptius experiri possim, ut et alias, occasionem hanc capitandi in dedicando illi Aureum hunc TRIPODEM, hoc est, tres Authores Chymicos, qui nunc sub proelo fervent."

80 Strieder, *Grundlage*, pp. 92-93: "Michaelis Maieri Aquila germanica, hoc est, universum corpus Germaniae Magnae, modernae, constans capite seu imperio, et membris, ordinariis, cum organicis sive X circulis, tum similaribus, partim ecclesiasticis, ut Elect. Archiepiscopis, Episcopis, Ordinum Magistris, Praepositis, Abbatibus, partim Secularibus ut Elect. Archiduc. Ducibus, Principibus, Comitibus, Baronibus, Nobilibus, Civitatibus liberis et aliorum dominio subjectis, nec non Extraordinariis; quo Topographiae, genealogiae, chronologiae seu Historiae praecipuorum locorum, personarum, rerum et factorum memorabilium continentur, demonstrantur et recensentur, ut debitum Patriae talentum solvatur, ex varie dispersis materiis in unam formam sibi debitam collectum et in XII. Sectiones dispositum et concinnatum."

81 Schiller, *Religion, Political Culture and the Emergence of Early Modern Society*, p. 78.

the Bohemian and German Protestant forces led by Prince Christian of Anhalt-Bernburg.[82] At the time Friedrich was residing nearby in his Star Palace (figure 28), an ornate hexagram structure fashioned on Hermetic principles; such was the haste of his retreat that his crown was left behind, and he is reported to have uttered the unhappy words, "I now know who I am."[83] Ferdinand's wrath in Bohemia was severe, and he personally rent the Letter of Majesty asunder and burnt its seal.[84] Thus began the thirty-year cycle of war, famine and pestilence that – in a strange confirmation of the Paracelsian prophecy – would cost the German states one third of their population.

4. The *Civitas Corporis Humani* – procuring a medicine of piety

Life went on for the 51 year-old Maier, albeit under conditions of increasing hardship. As Figala and Neumann note, there is no mention on the title page of Maier's *Civitas Corporis Humani* ('State of the Human Body,' 1621) of his status as 'Medicus und Chymicus von Hauß aus' at the court of Moritz the Learned, a fact which not only strongly suggests that he no longer held this position, but also raises the possibility that his services had been dispensed with for lack of result.[85] Nevertheless, Moritz remained a staunch supporter of Friedrich V after the Battle of the White Mountain; even the dissolution of the Protestant Union in 1621 did not deter him, and in that year a great part of his revenue was devoted to the cause of Count Ernst von Mansfeld and Duke Christian of Braunschweig, who raised two marauding armies of forty thousand ex-Union troops which skirmished and plundered their way through the heart of Germany.[86] With Spanish and Bavarian troops occupying the lands of the Palatinate and pressing hard on the borders of his own land, Moritz may have found little time or money for further patronage of Maier.

Whatever the reasons for his apparent departure from the princely court, it seems that Maier continued to make a living with his private medical practice; the *Civitas Corporis Humani* is a rather more sophisticated version

---

82   *Ibid.*, p. 85.
83   *Ibid.*
84   *Ibid.*, p. 86.
85   Figala and Neumann, "Michael Maier," p. 46.
86   Schiller, *Religion, Political Culture and the Emergence of Early Modern Society*, pp. 97 ff.; Moran, *Alchemical World of the German Court*, pp. 33-35: the reign of Moritz came to an end in 1627, when he abdicated in the face of military defeat, and in face of his own wife's bargaining with Catholic forces for a portion of his remaining land.

of a pharmacy window advertisement, in which Maier presents the sum total of his medical knowledge alongside extravagant promises aimed at those wealthy readers who might employ him. Rather than dedicating this work to a potential princely patron, Maier makes a general dedication to doctors, doctoral candidates, and whosoever may be concerned with the diseases of arthritis and gout – and amongst the latter, as Maier makes clear in his work, are those on whom his livelihood depends, i.e. the sufferers of these diseases.

In the course of his *Civitas Corporis Humani* Maier elaborates further on the correspondences between the princely state, the human body and the divine order mentioned in the *De Circulo Physico, Quadrato*, and he makes explicit the relationship between his own medicine and an ethic of piety. As in the macrocosm the 'citizens' of the universe are the stars, elements, angels and creatures, so in the microcosm of the human body each citizen is represented by the organs and limbs.[87] Together, these form the *civitas corporis humani*. Three states exist in the body politic – monarchy, aristocratic oligarchy and democracy – and although there may be variations of these principle forms, monarchy is clearly the most perfect amongst them.[88] Likewise, in the human body these three states also exist. Again, the most harmonious or temperate state is the monarchy – the rule of the heart, which Maier compares to the prince in the royal court of the thorax. The other members of the corporeal 'aristocracy' – the brain, lungs, liver and other principle organs – pay homage to the heart, as it is the heart that is the source of the body's *calor innatus*, which imparts to the corporeal state life

---

[87] Maier states that Galen observed the elegant order and functions of these 'citizens', even if he opposed the teachings of Moses and Christ; indeed, by his dissection of the human body Galen had made a greater sacrifice than if he had offered up a hundred oxen at the pagan altar, for in so doing he came to know God by His works: "De Mundo minore, seu Civitate humani corporis nostra intentio est dicere, cuius cives, seu viscera et membra, cum Ethnicus ille Galenus (Mosi, Christoque nostro, contrarius alias) per anatomiam rimaretur, eorumque concinnos ordines, officia, et functiones miraretur, in libro De usu partium, se maius DEO sacrificium hac descriptione praestitisse affirmat, quam si Hecatomben, seu centum bovum oblationem, ad aram instituisset: Certe huiuc Philosopho et Medico possibile fuit, DEUM ex operibus suis cognoscere, non qualis in essentia, et quantus secundum immensitatem suam DEUS sit, nec qualiter se in verbo creationis, redemptionis, et sanctificationis patefecit, sed tamen vere et mire secundum quid." Maier, *Civitas Corporis Humani*, pp. 23-24.

[88] *Ibid.*, pp. 33-34: "In tres omnino species Magistratus politicus olim, ut adhuc, divisus, usu ipso rerum magistro, invenitur, nempe in eum, quo unus omnibus praeficitur, sive Rex, sive Princeps, aut in quem Optimates plures consentiunt, aut quando populus ipse imperii habenas penes se habet: Prima species est regnum, vel principatus: Secunda dicitur Aristocratia: Tertia, Democratia. Hae, et non plures, a politicis omnis aevi admissi sunt, licet mixti dominatus ex his, vel etiam degeneres non raro legantur: Nullum est dubium, quin monarchia sit perfectissima Reipublicae forma, in qua potestas summa sit penes unum, sive Regem, sive Principem."

and heat (the equivalent of princely justice in the political state). The consent of the principle organs to the rule of the heart ensures that the common citizens – the limbs and extremities – remain "steadfast in their duty" and maintain their proper function.[89] However, if the heart becomes too powerful, and the other members of the 'aristocracy' such as the reasoning brain are overthrown, tyranny may result. Maier compares this state of affairs to a royal palace, in which love of power and immoderation has grown so strong that rubbish and filth pile up at the palace doors, and the common folk whose work it is to clean up after the monarch become overloaded with their burdens.[90] In the corporeal state such tyranny is brought about by an over-fondness for 'Bacchus and Venus', i.e. by immoderation in drinking, eating and sexual activity.[91]

Such is the source of the 'tyranny' of gout and arthritis,[92] which involves a breakdown of the natural order and may lead to "the utter destruction of the republic."[93] Immoderation produces an excessive downflow of humours from the brain, lungs, liver and stomach, which suffer from a paucity of the 'justice'-imparting *calor innatus*. If the body is not destroyed by a revolutionary 'democracy', it may become a tyrannical oligarchy, in which the impurities produced by an impious lifestyle build up in the pericranium and

---

89 *Ibid.*, pp. 34-35: "Ad Aristocratiam itaque mixtam cum principatu referimus, quemadmodum in Republica Veneta observamus, in qua Magnates dominantur, sed sub Principe limitatae potestatis: Cor, pulmo, thorax, nec non caput, seu cerebrum, cum visceribus aliis principalibus ad salutem corporis humani spectant; verum cordi, ut principi, plurima indulgentur vota, dignitas, et excubiae regales, ut sub eo reliqua omnia vegetabilia firma permaneant, in suis quaeque officiis. Cor fabricatur spiritus vitales in suis thalamis, per systolen et diastolen, hoc est, dilatationem et compressionem pulsuum in arteriis totius corporis sensibilium, eosque defert ad omnes partes, tam remotas, quam propinquas, ut sic illae vita et calore imbuantur, et perfundantur."

90 *Ibid.*, pp. 37-38: "Restant membra, vel viscera evehentia superfluitates et saburras corporis per sua emunctoria, quae, cum plebeia munia obeant, et non semper aequaliter a calore cordis et spiritibus vitalibus illustrentur, hinc fit, ut facile onerentur laboribus, et tardentur in functionibus; unde contingit, ut indies materia in nobilioribus visceribus generata ad haec mittatur: Quemadmodum enim in aula potentissimi Principis, ex singulis conclavibus sordes eiiciuntur foras, et quilibet a suis ostiis onera illa submovent, donec tandem ad loca ab aliis neglecta vel humilia devoluantur; sic quoque fit in humani corporis civitate nonnunquam, dum partes fortiores ad imbecilliores, cordi propinqui-ores, ad remotiores sua excrementa amandant: Quod si imbecilliores possent respondere suis viribus ad se translata, alio quoque mitterent."

91 *Ibid.*, p. 37.

92 Gout is a metabolic disease marked by a painful inflammation of the joints, deposits of urates in and around the joints, and commonly an excessive amount of uric acid in the blood; the term arthritis refers to a number of conditions involving inflammation of the joints due to infectious, metabolic or constitutional causes.

93 Maier, *Civitas Corporis Humani*, p. 38.

three coctions (the three sites of 'cooking' nutrients in the Galenic system, i.e. the stomach, liver and veins[94]) and overwhelm the extremities:

In the body politic the state of the aristocracy we have described degenerates into an oligarchy if the noblest suppress the inferiors and demand all work and little profit... In like manner it happens in the State of the human body that a paucity of innate heat and *spiritus vitalis* are supplied to the hands and feet, since those extremities are very remote from the heart, but nevertheless the superfluities which should be expelled elsewhere are transported to them. This occurs because the hands and feet are positioned in the lower places of the body, to which place the humours flow by their nature, nor do the extremities possess any other ways or indeed parts to which they may send the superfluities further. Hence the tyranny of the oligarchy prevails in the human body, which rages and frenzies most bitterly in the nerves and tendons of the hands or feet, which it lacerates, dislocates and swells like a torturer, and makes those organs useless and maimed.[95]

The deleterious results of decadence in the *civitas corporis humani* demonstrate the close relation of immorality to sickness in Maier's medicine, and the necessity of piety and sensual moderation for the maintenance of good health. If this early modern aetiology of arthritis seems strange to the contemporary reader, then the purgative remedies which Maier proposes might also strike us as being somewhat dangerous. Nevertheless, the *Civitas Corporis Humani* contains the most detailed description of Maier's 'mercurial medicine' and its mode of operation to be found in his works. Two principle remedies are described, the first being a golden powder, and the second a 'fixed yellow Quicksilver' composed of Mercury and Sulphur in equal parts, and apparently very similar in nature to the mercurial medicine Maier produced in Easter of 1604 during his first period of

---

[94] According to Galenic physiology, the first coction in the stomach turns food into chyle, which is transported through the veins of the intestine to the liver. In the liver the second coction transforms the chyle into blood, which issues forth to the various parts of the body. In these parts the third coction takes place, by which the material absorbed from the veins by the flesh is made flesh itself. In the Galenic system the coctions are assisted by the *calor innatus*, being thus analogous to domestic cooking. See Hall, A. Rupert. *The Scientific Revolution, 1500-1800: The Formation of the Modern Scientific Attitude.* Boston: Beacon Press, 1966, p. 133.

[95] Maier, *Civitas Corporis Humani*, pp. 38-39: "In Politia est status Aristocraticus ante relatus, qui in Oligarchicum degenerat, si Optimates supprimant inferiores, illisque omnia onera et perpauca commoda demandent... Similiter contingit in Civitate humani corporis, quod paucitas caloris nativi et spirituum vitalium manibus et pedibus suppeditetur, cum sint a corde eae extremae partes valde remotae, et nihilominus superfluitates pleraeque totius, quae evehi aliunde deberent, iis transmittantur; quod eo facilius contingit, quia in inferiori corporis situ collocatae sint, quorsum humores sua natura defluunt, nec habeant alias partes, aut vias, ad quas ipsae ulterius amandent: Hinc Tyrannis oligarchica in homine tum exoritur, quae saevit et furit acerbissime in nervos et tendones manuum aut pedum, eosque instar carnificum lacerat, extendit, luxat, et ad omnem usum motionis organa illa inutilia et manca reddit."

alchemical experimentation. This 'Quicksilver' is also imbued with solar or astral virtues, and the stages of the process used to obtain it again follow the traditional medieval sequence:

I have received the brightest mineral produced by Nature, which resembles ice, the most pure substance devoid of any heterogeneity, and if we may establish its physical anatomy, it will be discerned that it is composed of Mercury and Sulphur. That Mercury contains some grains of silver, and if it is bound together with the correct quantity of silver itself, will then secrete some grains of gold. This mineral is therefore the grandmother of gold, as it were, and the mother of natural silver, or rather it is sticky water impregnated with sulphur, which takes into itself the embryos of gold and silver. It is liquefied in a strong fire, and it is the ray of a higher sphere: it is pounded into the blackest powder, and it becomes somewhat white as it is heated by a slow fire in an earthen vessel, and it is made in nine months – not less – and at length by the tenth month it matures into a fixed yellow Quicksilver.[96]

This passage gives clear expression to the medieval alchemical conception of a cure for 'sick' metals and humans alike, and the notion of embryonic forms of silver and gold created through the 'impregnation' of Mercury with Sulphur, understood by Maier as the infusion of 'female' matter with 'male' form.[97] Hence the preparation period of nine months, after which "you will possess the yellow Mercurial substance, twofold by nature, both fixed and volatile, masculine and feminine, which is our said Medicine."[98] Maier also describes his golden powder as a 'mercurial medicine', and like the 'fixed yellow Quicksilver' it is also a strong purgative. As it is very potent, only three to six grains are to be well mixed with aniseed water, cinnamon water or *aqua vitae* (wine spirit), and are to be drunk before the grains subside to the bottom of the cup. This *aurum potabile* should be administered "when paroxysm is impending," but not when the patient is already vomiting. The draught should be washed down with one or two spoons of the same liquid medium, "so that nothing should be felt to have stuck in the mouth, throat or oesophagus, but the complete dose has descended into the stomach with the liquid." During treatment the patient should remain in bed, but avoid sleep or

---

[96] *Ibid.*, p. 67: "Accepi mineram a natura productam clarissimam, instar glaciei, absque ullis heterogeneis purissimam, cuius si anatomiam physicam instituamus, composita animadvertetur ex Mercurio et sulphure: Mercurius ille continet in se argenti aliquot grana, et ipsum argentum, si colligatur ad iustam quantitatem, aliquot auri grana iterum abscondit: Est itaque illa minera tanquam avia auri, et mater argenti naturalis, imo est aqua viscosa impraegnata a sulphure, donec hos conceperit embryones: Liquescit in igne valido, estque radius superioris sphaerae: In pulverem nigerrimum tunditur, et igne lento in vasis terreis tenetur, donec subalbescat, idque fit nono fere mense, non prius, ac tandem decimo mense maturatur in argentum vivum fixum subflavum."

[97] Maier, *Septimana Philosophica*, p. 74; see n. 25 above.

[98] Maier, *Civitas Corporis Humani*, p. 68: "...habebis Mercurialem substantiam citrinam, duplicem, fixam et volatilem, masculam et foemineam, quae est nostra dicta Medicina."

ingesting other fluids or solids.[99] The effects of the remedy on the patient are described in some detail:

The operation is usually accomplished in this manner: as soon as this little powder reaches the bottom of the stomach, it begins to attract the humours, at first from neighbouring parts, then from more remote parts; when an abundant amount has been attracted, a portion ascends through the oesophagus into the mouth, and fills it with sputum, which is continuously spat into a basin. But in fact the greater part of the same humour remains in the stomach, which it aggravates while it remains in abundance; there may be nausea, belching, and - by and by - light vomiting. Which as often and as frequently as it returns, then so often and of so great a magnitude the work will have been.[100]

In accordance with Galenic method, then, this 'work' is effected by a poison; and whilst we may discount Heisler's strange depiction of Maier as a poisoner-assassin embroiled in aristocratic intrigue at the court of James I,[101] it is an open question as to whether any of Maier's patients died of their 'cure' before he determined the non-fatal dose of his remedies. In the *Civitas Corporis Humani* Maier advises those patients who "do not greatly fear the use of this powder" to obtain a prescription from their local apothecary; and failing this, "a quantity pleasing for the price" may be received directly from the author.[102] Furthermore, we are told that arthritis is not the only ailment that this mercurial medicine is indicated for; Maier claims that his Quicksilver will cure *'quasi in una hora'* a host of diseases caused by the

---

[99] *Ibid.*, p. 53: "Volumus autem, ut grana iij. iiij. ad vj. usque, eius pulveris sumantur eo tempore, quando paroxysmus instat, nec dum iam incursionem fecerit, (quamuis in ipso paroxysmo et urgentibus doloribus idem optime revellendo et evacuando conveniat,) in aqua stillatitia qualitatis calidae; utpote aqua cinamoni, anisi, vitae spiritu vini, aut simili, cum cochleari, pulvisculo bene mixto, et per liquorem diffuso, ut, antequam subsideat, ebibatur, et post unum aut alterum cochlear eiusdem liquoris superbibatur, donec nihil in ore, vel faucibus, aut oesophago haesisse sentiatur, sed tota dosis cum liquore in ventriculum descendat: Teneat patiens se in lecto calide, et ab assumptione a somno, et aliarum rerum ingestione abstineat."

[100] *Ibid.*, p. 54: "Operatio hoc modo plaerumque perficitur: Quamprimum hic pulvisculus fundum stomachi attigerit, incipit attrahere humores primo viciniores, deinde remotiores in ventriculum; quorum copia cum adfuerit attracta, pars ascendit per oesophagum in os, et replet illud sputo, quod continue in pelvim expuendum est; maior vero pars eiusdem humoris manet in ventriculo, quem dum sua copia aggravat, sit nausea, ructus, et mox levis vomitio; quae toties redit, et in tanta frequentia, quoties et quanta opus fuerit."

[101] Heisler, Ron. "Michael Maier in England," in *The Hermetic Journal*, 1989.

[102] Maier, *Civitas Corporis Humani*, pp. 68-69: "Pulvis Aurelius ubi haberi possit? Si vero non cuiusvis sit Medici, aut patientis, tantum temporis, laboris, aut sumptus, huic operi impendere, et interim quis eius pulveris usum ad eradicationem tanti mali non reformidet, sed maxime desideret, is saltem proximum sibi pharmacopoeum moneat, ut ad praescriptam formam dictam medicinam praeparet, vel, si neque id tuto aut commode fieri possit, ut a nobis quantitatem placitam pro suo pretio accipiat, inque usus aliorum iterum divendat."

excessive downflow of humours, from fever, 'hypochondriac melancholy' and kidney stones to obstructions of the spleen, liver, gall bladder, mammary glands, urethra and uterus – and all for the price of "an easily tolerated sickness."[103]

There is a note of desperation, and a strong suggestion of charlatanism, in Maier's use of such exorbitant claims. His tone in the *Civitas Corporis Humani* is far removed from the elegant natural philosophical speculations of the *Septimana Philosophica* or the *De Circulo Physico, Quadrato*. Had Maier fallen upon hard times following the loss of his position at the court of Moritz? Such is confirmed not only by the assertion of the eighteenth century *Biographie Universelle* that Maier "sacrificed his time, his fortune and his reputation to a vain research"[104] – a statement that reflects the standard eighteenth century view of alchemy – but also by his posthumously published ethical tract *Ulysses* (1624), which appeared two years after his death with the melancholy subtitle, "Wisdom or intelligence, as a spark of heavenly joy, by which if one might be shipwrecked in fortune and health, one may happily make one's way to port with the oars of meditation and patience."[105] Indeed, the contents of Maier's *Ulysses* – no less than its posthumous appearance – give rise to the suspicion that Maier had been 'shipwrecked' in health, and that this tract was composed during a time of terminal illness.

5. Ulysses and the death of Maier

Maier's *Ulysses* was published with a foreword from his publisher, Lucas Jennis, announcing the death of 'the master' in Magdeburg:

Recently, friendly reader, I received a number of letters from learned men in various locations addressed to Master Doctor Maier, P. M., whom these men were imagining to be alive: on which account I could not tarry, but felt I must announce positively to one and all that the master himself, namely my friend and honoured patron, died in Magdeburg in the summer of 1622, the debt of Nature having been dutifully paid. When therefore I received

---

103 *Ibid.*, p. 69: "Quibus alias conveniat. Nec vero hoc remedium tantum arthriticis convenit, sed aeque omnibus ex humorum colluvie quacunque laboratibus auxiliatur, quasi in una hora omnem labem morbificam copiosissime cum aegri facili tolerantia educendo, ut sunt febres tertianae, quartanae, quotidianae, melancholia hypochondriaca, calculus, obstructio viscerum, lienis, epatis, vesiculae fellis, meseraicarum, emulgentium, ureterum, uteri, et in summa omnium humorum excessus, et ex his morbi, aut symptomata."

104 *Biographie Universelle*, Vol. 36, p. 232.

105 Maier, *Ulysses*, title page: "Sapientia seu intelligentia, tanquam coelestis scintilla beatitudinis, quod si in fortunae et corporis bonis naufragium faciat, ad portum meditationis et patientiae remigio feliciter se expediat."

the present little tract named *Ulysses* from that same man who was hitherto living, I was unwilling to submit it for publication on account of its humble size. Nevertheless, as I have said, when several of the most learned men took care that their letters to the deceased Dr. Maier be delivered to me (having expected that they would be passed on to him because I had printed the greater part of their works), I felt it would be worth the labour if, for the better information of everyone, and by issuing this little work itself, I might arrange [for Dr. Maier] a public departure from this miserable life to death. In doing so I fulfilled the task of a mother carrying out the last duties for her dead son. Granting, as I have said, this little work may be too slender in respect of pages, nevertheless with regard to its substance it is quite big enough, and worthy of being read...[106]

It seems from these solemn words that Maier died in 1622 between the date of the dedication of his *Cantilenae Intellectuales*, the 25th of August, and summer's end in the calendar, the 22nd of September. The cause of his death is not made clear by Jennis; nevertheless, his wording suggests sickness carried Maier away rather than accident or foul play. Chronic chemical poisoning was not uncommon for alchemists in the seventeenth century; thus the prolific author Glauber died of mercury poisoning, whilst Hermann Wolf (1562-1620), employed by Moritz of Hessen-Kassel as a physician and 'taster', fell seriously ill in 1619 after sampling a leaden *clyssi ex Saturni* for his prince, was 'revived' by an *aurum potabile Angelicanum*, but expired some months later after ingesting Moritz' very own 'lunar essence'.[107] Whether or not long-term exposure to 'Saturnus', mercury, antimony and other toxic substances explains Maier's untimely demise, there is certainly no justification for Åkerman's assertion that Maier "disappeared during the violent siege of Magdeburg by Imperial troops in 1622," as the city's declared neutrality was still holding in that year, and she was not put under

---

[106] *Ibid.*, p. 3-4: "Postquam, amice Lector, hactenus diversis ex locis aliquot Doctorum virorum, ad Dominum Doctorem Majerum, p.m. (quem in vivis adhuc esse certo sibi persuadebant) spectantes litterae ad me pervenissent: ea propter intermittere non potui, quin, illum ipsum Dominum Doctorem videlicet, Amicum et Favitorem meum honorandum, ANNI M.DC.XXII. tempore aestivo, Magdeburgi naturae debitum pie persolvisse, omnes et singulos certiores redderem. Cum igitur, ipso adhuc vivente, praesens opusculum, Ulyssis nomine inscriptum, ab eodem acceperim, illudque, ob parvitatem suam, praelo subijcere noluerim: nihilominus tamen cum, uti dictum, aliquot viri doctissimi literas suas, ad D. Majerum exaratas, ad me (ut pote qui, non abs re quidem, credebant, illas ipsas suas literas me hero suo certo transmissurum esse, idque eo magis, quod suorum operum majorem ad partem sumptibus meis imprimi operam dedissem) perferri curassent: operae pretium me facturum putavi, si, ad meliorem omnium informationem, publicatione huius sui opusculi mortalem ipsius ex misera hacce vita egressum testatum facerem. Qua sane in re matris alicuius, posthumum aliquem excludentis officio functus sum. Licet vero, uti dictum, opusculum illud papyri paucitate nimis tenue et parvum sit: nihilominus tamen respectu materiae satis magnum, lectuque dignum est..."

[107] Szydlo, Zbigniew. *Water which does not Wet Hands*. Warsaw: Polish Academy of Sciences, 1994, pp. 15-16; Moran, *Alchemical World of the German Court*, pp. 69-70.

siege or sacked until 1631.[108] The suggestion that Maier may have been executed by his enemies is only one amongst a number of myths that have grown up around his death. Despite the testimony of Jennis – or perhaps because of it, as he makes mention of Maier's purported 'admittance' into the ranks of the Rosicrucian Fraternity shortly before his death – the notion has recently arisen in esoteric circles that Maier did not die at Magdeburg at all, but changed his identity and continued his work under another name.[109] Whilst not disprovable, one cannot fail to note that similar myths have adhered to numerous personages in history, and are likely to reflect a religious impulse in their creators. Furthermore, the *Cantilenae Intellectuales* are dedicated to Duke Friedrich III of Schleswig-Holstein-Gottorf, the son of Carnarius' patron Duke Johann Adolf, and grandson of the patron of Peter Maier, King Friedrich II of Denmark. In that dedication Maier flatters the Duke for his "singular love of letters and those who cultivate them," and recalls the past generosity shown by the Duke's family to his own; he also states that he is hoping to return to his native Holstein with the help of the Duke's patronage, thus bringing to an end the fourteen years he has 'endured' in foreign lands "perfecting his Hermetic studies."[110] These are not the words of someone who had decided "the time was ripe to disappear for political and philosophical reasons," as de Rola has it.[111] Rather, they speak of a dying man's desire to see his homeland.

Alas, unlike the wandering Ulysses, the ailing Maier was not to make a heroic return to his native land after years of travelling. Given its clear parallels with Maier's own life of wandering and hardship, *Ulysses* may be understood in an autobiographical sense, and its subject – the Greek hero

---

[108] Wolter, F. A. *Geschichte der Stadt Magdeburg von ihrem Ursprung bis auf die Gegenwart*. Magdeburg: Faber, 1901, p. 149; Åkerman, *Rose Cross over the Baltic*, p. 91. Åkerman's statement echoes Yates' suggestive and misleading comment that Maier "disappeared at Magdeburg in 1622 when that city was in the hands of the troops;" Yates, *The Rosicrucian Enlightenment*, p. 81.

[109] This tradition seems to stem from Stanislas Klossowski de Rola, who writes: "Some biographers believe that Maier died at Magdeburg in 1622, but I do not. I believe that Maier felt the time was ripe to disappear for political and philosophical reasons, and this may well be why his last treatise (1624) was given out as posthumous." The idea of 'disappearing' may also stem from Yates; to be fair to de Rola, he rightly admits that this is "an unsubstantiated feeling." See de Rola, *The Golden Game*, p. 106.

[110] Maier, *Cantilenae Intellectuales*, pp. A4-A5: "Mei, quia Holsatus sim patria, quam ob studia Hermetica penitus absolvenda et apud exteros in diversis regionibus et populis exantlanda, ante 14. annos reliqui lubens et volens, non, ut spes est, in perpetuum, sed ad tempus, prout Deo et principi meo placuerit, aliquando reversurus: Meos autem, qui qualesque fuerint, non solum tota Nobilitas Holsata, sed et parens tuus, avusque Divae memoriae, quibus illi, quoad vixerunt, servitio fidelissimo astricti fuerunt, optime noverunt."

[111] De Rola, *The Golden Game*, p. 106.

Odysseus, or Roman Ulysses – reflects the ideals and self-perception of a man who is nearing the end of a long journey. Following the method of his *Arcana Arcanissima*, Maier portrays the figure of Ulysses as a hieroglyph, behind which lies veiled a higher truth – wisdom in the face of suffering. This wisdom takes the form of a paradox, as ill fortune and poor health may be transformed through the power of the intellect:

Nobody is happy, I believe, unless they are wise, and nobody unhappy or foolish, unless they do not skilfully use the intellect; for while good and evil things depend on fortune, they do not define a man or determine the boundary of happiness and unhappiness, since bad may be transformed into good for a man, and good into bad. I am willing to say the same concerning favourable or odious circumstances of the body, because they do not truly deliver happiness or sadness to a man. It is that better part of man, the mind, which determines whether he is happy or not; and even if this opinion seems at first sight to reveal a rather strong Stoic attitude, it does not contradict the truth of the Academic philosophy,[112] but rather approaches it very closely. And if this may be held to be the paradox of paradoxes, I take care to put it in a way that it might not be unpleasant – unless I am mistaken – to delicate ears.[113]

For all their reification of the intellect, these introductory words appear to be spoken from experience; and on account of his constancy in the face of hardship – be it shipwreck, battles with fabulous beasts, or seduction by the sirens – Ulysses is accounted "the symbol of absolute (human) wisdom, which exceeds all other mortals, and exalts itself in the ethereal realm, never crawling on the earth or seeking bestial practices, but sublime, truly intellectual and peculiar to man."[114] According to Maier the wisdom encapsulated in the figure of Ulysses has been 'imprinted' by God in the minds of a select few, and is not visible with the corporeal eye – by which he means to say that it may be discovered with 'the little eye of the soul' we

---

[112] Here Maier seems to allude to the Platonic Academy of ancient Greece, and to the fact that the Good of Platonic idealism is an absolute which cannot become its opposite; in another place he criticises the Stoics for arguing that God is subject to Fate and not entirely free; see Maier, *Themis Aurea*, p. 180.

[113] Maier, *Ulysses*, pp. 11-12: "Nemo est, me judice, beatus, nisi sapiens, et nemo infelix, nisi intellectu dextre non utens, aut insipiens: Nam quae bona et mala a fortuna dependent, hominem non definiunt aut ad finem beatitudinis aut infelicitatis non dirigunt, cum illa mala in bonum, et bona in malum virum transferri possint: Eadem de corporis accidentibus favorabilibus, aut odiosis dicta velim; quod nec illa vere felicem, haec miserum reddant hominem: In potiore hominis parte, mente, situm esse debet, a quo denominatio ejus beati vel contra petenda sit: Quae mea sententia liceat stoam duriorem primo aspectu praese ferat, veritati tamen Academicae neutiquam adversatur, sed proxime ad eam accedit: Hoc etsi paradoxon paradoxotaton haberi possit, tamen faxo, ut teneris etiam auribus non ingratum, nisi fallor, accidat."

[114] *Ibid.*, p. 30: "Ulysses itaque est sapientiae absolutae (humanae) symbolum, quae omnes alios supergreditur mortales, seque in aethereas exaltat domos, nunquam humi repens aut bestialia exercitia quaerens, sed sublimia, vere intellectualia et homini propria."

have discussed.[115] In accordance with Maier's Lutheran sensibilities, this wisdom is the foundation of morality, imparting both strength and piety to humankind, lest it falls into the immoderation of vice.[116]

In the figure of Ulysses Maier sees those aspects of a man's character he most admires; thus we are told that Ulysses was the most astute of men, the most eloquent, the most prudent, the most ingenious, the most distinguished in war, the most expedite in counsel, and the most patient in the face of toil and danger. In the course of the *Ulysses* he elaborates upon each of these seven characteristics with reference to various episodes in the hero's journey. In the manner of the *Arcana Arcanissima* Maier undertakes a curious rationalisation of the myth, for just as Ulysses represents the intellect, the divine faculty in humanity, so the men of his company are understood to be the faculties of vision, hearing, tasting, smelling, touching, imagination, memory and 'common sense' – that is to say, the sense in the Aristotelian schema binding the other senses together to give a common, unitary impression. Maier illustrates the relation of this schema to his medicine of piety through Ulysses' encounter on the island Aeaea with the sorceress Circe, who turns Ulysses' men into pigs with her magic wand. Although these men, as representatives of the base senses, are easily led into a 'bestial' existence, Ulysses as the intellect is rendered immune to Circe's sorcery by Hermes, who gives the hero the magical herb Moly – in Maier's eyes, a cipher for the Universal Medicine:

Ulysses protected himself with the herb Moly, lest he should be transformed by Circe into wild animals with his men. The men, as I have said, are the senses... and they are all defeated by the sorceress Circe, or the abyss of wickedness, and transformed into beasts. Ulysses alone, the intellect, being the exception, who used the most extraordinary amulet[117] to avert the sorcery. Here one might ask what this Moly, a white flower with black roots, might be? Without doubt it is a bittersweet virtue that must be searched for by the intellect and perfected by the will; it possesses a black and bitter root, but a sweet and lovely little white flower: through baseness to majesty, through toil to glory, through courage to immortal fame, it is striven for and it is reached. The same thing concerning Moly and its virtue is asserted by Gratian the Philosopher in the *Rosarium Philosophorum*: "and there is in our Art a certain noble body, which is moved from master to master, in the beginning of which will be misery with vinegar, but in the end gladness with joy." This herb arrives from a black root to a little white flower, from darkness to radiance, from immaturity to perfection; likewise the same [noble] body we

---

[115] *Ibid.*, pp. 30-31: "Haec est idaea paucorum mentibus impressa, quae si oculis corporeis conspici posset, miros sui amores apud quam plurimos relinqueret."

[116] *Ibid.*, p. 31: "Sapientia est, quae hominem exornat moribus, ditat opibus et temperat virtutibus, ne in extremitates vitiorum immoderatas irruat."

[117] Pliny makes mention of a *veneficiorum amuleta*, hung around the neck as a preservative against sickness.

have just mentioned tends from misery to pleasure, from vinegar to joy, like the completion of a comedy.[118]

Naturally Maier does not mention the fact that, in Homer's tale, Ulysses proceeds to the bed of Circe once she releases his men from the bondage of their swinish forms. Nevertheless, Maier's purpose here is to demonstrate the integral relation of piety to his alchemy, and its relation to the *coniunctio oppositorum*. The 'noble body' mentioned in the *Rosarium Philosophorum* is not only manifested in the preparation of the cathartic iatrochemical cure and its operation, but in a life of travelling and hardship, by which the corporeal realm is superseded and we approach divinity. On both cosmic levels the Philosophers' Stone stands in a paradoxical relationship with its opposite, "the abyss of wickedness," for as in the black phase of the alchemical process, so in the seductions and anguish of the body new life and wisdom are found.

Even if Maier found wisdom in the Great Work that was his life, it would be tempting to conclude that he did not find it in the laboratory, although he stubbornly persisted with his methods to the end. For Maier the figure of the ideal alchemist was to be found in Ulysses, as both are steadfast and courageous, "pushing on through the many waves of error to the haven of truth."[119] This is not the way of the "purely speculative philosopher," who regardless of the merits of his reasoning achieves nothing more than the formation of an abstract idea; rather, the ideal alchemist is "a practical physical philosopher, who is compelled to prove by the work itself that which

---

[118] *Ibid.*, pp. 21-22: "Sexto, idem se molii herba munit, ne in bestias cum sociis a Circe transformetur: socii, ut diximus, ipsius intellectus sunt sensus tam externi, visus auditus, gustatus, odoratus, tactaus, quam interni, communis, phantasia et memoria: Hi omnes a venefica Circe, seu vitiorum voragine superantur, in bestias mutantur, solo intellectu, Ulysse, excepto, qui amuleto prestantissimo ad veneficium avertendum usus est: Quid moly sit, flos albus cum radice nigra, hic quaeri posset? Certe est amara dulcis virtus tam intellectu investiganda, quam voluntate perficienda: Nigram habet radicem et amaram, sed flosculum album, amabilem et dulcem: Per angusta n. ad augusta, per laborem ad gloriam, per virtutem ad immortale nomen tenditur et pervenitur: De Moly que dicitur, et virtute, idem in Rosario Philosophorum a Gratiano Philosopho asseritur, nempe que sit in arte quoddam corpus nobile, que movetur de domino ad dominum, in cujus principio erit miseria cum aceto, sed in fine gaudium cum laetitia: Herba ea a radice nigra ad flosculum album, a tenebris ad candorem, ab immaturitate ad perfectionem pervenit; Eodem modo et iam dictum corpus a miseria ad gaudium, ab aceto ad laetitiam, quasi comoedia peracta, tendit."

[119] *Ibid.*, pp. 28-29: "Est enim Herois constantis, animosi et patientis praeclarum exemplar, quod poeta in Ulysse exprimere voluit: At nos meminimus, quod in Hieroglyph. libr. 6. ad philosophum retulerimus, qui per multos errorum fluctus ad veritatis portum contendat."

is speculated."[120] It seems that Maier attempts to rationalise his own failures when he describes this 'practical physical philosopher'. Thus he argues that nothing certain has been established when "the most learned doctor" strays from the mark in his diagnosis, and is not immediately able to remove an illness with his remedies, whilst "empiricists, charlatans and little old women" manage to heal difficult cases with mere audacity and persuasion, with a false theoretical basis, and without insight into the true causes of disease. There is a science (i.e. *chemia*) beyond the extremes of unlearned empiricism and Scholastic medicine, in which the practitioner is able to systematically learn from his errors – a science which is nevertheless open only to the most learned of the learned.[121] These words mark something of a departure from the exorbitant claims of the *Civitas Corporis Humani* and its promise of a cure, *quasi in una hora*, for diverse and serious diseases. Indeed, they are more reminiscent of the testimony of 'Bacsen' (the Arabic alchemist Baqsam) given in the *Turba Philosophorum*, and quoted in the thirty-ninth discourse of *Atalanta Fugiens*. After stating that the "seeker after the Art" needs a patient soul and persevering courage, Baqsam issues the following stern warning:

Woe unto you who seek the very great reward and treasure of God! Do you not know that for the smallest purpose in the world, earthly men will give themselves to death, and what, therefore, ought they to do for this most excellent and almost impossible offering? ...Woe unto you, sons of the Doctrine! For one who plants trees does not look for fruit, save in due season; he also who sows seeds does not expect to reap, except at harvest time... Learn O ye students, that which the Philosophers have long since intimated, saying that truth is not discerned but by error, and that nothing begets more grief to the heart than error in this work; for when a man thinks he has done and has the world, he shall find nothing in his hands.[122]

Strangely, it seems that *this* was the wisdom Maier found in his laboratory. In his discourse on this passage in the *Atalanta Fugiens*, Maier states that the

---

[120] *Ibid.*, p. 29: "Non intelligo philosophum mere speculativum, qui sive bene, sive male ratiocinatus sit, eundem effectum relinquit, nempe scientiam vel opinionem in mente, sed philosophum physicum practicum, qui opere ipso quod speculatus est, comprobare cogitur."

[121] *Ibid.*: "Verum cum in re medica saepe usu veniat, doctissimum medicum, causas rerum optime perscrutantem, a scopo aberrare, ut morbum suis remediis non statim tollat, et econtra indoctissimum quoque, Empyricum, agyrtam vel aniculam absque ulla causarum consideratione, ex falso fundamento, ex mera audacia, et persuasione non raro morbos desperatos medicis curare, hinc nihil certi hic statuendum arbitror: Est praeter medicinam alia scientia mere intellectualis, quae opus palpabile post se relinquit, nullis Empyricis, falsariis aut indoctis possibile vel imitabile, sed solis doctiorum doctissimis, in opere constantissimis, et errores suos emendare non detrectantibus."

[122] Waite, Arthur Edward. *The Turba Philosophorum, or the Assembly of Sages*. New York: Samuel Weiser, 1973, pp. 128-129; the final sentence here is taken from Maier, *The Flying Atalanta*, discourse 39.

same truth lies hidden behind the hieroglyph of the Sphinx, for those who fail to solve its riddles are destroyed – a fate he understands allegorically as the 'grief' occasioned by failure in the enigmatic alchemical Art.[123] In this complex of ideas we may discern the integral relation of Maier's laboratory practice to the *magnum opus* that was his life; for it was precisely his quest for the Universal Medicine and his endless struggle to find patronage which constituted the black phase of the work, an impossible task from which the final release could only be death. Thus in the *Atalanta Fugiens* Maier clearly states that "there is nothing that can restore youth to man but death itself, which is the beginning of eternal life that follows it."[124] This is the circular and paradoxical nature of Maier's spiritual alchemy, which like the *ouroboros* devours and emerges out of itself (figure 6).

6. The phoenix and the return of the long-absent traveller

In concluding our consideration of Maier's life and its relationship to his alchemy, we may turn again to his *Allegoria Bella*, in which the correspondence of laboratory process to his own personal odyssey through the world finds its clearest expression. This allegory forms part of the concluding chapter of the *Symbola Aureae Mensae* (1617); in accordance with his role as 'cook' for the banquet held in honour of 'Queen Chemia', the *Allegoria Bella* is offered up by Maier as the *bellaria* or 'dessert', i.e. a summation of the combined wisdom of the sages gathered around the Golden Table.[125] Although strictly speaking it is not an autonomous text, the *Allegoria Bella* counts amongst the most attractive and intriguing works of Maier, a fact which no doubt earned its separate publication in the *Musaeum Hermeticum* of 1678 and 1749 as *A Subtle Allegory concerning the Secrets of Alchemy*.[126]

Inspiration for Maier's allegory was undoubtedly drawn from the quintessential expression of early Rosicrucianism, Johann Valentin Andreae's *Chymische Hochzeit Christiani Rosenkreutz*, which appeared a year prior to

---

[123] Maier, *Atalanta Fugiens*, discourse 39: "...quod si aliquis monstrum praetereat, nil mali ab ipso patitur, qui vero animi vel ingenii audacia fretus ejus aenigmata dissolvere conetur, nisi id faciat, excidium sibi parat, hoc est, dolorem cordi et damnum rebus suis ex errore in hoc opere."

[124] *Ibid.*, discourse 9: "Hominem, quod rejuvenescere faciat, nihil est, nisi mors ipsa et sequentis aeternae vitae initium."

[125] The work's full title runs as follows: "Mensae Secundae seu Bellaria, Hoc est, Allegoria Bella, Vice recapitulationis aut conclusionis summariae totius operis posita, plurimum et perspicuae utilitatis et iucundae meditationis lectoris menti exhibens."

[126] See above, chapter I, n. 131.

the *Symbola Aureae Mensae*. That work describes the journey of Christian Rosenkreutz, the legendary founder of the Brotherhood of the Rosy Cross, who sets out to attend a mysterious royal wedding. His seven-day journey symbolises seven stages of the alchemical work, whilst the wedding itself denotes the perfection of the opus through the union of Mercury and Sulphur.[127] As we have mentioned, Maier's *Allegoria Bella* is constructed in a very similar fashion, portraying the alchemical process as the author's pilgrimage through four continents in search of the phoenix, the feathers of which constitute a cure for "anger and grief." However, given Maier's own unsettled life of roaming it is clear that this allegorical pilgrimage was not composed merely as a didactic analogy for the laboratory work; Maier tells us at the outset that he himself was "destined to imitate the natural progression of elements," which tend from density to subtlety – that is to say, the pattern of elemental transmutation described in Aristotle's *De Generatione et Corruptione* to which we have referred.[128] Thus he begins his quest in Europe (earth), travels through America (water) to Asia (air) and finally arrives in the deserts of Africa (fire) – for "air may not come from earth except by the mediation of water, and fire may not come from water except by the mediation of air."[129] Whilst Andreae's *Chymische Hochzeit* is replete with an intensely surreal imagery, Maier's allegory is permeated with a veritable cornucopia of bizarre facts drawn from history, astronomy, botany and zoology, each of which possesses a microcosmic or macrocosmic correspondence to laboratory process.

Maier begins his allegory with an explanation of the origins of his quest for the phoenix. Having spent the greater part of his life in the study of refined literature and the liberal arts, and having conversed with men of greater wisdom than the common folk, his contemplation of the masses had led him to the conclusion that they prefer ostentation, carnality and lust to

---

[127] In his *Elucidarius Major* (1617) Maier's contemporary Radtichs Brotofferr (Christoffer Rotbard 'the Exile') describes the *Chymische Hochzeit* as a 'very artful description' of the preparation of the Philosophers' Stone, and enumerates the seven stages of the alchemical process corresponding to the seven days of Christian Rosenkreutz' journey as distillation, solution, putrefaction, multiplication, fermentation, projection and 'the Medicine'. 'Rotbard' also gives a chemical explanation of the Rosicrucian manifestos in this work and the earlier *Elucidarius Chymicus*. Goßlar: Johann Vogt, 1616.

[128] See below, chapter VI, n. 3; in constructing this schema (see above, chapter II, n. 61) Aristotle elaborated upon similar theories proposed by the pre-Socratics. Thus, according to Heraclitus (535-475 BCE), the world is resolved out of fire (the *prima materia*) into water and then into earth ('the way downwards'), and then returns again from earth through water to fire ('the way upwards'). See Barnes, Jonathan. *Early Greek Philosophy*. Harmondsworth: Penguin Books, 1987, p. 107.

[129] Maier, *Symbola Aureae Mensae*, p. 572: "Ex terra autem non fit aer, nisi intermedio aquae, et ex aqua non fit ignis, nisi intermedio aeris."

honour, and esteem piety and virtue less than the pursuit of material wealth. When he discovered this melancholy truth, Maier tells us he was not sure whether he should follow the 'laughing Democritus'[130] or the 'weeping Heraclitus',[131] or indeed simply follow Solomon in declaring, "Vanity of vanities, all is vanity!"[132]

Nevertheless, upon reading the Bible he was inspired to investigate "the most useful things hidden in Nature and man," be that "at home in books bequeathed by others, which lead the way for meditation and experience, or to go out of the house and range through that great book of the world."[133] Although Maier's autobiographical testimony in the *De Medicina Regia* points to the medieval alchemists as the inspiration for his quest to uncover the structure of the cosmos and the Universal Medicine, his allusion here is to the harmony of the two great works of God – the Bible and the Book of Nature. This harmony is expressed in the *Allegoria Bella* in the figure of the phoenix, by which both Christ and the Universal Medicine are signified. The phoenix had constituted a symbol for Christ since the time of the *Physiologus*, an allegorical bestiary produced by Alexandrian Christians around the fourth century CE, and this significance would have been clear to many of Maier's Christian readers.[134] In Maier's eyes Jesus Christ was the

---

[130] Democritus (born c.460 BCE), founder of atomic theory and the Epicurean school of thought, was said to have laughed constantly; imagining him to be crazy, the local people called upon the great physician Hippocrates to tend to him, whereupon Democritus confessed that he was laughing at their foolishness.

[131] Heraclitus, despiser of democracy and the lower classes, was known as the 'weeping philosopher', in part for his theory of perpetual flux and his belief that 'war is the father of all things'.

[132] Maier, *Symbola Aureae Mensae*, pp. 561-562: "Cum iam potiorem vitae meae partem in literarum humaniorum, artiumque liberalium studiis, ac cum doctioribus quibuscunque, qui sapere quid prae vulgo viderentur, conversationibus transegissem, ita ut quid firmioris iudicii partim assidua lectione, partim ipso rerum usu acquisiuisse mihi viderer, cepi mecum considerare acutius varias hominum actiones, plaerumque vel ad pompam et libidinem aliis praedominandi et in honoribus anteferri, aut gulam et luxuriem corporis promovendam, aliaue eiusmodi enormia vitia spectantes, et quod plaerique per fas et nefas solis fere diuitiis cumulandis, omni conscientiae respectu, pietatis aut virtutis zelo posthabito, praeoccupati essent; Unde diu anceps et incertus haesitavi, an Democritico cachinno, an Heracletio fletui eandem ob causam subscriberem, an vero cum Ecclesiastico, Omnia vanitates vanitatum pronunciarem..." See *Ecclesiastes* 1.2.

[133] *Ibid.*, p. 562: "...Verum pensiculatis singulis tandem ad me reversus, post Dei Opti. Max. agnitionem, ex Fontibus Israelis seu sacris Bibliis haustam, nihil melius, prius aut antiquius inveni, quam rerum abditarum in natura existentium, hominique maxime utilium, investigationem, qualicunque modo institutam, sive domi per libros ab aliis relictos, meditatione praevia et experientia manuali pedisse qua, sive foris magnum illum Mundi codicem pervoluendo."

[134] *Physiologus*. Trans. Michael J. Curley. Austin: University of Texas Press, 1979, pp. 13-14; the phoenix-Christ analogy is also used by certain Church Fathers, such as Clement

greatest of physicians, and the agent of transmuting the hearts and minds of men, turning them from lives of sin to piety.[135] In his reference to the Bible, therefore, we may discern the experiential genesis of Maier's concern with a cure for anger, as Christ promises emancipation from base impulses of the kind that had once jeopardised his own career in Padua. Nevertheless, as a doctor Maier also understands that anger has a very physical basis, and that Christ has the temperance-imparting Universal Medicine as a physical corollary – for "the habits of the mind follow the temperament of the body," as Galen has stated, and just as the bravest soldier may be ground down by a long and squalid imprisonment, so also the mind of man, whilst not being otherwise predisposed to anger, may be overcome through 'contamination' with yellow bile or other humours.[136] The Universal Medicine also promises to assuage unspeakable sorrows such as those inflicted upon Maier by his 'harsh fortune'. For we are told in the *Allegoria Bella* that the phoenix is synonymous with *nepenthe*,[137] the cure of worldly cares given by the queen of Egypt to Helen of Troy, who administered it to the son of Odysseus, Telemachus:

...like Tantalus, the more I learnt, the more I thirsted: and I had heard moreover that there is a certain bird unparalleled in the entire sphere of the earth called the phoenix, and that its skin stripped away from its body (that is to say, its feathers) constitute the pre-eminent medicine of all medicines, as it is the remedy for anger and grief, or *Nepenthe*; concerning which it is written in the ancient texts, that Helena, having been seized by Paris to Troy, supplied it to Telemachus, who was rapt in the greatest joy, having forgotten all his past toils, cares and grief. Therefore I was forced to search for this bird – wherever it may have been hidden – by a certain impulse of Nature and my mind, as if willingly compelled. Not that I hoped to possess this bird in its entirety (for I could see that was impossible for me), but at least in order that I might obtain a little feather of it, whatever labour, expense or travel I may need to undergo.[138]

---

of Alexandria, *The First Epistle of Clement to the Corinthians*, ch. 25, "On the Phoenix as an Emblem of the Resurrection."

[135] The description of Christ as the greatest of physicians occurs in a number of places in Maier's works; see, for instance, Maier, *Septimana Philosophica*, p. 200: "Quanto enim honestius est, mederi malis et morbis hominum (quod aeternus Dei Filius hic in terris versans ante alia omnia elegit et perfecit divinitus) quam cupiditatibus propriis indulgere."

[136] Maier, *Symbola Aureae Mensae*, p. 564: "...Quod mores animi sequantur temperamentum corporis: Ut enim alias fortissimus et invictus miles diutino et squalido carcere enervari et conteri potest adeo, ut aegre seipsum sustineat, ita et mens hominis, alias nec irae nec furiosis affectibus mancipata, vitio solius corporis biliosi vel ab humoribus aliis contaminati, saepissime inficitur et vincitur."

[137] According to Pliny and Dioscorides, *nepenthe* was the herb borage, or *borago officinalis*, which was steeped in warm wine and drunk as a sedative.

[138] Maier, *Symbola Aureae Mensae*, p. 562: "A nullo horum inquirendae scientiae modo abstinui, sed nunc hic, nunc alteri indulgendo, quo plus hausi, eo magis, Tantali instar,

Having decided upon his quest, Maier left his hometown on the day of the vernal equinox, "when the moon and sun were in the sign of Aries near the head of the Dragon."[139] This is a reference to the most auspicious astrological moment for the commencement of the laboratory work, when the appropriate astral influences are at their peak. It is also the time of spring, which marks the beginning of life in the cycle of the year; in which case we may assume that 'the head of the dragon' refers not only to the constellation *Draco* which coincides with that of Aries, but also to the *ouroboros*, whose head marks the beginning and the end of the cyclical alchemical work.

According to Maier, Europe represents the element earth because she is the foundation and mother of the world; she also corresponds to the sun and gold, on account of the excellence of her people.[140] Giving further reign to his nationalistic sympathies, Maier describes the *Umbilicus Germanicus* that is the centre of the European 'virgin', from which both imperial power and occult wisdom extend:

This is the mother, who is always known as a virgin; this is the most talented nurse of the people, who has brought forth from herself in abundance many gifts invented by the most subtle art: in this Umbilicus Germanicus, as the immovable centre from which the axioms of imperial authority extend, so many arts issue forth as from the fruitful horn of Amalthea.[141]

Maier goes on to relate certain 'miracles' or hieroglyphic truths demonstrating the correspondence of Europe to the element of earth: thus in certain regions of Hungary men live underwater with the help of tufa, which is congealed out of water; and in the mountains of Karlsbad raging waters are

---

sitii: Audiveram vero inter caetera esse avem quandam in toto terrarum orbe saltem unicam, PHOENICE dictam, cuius corporis exuviae, hoc est plumae seu carnes haberentur Medicina omnium Medicinarum praestantissima, ut pote quae foret Remedium IRAE ET DOLORIS seu NEPENTHES, de quo legitur in antiquorum scriptis, quod Helena, a Paride Troiano rapta, id praebuerit Telemacho, quo ille omnes praeteritos labores, curas et dolores oblitus laetitia singulari exhilaratus est. Ad hanc itaque avem indagandam, ubicunque lateret, impetu quodam naturae meae mentisque raptus et quasi volens coactus sum; non quod sperarem potiri hac volucri integra (id enim mihi impossibile praevidi) sed saltem ut vel plumam exiguam eius, quocunque labore, sumptu et peregrinatione adipiscerer..."

[139] *Ibid.*, p. 572: "Egressus itaque solo patrio ipso AEQUINOCTII Vernalis die LUNA, cum Sole in ARIETIS signo circa caput Draconis..."

[140] *Ibid.*, pp. 573-574.

[141] *Ibid.*, p. 574: "Haec est ea mater, quae virgo semper agnoscitur: Haec est nutrix populorum ingeniosissima, quae multa dona artificio subtilissimo a se inventa suppeditavit: In hac Umbilicus Germanicus, veluti centrum immobile, consistit, a quo ut Axioma Imperialis Dignitatis dependet, ita multae artes, tanquam ex uberrimo Amaltheae cornu profluxerunt."

petrified in the same manner.[142] On the shores of Prussia pellucid and
fragrant amber is washed up by the waves, having been produced from
subterranean juices, and the coral-plants of the Sicilian sea harden into red
and white stony shoots when taken out of the water (figure 29).[143] Maier tells
us these examples are to be understood with the mind, and not only with the
ears – for Europe itself is akin to the fixed 'Lion Earth' of the alchemical
vessel, which is not resolved into air, nor is it destroyed by the fiercest fire,
but in the likeness of gold maintains an equilibrium of forces and yields to no
other power.[144]

For all the magnificence of Europe, Maier says that he did not find anyone
there who could tell him something more certain about the phoenix and its
medicine; indeed, he encountered many people who would rather jest with
him than aid him by word or deed. Some tell him the thing which he seeks is
nowhere to be found, and when he does find something it will not be what he
expects; they advise him to spare his labours, expenses and droning
questions, which are as insubstantial as Echo following Narcissus – the
implication being that Maier has fallen in love with the products of his own
imagination. Others say that life is too short, and that a man will die before he
finds such secret and intricate things.[145] Nevertheless, in his reply to these
nay-sayers Maier speaks of a certain allure that draws him on in the face of
such doubts – and in so doing he reveals something of the psychology lying
behind his quest:

---

[142] *Ibid.*: "In quibusdam Pannonia locis homines sub aquis habitare scribunt, quia ex aquis
induratis tophacei lapides concreverint: In montanis Carolinis aquae ferventes lapides-
cunt similiter."

[143] *Ibid.*, p. 575: "Quis non miretur succinum, lapidem pellucidum et odoriferum ex succis
subterraneis gigni et per maris fluctus littoribus appelli, ut in Sudavia, maritima
Borussiae ora? Ne quid dicam de Corallis Siculi maris, ex vegetabili seu frutice
indurescente extra aquam in lapideum rubrum vel album virgultum."

[144] *Ibid.*: "...sufficiat nobis Leoninam terram indicasse et intelligentibus, qui mente, non
auribus solum nostra dicta capiunt, innuisse. Terra insuper ut in igne perdurat, nec
resolvitur in aerem, licet flamma sit fortissima, sed Auri instar pretiosi, quibus libet
injuriis resistit, sic et Europa nostra suis potentiis aequata et serata, veluti Terminus
Deorum antiquissimus, nulli cedit." The reference to 'Terminus' here is to the ancient
Roman god of boundary stones.

[145] *Ibid.*: "Multis perreptatis celebr ioribus locis in nullum incidere potui, qui de Phoenice
eiusque Medicina me certiorem faceret, Verum quamplurimos offendi, qui me veluti
ludentem operam et oleum luserint potius, quam iuverint verbis, multo minus rebus:
Quod quaeris, dicebant, nusquam invenies, ac quod invenies, non est, quod quaeris:
Deceptus es ab aliis, qui te, quod non est, indagare impulerunt: Parce labori, sumptui et
inquisitioni vocalis sine pondere bombi, qui velut Echo te Narcissum proprii ingenii
admiratorem sequitur et ad omnia vocata, prout videntur, apta respondet, ad rem vero,
quam inquiris, ineptissima: Nonnulli eorum, haec est res abstrusior et intricatior, aiebant,
quem ut tibi, tuisque studiis conveniat: Demus enim, esse eiusmodi Medicinam ex
Phoenice petendam, at hominis vita per se admodum brevis perit, antequam indagetur."

Even if truly I may not possess such great gifts, nevertheless I do not know by which beckoning or command (surely divine, I believe) I am being swept into these troubles, at once willing and unwilling, with the unwavering and preconceived hope that the sought medicine will eventually be found through the benevolence of God. As any queen appears to her king, or a beautiful bride to her bridegroom, so this medicine is pleasing to me before all good things in the world, and with a certain magnetic power it enchants and draws my mind towards it, so that I might be willing to forego life, friends and family if I could hold it.[146]

Maier also defends his quest by stating that 'sweat' comes before virtue and fame, and "rest from labour will be reached through the earth":[147] another indication that his purifying peregrination through the world mirrors both the transmutation in the vessel and the action of the cathartic Medicine itself.

Having gained no useful information concerning the phoenix in Europe, Maier travels to the Canary Islands where he witnesses a royal wedding vaguely akin to that portrayed in Andreae's *Chymisches Hochzeit*.[148] From there he sails onwards to America on a ship with an eagle at its prow. The eagle is the symbol of St. John; yet its significance for Maier is also to be found in the forty-sixth emblem and discourse of the *Atalanta Fugiens*, in which Maier speaks of two eagles circumnavigating the globe: one comes from the east, and one from the west, which together signify the two principles (masculine Sulphur and feminine Mercury) necessary for the completion of the work (figure 30). Maier also likens the eagle to the *lapis philosophorum* because it is said to restore itself to youth by plunging itself three times into a fountain.[149] In this way the eagle is linked with the cyclical processes in the vessel, in which the alchemical subject eventually returns to the point of origin, albeit in a purified and renewed state. In the course of his peregrination Maier also returns to the place of his departure by circumnavigating the earth, a subject that figures prominently in the discourse of the 'sixth day' of his *Septimana Philosophica*. There it is said that Columbus, Americus and Magellan have fought the vast oceans in their quest for new worlds, sailing "with barely a hand's width between their lives and death;" the latter encircled the entire globe (figure 31), thus overcoming

---

[146] *Ibid.*, p. 576: "Etsi vero ego talia et tanta dona in me non agnoscam, tamen nescio quo ductu aut nutu (credo, certe divino) in has difficultate nolens volens rapior, spe indubitata praeconcepta, me Medicamentum quaesitum tandem, ex Dei gratia inventurum esse: Cuilibet Regi ut sua Regina, aut sponso sponsa pulchra videtur, sic mihi haec Medicina prae omnibus mundi bonis arridet et magnetica quadam virtute mentem meam sibi fascinat et astringit, ut vita et amicis cognatisque carere velim, si illa debeam."

[147] *Ibid.*, pp. 576-577: "Ratio est, quia pulchra difficilia, et sudor ante virtutem et gloriam positus sit: Per terram enim laboris tenditur ad quietem."

[148] *Ibid.*, pp. 578-579.

[149] Maier, *Atalanta Fugiens*, discourse 46.

human weakness through "steadfastness and greatness of soul" – a theme
familiar to us from Maier's *Ulysses*.[150]

In accordance with this theme, Maier's crossing of the Atlantic is described as a journey by night through the dark surges of the ocean, in which
perilous encounters with hurricanes and sea monsters mirror the black phase
of the processes within the vessel. At length, however, he arrives at the
shores of Brazil, "a great province of America covered with unbroken
forests," in which colonies are rare and men with knowledge of the liberal
arts such as Maier himself are entirely foreign.[151] Given that the natives of
that province have only recently received the art of reading and writing from
the Spanish, and hold it in low esteem as "the betrayal of deeds," Maier
wonders whom he might question concerning the phoenix. For although there
are birds of many species and diverse colours in Brazil, he knows that the
phoenix is of a different nature and is not to be found amongst them. In any
case, he takes to wandering through the fragrant and multi-coloured forests,
where the flowers and trees refresh his eyes and the "natural music" of the
birds frees his mind from troubles.[152] There he discovers an extraordinary and
marvellously elegant apple, on the side of which is the following inscription:

---

[150] Maier, *Septimana Philosophica*, pp. 199-200: "Magna fuit hominum illorum audacia
prudentiae coniuncta, qui, relicta terra, quae humanae genti incolenda concessa est, aliud
elementum, utpote vastum ingressi Oceanum, compactis lignis seu navibus, vitam suam,
ut a morte vix palmum distaret, crediderunt, alium quo quaererent orbem, animalibus,
hominibusque, veluti hunc, inhabitatum, quales fuere Columbus, Americus, et Magel-
lanus; quorum primus novas insulas invenit; alter Americam, de suo nomine sic dictam,
detexit et lustravit; tertius totum terrenum globum aquis undiquaque cinctum cir-
cumnavigavit, incredibili et pene humanam superante imbecillitatem magnanimitate et
constantia." Maier goes on to say that the physician is an explorer of the 'little world'
that is man, although he is not driven by greed for gold and the 'thirst of kings'; rather, it
is his aim to remedy the evils and illnesses of humankind, a task which the eternal Son of
God perfected whilst living here on earth.

[151] Maier, *Symbola Aureae Mensae*, p. 580: "Fluctibus Oceani de nocte horribiliter nigri-
cantibus emensis, multisque periculis a monstris marinis et adversis turbinibus ac
procellis inflictis, exantlatis; tandem ad Brasiliae littora laeti appulimus, quae magna
Provincia est Americae nemoribus continuis repleta. Mapalia colonorum rara, rarissima
oppida, et homines a doctrinis liberalium artium alienissimi sunt."

[152] *Ibid.*, pp. 580-581: "Quos hic, inquam, de arcanis naturae occultissimis consulam, ubi
incolae pro miraculo non ita pridem habuerunt lectionem Epistolae ab Hispanis invicem
scriptae et transmissae, putaruntque chartam loquacem et proditoriam factorum? Quem
perconter de Phoenice avium omnium rarissima? Hoc quidem indubitatum est, volucres
diversorum generum et colorum ibi reperiri, quales non in his locis aut terrae partibus
visantur, verum cum Phoenix sit longe alterius naturae et proprietatis, non est qui illum
inter vulgares aves quaeramus. Nemora hic ex odoratis et variae coloratis arboribus sunt
frequentia, in quae dum meditationibus occupatus aliquando deambularem; partim ut
laetiori arborum florumque aspectu oculos reficerem, partim ut naturali avium cantil-
lantium musica mentem a curis relaxarem..."

Within lies that which you may deliver to its grandmother,
Thence reappears the son which may enter the mother in embrace.
After a little while it will be born again into an excellent tree,
Which will give to the farmer progeny with golden foliage.[153]

After pondering for a while over this little riddle, Maier realises that the apple must come from the garden of the Hesperides, and that the grandmother in question is the earth – a line of reasoning familiar to us from the tale of Deucalion and Pyrrha in the *Themis Aurea*. Thus Maier plants a seed of the fruit in the earth, and after a short time a sapling grows up; then he looks nearby for another tree of the same genus (the mother) and grafts the two together. From this grafting there arises a more noble tree bearing the extraordinary fruit of the scion – an example, as Maier declares, of the perfection of Nature through art.[154] Maier goes on to relate a similar story concerning a sage who passed through the same region and taught the natives how to breed mules from horses and asses; an allegory which serves to demonstrate a natural or chemical law in the same manner as the tale of the apple.[155] For just as the leopard is born from the lioness and the panther (!), or new varieties of flowers are produced through interbreeding, so gold arises when Mercury is mixed with the Tincture or "red metal powder" in the fire. Maier's point here is to demonstrate that gold differs in kind from both its parents.[156]

Before taking his leave of America, Maier takes a valuable piece of ebony as a souvenir; in describing its properties he cites the work of Nicolas Bautista Monardes (c.1508-1588), a physician of Seville who first brought knowledge of the medicinal virtues of plants in South and Central America to Europe.[157] Maier also relates that the natives of Peru are in possession of a miraculous 'water' or *aqua Americana* which makes gold soft and malleable, yet does not burn the fingers – the reason, no doubt, why America answers to the element of water in his schema.[158]

---

[153] *Ibid.*, p. 581: "Intus adest aviae, quod tradas, inde resurgens/ Filius, amplexus matris inire potest./ Inde renascetur paulo post nobilis arbor,/ Agricolae foetus quae dabit auricomos."

[154] *Ibid.*

[155] *Ibid.*, pp. 581-583.

[156] *Ibid.*, p. 583: "Sunt nam qui dicant ex Pardo et Leaena sic generatum Leopardum, ex lupo et cane foemina, lyciscam, ex equo et asina hinnum seu mulam diversam a mulo; Ex surculo seu ramulo unius arboris et trunco alterius illi, non huic similem arborem, ex floribus certis coloribus mistis, alios flores coloratos, ex Tinctura seu pulvere metallico ruberrimo cum argento vivo in igne mixto, aurum, quae nec huic, nec illi per oina est simile, et sic de aliis censendum."

[157] The work Maier cites is the *Historia Medicinal de las cosas que se traen de nuestras Indias Occidentales*. Seville: Escrivano, 1574.

[158] Maier, *Symbola Aureae Mensae*, pp. 583-584.

Maier sails on towards Asia on a ship with a white unicorn at its prow – a medieval symbol for Christ – and by and by makes a landing in the Persian Gulf. On account of the moistness and warmth of this region Maier associates it with the element of air, and speaks of it as the mediator between hot and dry Africa and the frigid north (a slight variation on the association of regions with Aristotelian properties given in the *Theses Summam Doctrinae de Temperamentis Corporis Humani*).[159] Upon his arrival Maier makes his way towards Asia Minor, and to the place where Jason was said to have obtained the Golden Fleece. Coming to the field of Mars, which was the site of the palace of Jason's father-in-law Äetes (a descendant of the Sun), Maier meets an old man of venerable countenance with whom he strikes up a conversation. As this *senex* is clearly a wise and experienced man, Maier asks him if the stories related in poems and histories concerning Jason and his Golden Fleece are in fact true, or vain and false; for as facts they detract from faith, but as fictions they may at least represent moral expositions.[160] To this question the old man suddenly cries "Behold, I am Jason!", and proceeds to relate the story of his quest for the Golden Fleece, which had been 'gilded' by Mercury and hung in the grove of Mars by Äetes. As a dragon had been set to guard the fleece, Jason had subdued it with a narcotic supplied by Medea; he then sowed the dragon's teeth in ground tilled by fire-breathing bulls, whose fire he first extinguished by sprinkling "the clearest dripping water" into their jaws. Whilst Maier was "somewhat terrified" by the old man's revelation, nevertheless he was told not to be afraid, as it appears that the Greek hero was not in the habit of harming others, but rather sought to benefit them as a good physician.[161] In this way Maier receives a confirmation of his chemical interpretation of ancient myth – from the horse's mouth, as it were.

In time Maier journeys towards Ormuz (Jazireh-ye Hormoz) – a city on an island in the Persian Gulf that in Maier's time was a major Portuguese conduit for the Indian spice trade. In that city, which as we might expect is full of exotic fragrances, Maier becomes embroiled in the locals' quest for an 'earthly paradise', although he gathers little information from them

---

[159] *Ibid.*, pp. 584-585.

[160] *Ibid.*, p. 586: "Vellem autem lubens cognoscere, num illa, quae de Iasone, eiusque vellere Aureo a tot Poesis et historiis tradita, revera ita se habeant, an vero sint vana et falsa, solummodo ad delectandos homines introducta et huc usque ad nos propagata? Multi enim his, ceu factis, fidem detrahunt, sed saltem ut fictis moralem expositionem inducunt."

[161] *Ibid.*, pp. 586-587: "Ad quae ille renidens paululum, en ego, inquit, sum ipse Iason, de quo quaeris, qui tibi de me roganti omnium optime responsum dare ut possum, sic polliceor: Quo dicto, cum aliquantulum exhorrescerem, non est, ait ille, cur timeas; Ego enim et vivus nulli nocui, sed veluti Medicus bonus omnibus profui, sic nec vita defunctus, quamvis revera mortuus non sim, sed fama, ut semper, vegetus et superstes."

concerning its whereabouts.[162] Having crossed to the mainland of Persia he travels by road until he comes to a fork in the way, where there stands a statue of Mercury; like the "man of silver who becomes a man of gold" in the *Visions* of Zosimos, his body is made of silver and his head is golden, and with his right arm he gestures towards the 'earthly paradise' which Maier seeks.[163] Setting forth in this direction, Maier reaches a broad river – on the other shore lies a magnificent garden replete with the sound of birds, exotic fragrances, evergreen trees and flowers such as amaranths, lilies, roses and hyacinths. The parallels between the peregrination of the *Allegoria Bella* and Maier's own biography are demonstrated here when Maier also tells us he could see an organ in the Edenic garden driven by a water-wheel and windsocks, which gave forth wonderful multi-voiced melodies – a device that was very similar to one he once saw near Florence.[164] We may take this as another indication that the *peregrinatio academica* which Maier undertook some twenty years earlier served as an important experiential source for the pilgrimage described in the *Allegoria Bella*, as his only recorded visit to Florence occurred on that journey.[165]

Nevertheless, for want of a boat Maier is unable to cross the river to the earthly paradise, and so he decides to return to his quest for the phoenix, confident in the knowledge that he will one day come back to this magnificent place. In this passage we may see another reference to the secluded alchemical garden with its roses and lilies – a symbol for the perfection of the work, in which things heavenly and earthly coalesce. Nevertheless, in Maier's failure to reach his goal we may also see a very Christian allusion to the afterlife awaiting us when our earthly toils are at an end. Although the divine law of death and resurrection is to be observed in the microcosm of the vessel, and the *elixir vitae* Maier sought to procure partakes of the divine nature and power in some lesser measure, we have seen that Maier believed eternal life can ultimately be found only through our departure from this life. Thus the Edenic symbolism of the *Allegoria Bella* recalls the passage in *1 Corinthians* to which Maier alludes when describing the Rosicrucian Brotherhood's *Liber M.* in the third chapter of the *Themis*

---

[162] *Ibid.*, pp. 591-592.

[163] *Ibid.*, p. 592; see Taylor, "The Visions of Zosimos." A representation of the Work as a human figure with a golden head is to be found in the sixth parable and emblem of the *Splendor Solis*.

[164] *Ibid.*, p. 593: "Nec defuit Musica arte instrumentalis, quae facta erat cum rota suis clavis deprimente claviculas Organorum Musicorum, atque sic varias melodias 4 5 vel 6 vocum, veluti digitis humanis, causante; follibus ventum afflantibus, dictaque rota a rivo quodam aquae perenni, motis et circumductis, quemadmodum prope Florentiam Italiae in Pratolino olim vidimus et audivimus."

[165] Maier, *De Medicina Regia*, p. Aii *recto*.

Aurea: "For now we see through a glass, darkly; but then face to face; now I know in part; but then I shall know even as also I am known."[166]

The frustration of Maier's attempt to reach the 'earthly paradise' prefigures the outcome of his quest for the phoenix, which next takes him to the penultimate destination of his journey, 'hot and dry' Africa which answers to the element of fire. Maier's point of arrival is Eritrea, which he reaches by crossing the Red Sea from Arabia when "the sun has entered Leo for the second time, and the moon is holding in the height of the house of Cancer;" more than a year had elapsed since his departure from Europe, and the astrological signs seemed to augur well for him.[167] Maier begins the tale of his adventures in Africa by giving a description of a number of fabulous animals and semi-humans that live there; he also tells us that in the region by the Red Sea there dwells the 'Ortus':

In the same place close to the Eritrean sea a certain wild animal has been seen, called the Ortus, which has a red head with golden lines extending all the way to the neck, black eyes, white forefeet, blacker hindfeet, and a white face up to the cheeks. Whilst I was engaged in meditation on the exterior form of this creature, it occurred to me that the words of Avicenna the philosopher appear to concern an animal which is in all ways similar: namely, "What is that thing, whose head is red, feet white and eyes black? That is the magistery."[168]

This creature does not seem to appear in the *Hieroglyphics of Horapollo* or the bestiaries which Maier drew upon when compiling his *Tractatus de Volucri Arborea*; nevertheless, some clue as to the significance of the beast's name is given by the meaning of the Latin word *ortus*: variously 'a rising of the heavenly bodies', an 'origin' and 'a springing up' or 'growth'. Like the multi-coloured statue of Mercury this beast recalls the vitalistic fantasy represented in the fourth parable and corresponding emblem of the sixteenth century *Splendor Solis*, in which we see a humanoid figure with a red head and right arm, white left arm and black body emerging from a muddy swamp and accompanied by the caption, "it is a living thing that dies no more, for it is endowed with everlasting increase."[169] Maier's Ortus represents the

---

[166] *1 Corinthians* 13.12.

[167] Maier, *Symbola Aureae Mensae*, p. 594: "Cum in Africam appulissem, integro exacto anno et eo amplius, iam Sol iterum Leonem ingressus fuerat, Luna tenente Cancrum sui domicilii fastigium, quod magnam mihi spem optimi augurii fecit."

[168] *Ibid.*, pp. 594-595: "Ibidem iuxta Erythraeum mare fera quaedam visa est, ORTUS nomine, cuius caput rubeum lineis aureis ad cervicem usque pertinentibus, oculi nigri et pedes, praesertim priores, albi, posteriores nigriores, os usque ad genas candidum, fuere: Cuius exterioris formae consideratione dum detineor, occurrit, philosophi Avicennae dictum, quod de consimili animali videtur intelligi; nempe, Res, cuius caput rubeum est, et pedes albi et oculi nigri, quid est? Hoc est magisterium."

[169] Salomon Trismosin. *Splendor Solis*. Trans. Joscelyn Godwin, with an introduction and commentary by Adam McLean. Grand Rapids, Michigan: Phanes Press, 1991, p. 36.

progressive perfection of organic forms, in which the head as the centre of the most refined *spiritus* corresponds to the final phase of the work arising from the inferior, black and earthy parts of the body.

In a cave in the vicinity of the Red Sea there also lives the Erythræan (i.e. Eritrean) Sibyl – the pagan prophetess who, according to certain of the Church Fathers, predicted the coming of Christ.[170] Having heard of her presence there, Maier decides to pay her a visit in order to learn more from her concerning the whereabouts of the phoenix, and whether its feathers do indeed constitute a cure for anger and grief. Although she is somewhat startled by Maier's arrival and castigates him for approaching a lone virgin thus, the Sibyl consents to tell him what she knows. She begins her discourse by stating that the very land in which Maier now stands is the birthplace of the phoenix, and she goes on to describe the bird in order that Maier may better apprehend it:

In ancient times felicitous Arabia and its neighbour Egypt rejoiced in this bird, the neck of which is of flashing gold, the body is covered with purple feathers, and on the head there is a crest like a crown. It is sacred to the sun, and it lives 660 years; at which time, with old age approaching, it constructs a nest with twigs of cinnamon and frankincense which it fills with fragrance. Then it stirs up flames by shaking its wings towards the sun's rays, and is burnt to ashes. Out of these ashes there is produced a worm, and from thence a little bird, which gives its father a proper funeral by carrying the entire nest to Heliopolis in Egypt, the city sacred to the sun also known as Thebes, and there places it upon an altar. Those who regard this as a complete fantasy show themselves to be children and poor judges of things; those who take it to be historical fact just as the words sound are deceived by their judgement. For these things are Hieroglyphs and are spoken more to the mind than the ears, and are written to the mind rather than the eyes by means of certain figures and pictures like letters, which are said to be sacred. If you have no faith in my judgment alone on this matter, you should consult the Egyptian author Horus Apollo, amongst others...[171]

---

[170] Augustine. "City of God." In *The Fathers of the Church*, Vol. 24. Washington: Catholic University of America Press, 1954, pp. 114 ff. See also Theophilus and Lactantius; and Eusebius, from whom Maier quotes when introducing the Sibyl.

[171] Maier, *Symbola Aureae Mensae*, p. 598: "Arabia felix, eique adjacens Aegyptus antiquitus hac gaudebat volucri, cuius collum aureus fulgor, reliquum corpus purpureus color in   pennis cinxit: In capitibus crista, coronae instar, visa est: Soli sacra avis vivit annos 660 ad quam aetatem cum pervenerit senescens, casia thurisque surculis construit nidum, quem odoribus replet, conquassatisque ad solis radios alis flammam excitat, qua comburitur in cinerem: Ex hoc deinde prodit vermiculus et inde pullus, qui priori ceu patri funera iusta reddens, totum nidum defert in urbem Aegypti Heliopolim Soli sacram, alias Thebas dictam, ibique in ara deponit. Hoc, qui pro fabula omnino habent, pueri et iniqui rerum aestimatores videntur, qui pro historia, ut verba sonant, facta, et illi falluntur suo iudicio. Hieroglyphica enim sunt haec et menti potius dictantur, quam auribus, inscribunturque potius, quam oculis per certas figuras et picturas, quasi literas, quas sacras vocant: Qua de re si mihi fidem soli non adhibes, consule inter caeteros Orum Apollinem Aegyptium scriptorem..."

The Sibyl then cites the words of Horapollo in his *Hieroglyphics*, which interestingly are at variance with both the account of Pliny she had just delivered and the account of the *Hieroglyphics* given in Hoeschel's 1595 edition of that work: for the Sibyl states that the phoenix flies to Heliopolis when it is 500 years old, and if it reaches that city before it dies it is "cared for mystically" by the Egyptians. Although Hoeschel's edition merely mentions that when the phoenix dies "it is buried with great solemnity and ritual," the reasoning behind the 'mystical' wording of the Sibyl's account is clear; for she goes on to tell Maier that "these words are enough to teach you that the phoenix was understood mystically by the Egyptians, just as it was cared for 'mystically'."[172]

This 'mystical' significance of the phoenix becomes apparent when Maier is directed by the Erythræan Sybil to the seven mouths of the Nile, the dwelling-place of Mercury himself, who has "the power to show you the phoenix and the Medicine derived from it."[173] In using the Christ-prophesying Sybil to demonstrate the path to the phoenix in this way, it is clear that Maier understands the fabled bird as a symbol for both the alchemical Universal Medicine and Christ, whose life-giving power of renewal was manifested not only in His passion and resurrection, but also in the resurrection of those saved by Him. Thus, whilst en route to the mouths of the Nile, Maier passes by a famous hill where the bodies of a number of Christian martyrs are interred. We are told that on a certain day in May between the rising of the sun and midday the skeletons buried there rise up towards the surface of the earth until they are visible, then sink back into the earth as the sun wanes. Maier declares that those who might call this event diabolical rather than divine are impious, for they deny the will of the free and omnipotent God; furthermore, such a miracle presents evidence for the

---

[172] *Ibid.*, p. 598: "...'Phoenicem post quingentesimum annum, cum iam est morti propinqua, in Aegyptum remeare, ac si praeveniat ante obitum curari mystice ab Aegyptiis, et quaecunque aliis sacris animalibus tribuunt, haec et Phoenici omnia deberi: Gaudet enim sole maxime Phoenix in Aegypto praecipue, ut pote illic vehementi.' Haec Ori verba te satis erudiunt, quod mystice accipiatur Phoenix ab Aegyptiis, prout mystice curatur." Hoeschel's 1595 edition runs as follows: "Haec enim in Aegyptum, cum tempus mortis instat, quingentesimo demum anno regreditur: ubi si naturae debitum persolverit, magna solennitate ac ritu funeratur. Quaecunque enim in caeteris sacris animantibus religiose observant Aegyptii, ea et Phoenici tribui debent. Fertur siquidem Sole magis apud Aegyptios gaudere, quam apud caeteras gentes." *Hieroglyphica Horapollinis.* Trans. David Hoeschel. Augustae Vindelicorum: n.p., 1595, p. 44. For an English translation of this passage, see Boas, George. *The Hieroglyphics of Horapollo.* Princeton: Princeton University Press, 1993, p. 61.

[173] Maier, *Symbola Aureae Mensae*, p. 599: "Pater enim filio dedit potestatem monstrandi tibi Phoenicem et ex ea petendam Medicinam."

resurrection of the body at Judgment Day, "just as the new phoenix arises from the ashes of the dead."[174]

When Maier finally arrives at the Nile he finds his quest for Mercury frustrated at every juncture, as the inhabitants of the delta that once cradled the Great Library of Alexandria are sunk in a barbarous and abject state. Nevertheless, this is the place of which Zosimos once wrote:

> Go to the waters of the Nile; there you will find a stone which has a spirit; take it, cut it in two; put your hand in its interior and draw out the heart: because its soul is in its heart.[175]

Maier's point of arrival at the Nile is Canopus (i.e. modern Abu Qir on the outskirts of Alexandria), where he hears that Hermes once said Egypt

---

[174] *Ibid.*, p. 600: "Ad Canopicum primo me contuli, in qua via per collem sepulturae Christianorum a barbaris ibi quondam occisorum insignem profectus sum, cuius loci annua miracula, relatu dignissima, hic praeterire nequeo: Num certo quodam die Mensis Maii cadavera seu ossa sepultorum ab oriente sole usque in meridiem sensim ad superficiem usque tumbae elevantur ex sese, donec in conspectum eo concurrentium hominum devenerint, alicubi magis, alibi minus, tum a meridie versus occasum solis eodem modo deprimuntur, donec omnia ad pristinum statum redierint: Quae si quis non divina virtute, sed diabolica prorsus fieri affirmet, videat ne a superstitione nimium discedendo ad incredulitatem seu impietatem inclinet, Deique omnipotentiae et liberrimae voluntati haec aut his similia miraculosa facta deneget ac subtrahat: Haec si vera sunt, ut testantur multi, qui viderunt, suis scriptis publicatis, Resurrectionis corporum humanorum evidentissimum exemplar exhibent, quemadmodum quoque Phoenicis novi ex cinere mortui resuscitatio." Tertullian also used the phoenix as a symbol for the resurrection of the body in his *On the Resurrection of the Flesh*, ch. 13: "What can be more express and more significant for our subject; or to what other thing can such a phenomenon bear witness? God even in His own Scripture says: "*The righteous* shall flourish like the phoenix;" that is, shall flourish or revive, from death, from the grave – to teach you to believe that a bodily substance may be recovered even from the fire." However, the reference in the gospel of Matthew to which Tertullian refers only mentions a palm tree – a symbol associated with the phoenix.

[175] Zosimos of Panopolis. "Concerning Virtue and its Interpretation." In Berthelot, *Collection des Anciens Alchimistes Grecs*, p. 129: "Va vers le courant du Nil; tu trouveras là une pierre ayant un esprit; prends-la, coupe-la en deux; mets ta main dans l'intérieur et tires-en le cœur: car son âme est dans son cœur;" the saying is attributed by Zosimos to 'Ostanes'. Budge once argued that the very term 'alchemy' is ultimately Egyptian in origin, deriving from an ancient name for Egypt, 'Qemt' – a word meaning 'black' on account of the dark mud of the Nile's floodplains. According to Greek writers, quicksilver was utilised by Egyptian metalsmiths to separate gold and silver from the native ore, from which process there was produced a dark powder or substance. Not only was this powder believed to possess the individuality of the various metals; it was also identified with the body of Osiris during his journey to the underworld, and was held to possess life-giving powers. From the word 'Qemt' came the Greek 'Khemeia', or 'preparation of the black powder', to which the Arabs added the article 'al-'. Budge, Sir E. A. Wallis. *Egyptian Magic*. London: Kegan Paul, Trench, Trubner and Co. Ltd., 1899, pp. 19-20.

signifies the heavens, and that the seven mouths of the Nile refer to the seven planets; the Canopic mouth answers to the highest of the planets, Saturn, and as Mercury is his grandson Maier is told to look for him in another mouth of the Nile.[176] Given the correspondence of the planets to the metals, this allusion shows the reader of the *Allegoria Bella* that Maier's passage through the delta is akin to the progress of metallic development in the womb of the earth, and that Maier has begun his journey at Saturn or lead – which as Rhazes stated is the "first gate to the arcana."[177]

Nevertheless, upon searching all the other mouths of the Nile – the Bolbitic, Sebbenitic, Pelusian, Tanitic, Phanitic and Mendesian – the dwelling of the elusive Mercury is nowhere to be found, and the inhabitants are equally elusive in their answers to Maier's queries. Whilst the Sibyl had issued a warning that Mercury has no 'fixed' habitation, and is to be found in different places at different times, Maier begins to believe that she has deceived him out of some hatred for strangers, and thrown him into this 'labyrinth' in order to lead him around with the false hope of reward.[178] Similarly, it seems to him that the deceptions of the delta's inhabitants are also born of some loathing of foreigners; but considering this matter carefully, he decides to follow the opposite of their advice, and begins to retrace his steps towards the Canopic mouth. Before reaching that mouth he finally finds Mercury in a place where the inhabitants had previously said he was not to be seen – in all likelihood the fifth Tanitic mouth, which corresponds to the fourth planet from Saturn (i.e. Mercury) in Maier's cosmology, and where the locals had actively denied Mercury's presence rather than disowning any knowledge of the matter.[179]

Having received instructions from Mercury (about whose visage nothing is said), the time is ripe for the fulfilment of Maier's destiny as it was prefigured in the augury of his birth. However, when he finally arrives at the abode of the phoenix, he finds it has "gone abroad" for a few weeks, and so

---

[176] Maier, *Symbola Aureae Mensae*, pp. 600-601.

[177] See above, p. 42.

[178] Maier, *Symbola Aureae Mensae*, p. 603: "Atque sic septem ex ordine Nili ostiis perlustratis, quem quaesivi, cum non offenderim, deceptum me a Sibylla arbitratus sum, quae saltem in hosce labyrinthos iniecerit, ut animum falsa spe lactatum circumduceret, forte ex invidia aut odio erga alienos praeconcepto."

[179] *Ibid.*: "Verum cum singula, quae contigerant in itinere, revolverem; me forte ab inquilinis quorumcunque locorum pessime deceptoria responsione circumventum conjectavi, ea ratione quod innata quadam ferocia omnes peregrinos fastidirent ac odissent: Ideoque quid circa primum, secundum ac tertium, aliaque ostia, ab illis responsum fuerit, bene consideravi, ex quibus quam plurima occurrerunt, quae dubium ante conceptum augerent potius, quam eximerent: Unde retorsum vestigia relegendo ab ultimo versus primum regressus sum, ac tandem antequam ad primum redierim Mercurium inveni, in aliquo ostiorum, ubi incolae visi essent antea negasse."

he returns empty-handed to Europe. The phoenix has taken flight – just as a dove once flew beyond the grasp of Maier's mother's hands – and the oft-repeated warning of the alchemists has been realised: when the seeker thinks the Art is finally perfected, "he will find nothing in his hands." Nevertheless, in one of Maier's typically enigmatic and witty asides, we are told that the phoenix is absent because it has been "appointed arbiter between the owl and the other birds attacking her, which conflict we have elsewhere put on record" – an oblique reference to the 'Rosicrucian' Owl and its detractors described in Maier's *Jocus Severus*.[180] In his lengthy analysis of the *Allegoria Bella* Carl Gustav Jung found it tragic that, at the end of his long journey, Maier was left with nothing but a feather, i.e. "his own quill pen."[181] But for those of Maier's readers well acquainted with the *Hieroglyphics of Horapollo*, it is clear that the author has found the phoenix in the face of its very absence. For in allowing the Erythræan Sibyl to give voice to Horapollo's pronouncements on the phoenix, Maier has nevertheless withheld the crux of that particular passage, which is the significance of the hieroglyph and the key to Maier's allegory – "to indicate a traveller who returns from a long journey to his native land, again do the Egyptians draw a phoenix."[182]

Apart from offering concise insight into the nature of Maier's spiritual alchemy, the *Allegoria Bella* sets forth that admixture of vitalism, solar mysticism and pietist Christian sentiments that is so characteristic of Maier's thought. Although we must continue to designate Maier's doctrines as 'pseudo-Egyptian' due to the transformation of Egyptian religion by both ancient and Renaissance Neoplatonism, his works display a very Egyptian and pagan fascination with gold, the sun and eternal life. In other passages in the *Hieroglyphics of Horapollo* from which Maier does not quote, the phoenix is also said to denote the sun, the immortality of the soul and a 'long enduring restoration', "for when this bird is born, there is a renewal of things."[183] Despite the Neoplatonising nature of the *Hieroglyphics*, these meanings are congruent with ancient Egyptian depictions of the phoenix or *bennu*, which show the bird as a type of heron with two long feathers streaming from the back of its head, and which associate it with the rising

---

[180] *Ibid.*, p. 603-604: "Phoenicem inprimis demonstravit, ubi conveniri deberet, quem in loco, de quo ne cogitassem antea latere apertissime narravit, quo cum pervenissem, meo infortunio, exierat foras, (forte tum Arbiter constitutus inter Noctuam et volucres alias eam insectantes, de quo praelio alibi tradidimus) at post aliquot dies, paucasue septimanas rediturus."

[181] Jung, *Psychology and Alchemy*, p. 431.

[182] Horapollo, *Hieroglyphica Horapollinis*, p. 44: "Quin et eum innuentes, qui longo tempore peregrinatus tandem in solum natale remeet, rursum Phoenicem avem pingunt."

[183] *Ibid.*, pp. 42-44, 96.

sun. Hieroglyphic inscriptions speak of the phoenix as "the soul of Ra" and "the heart of the renewed Ra;" the *Papyrus of Ani* also relates the creature to the cult of the resurrected Osiris, and Egyptian funerary trappings represent the deceased with the words "I am in the form of the phoenix."[184] In this way the phoenix represents a typically pagan concern with natural cyclical processes of ebb and flow, death and resurrection – processes that appear to have first given rise to the association of the *bennu* with the returning sun in ancient Egypt, as the meaning of the "returning traveller" given by Horapollo derives from the said heron's periodic migrations.[185] When we view these facts in light of Maier's discourse in the *Allegoria Bella* on the "model of peregrination" set for man by birds and the sun,[186] it is clear that for all Maier's errors the ethos of the Egyptian cults was not entirely lost to him.

As we have seen, Maier did not consider his 'true home' to be Europe, or even his native Holstein. Maier's homecoming came when death overtook him as he was returning to Holstein, i.e. through another frustration of his earthly designs, a fate that seems to have been prefigured in the alchemical augury appearing at his birth. After the many years he had spent in foreign lands 'perfecting' his unattainable Art, living amongst strangers as hostile to his quest as the inhabitants of the Nile delta in the *Allegoria Bella*, the spirit of this 'long-absent traveller' had finally returned to its origins. This is the 'rotation of the circle' of which Maier spoke in his *De Circulo Physico, Quadrato*, the cyclical return to the beginning in the great vessel that is God's Creation – for just as the *spiritus* descended as a dove at Maier's birth, so it ascended at death as Maier returned to his true heavenly home. All things stem from God, and all return to God; the *spiritus* moves through the sun to gold and the human heart, and then returns again to its source. Alternatively, it is the 'return to the Monad' of the *Atalanta Fugiens*, the 'unity and eternal peace' following the purification of the matter in the vessel – "make a circle out of a man and a woman, derive from it a square, and from the square a triangle: make a circle again and you will have the Philosophers' Stone."

---

[184] Cook, Albert Stanburrough. *The Old English Elene, Phœnix and Physiologus*. New Haven: Yale University Press, 1919, pp. xxxviii ff.

[185] *Ibid.*, p. xxxix; according to Cook, the etymological origin of *bennu* lies in a root verb meaning 'to turn'.

[186] See above, p. 56.

VI. Conclusion: Maier and the historiography of alchemy

1. Piety and the *coniunctio oppositorum*

Let us now return to the conjectures of Principe and Newman, and in particular to their argument that the notions of piety and "exhortations to morality" to be found in the literature are epiphenomena with little or no relation to the central goal of the early modern alchemist, who merely worked on "material substances towards material goals."[1] As we have seen in our analysis of the life and work of a significant laboratory worker and influential writer on the nature of alchemical *Decknamen*, notions of morality held an important place in the early modern medical worldview. This holds true not only for Maier, but also for other alchemists of his time, such as Raphael Eglinus, Oswald Croll, Joseph Duchesne and Heinrich Noll.[2] In Maier's eyes disease was closely associated with impiety and a sinful lifestyle; and the Universal Medicine which he strove to uncover imparted 'temperance' to the human body, a term which refers simultaneously to a somatic and a psychic or moral state. The imbalance of humours in the body that Maier sought to treat was the direct result of overindulgence in sensual pleasures, such as the drinking of alcohol, sexual debauchery and gluttony. Likewise, impious urges such as anger are the result of just such a disequilibrium in the four bodily fluids, which may be remedied by the temperance-imparting *lapis* just as metals may gain a more perfect proportion or balance of opposing elements. Furthermore, the operation of Maier's alchemical remedies depends upon the 'virtue' of divine origins inhering in the rays of the sun, be it directly received or reflected; and in the term *virtus* itself we may also see something of the holistic sense that has been largely lost to contemporary science, i.e. the dual meaning of 'strength' or 'power' and 'moral virtue'. Hence the relation of the body to the princely state in Maier's work, and the nature of his appeals to the patronage of his Calvinist master in the *De Circulo Physico, Quadrato.*

Central though piety was to Maier's alchemical physic, there is nothing in this fact *per se* which would justify the application to his work of the phrase 'spiritual alchemy' as we have defined it. Nevertheless, in Maier's

---

[1] Principe and Newman, "Some Problems with the Historiography of Alchemy," p. 397.
[2] On this point see Moran, *Alchemical World of the German Court*, pp. 122-125.

work alchemical *Decknamen* refer not only to chemical processes narrowly conceived in the manner of Principe and Newman, but also to a process of personal transmutation from a base, earthly state into "a more noble, more spiritual, more moral, or more divine state" – i.e., a 'spiritual alchemy'. Thus Maier believed that he was "destined to imitate the natural succession of elements" to be observed within the vessel, moving from a denser 'earthly' state to a finer 'spiritual' state.[3] From the perspective of the history of ideas, these sentiments are a natural extension of the Hermetic theory of microcosmic-macrocosmic correspondence, and the traditional alchemical conception of an agent able to transmute metals and humans alike; in Maier's time they were fortified on the one hand by the Protestant emphasis on reflexivity and the religion of the individual, and on the other by pansophic concerns with the integration of disparate fields in a unified science. Whilst Newman has briefly considered in his work the court of Rudolf II, the centre of pansophic thought in the early modern period, it is only to state that "the cult of emblems" adhered to by Maier encouraged the trend of employing 'verbal conceits' and 'tropes' current in medieval European alchemy![4] In the pansophist imagination, the relation of the processes in the alembic to soteriological and spiritual matters was one of *correspondence*, and not merely didactically employed analogy. Indeed, when reading Maier's works one has the sense that the underlying reality of the cosmos is 'chemical' in his eyes, and that 'chemical' research was concerned with uncovering laws which govern all aspects of the macrocosm and the microcosm – including the life of the soul.

Whilst Jung's ahistorical methodology failed to expose the integral relation of laboratory practice with 'spiritual' alchemical notions of the transformation of the psyche or soul, we have seen that in Maier's work the one emerges from and complements the other. On the one hand, Maier hoped to achieve something of a moral transformation in his patients through the application of his cathartic, purgative medicine; more importantly, however, it was precisely the hopeless quest for the Philosophers' Stone that formed the black phase of the work that was Maier's life, a peregrination in search of the arcana in which a finer spirit was distilled through the trials and seductions of earthly existence. In this sense Maier's thought conforms to the ethos of the later German Romantics, who utilised the alchemical symbol of the blue flower to signify an elusive wisdom that withers away before it can be grasped. Herein lies the most profound expression of the alchemical

---

[3]   Maier, *Symbola Aureae Mensae*, p. 572: "Cur vero hunc ordinem suscipiendi itineris de una parte in aliam transeundi, animo praeconceperim, haec causa sufficiens mihi visa est, quod naturalem elementorum seriem, qua illa ex crassis in subtilia, ex ponderosis in levia migrant, imitari debeam."

[4]   Newman, "*Decknamen* or Pseudochemical Language?," pp. 162-163.

coniunctio oppositorum; for Maier's great and fruitless labour to reach the eighteenth rung of the alchemical ladder, and the sometimes inglorious and near-fraudulent means he employed to extract gold from his patrons and patients, formed the means of knowing "the nature of this transitory life, and the nature of the everlasting happiness to come." Whosoever denies the lessons imparted by the *liber mundi*, Maier writes, is in need of "a dose of Hellebore."[5]

2. *Chymia* and *alchemia*

Given that Maier names his own Art *chemia* or *chymia* and uses *alchemia* in reference to the work of those vulgar practitioners and *Betrüger* who have brought the true Art of transmutation into disrepute, should we dispense with the term 'alchemy' when describing his work? Or should we dispense with the term altogether when referring to the early modern period, as Principe and Newman recommend? Whilst these authors have shown that a clear and consistent distinction between the terms *alchemia* and *chemia* did not appear until the anti-chrysopoeian Lemery elaborated upon Ruland's mistaken etymology in the late seventeenth century, Maier was already distinguishing between the two terms on the basis of charlatanism by the early seventeenth century. In itself this fact suggests that the eventual widespread distinction between the two terms – the one referring to the procurement of the *lapis philosophorum*, the other to a chemical research rejecting metallic transmutation and the feasibility of an *elixir vitae* – was not merely the result of an etymological error, but may also have emerged through earlier attempts to distinguish unlearned from legitimate chemical research. Maier's discarding of the term *alchemia* in favour of *chemia* is in accord with the rationalising aspect of his work, and may indicate that the exotic otherness imparted by the Arabic definite article 'al' was beginning to be associated in his time with equally outlandish and spurious claims (hence the widespread seventeenth century misunderstanding of 'al' as signifying the 'great' or 'sublime' nature of the Art).[6] Whatever the case may be, with the progressive 'disenchantment of the world' associated with the rise of modernity the term *alchemia* became associated exclusively with transmutational pursuits excluded from the domain of 'legitimate' chemical research.

In her study of Maier's *Atalanta Fugiens* de Jong has also made note of the fact that Maier eschewed the term 'alchemy' in favour of *chemia* or

---

5 See above, chapter V, n. 15; Hellebore was a plant with violent emetic and cathartic properties much used by the ancients as a remedy for mental disease; it has been used as a term of invective through the centuries.

6 C.f. Principe and Newman, "Alchemy vs. Chemistry," *passim*.

chymia in his work; nevertheless, she continues to use the term herself because Maier draws from sources prior to the widespread emergence of the term *chymia*, and because his iatrochemical goals bear a strong resemblance to those of his medieval predecessors (i.e. the production of a Universal Medicine which imparts its virtue to metals and the human body alike).[7] It behoves us to follow this sound reasoning when considering the continuity existing between Maier's work and subsequent esoteric pursuits sequestered from the scientific mainstream in the course of the eighteenth century. If we were to cease utilising the term 'alchemy' in favour of *chymia* on the grounds that such use would constitute a 'presentist' projection of contemporary categories into a time when they did not exist, we would be left with a medieval 'alchemy', an early modern *chymia*, and a modern 'alchemy', with no sense left of the clear ideological continuity between them. Likewise, the term 'alchemy' could not be applied to the pre-Arabic pursuit of metallic and spiritual transmutation. Given these difficulties inherent in Principe and Newmans' proposal, one may legitimately speak of Maier's place in an esoteric tradition of 'alchemy'; for just as the retrospectively-constructed term 'humanism' would have proved a strange conception in the Renaissance and early modern periods, so the term 'alchemy' – whilst possessing negative connotations in Maier's work – is indispensable as a category in the history of Western esotericism. In making sense of the alchemical past we cannot fail to be 'presentist', as our own schismatic understanding of science and religion is grounded in developments which were nascent in the early modern era but which had not fully crystallised by that time.

On this count there can be no doubt that Maier stood at a crossroad in the history of ideas, as Jung suggested; for whilst the rationalising elements present in his work led Peuckert to speak of Maier's "philosophy of the laboratory" which "must lead in the end to Newton,"[8] it is also clear that the spiritual alchemy, vitalism, pietism and pseudo-Egyptianism drawn from his work by the eighteenth century *Gold- und Rosenkreutz* lay on the wrong side of the *Aufklärung* (a fact demonstrated by that Order's inter-Masonic conflict with the Illuminati). But of course, in the eyes of Principe and Newman there is no continuity between early modern laboratory alchemy and the later esoteric traditions, as the alchemical *Decknamen* of the seventeenth century became 'meaningless' in the hands of the secret societies.[9]

---

7   de Jong, *Michael Maier's Atalanta Fugiens*, p. 11.

8   Peuckert, *Pansophie* (1936 edition), pp. 107-108.

9   Principe and Newman, "Some Problems with the Historiography of Alchemy," p. 387.

3. The 'Tradition' and the fate of Maier's thought

In order to offer a corrective to this claim, let us proceed to chart the history of the reception of Maier's thought amongst later writers. When delving through this history and uncovering the myriad verdicts pronounced concerning the value of Maier's labour or the moral standing of this man, it must be said that a mercurial figure emerges. Maier has been the subject of a spate of recent academic studies, many of which have focussed on his work of multimedia, the *Atalanta Fugiens*, which has been described as "the strangest, the most beautiful and the most innovative work of esoteric alchemy in the seventeenth century."[10] Maier has also figured in recent works of popular fiction, in which he has been playfully portrayed as the erstwhile correspondent of John Dee, or the purveyor of an elusive wisdom.[11] Amongst Protestant writers of the last century the judgment was mixed; thus Montgomery perceived in Maier's work inclinations towards "an existential Christ mysticism," yet the Reverend Craven felt that Maier's desire for "earthly riches" led him away from "higher studies."[12] And in the esoteric circles of contemporary Rosicrucianism and Freemasonry, Maier is accepted as an initiate of the mysteries and a representative of the 'Tradition', even if his enigmatic style has eluded some writers.[13]

The conception of a Tradition prevalent in contemporary esoteric circles stems in part from the Renaissance, and the attempt to identify the chain of

---

[10] *Kindlers Literatur Lexikon*. Vol. 8. Weinheim: Zweiburgen Verlag, 1982, p. 10478; in addition to those works already cited above, we may mention Mödersheim, Sabine. "Mater et Matrix: Michael Maiers alchimistische Sinnbilder der Mutter." In *Mutter und Mütterlichkeit: Wandel und Wirksamkeit einer Phantasie in der deutschen Literatur*. Würzburg: Königshausen und Neumann, 1996, pp. 31-56; Rebotier, Jacques. "La Musique Cachée de l'Atalanta Fugiens," *Chrysopoeia*, Vol. 1, 1987, pp. 56-76; Allen, Sally G. "Outrunning Atalanta: Feminine Destiny in Alchemical Transmutation," *Journal of Women in Culture and Society*, Vol. 6, 1980, pp. 210-221; Streich, Hildemarie. "Musikalische und psychologische Entsprechungen in der *Atalanta Fugiens* von Michael Maier." In *Correspondences in Man and World*. Eranos Yearbook, 1973. Leiden: E. J. Brill, 1975, pp. 361-426. Forthcoming studies on Maier will appear from Erik Leibenguth of Universität Heidelberg (*Cantilenae Intellectuales*) and Bernhard Zagler of Technische Universität München (*Theses Summam Doctrinae de Temperamentis Corporis Humani*).

[11] Umminger, Walter. *Das Winterkönigreich*. Stuttgart: Klett-Cotta, 1994; Eco, Umberto. *Das Foucaultsche Pendel*. München: Carl Hanser Verlag, 1989.

[12] Montgomery, *Cross and Crucible*, p. 19; Craven, *Count Michael Maier*, p. 11.

[13] Thus the *Ancient Mystical Order Rosae Crucis* (AMORC) recently established a 'Michael Maier' branch in Seattle; the Freemasonic writer Manly P. Hall once stated that Maier was one of a small group of adepts residing at the House of the Holy Spirit, but he "concealed his knowledge so cunningly that it is exceedingly difficult to extract from his writings the secrets which he possessed;" Hall, Manly P. *Lectures on Ancient Philosophy*. Los Angeles: Hall Publishing Co., 1929, p. 411.

initiates who transmitted the *philosophia perennis* from the time of the Jewish Patriarchs onwards; medieval alchemical texts also produced lists of those adept in the alchemical Art.[14] As we have seen, the identification of just such a Tradition was the central concern of Maier's *Symbola Aureae Mensae*, as it also was in the fifth and sixth chapters of his *Silentium post Clamores*, in which the Rosicrucian 'Brethren' were portrayed as only the latest representatives of a long line of purveyors of the *prisca sapientia*. As Faivre argues, the task of the scholar of esoteric studies is not to prove the existence of a *philosophia perennis* reaching beyond the Renaissance into antiquity, but rather to describe the different facets of the emergence of this idea as it appears in post-Renaissance discourse.[15] On this count we may note that in the decades following his death, Maier himself came to be regarded as an expositor of the Tradition amongst the proponents of Hermetic philosophy.

One of the earliest figures in this regard was Daniel Stoltzius von Stoltzenberg (c.1597-c.1644), a Bohemian alchemist who has been rather enthusiastically described by Read as "a humble disciple of the great Michael Maier."[16] Stoltzius studied at Charles University in Prague and at the University of Marburg, an important centre of 'Rosicrucian' activity; later in his life he would find employment in Constantinople.[17] Whilst in Frankfurt-am-Main Stoltzius visited Maier's publisher, Lucas Jennis; it seems Jennis himself arranged a viewing for the young man of certain alchemical emblems from the books of Maier and his fellow physician at the court of Moritz the Learned, Johann Daniel Mylius. According to Stoltzius, his soul was delighted by the "mystical sense" of these ingenious pictures; they provided some solace in the face of his flight from war-torn Bohemia, which seems to have coincided with the defeat and exile of Friedrich V. Having seen how much these copperplate engravings pleased the young man, Jennis suggested that he compose short verses to accompany their republication – the end result being the beautiful *Viridarium Chymicum* (*Chemical Pleasure-Garden*, 1624).[18] In the foreword to this work Stoltzius pays tribute to the pious

---

[14] Faivre, *Access to Western Esotericism*, p. 37.

[15] *Ibid.*, p. 51.

[16] Read, *Prelude to Chemistry*, p. 197.

[17] See Hild, Heike. *Das Stammbuch des Medicus, Alchemisten und Poeten Daniel Stoltzius als Manuskript des Emblembuches Viridarium Chymicum (1624) und als Zeugnis seiner Peregrinatio Academica*. Doctoral Thesis, Technische Universität München, 1991; also Karpenko, Vladimir. "Viridarium Chymicum: The Encyclopedia of Alchemy," *The Journal of Chemical Education*, Vol. 50, No. 4, April 1973, p. 272.

[18] Stoltzius, Daniel. *Viridarium Chymicum Figuris Cupro Incisis Adornatum et Poeticis Scripturis Illustratum: Ita ut non tantum oculorum et animi recreationum suppeditet, sed et profundiorem rerum naturalium considerationem excitet, ad haec forma sua oblonga Amicorum Albo inservire queat*. Frankfurt am Main: Lucas Jennis, 1624, p. A4: "Desiderabam igitur talem mihi Philothecam comparare, quae et oculos meos artificiosa

memory of Michael Maier, a celebrated doctor and a "most brilliant and learned man," and he speaks of the importance of embracing the "great treasure" that has been bequeathed through his work.[19] In a particularly poetic passage, Stoltzius describes his re-issuing of the emblems as the transmission to posterity of a tradition based on reason and experience:

With this flame before us, we shall not stray into darkness; leaning on this staff, we shall not fall in the slippery way; nor will we swear by someone's lengthy words or inane phantasms, but having been guided by Nature, we will examine everything with the precise touchstone of reason and pyrotechnic experiment, eagerly seizing the truth and rejecting falsehood. And by examining closely the unexhausted abysses of Nature, and the immense miracles in this great amphitheatre of the contemplated universe, we will be inspired to sing to the praise and glory of its Author.[20]

Here Stoltzius expresses a similar sentiment to that of the forty-second emblem and discourse of Maier's *Atalanta Fugiens* (1617), in which it is said that Nature, reason, experience and reading should be 'guide, staff, spectacles and lamp' to those who are employed in alchemical affairs (figure 32). The first intention of the alchemist, Maier writes, must be to discover "through intimate contemplation how Nature proceeds in her operations."[21] This was a staple theme of the medieval alchemical literature, and one that was reinforced by the Paracelsian emphasis on observation and experiment. Stoltzius adds that such knowledge of Nature aids our proximity to God, and that all our labours should be made to repay His love for us – a restatement of Maier's belief that we may know God through His works. The reading of the *liber mundi* remained a central concern of the Tradition as it appeared in later Paracelsian *Naturphilosophie* and eighteenth century Rosicrucianism.

---

pictura recrearet, et mystico sensu animum oblectaret: potissimum in hac Medicinae ergo suscepta peregrinatione, in qua Patriae meae mirandos et miserandos casus cum moerore audio, et turbis illis Martialibus hinc et inde dispersis, non sine gravi dolore, saepissime interturbor. Has ergo cupro incisas imagines Francofurti apud Dn. Lucam Jennisium praeter spem inveni, et cum mihi arriserint, eidem desiderium meum aperui. Propositum ille comprobavit, meque mei voti compotem reddidit, simulque ut figuras illas brevissimo Carmine describerem, et tecum, Lector Humaniss. communicarem, rogavit."

[19] *Ibid.*, p. A6.

[20] *Ibid.*: "Hac enim face praeeunte, in tenebris non aberrabimus; hoc baculo innixi, in via lubrica non cademus, neque amplius in alicujus sesquipedalia verba, et inania phantasmata jurabimus, sed naturae ductum sequendo, ad rationis et experientiae pyronomicae trutinam omnia examinabimus, verum avide arripiemus, falsum abjiciemus, Inexhaustas Naturae abyssos, et miracula immensa in hoc totius Universitatis Amphitheatro intuendo, ad laudem et gloriam Conditori decantandam excitabimur."

[21] Maier, *Atalanta Fugiens*, discourse 42: "Prima itaque intentio est, naturam intime contemplati quomodo procedat in suis operationibus eo fine, ut subjecta Chymiae naturalia absque defectu aut superfluitate haberi queant."

The conception that knowledge of Nature leads to knowledge of things divine was succinctly expressed by another early appraiser of Maier, the French alchemist Jean d'Espagnet (1564-c.1637). In his *Enchiridio Physicae Restitutae* ('Summary of the Restored Physics,' 1623), written a year after Maier's death, d'Espagnet tells us that the ancients knew the world was prefigured in its Archetype, which is God; before Creation He was like unto "a book rolled up in Himself," but by giving birth to the world His mind was made manifest, so that Nature is nothing else but "the disclosed image of an occult Deity."[22] In his writings d'Espagnet gives alchemical meanings to Greek and Egyptian myth in a style reminiscent of Maier's; he also recommends that those who have not understood the alchemists should inspect the writings of Maier on account of their perspicuity:

Philosophers do usually expresse themselves more pithily in types and aenigmaticall figures (as by a mute kind of speech) then by words; for example, Senior's Table, the allegoricall Pictures of Rosarius, the Schemes of Abraham Judaeus in Flamellus: of the later sort, the rare Emblemes of the most learned Michael Maierus, wherein the mysteries of the Ancients are so fully opened, that as new Perspectives they can present antiquated truth, and remote from our age as near unto our eies, and perfectly to be seen by us.[23]

Although Schick once asserted that Maier was a 'theosopher',[24] the thought of laboratory alchemists such as Maier or d'Espagnet is more often described as 'pansophist' due to its emphasis on knowing divinity through Nature, rather than using gnosis or theosophical speculation on cosmogony as a point of departure.[25] Nevertheless, there were a variety of worldviews grouped under the rubric of the term *theosophia* in early modern Germany, some of which grew directly from alchemical labours before the furnace fire. Maier's contemporary and fellow Lutheran, Khunrath, spoke of theosophy in terms of the mystical perception of a universal, external and visible fire of Nature, and its complement in a universal, internal and invisible fire – that is to say, in terms of both a knowledge and a life-imparting entity that transcends the

---

[22] d'Espagnet, Jean. *Enchyridion Physicae Restitutae, or, A Summary of the Physicks Recovered.* Ed. Thomas Willard. New York: Garland Publishing, Inc., 1999, p. 10.

[23] Ashmole, Elias. *Fasciculus Chemicus: or, Chymical Collections. Expressing the Ingress, Progress, and Egress, of the Secret Hermetick Science, out of the Choisest and most Famous Authors. Collected and digested in such an order, that it may prove to the advantage, not onely of the Beginners, but Proficients of this high Art, by none hitherto disposed in this Method. Whereunto is added, the Arcanum or Grand Secret of Hermetick Philosophy. Both made English by James Hasolle, Esquire, Qui est Mercuriophilus Anglicus.* London: Printed by J. Flesher for Richard Mynne, at the sign of St.Paul in Little Britain, 1650, p. 169.

[24] Schick, *Das Ältere Rosenkreuzertum*, p. 250.

[25] On this point see Faivre, *Access to Western Esotericism*, pp. 23-32.

apparent division between the interior and exterior worlds.[26] Similarly, Maier's own use of the term 'theosophy' in the *De Theosophia Aegyptiorum* denotes a knowledge of divine things acquired through the reading of 'hieroglyphs' present in both the microcosm and the macrocosm, which proceeds from the gnostic and revelatory operation of the 'little eye of the soul'. Whilst there is nothing in the way of explicit theological speculation in Maier's works, given the complementarity of the Light of Nature and the Light of Grace (the latter being the inspiration of theosophers proper such as Boehme and Weigel), later theosophically-oriented Paracelsians could comfortably portray Maier as a 'chymico-theologian'.

Whilst Rosicrucianism underwent something of a lull in Germany after its initial efflorescence, across the English Channel Maier's reputation in Britain as an expositor of Rosicrucian knowledge was furthered by Nathaniel and Thomas Hodges' 1656 translation of his *Themis Aurea*, entitled *The Laws of the Fraternity of the Rosie Crosse*.[27] The dedicatee of this translation was "the most excellently accomplish't, the onely Philosopher in the present age: the Honoured, Noble, Learned, Elias Ashmole, Esq.," who as we have mentioned was an early English Freemason and a member of the Royal Society. In accordance with their concern to establish an unbroken lineage of adepts, in the eyes of later esoteric writers England became the nexus for the transmission of Rosicrucian ideas through the fictitious Maier-Fludd-Ashmole chain we have discussed.[28] Whether or not Freemasonry was influenced by Rosicrucian ideas at this early stage, the currency of Maier's thought in 'Rosicrucian' circles is demonstrated by Thomas Vaughan's citations from the *Themis Aurea* in his preface to the English edition of the *Fama Fraternitatis* (1652). Furthermore, the 1618 version of the *Themis Aurea* had a preface addressed to a certain S. P. D., who was described as "Theod. Verax., Theophil. Caelnatus;" after the publication of Vaughan's version of the *Fama Fraternitatis* an open letter appeared in reply from

---

[26] Khunrath, Heinrich. *De Igne Magorum Philosophorum.* Strassburg: Lazarus Zetzner, 1608, pp. 87-88.

[27] Maier, Michael. *Themis Aurea: The Laws of the Fraternity of the Rosie Crosse. Written in Latin by Count Michael Maierus, And now in English for the Information of those who seek after the knowledge of that Honourable and mysterious Society of wise and renowned Philosophers... Whereto is annexed an Epistle to the Fraternity in Latine, from some here in England.* London: Printed for N. Brooke at the Angel in Cornhill, 1656.

[28] Hence William Wynn Westcott, writing in 1926 in his capacity as Supreme Magus of the *Societas Rosicruciana in Anglia*, stated that Maier "admitted Robert Fludd, M. A. and M. D. Oxon. to Rosicrucian Adeptship;" Fludd became "First Magus" in England, followed by Sir Kenelm Digby, whilst Ashmole received the torch of occult truth from William Backhouse, "a renowned Rosicrucian and Chemist:" introduction to Gardner, F. Leigh. *A Catalogue Raisonné of Works on the Occult Sciences.* Vol. 1. N.p.; n.p., 1923, pp. xviii-xix.

"Theodosius Verax and Theophilus Caelnatus," a clear indication that the German edition of the *Themis Aurea* was in circulation in England prior to the appearance of the English *Fama Fraternitatis*.[29] Maier's *Lusus Serius* was also published in English at this time as *The Serious Jest* (1654),[30] and there exist two English manuscript translations of the *Atalanta Fugiens* dating to the seventeenth century.[31]

Following the devastation wreaked by the Thirty Years War in Germany, the thought of Maier re-appeared in an interesting series of dialogues concerning the true nature of alchemy and the possibility of the transmutation of metals. In 1673 the renowned German encyclopaedist and professor of history at the University of Kiel, Daniel Morhof (1639-1691), published a lengthy letter concerning the transmutation of metals (*De Metallorum Transmutatione*) he had earlier sent to the chief physician at the court of Schleswig-Holstein, Joel Langelott (1617-1680). In this letter he advises caution in the pursuit of metallic transmutation, arguing agnostically that the secrets of *chrysopoeia* or gold-making will probably remain forever unknown, just as the processes of metallic formation in the womb of the earth must remain hidden from human eyes.[32] Whilst acknowledging the many benefits of *chymia*, Morhof argues that prudence should prevail before spending time and money on the uncertain quest for transmutation. He goes on to impugn those pseudo-chemists who set out to deceive even the most observant clients by concealing gold dust in the coals of their fires, or within the instruments with which they work. On this count he mentions the *Examen Fucorum Pseudo-chymicorum* of the 'learned' Michael Maier, in which are enumerated over fifty such ingenious frauds:

...I have recommended that his book be read, lest we may be deceived by those impostors, whose sole labour it is, to seek wealth of their own by imposing the hope for wealth on others: a practice by which the harmless study of alchemy is led into odium, and honest men come to perceive this Art as an empty mockery, or curse all chymists as fraudulent.[33]

---

[29] Waite, *Brotherhood of the Rosy Cross*, pp. 329, 386; according to Heisler, there is an English manuscript translation of portions of the *Themis Aurea* dating to 1623.

[30] Maier, Michael. *Lusus Serius, or, Serious Passe-time. A Philosophical Discourse concerning the Superiority of Creatures under Man*. London: Moseley and Heath, 1654.

[31] Maier, *The Flying Atalanta*, is held by the British Library; Yale University Library houses *Atalanta Running, that is, New Chymicall Emblems relating to the Secrets of Nature*. Yale University Library, MS 48; this latter work may have been a rough draft for a planned English edition that never emerged.

[32] Morhof, D. G. *De Metallorum Transmutatione, ad Virum Nobilissimum et Amplissimum Joelem Langelottum, Serenissimi Principis Cimbrici Archiatrum Celeberrimum, Epistola*. Hamburg: Ex Officina Gothofredi Schultzen, 1673, p. 83.

[33] *Ibid.*, pp. 84-85: "Talibus enim operandi modis plerumque dignoscendi Pseudo Chemici, qui adeo speciose fraudes suas tegere possunt, ut vel oculatissimos nonnunquam fallant: per infidias enim auri pulverem vel carbonibus, vel instrumentis, quibus operantur,

Here Morhof uses the terms *alchemia* and *chymia* to denote the *iatrochemia* formerly pursued by the 'learned' Maier, and now practised by his friend Langelott; this 'alchemy' stands in contrast with *chrysopoeia*, which had been so thoroughly tainted by fraud. Later in his letter Morhof also commends Maier's *Arcana Arcanissima*. Although he feels Maier ascribed a little too much ingenuity to the Egyptians as the concealers of chemical truth with myth and hieroglyph, Morhof notes that Maier's argument is followed by Vigenerius, Johannes Petrus Faber, Conringius, and the 'father' of early Egyptology, Athanasius Kircher.[34] In his *Oedipus Aegyptiacus* (1653), in the chapter entitled *De Alchymia Aegyptiaca*, Kircher argued that the hieroglyphs referred symbolically to "a certain quintessence" that cures illness and imparts abundant happiness, on account of which it is known as "the highest subtlety and perfection;" he also makes brief mention of Maier's *Arcana Arcanissima*, although his status as a Jesuit seems to have hindered him from citing more freely from a book that was to earn a place on the Index in 1667.[35]

Despite the decline of early Rosicrucianism in the German-speaking lands, the Paracelsian alchemy which was the life-blood of its eighteenth century revival remained. A rejoinder to the dialogue between Morhof and Langelott was made by Johann Ludwig Hanneman (1640-1724), a professor of natural philosophy at Köln patronised by Christian Albert, King of Norway and ruler of Schleswig-Holstein. Hanneman was a believer not only in the Universal Medicine but also in the possibility of the transmutation of metals, and there is a strong mystical streak in his work, whereby chemistry and

---

recondunt, ut arte factum quis putet, quod verum est et nativum. Quoru. quinquaginta et amplius fraudes sane ingeniosissimas recenset Michael Meierus in Examine Fucorum Pseudo-Chemicorum detectorum: quem vel ideo librum legendum suaserim, ne fallamur ab agyrtis istis et impostoribus, quorum unicus labor est, spe lucri aliis ostensa sibi lucrum quaerere: quo fit, ut innoxia Alchemiae studia in invidiam adducantur, honestique homines vel ut res inanes ludibrio habeant, vel ut fraudulentas detestentur."

[34] *Ibid.*, p. 104: "Hinc plurimas Graecorum fabulas natas fuisse verosimile est, quas ingeniose satis ad Chemicos sensus explicat Michael Mejerus, Vir doctus, in *Arcanis suis arcanissimis sive Hieroglyphicus Aegyptio-Graecis vulgo nondum cognitis*, qui tamen ob amorem artis fortassis nimium ingenio suo indulget. Quem sequuntur in hoc instituto *Vigenerius commentario in Philostrati tabulas et Pet. Ioh. Faber in Pan-Chymico suo.* Negare certe ipse Conringius non potest, docendi ac scribendi rationem apud Aegyptios, Chemicorum ordini semper familiarem, et ad hos ab illis derivatam videri posse. Kircherus vero noster quasi e tripode pronunciat (*Oedip. Aegyptiac. tom. 2. classe 10. de Alchymica Aegyptiaca*) Aegyptios praxin lapidis Philosophorum haud intendisse, sed rem quandam in inferiori mundo Soli analogam et quintam quandam essentiam pro morbis omnibus curandis et vita in omni felicitate traducenda."

[35] Kircher, Athanasius. *Oedipus Aegyptiacus*. Vol. 2. Rome: Vitalis Mascardi, 1653, p. 399; Moller, *Cimbria Literata*, p. 379: "E vocibus Praefationis: *Salvifico verbo*, priorem *Salvifici Index Expurg. Hispanicus,* ab Ant. Sotomajore Madriti A. 1667 editus, p. 787., ridicule jubet expungi."

theology are brought into close proximity. In his *Cato Chemicus Tractatus* (1690) he set out to distinguish between "the true and genuine hermetic philosophy, and the counterfeit and sophistical pseudo-chemistry, as well as the characteristics of the masters of both."[36] There the *Examen Fucorum Pseudo-chymicorum* is specified as the means by which these two lineages may be distinguished; Hanneman also recommends Heinrich Khunrath (c.1560-1605), whose warnings concerning the *Betrüger* were translated from the vernacular into Latin by Maier and quoted at length in his own polemic. Great praise is lavished on Maier in Hanneman's *Ovum Hermetico-Paracelsico-Trismegistum* ('Hermetic-Paracelsian-Trismegistian Egg,' 1694); and whilst there is no reason to doubt the sincerity of Hanneman's beliefs, his love of Maier ("O most serene and merciful master!") is certainly motivated in part by ethnic pride. Amongst learned men, Maier is "a star of the first magnitude" not only in Jutland but in all Europe, and through him Jutland shines as the possessor of that 'sublimer' Hermetic Art.[37] As a number of erudite persons have flourished in Jutland under the name of Maier, Hanneman suggests further research should be made into his lineage by means of baptismal records, and he also muses that some material may one day be found concerning the nature of his death in Magdeburg.[38]

---

[36] Hanneman, Johann Ludwig. *Cato Chemicus Tractatus: Quo Verae ac Genuinae Philosophiae Hermeticae, et Fucatae ac Sophisticae Pseudo Chemiae et utriusque Magistrorum Characterismi accurate delineantur.* Hamburg: Gothofried Liebernickel, 1690.

[37] Hanneman, Johann Ludwig. *Ovum Hermetico-Paracelsico-Trismegistum, i.e. Commentarius-Philosophico-Chemico-Medicus, In quandam Epistolam Mezahab Dictam de Auro. Et Historia Philosophico Chemico-Medica de eodem metallo nativo et artificiali. In quo et 108. Quaestiones Chemicae ab Excellentiss. D. D. Morhofio propositae ab Autore solvuntur. Omnia, juxta adeptae Paracelsicae et Eclecticae Philosophiae principia.* Frankfurt am Main: Friderich Knoch, 1694, pp. C1a-C1b: "Multi sunt ex omnium facultatum et scientiarum Professoribus, qui pro ejus divinioris artis veritate pugnarunt, ac doctissima apologemata conscripserunt. Ex quorum numero duo instar omnium, qui et Cymbriae nostrae, imo universae Europae stellae primae magnitudinis fuerunt, esse possunt. Quos et jam ex nube testium in hoc theatro sisto, ut puta DD. Michaelem Meyerum, qui O serenissime Princeps ac Domine clementissime! primam suae vitae auram Tuae Cymbriae, in hac enim dicitur natus, tuusque vel et beatae memoriae Divi Parentis subditus fuit, ut hoc pluribus in commentarii hujus contextu asserui. Sicque haec nostra Chersonesus Cymbrica consummatissimo istius Hermeticae sublimioris possessore superba fulget. Huic a latere jungimus DD. Morhofium, o candidum olim amicitiae nostrae pectus!"

[38] *Ibid.*, p. 133: "Forsan adhuc Magdeburgi aliqua notitia de eo haberi posset. Esset revera operae pretium, anxius quis inquireret in ejus familiam, ad quamnam *Mejeranam* esset relegandus. Aluit enim alias nostra Cimbria Eruditos Mejeros Criticos, Mathematicos, Rectores, Gymnasiarchas, Poetas, Concionatores et id genus Eruditos. Ad aliquam autem familiam Mejeranam hic noster Philosophus adeptus afferendus. Quod si inquirerentur

In the course of his *Ovum Hermetico-Paracelsico-Trismegistum* Hanneman refers to the "chemical questions" proposed by the sceptical Morhof, which he seeks to answer "in accordance with the principles of Paracelsian and eclectic philosophy."[39] These questions seem to have arisen not only from the publication of Morhof's *De Metallorum Transmutatione*, but also because Morhof had personally shown Hanneman a letter from Maier (now apparently lost) to a certain doctor in Lübeck condemning alchemical *Betrügerei*.[40] In his reply to Morhof, Hanneman counts Maier amongst the *adeptae*, who in his eyes possessed the means to transmute both metallic and human bodies. In his *Ovum* he sets forward four (slightly shaky) reasons for this assertion. Firstly, Maier was physician to Emperor Rudolf II, a man who was himself most experienced in chemical matters, and who promoted Maier to the position of Count Palatine on account of his fine service; secondly, because the Emperor granted Maier nothing less than the 'symbol of Avicenna', the representation of the magistery that appears on Maier's coat-of-arms – an honour that would never have been granted unless Maier had possessed that magistery; thirdly, because clear and manifest testimonies concerning the arcana are given in Maier's *Viatorium, Symbola Aureae Mensae* and *Arcana Arcanissima*; and fourthly, because Maier is counted amongst the adepts by other adepts, such as the author of the *Experimentum Osiandrinorum*.[41] Here Hanneman refers to the *Osiandrische Experiment* (1659), in which the anonymous author writes of his efforts to repeat the purported experimental production of the Philosophers' Stone by Lucas

---

Matriculae Ecclesiasticae, quibus recens baptisati infantes inscribi solent. Quilibet Pastor alicujus Parochiae tantum temporis facile impenderet ut suae Ecclesiae matriculam perlustraret, anne ex ea aliquid luminis huic dubio accendi posset."

[39] Hanneman also addressed Morhof's doubts concerning *chrysopoeia* in a book-length commentary on the *Arcanum Hermeticae Philosophiae* of d'Espagnet entitled *Instructissima Pharus*. Kiel: n.p., 1712, p. 190.

[40] Hanneman, *Ovum Hermetico-Paracelsico-Trismegistum*, p. 131: "Mihi aliquando praelaudatus Morhofius concessit literas ipsius Michaelis Meyeri manu hic Kiliae exaratas ad quendam Chymicum Lubecae commorantem, in quo vehementius expostulat de dolo, quo ipsi Chymicus pessime imposuerat; in istius Epistolae contextu multa occurrebant, quae ipsum Cimbriae nostrae asserebant."

[41] *Ibid.*, pp. 130-131: "(1) Quia fuit Archiater ipsius Imperatoris, qui istorum naturae Mysteriorum fuit peritissimus, ejus autem clementia luculentissime esse usum, probat quod ab eo Autore in Comitem Palatinum fuerit promotus. (2) Quod ipsi Imperator ad insignia concesserit symbolum Avicennae, quo hoc Magisterium adumbratur: et est: *Aquila volans per aerem et Bufo gradiens per terram est Magisterium;* scilicet Aquila catena Bufoni alligata est. Nunquam autem suis insignibus hoc symbolum inseruisset, nisi istius artis vel Magisterii fuisset Possessor. (3) Idem et probant ejus scripta, cumprimis Viatorium; symbolae aureae mensae; Arcana arcanissima etc. in quibus evidentia et perspicua testimonia istius arcani exstant. (4) ab omnibus inter Adeptos refertur, quoque iis eum annumerat Author Experimentorum Osiandrinorum, et alii multi."

Osiander (1534-1604), a Lutheran professor of theology and chancellor at the University of Tübingen; in that work the *lapis* is conceived of as both a Tincture for metals and a miraculous medicine, and the lineage of twelve nations given in Maier's *Symbola Aureae Mensae* is reiterated.[42]

When enumerating these proofs, perhaps Hanneman was unaware of the fact that Maier had only reached the seventeenth rung of the alchemical ladder leading to the Philosophers' Stone. Nevertheless, his aim was to establish and define for his own purposes an authoritative Tradition in which Maier himself appears as a representative, thus lending credence to his own conception of the alchemical Art as the means of metallic and human transmutation. Thus Hanneman also identifies in detail an "unbroken chain" of German adepts, because "our Germany has brought forth so many who have acquired that golden harvest, and it may in future bring forth more."[43] This chain is led by Albertus Magnus, the Swabian Dominican and eminent scientist whose name adorns a number of alchemical works from the fourteenth and fifteenth centuries; it moves through Bernard of Trevisan, Basil Valentine of Alsatia, Isaac Hollandus, Johannes Pontanus, Jodocus Greverus, Paracelsus, Borrichius, Abbot Trithemius, Johannes Rhenanus, Valentin Weigel, Heinrich Khunrath, and comes to Michael Maier. We cannot fail to note the inclusion in this list of the theosopher Weigel, who was not a laboratory worker but whose work is congruent in Hanneman's eyes with a practical alchemical endeavour. For Hanneman, Maier was "an incomparable priest of the mysteries," a revealer of that sacred knowledge held by the pre-Christian pagans which Maier himself terms a 'theosophy'.[44] Thus Hanneman also lauds *Arcana Arcanissima* ("O most learned of writings!") and he suggests (in concert with Moller) that the fame of the Jesuit Athanasius Kircher has derived in no small part from Maier's own findings in that work.[45]

---

[42] *Osiandrische Experiment von Sole, Luna et Mercuria, Welche in fürnehmer Herren laboratoriis probirt worden darauß mehr per Exempla als Rationes, oder durch viel verwirzte Proceß verkehrte Sophistische und unnütze Bücher verschrauffte Wort und subtile Reden und die wahre Philosophische Materi, rechte Solution, Gewicht, Glas, Ofen und Regierung des Feuers zu fassen, und zumal man richtige Anleitung hat, dem Werck zur Tinctur und Arztnei weiter nachzudencken und zuergründen.* Nürnberg: Johann Andreas, 1659, p. 39.

[43] Hanneman, *Ovum Hermetico-Paracelsico-Trismegistum*, p. 127.

[44] *Ibid.*, p. 130: "Locum decimum sextum sibi vindicat DD. Michael Mejerus Archiater Rudolphi Imperatoris; de quo sibi nostra gratulatur Cimbria, qua hic magnus Vir oriundus, adeptae Philosophiae ac arcanioris sapientiae mysta incomparabilis, perspicua dictione usus est, et caeteris luculentius scripsit; Quare autem ipsum Adeptum faciamus nos sequentes rationes movent."

[45] *Ibid.*, pp. B5b-B6a: "Asserit id mecum incluta et Nobilissima Virorum triga, quae rei literariae nostri seculi fulgidissima lumina fuerunt, ut puta praelaudatus DD. Michael Mayerus adeptus Holsatus; DD. Morhofius et DD. Jacobus Toll; iste in suis arcanis

An increasing antagonism emerged in the course of the eighteenth century towards *chrysopoeia* and the claims of gold-makers such as Hanneman, and it is interesting that the name of Maier was also invoked by those who wished to discredit alchemy altogether. One of the most intriguing references to Maier in this regard comes from a certain 'Tharsander', or the physician Georg Wilhelm Wegner, in his amusingly entitled *Adeptus Ineptus* (1744). The subtitle of his work reads:

An exposé of the falsely celebrated art known as Alchemy, wherein the inanity of this art is clearly proven, the principles of the alchemists scrutinised and refuted, their beguiling exposed, and the likelihood of the impossibility of metallic transmutation is set forth...[46]

In the course of his polemic Wegner does not distinguish between *chrysopoeia* and the quest for the Universal Medicine, which he also impugns as a delusion. His definition of alchemy runs as follows:

By alchemy I understand that art which teaches the means of transmuting metals, and of bringing imperfect metals to their maturity, or making Gold or Silver from imperfect metals. Or it is the art of preparing the Philosophers' Stone, which not only makes imperfect metals into Gold and Silver, but also works in the human body as a general medicament for the preservation of health and life. I speak therefore not of *Chimia*, which is the art of opening the natural body, of separating, purifying, and setting it together again, thereby making it more amenable to medicine and other useful applications. I have deemed it necessary to state this in order that no-one should believe that I reject and disapprove of *Chimia*, which I do in fact hold to be the most highly useful art.[47]

---

arcanissimis (o doctissimum scriptum) in quibus Aegyptiorum Mythologiam, idololatriam de hac arte felicissime explicavit, ut de *Athanasio Kirchero* scribat *Casalius Romanus* lib. II. de Ritibus Veter. Aegyptiorum c. 10 p. 35. *Difficillimam hanc antiquitatum Aegyptiarum, sacrorumque mysteriorum sub hieroglyphicis disciplinis latentium, a nemine hucusque tentatam investigationem etc.* Verum nisi arasset Vitulo nostri Mayeri haud tanto elogio dignus esset. Preter haec arcana arcanissima edita Mejeri, restat adhuc aliud Msc. ejusdem Autoris in eodem argumento conscriptum."

[46] Wegner, *Adeptus Ineptus*, title page.: "Adeptus Ineptus, Oder Entdeckung der falsch berühmten Kunst ALCHIMIE genannt: Darin die Nichtigkeit solcher Kunst klärlich erwiesen, der Alchimisten Principia untersucht und widerlegt, ihre Betrügereyen eröffnet, und die Unmöglichkeit der Metallen-Verwandlung wenigstens auf das wahrscheinlichste dargethan, Wie auch von der Universal-Medicin und anderen vorgegebenen Alchimistischen Kunst-Stücken gehandelt wird."

[47] *Ibid.*, p. 9: "Durch die Alchimie verstehe ich diejenige Kunst, welche lehret die Metallen zu verwandlen, und die unvollkommenen zu ihrer Reife zu bringen, oder aus denen unvollkommenen Metallen Gold und Silber zu machen. Oder es ist eine Kunst den Stein der Weisen zu bereiten, welcher nicht allein die unvollkommene Metallen zu Gold und Silber macht, sondern auch in dem menschlichen Cörper, als eine allgemeine Artzney, zur Erhaltung der Gesundheit und des Lebens würket. Ich rede also nicht von der Chimie, welches eine Kunst ist die natürlichen Cörper aufzuschliessen, zu scheiden, zu reinigen, sie wieder zusammen zu setzen, und dadurch zur Artzney und anderm nützlichen Gebrauch tüchtig zu machen. Solches habe ich zu erinnern für nöthig geachtet, damit

Thus Wegner makes a clear demarcation between a non-vitalistic conception of '*chimia*' and a vitalistic '*alchemy*' which has as its goal the isolation of a universal agent of transmutation. He distinguishes between two types of deception carried out by the alchemists – the conscious deception of others, and a self-deception brought about by the obscurity of the alchemical corpus combined with the alchemists' greed for worldly wealth.[48] Wegner states that such laboratory workers are not only thieves to themselves, but also deprive their needy neighbours through their wasteful practices; he suggests that if one could only gather together all the money that has been frittered away by alchemists through the ages, one could buy not only great cities such as London, Amsterdam and Paris, but entire kingdoms.[49]

In the passage pertaining to Michael Maier, Wegner rather unkindly states that those who eventually recognise their self-deception imagine they have thereby achieved something important, and some have flattered themselves by relating their experiences in print.[50] On this count he presents a tract which he attributes to Maier, the "famous Rosicrucian" who was known on occasion to "run around the German courts with the Gold-spear."[51] The name of this tract is the *Treuhertzige Warnungs-Vermahnung*, which also appears in the late compendium of alchemical texts, the *Deutsches Theatrum Chemicum* (1728);[52] it is dedicated to "all lovers of *Alchymie Transmutatoriae*" from a certain "faithful lover of Truth" named 'Riceni Thrasibuli'. Although Ferguson followed Wegner in attributing this work to Maier in his *Bibliotheca Chemica*,[53] Riceni Thrasibuli is actually a pseudonym of Heinrich Khunrath; the tract itself appears in Khunrath's *Von Hylealischen, Das ist Pri-Materia-lischen Catholischen, oder Algemeinem Natürlichen Chaos* (1597). Nevertheless, we have seen that extracts from

---

man nicht meyne, als ob ich die Chimie verwerffen und widerlegen wolte, die ich doch für eine höchst nützliche Kunst halte."

[48] *Ibid.*, pp. 79 ff.

[49] *Ibid.*, p. 80: "Das ist ein großer Selbstbetrug, welcher dabey noch sündlich ist: Denn solche Laboranten werden zu Dieben an sich selbst, und auch an ihren nothleidenden Nächsten, dem sie von ihren reichlichen Vermögen hätten einiger maßen dienen können... Wann ich nur das Geld zusammen haben mögte, welches jemahls durch die Alchimisten liederlich verlaboriret ist, wolte ich nicht nur fragen ob London, Amsterdam und Paris feil waren? Sondern ich getrauete mich ganze große Königreiche damit zu bezahlen, und wenn sie zu Kauf stünden an mich zu handeln."

[50] *Ibid.*, pp. 80-81.

[51] *Ibid.*, p. 94: "...der bekannte Rosen-Creuzer Michael Maier, der hin und wider mit dem Gold-Spieß, an den teutschen Höfen, weidlich herum gelaufen..."; I have not been able to identify the precise meaning of this derogatory expression.

[52] Khunrath, Heinrich. "Treuhertzige Warnungs-Vermahnung an alle Liebhaber der Natur-gemesen Alchemie Transmutatoriae." In *Deutsches Theatrum Chemicum*. Nürnberg: Adam Jonathan Felßecker, 1728, pp. 289-313.

[53] Ferguson, John. *Bibliotheca Chemica*. London: Starker Brothers, 1906, p. 66.

the *Treuhertzige Warnungs-Vermahnung* do in fact feature prominently in Maier's *Examen Fucorum Pseudo-chymicorum*.[54] Wegner bases his attribution of the work to Maier on a remark made by a certain Felix Maurer, who states that Maier had compiled in one of his works "the most remarkable intrigues and trickery" that he had met with in the German courts – a work which Maurer believed should be "included as a foreword to all alchemical texts hitherto printed."[55] It seems his reference was to the *Examen Fucorum Pseudo-chymicorum*, with which Wegner was clearly not acquainted.

4. Alchemy and the re-emergence of Rosicrucianism

Despite the protests of an increasing number of sceptics such as Wegner, the practical laboratory quest for the Philosophers' Stone survived until at least the end of the eighteenth century in Germany – chiefly amongst the inheritors of the Rosicrucian mantle, the members of the *Gold- und Rosenkreutz*. This survival forms a bridge between early modern and nineteenth century conceptions of alchemy – a critical link missing from Principe and Newmans' historiography.

The first sign of the emergence of the *Gold- und Rosenkreutz* is the *Warhaffte und vollkommene Bereitung des Philosophischen Steins der Brüderschafft aus dem Orden des Gülden- und Rosen-Creutzes* ('The True and Complete Preparation of the Philosophers' Stone of the Brotherhood, from the Order of the Golden and Rosy Cross,' 1710), a tract that appeared under the pseudonym of 'Sincerus Renatus' ('genuine rebirth').[56] The author is generally held to be a Protestant pastor from Hartmannsdorf in Silesia by the name of Samuel Richter. True to the example set by seventeenth century Rosicrucian literature, it is not clear whether an actual secret society lay behind Richter's work. Waite suggested the laws of the Fraternity appended to the text demonstrate that "something had been growing up in the silence," and the recent discovery of late seventeenth century Italian documents

---

[54] See above, pp. 106-107.

[55] Wegner, *Adeptus Ineptus*, p. 94: "...er die merckwürdigsten Räncke und Taschen-Spielerey, so dabey fürgehen, in ein Buch zusammen gebracht, welches meritirte, daß es allen alchimistischen Schriften als eine Vorrede von neuen angedruckt würde."

[56] Richter, Samuel. *Die Warhaffte und vollkommene Bereitung des Philosophischen Steins/ Der Brüderschafft aus dem Orden des Gülden- und Rosen-Creutzes/ Darinne die Materie zu diesem Geheimniß mit seinem Nahmen genennet/ auch die Bereitung von Anfang bis zu Ende mit allen Hand-Griffen gezeiget ist/ Dabey angehänget die Gesetz oder Regeln/ welche die gedachte Brüderschafft unter sich hält/ Denen Filiis Doctrinae zum Besten publiciret von S.R.* Breslau: Fellgiebel, 1710.

referring to a 'gold and rosy cross' seems to confirm his intuition.[57] In any case, the alchemical and theosophical ideology presented by Richter in the course of his work demonstrates a clear continuity of thought with earlier Rosicrucianism, and can hardly be dismissed as 'meaningless'.[58]

In his introduction Richter states that "some years ago" the Brethren had taken their leave of Europe and settled in India "to live there in greater peace" – a reference taken from a *Kampfschrift* that appeared in the initial Rosicrucian furore.[59] The main body of the work is concerned with laboratory alchemical procedure; drawing on the thought of Paracelsus, van Helmont and Basil Valentine, Richter demonstrates the means of obtaining a 'perfect metal' through repeated projection of the *lapis*.[60] The appendix of laws begins by stating that in 1624 the Fraternity made an effort to summon their Brethren from across the world, but that only nine new members and two apprentices were found due to the strict criteria of admission; in time a decision was made to increase the Fraternity's membership and construct a new set of laws, in order that such an "invaluable treasure" as was held by the Brethren should not be lost to the world.[61] Thus, in contrast to the anti-Catholic emphasis of the manifestos, a 'don't ask, don't tell' policy concerning the religious affiliation of members is prescribed; mention is also made of the fact that the society has been divided into two branches, the Rosy Cross and the Golden Cross.[62] Most of the laws govern the use of the Philosophers' Stone, which imparts sixty years to the lifespan of those who

---

[57] C.f. chapter I, n. 125 above.

[58] Waite, *Brotherhood of the Rosy Cross*, p. 403.

[59] *Ibid.*

[60] Richter, *Die Warhaffte und vollkommene Bereitung des Philosophischen Steins*, p. 57: "Diese Materie der andern Ordnung/ wird auf eine andere Art projectiret/ als wie oben gesagt/ dreymahl rectificiret/ und reincrudiret worden/ alsdenn sie von vielen grössern Kräfften zusammen gesetzet. Nimm also I. Theil dieses rectificirten Steines/ und trage ihn auf 100. Theil geflossen Metall/ diese 100. auf 1000./ diese 1000. auf 10000./und diese 10000 auf 1000000. Und also procedire biß auf die 10. Projection, so wird 1. Theil auf hundert fallen/ und ein perfectes Metall von allen Proben seyn."

[61] *Ibid.*, pp. 99-100: "Diese unsre Congregation war vor diesem von unsern alten Helden mit sehr strengen Clausuln und Gesetzen auffgerichtet worden/ durch welche unsere neue Brüderschaft wahrgenommen/ daß dieses allein die Ursach sey/ warum ietzo so wenig derselben gefunden werden/ deßwegen haben sie um das Jahr 1624. durch die ganze Welt ihr Votum und Stimme ergehen lassen/ um die Brüder zu beruffen/ von welchen nur ihren 9. und 2. Lehrlinge gefunden worden/ welche nach langer und reiffer Unterredung endlich beschlossen haben/ daß man diese Brüderschafft vermehren müsse/ damit ein so unschätzbares Kleinod/ als dieses/ so das allergröste ist/ unter denen zeitlichen Gütern dieser Welt/ nicht verlohren gehen möchte. Darum auch die ganze Zusammenkunfft übereinstimmig worden/ und confirmiret/ nach folgende Puncta zu halten."

[62] *Ibid.*, p. 102.

ingest it.[63] When undertaking their 'renewal' in this manner the brethren must permanently remove themselves to another country; they are also enjoined not to use the *lapis* whilst hunting.[64]

Whilst these peculiar edicts mitigate against the possibility that there existed behind Richter's work an actual cult centred on the miraculous powers of the *lapis*, the *Warhaffte und vollkommene Bereitung des Philosophischen Steins* was an influence on the emergence of later Rosicrucianism within Freemasonic circles around the middle of the eighteenth century.[65] The first German Freemasonic Lodge was founded in 1737; in the following decades there emerged a variety of higher degrees augmenting the three Craft degrees (Entered Apprentice, Fellowcraft, Master Mason) established in English Freemasonry. The higher degrees differed from group to group, and have been categorised by McIntosh according to three different tendencies; a secular, egalitarian and Enlightenment-orientated tendency, a 'Templar' chivalric strain, and a Rosicrucian variety marked by an emphasis on alchemy, secret gnosis and anti-democratic or theocratic sentiments.[66] According to McIntosh, evidence of the emergence of this latter tendency occurs in a Czech manuscript of 1761, which draws from the *Aureum Vellus* ('Golden Fleece,' 1749) of Hermann Fictuld and contains seven grades and rituals of the *Gold- und Rosenkreutz*.[67] Fictuld was a correspondent with the famous theosopher Friedrich Christoph Oetinger (1702-1782), and has been touted as a possible 'founder' of the *Gold- und Rosenkreutz*.[68] In the *Aureum Vellus* he made mention of *die goldenen Rosen-kreutzer* as the inheritors of the 'Golden Fleece' sought by Jason and the Argonauts; the work as a whole dealt with the alchemical significance of Greek and Egyptian mythology in the tradition of Michael Maier's *Arcana Arcanissima*, and gave an alchemical reading of the symbolism of the fifteenth century Order of the Golden Fleece (which we also find in the sixteenth chapter of Maier's *Themis Aurea*, albeit in passing).[69] A similar alchemical treatment of pagan mythology drawing directly from Maier's *Arcana Arcanissima*, *Symbola Aureae Mensae* and *Atalanta Fugiens* is to be found in the *Fables Égyptiennes et Grecques Dévoilées* (1758) of Antoine Joseph Pernéty, who would become librarian to the most prominent member

---

[63] *Ibid.*, p. 103.

[64] *Ibid.*, p. 106.

[65] McIntosh, *The Rose Cross and the Age of Reason*, pp. 33-34.

[66] *Ibid.*, pp. 39, 44.

[67] *Ibid.*, pp. 46-47.

[68] *Ibid.*; Faivre, *Access to Western Esotericism*, pp. 179-180.

[69] Faivre, *Access to Western Esotericism*, pp. 76, 186; on Maier's reading of the myth of the Golden Fleece in his *Arcana Arcanissima*, *Symbola Aureae Mensae* and *Atalanta Fugiens*, see also Faivre, *The Golden Fleece and Alchemy*, pp. 24-26.

of the *Gold- und Rosenkreutz*, King Friedrich Wilhelm II of Prussia (r.1786-1797).[70]

Following the collapse due to scandal of Baron von Hund's 'Strict Observance' Templar strain of Freemasonry in 1782, the *Gold- und Rosenkreutz* became the dominant force within the German Craft, alongside the 'Illuminati' who represented the secular, rationalising tendency we have mentioned.[71] The *Gold- und Rosenkreutz* was marked by its anti-Enlightenment stance and its emphasis on Christian piety and alchemy. Alchemical ideas and symbols were incorporated into the rituals of initiation and the teachings that accompanied each grade; laboratory alchemy was also an important part of the work of the order from the third degree onwards, and those members reaching the seventh grade were deemed to have knowledge of the Philosophers' Stone.[72] Paracelsian and Valentinian alchemy were the order of the day, although there were some members who denied the *tria prima* of Paracelsus and worked with the traditional sulphur-mercury theory as Maier had done.[73] Ideologically speaking, we find a marked similarity with the thought of early modern alchemists such as Maier, i.e. vitalistic conceptions of a correspondence between gold, the sun and God, and a belief in a vital spirit conveyed by the blood which is the basis of a miraculous medicine and tincture for metals.[74] Members of the *Gold- und Rosenkreutz* also defended the complementarity of pagan and Christian belief in the manner of their predecessors; thus Biblical authority was upheld alongside the authority of a Tradition stretching back to ancient Egypt.[75]

In the work that has been described as the 'Bible' of the *Gold- und Rosenkreutz* Order, the *Compaß der Weisen* (1779), we find an extensive survey of alchemical and Rosicrucian writings, compiled by a *frater Roseae et Aureae Crucis* with the partial aim of making them comprehensible within the context of Freemasonry. The author names a number of early modern writers as authorities, including Michael Maier, Heinrich Khunrath, Robert Fludd, Thomas Vaughan, Gerhard Dorn, Basil Valentine and Adrian von Mynsicht. The introduction deals with the occult knowledge of the Egyptians,

---

[70] Pernéty, Antoine Joseph. *Fables Égyptiennes et Grecques Dévoilées*. Paris: Chez Bauche, 1758, pp. 13, 243, 259, 382, 495, 513, 529 *et passim*; Faivre, *Access to Western Esotericism*, pp. 76, 178.

[71] McIntosh, *The Rose Cross and the Age of Reason*, p. 42.

[72] On this subject see McIntosh, Christopher. "Alchemy and the *Gold- und Rosenkreutz*." In Martels, Z. R. W. M. von. *Alchemy Revisited: Proceedings of the International Conference on the History of Alchemy at the University of Groningen*, 17-19 April 1989. Leiden: E.J. Brill, 1990, pp. 239-244.

[73] Beyer, *Das Lehrsystem des Ordens der Gold- und Rosenkreuzer*, p. 21.

[74] McIntosh, "Alchemy and the *Gold- und Rosenkreutz*," pp. 241-243.

[75] McIntosh, *The Rose Cross and the Age of Reason*, p. 52.

Greeks, Brahmans, Druids et. al., and there Maier is named next to the antique authors Macrobius and Diodorus Siculus as an authority on mythology and the mystery cults, as well as being noted for his Rosicrucian apologies.[76] In the main body of the text particular attention is directed towards the *Symbola Aureae Mensae* as a source for information on medieval alchemical authors,[77] and as a guide to alchemical procedure itself.[78] On this count the *Allegoria Bella* is cited concerning the most astrologically propitious moment for the commencement of the work, i.e. "when the moon and sun are in the sign of Aries near the head of the Dragon."[79] The *Atalanta Fugiens* is referred to concerning the nature of certain *Decknamen*,[80] as well as a passage from an unidentified work of Maier's concerning the relation of the alchemical work to the (Aristotelian) properties of the north and west winds.[81]

5. The historiography of alchemy

This brief sketch of the re-emergence of Rosicrucianism should serve to establish that the alchemy of early modern practitioners such as Maier did not become 'meaningless' in the hands of later esoteric groupings, as Principe and Newman assert. Our goal here has not been to demonstrate the transmission of a Tradition, passed from master to initiate from the time of Maier to our own; rather, it is to show that there exists an ideological congruence in the history of esotericism pertaining to matters of alchemy. When nineteenth century writers such as Buhle, Katsch and von Murr looked to Maier as a key figure in the emergence of later Rosicrucianism and Freemasonry, they may have erred in constructing their 'lineage'; nevertheless, their error was prompted by the broad similarities existing between Maier's thought and that of the secret societies of their own time. These similarities may be enumerated as follows:

---

[76] Jolyfief, *Der Compaß der Weisen*, pp. 93-94, 114.

[77] *Ibid.*, pp. 151-152, 311-313, 335.

[78] *Ibid.*, pp. 164, 311-313.

[79] *Ibid.*, p. 373.

[80] *Ibid.*, p. 402.

[81] *Ibid.*, pp. 376-377: "Michael Meier sagt, man müsse Achtung geben, daß der Vulcan die Sonnenhitze, die ohnehin schon von Natur trocken und warm sey, nicht zu stark überhand nehmen lasse, daher sey es rathsam die Arbeit anzufangen, wenn ein nicht zu rauher Nordwind wehet, welcher von den hohen Bergen seinen Ursprung nimmt, damit die starke Hitze dieses göttlichen Feuers in etwas nachlassen möge, und die angenehmen Westwinde eine gebührende Mäßigung der Kälte und Wärme, Nässe und Trockne mit sich bringen."

1. A vitalistic conception of alchemy as a universal science, which also encompasses the life of the human soul as a 'spiritual alchemy' with pietistic overtones. In the Freemasonic and later Rosicrucian traditions this alchemy was integrated with the Freemasonic system of initiatory grades designed to accomplish a moral transformation in the adept.

2. An alchemical philosophy of Nature focussing on celestial virtues, solar mysticism, cyclical natural processes and correspondences between the macrocosm and the microcosm. As McIntosh and Peuckert have argued, above all other authors it was Maier who effected a definitive binding of such alchemical conceptions with the Rosicrucian tradition, as alchemy had formed only a part of the message of the original manifestos and rejoinders.[82]

3. A concern with the deciphering of 'hieroglyphs', in the pansophist sense of signs in Nature pointing to universal, divinely instituted laws.

4. A pseudo-Egyptianism with its origins in the *prisca sapientia* doctrine of the Renaissance. This doctrine was associated with a syncretic tendency to harmonise Christian and pagan thought in a unitary Tradition, and an eclectic attitude towards the integration of diverse occult and religious ideologies; Jewish patriarchal origins were also heavily emphasised.

As we have shown in our introductory preamble to the current work, this conjunction of alchemical and associated ideological elements continued to prevail in the esoteric circles of the nineteenth century, and formed the basis for the alchemical hermeneutic proposed first by Silberer and then by Jung.

In attempting to evaluate Jung's historiography and his claims concerning the nature of alchemy, it is pertinent to note that his argument for the existence of a coherent 'tradition' extending from his own psychology via alchemy to ancient Gnosticism is far from new. Indeed, similar ideas are to be found in the *Unpartheyische Kirchen- und Ketzer- Historie* ('Impartial History of the Church and Heretics,' 1699) of the Pietist Gottfried Arnold, in which Rosicrucian and alchemical currents are also traced to the Gnostics, who were to Arnold's mind the 'true' Christians and forebears of the Reformation.[83] But even if we grant that Paracelsus and his followers were

---

[82] McIntosh, Christopher. *The Rosicrucians: The History, Mythology and Rituals of an Occult Order*. Wellingborough: Crucible, 1987, pp. 54-56; Peuckert, *Pansophie* (1936 edition), p. 152.

[83] The prevalence of alchemical practice in Pietist circles is demonstrated by the fact that Goethe himself was healed as a young man by an alchemical medicine produced by the Pietist Moravian Brotherhood – the origins of a fascination with alchemy that was to play a central role in German culture, particularly through his *Faust*.

branded as revivers of Gnostic heresy by their contemporaries,[84] a survey of the medieval sources utilised by Maier confirms Obrist's view that the soteriological and Christological motifs therein serve a primarily rhetorical purpose, and that Jung's views have their origins in the alchemy of the post-Reformation era. Certainly, a great deal of medieval texts speak of the necessity of divine inspiration in the Art, and the importance of leading a moral life if one wishes to be granted the divine secrets of the Philosophers' Stone. There are also widespread conjectures concerning the nature of the *prima materia* and the cyclical transmutation of the four elements, which in their original antique philosophical context were inseparable from religious speculation on the nature of God and the human soul. But it is only subsequent to the late fifteenth century flowering of Neoplatonism in Italy, the emergence of a syncretic Renaissance Hermeticism with its elaborate theories of sympathy and correspondence, and the re-appearance of overtly gnostic and individualistic sentiments in the course of the Reformation, that certain alchemies again attained the overt religiosity of their Hellenistic Egyptian and Gnostic counterparts.[85]

It should be noted, however, that Jung placed his own work in the context of a lineage of *symbolic* import rather than a Tradition *per se*, as he argued that psychological or 'spiritual' elements in alchemical practice prior to the sixteenth century 'fission' of *physica* and *mystica* remained largely unconscious to the 'adepts'. On this matter we might follow the good advice of the historian of alchemy E. J. Holmyard, who stated that "it must be left to the psychologists" to pronounce judgment on the "profound psychological study" put forward by Jung, rather than intruding into fields which are not our rightful domain.[86] We should also keep in mind Holmyard's accurate depiction of Jung's view of medieval alchemy as a "chemical research work into which there entered, by way of projection, an admixture of unconscious psychic material;"[87] as we have shown, when Principe and Newman speak of "Jung's assertion that alchemy ceases to be alchemy when it becomes clear enough to be understood in chemical terms," they betray their fundamental misunderstanding of the psychology of the unconscious.[88]

---

[84] Pagel, *Paracelsus*, p. 315.

[85] Whilst Merkur has recently argued for a medieval origin to 'spiritual alchemy' with reference to the theoretical relation of the quintessence to the soul, his terms are not well defined, and an explicit medieval work on alchemy as a process of spiritual transmutation within the adept is yet to be uncovered. See Merkur, Dan. "The Study of Spiritual Alchemy: Mysticism, Gold-Making, and Esoteric Hermeneutics," *Ambix*, Vol. 37, No. 1, March 1990, pp. 35-45.

[86] Holmyard, *Alchemy*, p. 160.

[87] *Ibid.*, p. 159.

[88] Principe and Newman, "Some Problems with the Historiography of Alchemy," p. 414.

Whilst it is true that the pursuit which we have defined as 'spiritual alchemy' remains a subset of the whole that is early modern alchemy, it is by no means an insignificant element in the history of ideas, nor was it limited to non-laboratory practitioners such as Boehme or Weigel. Furthermore, there can be no doubt that the seeds of the early modern emergence of 'spiritual' alchemies were contained in medieval alchemy. When dealing with the presence (or perceived absence) of spiritual alchemies amongst laboratory practitioners of the early modern period, Principe and Newman make mention of a little known 'supernatural alchemy' which developed in seventeenth century England, and which held that certain alchemical products had supernatural effects; their point is to show that such a pursuit has little in common with the spiritual alchemies of the nineteenth and twentieth centuries.[89] It is self-evident that this particular alchemy cannot be placed under the rubric of 'spiritual alchemy' in the manner of Maier's practice, and that nothing has been proved by the example. The historiography proposed by Principe and Newman can only be upheld by portraying early modern laboratory alchemy as a purely 'chemical' research (conceived in crypto-positivist terms), and by erasing from history the development of alchemical thought subsequent to the seventeenth century. For researchers in the history of Western esotericism, this *modus operandi* is entirely inadequate. Rather, it is apparent that the categories we encounter in the debate concerning the true import of the ambiguous symbols of the alchemical corpus are not new, and that we are embarking upon the study of living traditions; for just as certain voices in the early modern period called for the separation of matters theological and scientific, so today we find that schismatic outlook expressed by apologists (witting or otherwise) for the dominant scientific paradigm.

---

[89] *Ibid.*, pp. 399-400.

Bibliography

1. Primary Sources

A. *Printed works of Maier*

The following is a list of Maier's printed works cited in the foregoing pages. A forthcoming bibliography prepared by Prof. Dr. Karin Figala and Dr. Ulrich Neumann of the Technische Universität München promises to be an exhaustive inventory of Maier's known printed works and manuscripts.

Maier, Michael. *Arcana Arcanissima, hoc est, Hieroglyphica Aegyptio-Graeca, vulgo necdum cognita, ad demonstrandam falsorum apud antiquos deorum, dearum, heroum, animantium et institutorum, pro sacris receptorum, originem, ex uno Aegyptiorum artificio, quod aureum animi et Corporis medicamentum peregit, deductam, Unde tot poëtarum allegoriae, scriptorum narrationes fabulosae et pertotam Encyclopaediam errores sparsi clarissima veritatis luce manifestantur, suaeque tribui singula restituuntur, sex libris exposita.* London: Creede, c. 1614.

— *Atalanta Fugiens, hoc est, Emblemata nova de secretis naturae chymica, accommodata partim oculis et intellectui, figuris cupro incisis, adjectisque sententiis, Epigrammatis et notis, partim auribus et recreationi animi plus minus 50 Fugis musicalibus trium Vocum, quarum duae ad unum simplicem melodiam distichis canendis peraptam, correspondeant, non absque, singulari jucunditate videnda, legenda, meditanda, intelligenda, dijudicanda, canenda et audienda.* Oppenheim: Johann Theodor de Bry, 1617.

— *Cantilenae Intellectuales, in Triadas 9. distinctae, De Phoenice Redivivo, hoc est, Medicinarum omnium pretiosissima, (quae Mundi Epitome et Universi Speculum est) non tam alta voce, quam profunda mente dictatae, et pro CLAVE Ternarum irreserabilium in Chymia arcanum rationalibus ministratae.* Rostock: Mauritii Saxonis, 1622.

— *Civitas Corporis Humani, a Tyrannide Arthritica vindicata: Hoc est, Podagrae, Chiragrae, et Gonagrae, quae, velut tyranni immanissimi artus extremos obsident, et excruciant, Methodica Curatio. Duobus auxiliis potissimum instituta, ac deinde latius clarissimorum, praesertim GERMANIAE, Medicorum testimoniis comprobata, inque Medicinae Candidatorum gratiam atque utilitatem concinnata et edita.* Frankfurt am Main: Lucas Jennis, 1621.

— *De Circulo Physico, Quadrato: Hoc est, AURO, Eiusque virtute medicinali, sub duro cortice instar nuclei latente; An et qualis inde petenda sit, Tractatus haud inutilis.* Oppenheim: Lucas Jennis, 1616.

— *De Medicina Regia et vere heroica, Coelidonia.* Copenhagen, Royal Library, 12,-159, 4°. Prague: n.p., 1609.

— *Examen Fucorum Pseudo-chymicorum detectorum et in gratiam veritatis amantium succincte refutatorum.* Frankfurt am Main: Johann Theodor de Bry, 1617.

— *Hymnosophia, seu Meditatio Laudis Divinae, pro Coelidonia, Medicina mystica, voarchadumica etc.* Prague: n.p., n.d.

— *Jocus Severus, hoc est, Tribunal aequum, quo noctua regina avium, Phoenice arbitro, post varias disceptationes et querelas volucrum eam infestantium pronunciatur.* Frankfurt am Main: Johann Theodor de Bry, 1617.

— *Lusus Serius, quo Hermes sive Mercurius rex mundanorum omnium sub homine existentium, post longam disceptationem in concilio octovirali habitam, homine rationali arbitro, judicatus et constitutus est.* Oppenheim: Lucas Jennis, 1616.

— *Septimana Philosophica, qua aenigmata aureola de omni naturae genere a Salomone Israëlitarum sapientissimo rege, et Arabiae regina Saba, nec non Hyramo, Tyri principe, sibi invicem in modum colloquii proponuntur et enodantur: ubi passim novae, at verae, cum ratione et experientia convenientes, rerum naturalium causae exponuntur et demonstrantur, figuris cupro incisis singulis diebus adjectis.* Frankfurt am Main: Lucas Jennis, 1620.

— *Silentium post Clamores, hoc est, Tractatus apologeticus, quo causae non solum clamorum seu revelationum Fraternitatis Germanicae de R.C. sed et silentii, seu non redditae ad singulorum vota responsionis, una cum malevolorum refutatione, traduntur et demonstrantur.* Frankfurt am Main: Lucas Jennis, 1617.

— "Subtilis Allegoria super Secreta Chymiae." In *Museum Hermeticum Reformatum et Amplificatum.* Frankfurt am Main: Sande, 1678, pp. 701-740.

— *Symbola Aureae Mensae Duodecim Nationum. Hoc est, Hermaea seu Mercurii Festa ab Heroibus duodenis selectis, artis chymicae usu, sapientia et authoritate paribus celebrata, ad Pyrgopolynicem seu Adversarium illum tot annis iactabundum, virgini Chemiae Iniuriam argumentis tam vitiosis, quam conuitiis argutis inferentem, confundendum et exarmandum, Artifices vero optime de ea meritos suo honori et famae restituendum. Ubi et artis continuatio et veritas invicta 36 rationibus, et experientia librisque authorum plus quam trecentis demonstrantur. Opus, ut Chemiae, sic omnibus antiquitatis et rerum scitu dignissimarum percupidis, utilissimum, 12 libris explicatum et traditum, figuris cupro incisis passim adjectis.* Frankfurt am Main: Lucas Jennis, 1617.

— *Themis Aurea, das ist, von den Gesetzen und Ordnungen der löblichen Fraternitet R. C.* Frankfurt am Main: Lucas Jennis, 1618.

— *Themis Aurea, hoc est, de Legibus Fraternitatis R. C. tractatus, quo earum cum rei veritate convenientia, utilitas publica et privata, nec non causa necessaria, evolvuntur et demonstrantur.* Frankfurt am Main: Lucas Jennis, 1618.

— *Themis Aurea, hoc est, de Legibus Fraternitatis R. C. tractatus, quo earum cum rei veritate convenientia, utilitas publica et privata, nec non causa necessaria, evolvuntur et demonstrantur.* Frankfurt am Main: Lucas Jennis, 1624.

— "Theses de Epilepsia." Universitätsbibliothek Basel, *Disputationum Medicarum Basiliensium,* Vol. 3, No. 92.

— *Tractatus de Volucri Arborea, absque patre et matre, in insulis Orcadum forma anserculorum proveniente, seu de ortu miraculoso potius quam naturali vegetabilium, animalium, hominum et supranaturalium quorundam.* Frankfurt am Main: Lucas Jennis, 1619.

— *Tractatus Posthumus, sive Ulysses, hoc est, Sapientia seu intelligentia, tanquam coelestis scintilla beatitudinis, quod si in fortunae et corporis bonis naufragium faciat, ad portum meditationis et patientiae remigio feliciter se expediat. Una cum annexis tractatibus de fraternitate Roseae Crucis.* Frankfurt am Main: Lucas Jennis, 1624.

— *Tripus Aureus, hoc est, Tres tractatus chymici selectissimi, nempe I. Basilii Valentini, Benedictini ordinis monachi, Germani. Practica una cum 12. clavibus et appendice, ex Germanico; II. Thomae Nortoni, Crede mihi seu Ordinale, ante annos 140 ab authore scriptum, nunc ex Anglicano manuscripto in Latinum translatum, phrasi cuiusque authoris ut et sententia retenta; III. Cremeri cuius Abbatis Westmonasteriensis Angli Testamentum, hactenus nondum publicatum, nunc in diversarum nationum gratiam editi, et figuris cupro affabre incisis ornati opera et studio Michaelis Maieri. Phil. et Med. D. Com. P. etc.* Frankfurt am Main: Lucas Jennis, 1618.

— *Verum Inventum, Hoc est, Munera Germaniae, Ab ipsa primitus reperta (non ex vino, ut calumniator quidam scoptice inuehit, sed vi animi et corporis) et reliquo ORBI communicata, quae tanta sunt, ut plaeraque eorum mutationem Mundo singularem attulerint, universa longe utilissima extiterint, Tractatu peculiari evoluta et tradita.* Frankfurt am Main: Lucas Jennis, 1619.

— *Viatorium, Hoc est, de Montibus Planetarum septem seu metallorum; Tractatus tam utilis, quam perspicuus, quo, ut Indice Mercuriali in triviis, vel Ariadneo filo in Labyrintho, seu Cynosura in oceano chymicorum errorum immenso, quilibet rationalis, veritatis amans, ad illum, qui in montibus sese abdidit De Rubeapetra Alexicacum, omnibus medicis desideratum, investigandum, uti poterit.* Oppenheim: Johann Theodor de Bry, 1618.

B. *Manuscripts relating to Maier*

Hessisches Staatsarchiv Marburg, Bestand 4b, Nr. 266. Draft of Maier's appointment as *Medicus und Chymicus von Haus Auß* at the court of Moritz of Hessen-Kassel.

— Bestand 4g, Paket 57- 1619. A letter from Maier to Moritz of Hessen-Kassel dated 18th January, 1619.

Kassel, Gesamthochschul-Bibliothek, 2° MS Chem. 11, 1, pp. 47 *recto*- 64 *verso*. "Scala Arcis Philosophicae, Gradibus Octodecim Distincta." A manuscript from Maier to Moritz of Hessen-Kassel dating to shortly before 29th April, 1611.

— 2° MS Chem. 19, 1, pp. 279 *recto*- 280 *verso*. A manuscript from Maier to Moritz of Hessen-Kassel containing four memoranda and dating to around 1618-1619.

— 2° MS Chem. 19, 1, pp. 283 *recto*- 284 *recto*. A letter from Maier to Moritz of Hessen-Kassel dated March 16th 1611.

— 2° MS Chem. 19, 1, pp. 285 *recto*- 286 *verso*. A letter from Maier to Moritz of Hessen-Kassel dated 17th April, 1618.

— 2° MS Chem. 19, 1, pp. 287 *recto*- 287 *verso*. A letter from Maier to Moritz of Hessen-Kassel dated 29th April, 1611.

Universitätsbibliothek Leipzig, MS 0396. Maier, Michael. "De Theosophia Aegyptiorum."

Vienna, Allgemeines Verwaltungsarchiv: Palatinat, Prag 29. IX. 1609, (R) u. (WB II, 114), pp. 1 *recto*- 12 *verso*. Patent of nobility from the imperial court listing the privileges and obligations associated with Maier's title of Imperial Count Palatine, 1609.

— Palatinat, Prag 29. IX. 1609, (R) u. (WB II, 114), pp. 24 *recto*- 25 *recto*. A copy of Maier's letter to Emperor Rudolf requesting the symbol of Avicenna, 1609.

C. *Other manuscripts*

Abbot Cremer, Pseudo-. "A Book of the Transmutation of Metals." Bodleian Library, MS Ashmole 1415.

— "Testamentum." Wellcome Institute Library, MS 3557.

Arnoldus de Villanova, Pseudo-. "A Chymicall treatise of the Ancient and highly illuminated Philosopher, Devine and Physitian, Arnoldus de Nova Villa." Bodleian Library, MS Ashmole 1415, pp. 130-146.

Dorn, Gerhard. "A Treatise of John Tritheme concerning the Spagirick Artifice exposed & interpreted by Gerhard Dorn." British Library, MS Sloane 632, pp. 6-10.

Khunrath, Heinrich. "A Naturall Chymicall Symbolum, or a Short Confession of Henry Kunwrath of Lipsicke, Doctor of Phisick." Bodleian Library, MS Ashmole 1459, II, pp. 99-106.

Maria Prophetissa, Pseudo-. "The Practice of Mary the Prophetess in the Alchemical Art." British Library, MS Sloane 3641, 17th century, pp. 1-8.

Merlin, Pseudo-. "The Allegory of Merlin." British Library, MS Sloane 3506, 17th century, pp. 74-75.

Morienus Romanus. "Morieni Romani Eremitae Hierosolymitani Sermo." British Library, MS Sloane 3697, 17th century.

Norton, Thomas. "The Ordinall of Alchimy written by Thomas Norton of Bristoll." Bodleian Library, MS Ashmole 57, 1577.

D. *Other primary sources*

Albertus Magnus, Pseudo-. "Scriptum Alberti super Arborem Aristotelis." In *Theatrum Chemicum*. Vol. 2. Strasbourg: Zetzner, 1659, pp. 457-458.

al-Irāqī, Abu'l-Qāsim Muhammad ibn Ahmad. *Book of the Knowledge Acquired Concerning the Cultivation of Gold*. Trans. E. J. Holmyard. Paul Geuthner: Paris, 1923.

Andreae, Johann Valentin. *Turris Babel, sive Judiciorum de Fraternitate Rosaceae Crucis CHAOS*. Strasbourg: Lazarus Zetzner, 1619.

Anthony, Francis. *Apologia Veritatis Illucescentis, pro Auro Potabili: seu Essentia Auri ad medicinalem potabilitatem absque corrosivis reducti; ut fere omnibus humani corporis aegritudinibus, ac praesertim Cordis corroborationi, tanquam Universalis Medicina, utilissime adhiberi possit; una cum rationibus intelligibilibus, testimoniis locupletissimis, et modo convenienti in singulis morbis usurpandi, producta.* London: Johannes Legatt, 1616.

— *Medicinae Chymicae, et Veri Potabilis Auri Assertio.* Cambridge: Ex officina Cantrelli Legge, 1610.

Arisleus. "Visio Arislei." In *Artis Auriferae.* Vol. 1. Basel: Petrum Pernam, 1572, pp. 146-154.

Arnold, Gottfried. *Unpartheyische Kirchen– und Ketzer– Historie, Vom Anfang des Neuen Testaments biß auf das Jahr Christi 1688.* Hildesheim: Georg Olms, 1967.

Ashmole, Elias. *Fasciculus Chemicus: or, Chymical Collections. Expressing the Ingress, Progress, and Egress, of the Secret Hermetick Science, out of the Choisest and most Famous Authors. Collected and digested in such an order, that it may prove to the advantage, not onely of the Beginners, but Proficients of this high Art, by none hitherto disposed in this Method. Whereunto is added, the Arcanum or Grand Secret of Hermetick Philosophy. Both made English by James Hasolle, Esquire, Qui est Mercuriophilus Anglicus.* London: Printed by J. Flesher for Richard Mynne, at the sign of St.Paul in Little Britain, 1650.

Augustine. "City of God." In *The Fathers of the Church*, Vol. 24. Trans. Demetrius B. Zema et. al. Washington: Catholic University of America Press, 1954.

Bacon, Roger. *The Mirror of Alchimy.* London: Richard Olive, 1597.

Basil Valentine. *Letztes Testament und Offenbahrung der Himmlischen und irdischen Gehmeimniß.* Jena: Eyring, 1626.

Benedictus Hilarion. *Echo Colloquii Rhodo-staurotici, Das ist: Wider-Schall/ oder Antwort/ auff das newlicher zeit außgegangene Gespräch Dreyer Persohnen, die Fraternitet vom RosenCreutz betreffendt. Darinnen zu sehen, Wohin, nicht allein der Author ermeldtes Gespräches, im Schreiben geziehlet, sondern auch, wie es eigentlich, umb ermeldte Fraternitet beschaffen sey. Auff Befehl seiner Obern verfertigt Durch Benedictum Hilarionem, Fr. Colleg. etc.* N.p.: n.p., 1622.

— *Echo Colloquii Rhodo-Staurotici, hoc est: Resolutio sive Responsio ad nupero tempore editum trium personarum Colloquium Fraternitatem Roseae Crucis concernens.* Frankfurt am Main: Lucas Jennis, 1624.

Berthelot, Marcellin Pierre Eugene (ed., trans.). *Collection des Anciens Alchimistes Grecs.* London: Holland Press, 1963.

B. M. I. (Raphael Eglinus?). *Assertio Fraternitatis R. C. Quam Roseae Crucis vocant, a quodam Fraternitatis eius Socio Carmine expressa.* Frankfurt am Main: Johann Bringer, 1614.

Borelli, Petrus. *Bibliotheca Chimica.* Heidelberg: Samuel Broun, 1656.

C., Ro. *A True Historicall Discourse of Muley Hamets rising to the three Kingdomes of Moruecos, Fes and Sus: the dis-union of the three Kingdomes, by civill warre, kindled amongst his three ambitious Sonnes, Muley Sheck, Muley Boferes, and Muley Sidan.* London: Thomas Purfoot, 1609.

Campion, Thomas. *Thomae Campiani Epigrammatum libri primus.* London: E. Griffin, 1619.

Carrichter, Bartholomaeus. *Kräutterbuch des Edelen und Hochgelehrten Herzen Doctoris Bartholomei Carrichters.* Straßburg: Antony Bertram, 1609.

C. V. A. I. B. F. *Colloquium Rhodo-Stauroticum trium personarum, per Famam et Confessionem quodammodo revelatum, de Fraternitate Roseae Crucis.* Frankfurt am Main: Lucas Jennis, 1624.

— *Colloquium Rhodo-Stauroticum, Das ist: Gespräch dreyer Personen/ von der vor wenig Jahren/ durch die Famam et Confessionem etlicher massen geoffenbarten Fraternitet deß Rosen Creuzes; Darinnen zu sehen/ Was endlich von so vielen unterschiedlichen in ihrem Namen publicirten Schriefften/ und denn auch von der Brüderschafft selbsten zu halten sey. Allen trewherzigen/ und aber durch so vielerhand Schreiben irrgemachten Christlichen Lesern zu lieb in druck gegeben.* N.p.: n.p., 1621.

d'Espagnet, Jean. *Enchyridion Physicae Restitutae, or, A Summary of the Physicks Recovered.* Ed. Thomas Willard. New York: Garland Publishing, Inc., 1999.

Dorn, Gerhard. "Physica Trithemii." In *Theatrum Chemicum*, Vol. 1. Strasbourg: Zetzner, 1656, pp. 388-399.

Ecker und Eckhoffen, Hans Heinrich von (Magister Pianco). *Der Rosenkreuzer in seiner Blösse.* Amsterdam: n.p., 1782.

Fama Fraternitatis: Das Urmanifest der Rosenkreuzer Bruderschaft. Ed. Kooij, Pleun van der and Carlos Gilly. Haarlem: Rozekruis Pers, 1998.

Fama Fraternitatis, oder Entdeckung der Bruderschafft deß löblichen Ordens deß Rosen Creutzes/ Beneben der Confession Oder Bekantnuß derselben Fraternitet/ an alle Gelehrte und Haüpter in Europa geschrieben. Kassel: n.p., 1616.

Favaro, A. (ed.). *Atti della Nazione Germanica Artista nello Studio di Padova.* Vol. 2. Padua: Antenore, 1967.

Fersius, Johannes. *Commendatio Martyrii Beatorum Martyrum Ioannis Hussi et Hieronymi Pragensis.* Wittemberg: Johannes Cratonis, 1586.

— *Theses Summam doctrinae de Temperamentis Corporis humani breviter complexae, ad disputandum publice; Propositae a M. Iohanne Fersio Strelensis, de quibus iuvante Deo respondebit Michael Meierus Holsatus.* Frankfurt am Main: Sciurianis, 1592.

Fludd, Robert. *Apologia Compendiaria, Fraternitatem de Rosea Cruce suspicionis et infamiae maculis asspersam* [sic]*, veritatis quasi Fluctibus abluens et abstergens.* Leiden: Gottfried Basson, 1616.

— *Tractatus Apologeticus Integritatem Societatis de Rosea Cruce defendens. In qua probatur contra D. Libavii et aliorum eiusdem farinae calumnias, quod admirabilia nobis a Fraternitate R. C. oblata, sine improba Magiae impostura, aut Diaboli praestigiis et illusionibus praestari possint.* Leiden: Gottfried Basson, 1617.

Garasset, François. *La Doctrine Curieuse des Beaux Esprits de ce Temps, ou Pretendus Tels. Contenant Plusieurs Maximes pernicieuses à l'Estat, à la Religion, et aux bonnes Moeurs. Combattue et Renversee par le P. François Garassus de la Compagnie de JESUS*. Paris: Sebastien Chappelet, 1623.

Goethe, Johann Wolfgang von. *Poetry and Truth*. Vol. 1. Trans. Minna Smith. London: G. Bell & Sons Ltd., 1911.

Grasshoff, Johannes. *Aperta Arca Arcani Artificiosissimi*. Frankfurt am Main: Johan Carl Unckel, 1617.

— "Ein güldener Tractat vom Philosophischen Steine." In *Geheime Figuren der Rosenkreuzer aus dem 16ten und 17ten Jahrhundert*. Vol. 2. Altona: n.p., c. 1785-1790.

— "Ein güldener Tractat vom Philosophischen Steine." In *Dyas Chymica Tripartita*. Frankfurt am Main: Lucas Jennis, 1625, pp. 55-66.

Greverus, Iodocus. "Secretum Nobilissimum et Verissimum." In *Theatrum Chemicum*. Ursel: Zetzner, 1602, pp. 783-810.

Grick, Friedrich (Irenaeus Agnostus). *Prodromus Fr. R. C. Das ist: Ein vorgeschmack und beyläuffige Anzeig der grossen außführlichen Apologi εισ φανεραν ομολογησιν, welche baldt folgen sol, gegen und wider den Zanbrecher, und Fabelprediger Hisaiam sub Cruce*. N.p.: n.p., 1620.

Gwinne, Matthew. *Aurum non Aurum: In assertorem chymicae, sed verae medicinae desertorum, Frac. Anthonivm, Matthaei Gwynn succincta adversaria*. London: R. Field, 1611.

Hanneman, Johann Ludwig. *Cato Chemicus Tractatus: Quo Verae ac Genuinae Philosophiae Hermeticae, et Fucatae ac Sophisticae Pseudo Chemiae et utriusque Magistrorum Characterismi accurate delineantur*. Hamburg: Gothofried Liebernickel, 1690.

— *Instructissima Pharus*. Kiel: n.p., 1712.

— *Ovum Hermetico-Paracelsico-Trismegistum, i.e. Commentarius-Philosophico-Chemico-Medicus, In quandam Epistolam Mezahab Dictam de Auro. Et Historia Philosophico Chemico-Medica de eodem metallo nativo et artificiali. In quo et 108. Quaestiones Chemicae ab Excellentiss. D. D. Morhofio propositae ab Autore solvuntur. Omnia, juxta adeptae Paracelsicae et Eclecticae Philosophiae principia*. Frankfurt am Main: Friderich Knoch, 1694.

Hartmann, Johannes. *Disputationes Chymico-Medicae: Pleraeque sub Praesidio Joh. Hartmanni, Med. D. et Chymiatriae in Academia Marpurgensi Professoris Publici, ab aliquot Medicinae Candidatis et Studiosis, ibidem censurae publicae expositae...* Marburg: Paul Egenolph, 1614.

Hermes Trismegistus, Pseudo-. "Tractatus Aureus de Lapidis physici secreto." In *Theatrum Chemicum*. Vol. 4. Straßburg: Zetzner, 1613, pp. 672-797.

Homer. *The Iliad*. Trans. Martin Hammond. Harmondsworth: Penguin Books, 1987.

Horapollo. *Hieroglyphica Horapollinis*. Trans. David Hoeschel. Augustae Vindelicorum: n.p., 1595.

Horapollo. *The Hieroglyphics of Horapollo.* Trans. George Boas. Princeton: Princeton University Press, 1993.

Iamblichus. *Iamblichus on the Mysteries of the Egyptians, Chaldeans, and Assyrians.* Trans. Thomas Taylor. London: Stuart and Watkins, 1968.

Jolyfief, Augustin Anton Pocquières de. *Der Compaß der Weisen, von einem Mitverwandten der innern Verfassung der ächten und rechten Freymäurerey.* Leipzig: Christian Ulrich Ringmacher, 1782.

Kepler, Johannes. *De Stella Nova in Pede Serpentarii.* Prague: Pauli Sessii, 1606.

Khunrath, Heinrich. *Amphitheatrum Sapientiae Aeternae. The Amphitheatre Engravings of Heinrich Khunrath.* Trans. Patricia Tahil. Edinburgh: Magnum Opus Hermetic Sourceworks, 1981.

— "Treuhertzige Warnungs-Vermahnung an alle Liebhaber der Naturgemesen Alchemie Transmutatoriae." In *Deutsches Theatrum Chemicum.* Nürnberg: Adam Jonathan Felßecker, 1728, pp. 289-313.

— *Von Hylealischen, Das ist Pri-Materia-lischen Catholischen, oder Algemeinem Natürlichen Chaos.* Magdeburg: n.p., 1597.

Kircher, Athanasius. *Oedipus Aegyptiacus.* Vol. 2. Rome: Vitalis Mascardi, 1653.

Maier, Michael. "A Subtle Allegory concerning the Secrets of Alchemy." In *The Hermetic Museum, Restored and Enlarged.* Trans. Arthur Edward Waite. London: J. Elliott and Co., 1893, pp. 199-233.

— *Intellectual Cantilenae in Nine Triads upon the Resurrection of the Phoenix.* Trans. Mike Dickman. Magnum Opus Hermetic Sourceworks No.25. Glasgow: Magnum Opus Hermetic Sourceworks, 1997.

— *Lusus Serius, or, Serious Passe-time. A Philosophical Discourse concerning the Superiority of Creatures under Man.* London: Moseley and Heath, 1654.

— "The Flying Atalanta, Or Philosophical Emblems of the Secrets of Nature." British Library, MS Sloane 3645, 17th century, pp. 51-102.

— *Themis Aurea: The Laws of the Fraternity of the Rosie Crosse. Written in Latin by Count Michael Maierus, And now in English for the Information of those who seek after the knowledge of that Honourable and mysterious Society of wise and renowned Philosophers... Whereto is annexed an Epistle to the Fraternity in Latine, from some here in England.* London: Printed for N. Brooke at the Angel in Cornhill, 1656.

Maria Prophetissa, Pseudo-. "Practica Mariae Prophetissae in Artem Alchimicam." In *Artis Auriferae.* Vol. 1. Basel: Conradi Vvaldkirchii, 1593, pp. 319-324.

Merlin, Pseudo-. "Merlini Allegoria Profundissimum Philosophici Lapidis Arcanum Perfecte Continens." In *Artis Auriferae.* Vol. 1. Basel: Conrad Waldkirch, 1593, pp. 392-396.

Molther, Georg (E. D. F. O. C. R. Sen.). *Antwort, der Hochwürdigen und Hocherleuchten Brüderschafft deß RosenCreutzes.* N.p.: n.p., 1617.

— *De quodam peregrino, qui anno superiore MDCXV imperialem Wetzslariam transiens, non modo se fratrem R. C. confessus fuit verum etiam multiplici rerum scientia, verbis et factis admirabilem se praestitit.* Frankfurt am Main: Johann Bringer, 1616.

— "Von einer frembden Mannsperson/ Welche inn jüngst verflossenem M. DC. XV. Jahr durch deß H. Reichs Statt Wetzslar gereißt/ und sich nicht allein für ein Bruder deß Ordens deß Rosen Creuzes außgegeben/ sondern auch durch vielfältige Geschickligkeit/ unnd allerhand Sachen Wissenschafft/ mit Worten unnd Wercken sich also erzeigt hat/ daß man sich ab ihme verwundern müssen/ Gründtliche Relation." In *Fama Fraternitatis, oder Entdeckung der Bruderschafft deß löblichen Ordens deß Rosen Creutzes... Sampt dem Sendtschreiben Iuliani de Campis, und Georgii Moltheri Med. D. und Ordinarii zu Wetzlar Relation/ von einer diß Ordens gewissen Person.* Frankfurt am Main: Johann Bringer, 1617.

Monardes, Nicolas Bautista. *Historia Medicinal de las cosas que se traen de nuestras Indias Occidentales.* Seville: Escrivano, 1574.

Morhof, D. G. *De Metallorum Transmutatione, ad Virum Nobilissimum et Amplissimum Joelem Langelottum, Serenissimi Principis Cimbrici Archiatrum Celeberrimum, Epistola.* Hamburg: Ex Officina Gothofredi Schultzen, 1673.

Morienus Romanus. "Liber de Compositione Alchemiae quem edidit Morienus Romanus." *Artis Auriferae.* Vol. 2. Basel: Conrad Waldkirch, 1593.

Mynsicht, Adrian von (Hinricus Madathanus). "Aureum Seculum Redivivum," in *Dyas Chymica Tripartita, das ist: Sechs Herzliche Teutsche Philosophische Tractätlein.* Frankfurt am Main: Lucas Jennis, 1625, pp. 74-87.

Nichols, J. *The Progresses, Processions and Magnificent Festivities of King James the First.* Vol. II. London: Nichols, 1828.

Norton, Thomas. *Thomas Norton's Ordinal of Alchemy.* Ed. John Reidy. Oxford: Oxford University Press, 1975.

Osiandrische Experiment von Sole, Luna et Mercuria, Welche in fürnehmer Herren laboratoriis probirt worden darauß mehr per Exempla als Rationes, oder durch viel verwirzte Proceß verkehrte Sophistische und unnütze Bücher verschrauffte Wort und subtile Reden und die wahre Philosophische Materi, rechte Solution, Gewicht, Glas, Ofen und Regierung des Feuers zu fassen, und zumal man richtige Anleitung hat, dem Werck zur Tinctur und Arztnei weiter nachzudencken und zuergründen. Nürnberg: Johann Andreas, 1659.

Pernéty, Antoine Joseph. *Fables Égyptiennes et Grecques Dévoilées.* Paris: Chez Bauche, 1758.

Physiologus. Trans. Michael J. Curley. Austin: University of Texas Press, 1979.

Rawlin, Thomas: *Admonitio Pseudo-chymicis: seu Alphabetarium Philosophicum: omnibus doctrinae filiis, et philosophicae medicinae studiosis, verissime, sincere, et plusquam laconica brevitate conscriptum, et in bonum publicum emissum: in quo D. D. Antonii aurum potabile obiter refutatur, et genuina veri auri potabilis, in omnibus creatis delitescentis, praeparatio proponitur.* London: Allde, 1612.

Richter, Samuel. *Die Warhaffte und vollkommene Bereitung des Philosophischen Steins/ Der Brüderschafft aus dem Orden des Gülden- und Rosen-Creutzes/ Darinne die Materie zu diesem Geheimniß mit seinem Nahmen genennet/ auch die Bereitung von Anfang bis zu Ende mit allen Hand-Griffen gezeiget ist/ Dabey angehänget die Gesetz oder Regeln/ welche die gedachte Brüderschafft unter sich hält/ Denen Filiis Doctrinae zum Besten publiciret von S.R.* Breslau: Fellgiebel, 1710.

Rotbard, Christoffer (Radtichs Brotofferr). *Elucidarius Chymicus.* Goßlar: Johann Vogt, 1616.

— *Elucidarius Major, Oder Erleuchterunge uber die Reformation der ganzen weiten Welt/ F. C. R. auß ihrer Chymischen Hochzeit- und sonst mit viel andern testimoniis Philosophorum/ sonderlich in appendice/ dermassen verbessert/ daß beydes materia et praeparatio lapidis aurei/ deutlich genug darinn angezeigt werden.* Lüneburg: bey den Sternen Buchf., 1617.

Ruland, Martin. *Lexicon Alchemiae sive Dictionarium Alchemisticum.* Frankfurt am Main: Zachariae Palthenii, 1612.

Salmon, William. *Medicina Practica.* London: J. Harris at the Harrow in the Poultrey, 1692.

Salomon Trismosin, Pseudo-. *Splendor Solis.* Trans. Joscelyn Godwin, with an introduction and commentary by Adam McLean. Grand Rapids, Michigan: Phanes Press, 1991.

Stoltzius, Daniel. *Viridarium Chymicum Figuris Cupro Incisis Adornatum et Poeticis Scripturis Illustratum: Ita ut non tantum oculorum et animi recreationum suppeditet, sed et profundiorem rerum naturalium considerationem excitet, ad haec forma sua oblonga Amicorum Albo inservire queat.* Frankfurt am Main: Lucas Jennis, 1624.

Theatrum Chemicum Britannicum. Ed. Elias Ashmole. London: J. Grismond, 1652.

The Fame and Confession of the Fraternity of R: C:, commonly, of the Rosie Cross. With a Praeface annexed thereto, and a short Declaration of their Physicall Work. Trans. Thomas Vaughan (Eugenius Philalethes). London: Giles Calvert, 1652.

Vaughan, Thomas (Eugenius Philalethes). *Anima Magica Abscondita: or A Discourse of the universall Spirit of Nature, With his strange, abstruse, miraculous Ascent, and descent.* London: H.B., 1650.

Wegner, Georg Wilhelm (Tharsander). *Adeptus Ineptus, Oder Entdeckung der falsch berühmten Kunst ALCHIMIE genannt.* Berlin: Ambrosius Haude, 1744.

Widmore, Richard. *An History of the Church of St. Peter Westminster, commonly called Westminster Abbey.* London: J. Fox and C. Tovey, 1751.

2. Secondary Sources

Achelis, Thomas Otto. *Die Ärzte im Herzogtum Schleswig bis zum Jahre 1804*. Schleswig-Holsteinische Gesellschaft für Familienforschung und Wappenkunde e.V. Kiel: Kiel, 1966.

Åkerman, Susanna. *Rose Cross over the Baltic: The Spread of Rosicrucianism in Northern Europe*. Leiden: Brill, 1998.

Allen, Sally G. "Outrunning Atalanta: Feminine Destiny in Alchemical Transmutation," *Journal of Women in Culture and Society*, Vol. 6, 1980, pp. 210-221.

Arnold, Paul. *Histoire des Rose-Croix et les Origines de la Franc-Maçonnerie*. Paris: Mercure de France, 1954.

Barnes, Jonathan. *Early Greek Philosophy*. Harmondsworth: Penguin Books, 1987.

Beck, Wolfgang. *Michael Maiers Examen Fucorum Pseudo-Chymicorum – Eine Schrift wider die falschen Alchemisten*. Doctoral thesis, Zentralinstitut für Geschichte der Technik der Technischen Universität München, 1992.

Beyer, Bernhard. *Das Lehrsystem des Ordens der Gold- und Rosenkreuzer*. Leipzig: Pansophie-Verlag, 1925.

Biographie Universelle. Paris: L. G. Michaud, 1820.

Biographisches Lexikon der Hervorragenden Ärzte aller Zeiten und Völker. Berlin: Urban & Schwarzenberg, 1962.

Borggrefe, Heiner, Vera Lüpkes and Hans Ottomeyer (eds.). *Moritz der Gelehrte: Ein Renaissancefürst in Europa*. Eurasburg: Edition Minerva, 1997.

Brann, Noel. "Alchemy and Melancholy in Medieval and Renaissance Thought: A Query into the Mystical Basis of their Relationship," *Ambix*, Vol. 32, No. 3, November 1985, pp. 127-148.

Bricaud, Joanny. "Historique du Mouvement Rosicrucien," *Le Voile d'Isis*, Vol. 91, July 1927, pp. 559-574.

British Biographical Archive. Microfiche Edition. München: Sauer, 1984.

Budge, Sir E. A. Wallis. *Egyptian Magic*. London: Kegan Paul, Trench, Trubner and Co. Ltd., 1899.

Buhle, Johann Gottlieb. *Ueber den Ursprung und die vornehmsten Schicksale der Orden der Rosenkreuzer und Freymaurer. Eine Historisch-kritische Untersuchung*. Göttingen: Johann Friedrich Röwer, 1804.

Butterfield, Herbert. *The Origins of Modern Science, 1300-1800*. New York: MacMillan, 1952.

Cameron, Euan. *The European Reformation*. Oxford: Clarendon Press, 1991.

Cohn, Henry J. "The Territorial Princes in Germany's Second Reformation, 1559-1622." In *International Calvinism 1541-1715*. Oxford: Clarendon Press, 1986, pp. 135-165.

Cook, Albert Stanburrough. *The Old English Elene, Phœnix and Physiologus*. New Haven: Yale University Press, 1919.

Coudert, Allison P. (ed.). *The Language of Adam/ Die Sprache Adams: Proceedings of a Conference held at the Herzog August Bibliothek, Wolfenbüttel, May 30-31, 1995*. Wiesbaden: Harrassowitz, 1999.

Craven, J. B. *Count Michael Maier, Doctor of Philosophy and of Medicine, Alchemist, Rosicrucian, Mystic: Life and Writings*. Kirkwall: William Pearce and Son, 1910.

Crosland, Maurice. *Historical Studies in the Language of Chemistry*. New York: Dover, 1962.

de Jong, H. M. E. *Michael Maier's Atalanta Fugiens: Sources of an Alchemical Book of Emblems*. Leiden: E.J. Brill, 1969.

de Rola, Stanislas Klossowski. *The Golden Game: Alchemical Engravings of the Seventeenth Century*. New York: George Braziller, Inc., 1988.

Debus, Allen G. "Chemists, Physicians, and Changing Perspectives on the Scientific Revolution," History of Science Society Distinguished Lecture, *Isis*, Vol. 89, No.1, March 1998, pp. 66-81.

— *The English Paracelsians*. London: Oldbourne, 1965.

Dictionary of National Biography. Vol. 1. London: Smith and Elder, 1885.

Dobbs, Betty Jo Teeter. "Newton's *Commentary* on the *Emerald Tablet* of Hermes Trismegistus: its Scientific and Theological Significance." In Merkel, Ingrid and Allen G. Debus (eds.). *Hermeticism and the Renaissance: Intellectual History and the Occult in Early Modern Europe*. Cranbury: Associated University Presses, 1988, pp. 182-191.

— *The Foundations of Newton's Alchemy*. Cambridge: Cambridge University Press, 1975.

Eco, Umberto. *Das Foucaultsche Pendel*. München: Carl Hanser Verlag, 1989.

— *The Limits of Interpretation*. Bloomington, Ind.: Indiana University Press, 1990.

Edighoffer, Roland. *Die Rosenkreuzer*. München: C. H. Beck, 1995.

— *Rose-Croix et Société Ideale selon Johann Valentin Andreae*. Paris: Arma Artis, 1982.

Ellenberger, Henri. *The Discovery of the Unconscious*. New York: Basic Books, 1970.

Evans, R. J. W. "Rantzau and Welser: Aspects of Later German Humanism," *History of European Ideas*, Vol. 5., No. 3, 1984, pp. 257-272.

— *Rudolf II and his World: A Study in Intellectual History, 1576-1612*. Oxford: Oxford University Press, 1973.

Faivre, Antoine. *Access to Western Esotericism*. Albany: State University of New York, 1994.

— "Mystische Alchemie und Geistige Hermeneutik." In *Correspondences in Man and World*. Eranos Yearbook, 1973. Leiden: E. J. Brill, 1975, pp. 323-360.

— *The Golden Fleece and Alchemy*. Albany: State University of New York Press, 1993.

Faivre, Antoine and Voss, Karen-Claire. "Western Esotericism and the Science of Religions," *Numen*, Vol. 42, 1995, pp. 48-77.

Farber, Eduard. *The Evolution of Chemistry*. New York: The Ronald Press Company, 1952.

Ferguson, John. *Bibliotheca Chemica: A Bibliography of Books on Alchemy, Chemistry and Pharmaceutics*. London: Starker Brothers, 1906.

Figala, Karin. "Die Exakte Alchemie von Isaac Newton." In *Verhandlungen der Naturforschenden Gesellschaft in Basel*. Vol. 94. Basel: Birkhäuser Verlag, 1983, pp. 157-227.

Figala, Karin and Neumann, Ulrich. "'Author cui Nomen Hermes Malavici': New Light on the Bio-Bibliography of Michael Maier (1569-1622)." In Rattansi, Piyo and Antonio Clericuzio (eds.). *Alchemy and Chemistry in the 16th and 17th Centuries*. Dordrecht: Kluwer Academic Publishers, 1994, pp. 121-148.

— "Michael Maier (1569-1622): New Bio-Bibliographical Material." In Martels, Z. R. W. M. von. *Alchemy Revisited: Proceedings of the International Conference on the History of Alchemy at the University of Groningen, 17-19 April 1989*. Leiden: E. J. Brill, 1990, pp. 34-50.

Foucault, Michel. *The Order of Things: An Archaeology of the Human Sciences*. London: Tavistock Publications, 1970.

Frick, Karl R. H. Introduction to the reprint of *Symbola Aureae Mensae Duodecim Nationum*. Graz: Akademische Druck- und Verlagsanstalt, 1972.

Fuchs, Thomas. *Die Mechanisierung des Herzens*. Frankfurt am Main: Suhrkamp, 1992.

Gardner, F. Leigh. *A Catalogue Raisonné of Works on the Occult Sciences*. Vol. 1. N.p.: n.p., 1923.

Gellner, G. *Životopis Lékaře Borbonia a Výklad Jeho Deníků*. Prague: Nákladem Českě Akademie Věd a Umění, 1938.

Gilly, Carlos. *Adam Haslmayr: Der Erste Verkünder der Manifeste der Rosenkreuzer*. Stuttgart: Frommann, 1994.

— *Cimelia Rhodostaurotica: Die Rosenkreuzer im Spiegel der zwischen 1610 und 1660 entstandenen Handschriften und Drucke*. Ausstellung der Bibliotheca Philosophica Hermetica Amsterdam und der Herzog August Bibliothek Wolfenbüttel. Amsterdam: In de Pelikaan, 1995.

— "Iter Rosicrucianum: Auf der Suche nach Unbekannten Quellen der Frühen Rosenkreuzer." In *Das Erbe des Christian Rosenkreutz: Vorträge gehalten anläßlich des Amsterdamer Symposiums 18.-20. November 1986*. Amsterdam: In de Pelikaan, 1988, pp. 63-89.

Godwin, Joscelyn (ed.). "A Context for Michael Maier's 'Atalanta Fugiens' (1617)," *The Hermetic Journal*, 1985, pp. 4-10.

— *Atalanta Fugiens: An Edition of the Fugues, Emblems and Epigrams*. Grand Rapids, Mi.: Phanes Press, 1989.

Gould, Robert Freke. *The History of Freemasonry: Its Antiquities, Symbols, Constitutions, Customs, etc. Embracing an Investigation of the records of the Organisations of the Fraternity in England, Scotland, Ireland, British Colonies, France, Germany, and the United States*. Vol. 2. Edinburgh: T.C. & E.C. Jack, Grange Publishing Works, 1885.

Graesse, Johann Georg Theodor. *Orbis Latinus*. Berlin: Schmidt, 1922.

Granada, Miguel A. "Christoph Rothmann und die Auflösung der himmlischen Sphären. Die Briefe an den Landgrafen von Hessen-Kassel 1585." In *Beiträge zur Astronomie-*

geschichte, Vol. 2. Edited by Dick, Wolfgang R. and Jürgen Hamel. Frankfurt: Deutsch, 1999, pp. 34-57.

Haage, Bernhard Dietrich. *Alchemie im Mittelalter*. Düsseldorf: Artemis und Winkler, 2000.

Hall, A. Rupert. *The Scientific Revolution, 1500-1800: The Formation of the Modern Scientific Attitude*. Boston: Beacon Press, 1966.

Hall, Manly P. *Lectures on Ancient Philosophy*. Los Angeles: Hall Publishing Co., 1929.

Halleux, Robert. *Les Textes Alchimiques*. Brepols: Turnhout, 1977.

Hanegraaff, Wouter. "Beyond the Yates Paradigm: The Study of Western Esotericism between Counterculture and New Complexity," *Aries*, Vol. 1, No. 1, 2001, pp. 5-37.

— "Empirical Method in the Study of Esotericism," *Method and Theory in the Study of Religion*, Vol. 1, No. 2, 1995, pp. 99-129.

Hannaway, Owen. "Laboratory Design and the Aim of Science: Andreas Libavius versus Tycho Brahe," *Isis*, Vol. 77, 1986, pp. 585-611.

Hansen, Reimer. "Der Friedensplan Heinrich Rantzaus und die Irenik in der Zweiten Reformation." In Schilling, Heinz (ed.). *Die reformierte Konfessionalisierung in Deutschland – Das Problem der "Zweiten Reformation"*. Gütersloh: Gerd Mohn, 1986, pp. 359-372.

Heidorn, Günter. *Geschichte der Universität Rostock 1419-1969: Festschrift zur Fünfhundertfünfzig-Jahr-Feier der Universität*. Vol. I. Berlin: Deutscher Verlag der Wissenschaften, 1969.

Heisler, Ron. "Michael Maier in England," in *The Hermetic Journal*, 1989.

Heym, Gerhard. "Review. Paracelsica, Zwei Vorlesungen über den Arzt und Philosophen Theophrastus," *Ambix*, Vol. 2, No. 3, December 1946, pp. 196-198.

Hild, Heike. *Das Stammbuch des Medicus, Alchemisten und Poeten Daniel Stoltzius als Manuskript des Emblembuches Viridarium Chymicum (1624) und als Zeugnis seiner Peregrinatio Academica*. Doctoral Thesis, Fakultät für Chemie, Biologie und Geowissenschaften der Technischen Universität München, 1991.

Hitchcock, Ethan Allen. *Remarks upon Alchemy and the Alchemists*. Boston: Crosby, Nichols, and Co., 1857.

Holmyard, E. J. *Alchemy*. Harmondsworth: Penguin Books, 1957.

Hubicki, W. "Maier, Michael." In *The Dictionary of Scientific Biography*. Vol. 9. New York: Scribner, 1974, p. 23.

Hutch, Richard A. *The Meaning of Lives: Biography, Autobiography, and the Spiritual Quest*. London: Cassell, 1997.

Iversen, Erik. *The Myth of Egypt and its Hieroglyphs in European Tradition*. Princeton: Princeton University Press, 1993.

Jöcher, Christian Gottlieb. *Allgemeines Gelehrten-Lexicon*. Vol. 2. Leipzig: Gleditsch, 1750.

Jung, Carl Gustav. "Aion – Researches into the Phenomenology of the Self." *The Collected Works of C. G. Jung*. Vol. 9, Part 2. Trans. R. F. C. Hull. London: Routledge, 1991.

— "Alchemical Studies." *The Collected Works of C. G. Jung.* Vol. 15. Trans. R. F. C. Hull. Princeton: Princeton University Press, 1967.

— "A Psychological Approach to the Trinity." In *The Collected Works of C. G. Jung*, Vol. 11. Trans. R. F. C. Hull. Princeton: Princeton University Press, 1969, pp. 107-200.

— *Die Erlösungsvorstellungen in der Alchemie.* Eranos Yearbook, 1936. Zurich: Rhein, 1937.

— *Erinnerungen Träume Gedanken.* Stuttgart: Rascher Verlag, 1962.

— *Letters.* Adler, Gerhard and Aniela Jaffé (eds.). Vol. 1. Princeton: Princeton University Press, 1973.

— *Mysterium Coniunctionis.* Vol. 2. Düsseldorf: Walter Verlag, 1995.

— "Mysterium Coniunctionis." *The Collected Works of C. G. Jung.* Vol. 14. Trans. R. F. C. Hull. Princeton: Princeton University Press, 1976.

— "On the Nature of the Psyche." In *The Collected Works of C. G. Jung*, Vol. 8. Trans. R. F. C. Hull. Princeton: Princeton University Press, 1972, pp. 159-234.

— "On the Psychology of the Unconscious." In *The Collected Works of C. G. Jung*, Vol. 7. Trans. R. F. C. Hull. Princeton: Princeton University Press, 1966, pp. 1-119.

— "Psychologie und Alchemie." *C. G. Jung Gesammelte Werke.* Vol. 12. Freiburg im Breisgau: Walter-Verlag, 1972.

— "Psychology and Alchemy." *The Collected Works of C. G. Jung.* Vol. 12. Trans. R. F. C. Hull. London: Routledge and Kegan Paul, 1968.

— "Studien über Alchemistische Vorstellungen." *C. G. Jung Gesammelte Werke.* Vol. 13. Freiburg im Breisgau: Walter-Verlag, 1978.

— "Symbols of Transformation." *The Collected Works of C. G. Jung.* Vol. 5. Trans. R. F. C. Hull. Princeton: Princeton University Press, 1967.

— "Synchronicity: An Acausal Connecting Principle." In *The Collected Works of C. G. Jung*, Vol. 8. Trans. R. F. C. Hull. Princeton: Princeton University Press, 1972, pp. 417-531.

— "The Concept of the Collective Unconscious." In *The Collected Works of C. G. Jung*, Vol. 9, Part 1. Trans. R. F. C. Hull. Princeton: Princeton University Press, 1968, pp. 42-53.

— *The Integration of the Personality.* New York: Farrar & Rinehart, 1939.

— *Traumsymbole des Individuationsprozesses.* Eranos Yearbook, 1935. Zurich: Rhein, 1936.

— "Wotan." In *The Collected Works of C. G. Jung*, Vol. 10. Trans. R. F. C. Hull. Princeton: Princeton University Press, 1970, pp. 179-193.

Karpenko, Vladimír. "Between Magic and Science: Numerical Magical Squares," *Ambix*, Vol. 40, No. 3, November 1993, pp. 121-128.

— "Viridarium Chymicum: The Encyclopedia of Alchemy," *The Journal of Chemical Education*, Vol. 50, No. 4, April 1973, pp. 270-272.

Katsch, Ferdinand. *Die Entstehung und der wahre Endzweck der Freimaurerei.* Berlin: E. S. Mittler und Sohn, 1897.

Kiesewetter, Carl. Untitled article in *Sphinx: Monatschrift für die Geschichtliche und Experimentale Begründung der Übersinnlichen Weltanschauung auf Monistischer Grundlage.* Leipzig: Vol. 1, January, 1886, pp. 42-54.

Kindlers Literatur Lexikon. Vol. 8. Weinheim: Zweiburgen Verlag, 1982.

Kiple, K. F. (ed.). *The Cambridge World History of Disease.* Cambridge: Cambridge University Press, 1993.

Kirsch, Thomas B. "The Rose, the Cross and the Analyst," *Anima,* vol. 21, 1994, pp. 67-69.

Kleinpaul, Johannes. *Das Nachrichtenwesen der deutschen Fürsten im 16. und 17. Jahrhundert.* Leipzig: Adolf Klein, 1930.

Klibansky, Raymond et. al. *Saturn and Melancholy: Studies in the History of Natural Philosophy, Religion and Art.* Nelson: London, 1964.

Krabbe, Otto. *Die Universität Rostock im Fünfzehnten und Sechzehnten Jahrhundert.* Vol. 1. Rostock: Adler's Erben, 1854.

Lennhoff, Eugen. *Die Freimaurer.* Nachdruck der Ausgabe von 1929. Wien: Löcker Verlag, 1981.

Lippman, E. O. von. *Entstehung und Ausbreitung der Alchemie.* Hildesheim: G. Olms, 1978.

Macguire, W. et. al. (eds.) *Alchemy and the Occult: A Catalogue of Books and Manuscripts from the Collection of Paul and Mary Mellon given to Yale University Library.* Vol. 2. New Haven: Yale University Press, 1968.

Martin, Luther H. "A History of the Psychological Interpretation of Alchemy," *Ambix,* Vol. 22, No. 1, 1975, pp. 10-20.

Matton, Sylvain. "Le Phénix dans l'Oeuvre de Michel Maier et la Littérature Alchimique." In Bailly, J. C. (ed.). *Chansons Intellectuelles sur la Résurréction du Phénix par Michel Maier.* Paris: Gutenberg Reprints, 1984.

McIntosh, Christopher. "Alchemy and the Gold- und Rosenkreutz." In Martels, Z. R. W. M. von. *Alchemy Revisited: Proceedings of the International Conference on the History of Alchemy at the University of Groningen,* 17-19 April 1989. Leiden: E.J. Brill, 1990, pp. 239-244.

— *The Rose Cross and the Age of Reason: Eighteenth-Century Rosicrucianism in Central Europe and its Relation to the Enlightenment.* Leiden: E. J. Brill, 1992.

— *The Rosicrucians: The History, Mythology and Rituals of an Occult Order.* Wellingborough: Crucible, 1987.

McLean, Adam. "A Rosicrucian Manuscript of Michael Maier," *The Hermetic Journal,* 1979, pp. 5-7.

Menk, Gerhard. "Die 'Zweite Reformation' in Hessen-Kassel: Landgraf Moritz und die Einführung der Verbesserungspunkte." In Schilling, Heinz (ed.). *Die reformierte Konfessionalisierung in Deutschland – Das Problem der "Zweiten Reformation".* Gütersloh: Gerd Mohn, 1986, pp. 154-183.

Merkur, Dan. "The Study of Spiritual Alchemy: Mysticism, Gold-Making, and Esoteric Hermeneutics," *Ambix,* Vol. 37, No. 1, March 1990, pp. 35-45.

Mertens, Michèle. "Sur la Trace des Anges Rebelles dans les Traditions Ésotériques du Début de notre Ère jusqu'au XVIIe Siècle." In Ries, Julien and Henri Limet (eds.). *Anges et Démons: Actes du Colloque de Liège et de Louvain-la-Neuve, 25-26 Novembre 1987*. Louvain-la-Neuve: Centre D'Histoire des Religions, 1989, pp. 383-389.

Metzger, Hélène. "L'évolution du règne métallique d'après les alchimistes du XVIIe siècle," *Isis*, Vol. 4, 1922, pp. 466-482.

Meyers Grosses Universal Lexikon. Vol. 1. Mannheim: Bibliographisches Institut, 1981.

Meyers Lexikon. Vol. 1. Leipzig: Bibliographisches Institut, 1924.

Mitchell, Kenneth Stephen. *Musical Conceptions in the Hermetic Philosophy of Robert Fludd: Their Nature and Significance in German Baroque Muscial Thought*. Doctoral thesis, Washington University, 1994.

Mödersheim, Sabine. "Mater et Matrix: Michael Maiers alchimistische Sinnbilder der Mutter." In *Mutter und Mütterlichkeit: Wandel und Wirksamkeit einer Phantasie in der deutschen Literatur*. Würzburg: Königshausen und Neumann, 1996, pp. 31-56.

Moller, Johannis. *Cimbria Literata, sive Scriptorum Ducatus Utriusque Slesvicensis et Holsatici, Quibus et Alii vicini quidam accensentur, Historia Literaria Tripartita*. Vol. 1. Havniae: Orphanotrophius, 1744.

Montgomery, John Warwick. *Crisis in Lutheran Theology*. Grand Rapids, Mich.: Baker Book House, 1973.

— *Cross and Crucible: Johann Valentin Andreae (1586-1654), Phoenix of the Theologians*. Vol. 1. The Hague: Martinus Nijhoff, 1973.

— "The World-view of Johann Valentin Andreae." In *Das Erbe des Christian Rosenkreutz*. Amsterdam: In de Pelikaan, 1988, pp. 152-169.

Moran, Bruce T. *The Alchemical World of the German Court: Occult Philosophy and Chemical Medicine in the Circle of Moritz of Hessen (1572-1632)*. Stuttgart: Franz Steiner Verlag, 1991.

Morhof, Daniel Georg. *Polyhistor Literarius Philosophicus et Practicus*. Lübeck: Peter Böchmann, 1714.

Morienus Romanus. *A Testament of Alchemy*. Trans., ed., Lee Stavenhagen. Hanover: University Press of New England, 1974.

Muhlack, Ulrich. "Die Germania im deutschen Nationalbewußtsein vor dem 19. Jahrhundert." In *Beiträge zum Verständnis der Germania des Tacitus*. Göttingen: Vandenhoeck & Ruprecht, 1989, pp. 128-154.

Murr, Christoph Gottlieb von. *Über den Wahren Ursprung der Rosenkreuzer und des Freymaurerordens*. Sulzbach: Johann Esaias Seidel, 1803.

Naudon, Paul. *Les Origines de la Franc-Maçonnerie: Le métier et le sacré*. Nouvelle édition entièrement refondue des *Origines Religieuses et Corporatives de la Franc-Maçonnerie* (1953). N.p.: Dervy, 1991.

Neue Deutsche Biographie. Vol. 5. Berlin: Duncker und Humblot, 1961.

Neumann, Ulrich. "Johann Valentin Andreae." In Figala, Karin and Claus Priesner (eds.). *Alchemie: Lexikon einer hermetischen Wissenschaft*. München: C. H. Beck, 1998, pp. 46-47.

Newman, William R. "*Decknamen* or Pseudochemical Language? Eirenaeus Philalethes and Carl Jung," *Revue D'Histoire des Sciences*, Vol. 49, No. 2, 1996, pp. 159-188.

— "The Corpuscular Theory of J. B. Van Helmont and its Medieval Sources," *Vivarium*, Vol. 31, 1993, pp. 161-191.

Noll, Richard (ed.). *Bizarre Diseases of the Mind*. Berkeley: Berkeley Publishing Group, 1990.

— "C. G. Jung and J. B. Rhine: Two Complementary Approaches to the Phenomenology of the Paranormal." In Shapin, Betty and Lisette Coly (eds.). *Parapsychology and Human Nature*. New York: Parapsychology Foundation, 1989.

— *Encyclopedia of Schizophrenia and the Psychotic Disorders*. New York: Facts on File, 2000.

— "Multiple Personality, Dissociation, and C. G. Jung's Complex Theory," *Journal of Analytical Psychology*, Vol 34, No. 4, October 1989, pp. 353-370.

— *The Aryan Christ: The Secret Life of Carl Jung*. New York: Random House, 1997.

— *The Jung Cult – Origins of a Charismatic Movement*. Princeton: Princeton University Press, 1994.

— "The Rose, the Cross and the Analyst," *The New York Times*, October 15, 1994, p. 19.

Obrist, Barbara. *Les Débuts de l'Imagerie Alchimique (XIVe – XVe siècles)*. Paris: Le Sycomore, 1982.

Oestreich, Gerhard. "Clapmarius." In *Neue Deutsche Biographie*. Vol. 3. Berlin: Duncker & Humblot, 1957, p. 260.

Pagel, Walter. "Jung's Views on Alchemy," *Isis*, Vol. 39, No. 1, May 1948, pp. 44-48.

— *Paracelsus: An Introduction to Philosophical Medicine in the Era of the Renaissance*. Basel: Karger, 1982.

— *William Harvey's Biological Ideas*. New York: Karger, 1967.

Peuckert, Will-Erich. *Die Rosenkreuzer: zur Geschichte einer Reformation*. Jena: Eugen Diedrichs, 1928.

— *Pansophie*. Vol. 3. Berlin: Erich Schmidt Verlag, 1973.

— *Pansophie: ein Versuch zur Geschichte der weissen und schwarzen Magie*. Stuttgart: Kohlhammer, 1936.

Po-Chia Hsia, R. *Social Discipline in the Reformation: Central Europe 1550-1750*. London: Routledge, 1989.

Powell, Neil. *Alchemy: the Ancient Science*. London: Aldus Books, 1976.

Praz, Mario. *Studies in Seventeenth-Century Imagery*. Vol. 1. London: The Warburg Institute, 1939.

Principe, Lawrence M. and Newman, William R. "Alchemy vs. Chemistry: The Etymological Origins of a Historiographic Mistake," *Early Science and Medicine*, Vol. 3, No. 1, 1998, pp. 32-65.

— "Some Problems with the Historiography of Alchemy." In Newman, William R. and Anthony Grafton (eds.). *Secrets of Nature: Astrology and Alchemy in Early Modern Europe*. Cambridge, Ma.: MIT Press, 2001, pp. 385-431.

Quispel, Gilles. "Gnosis and Culture." In Barnaby, Karin and Pellegrino D'Acierno (eds.). *C. G. Jung and the Humanities*. Princeton: Princeton University Press, 1990, pp. 11-52.

Read, John. *Prelude to Chemistry*. London: G. Bell and Sons, 1936.
— *The Alchemist in Life, Literature and Art*. London: Thomas Nelson and Sons Ltd., 1947.
Rebotier, Jacques. "La Musique Cachée de l'Atalanta Fugiens," *Chrysopoeia*, Vol. 1, 1987, pp. 56-76.
Roberts, Gareth. *The Mirror of Alchemy: Alchemical Ideas and Images in Manuscripts and Books from Antiquity to the Seventeenth Century*. London: The British Library, 1994.
Ruska, Julius and E. Wiedemann. "Alchemistische Decknamen," *Beiträge zur Geschichte der Naturwissenschaften*. Vol. 67, 1924, pp.17-36.

Schama, Simon. *Landscape and Memory*. New York: Alfred A. Knopf, 1996.
Schick, Hans. *Das Ältere Rosenkreuzertum: Ein Beitrag zur Entstehungsgeschichte der Freimaurerei*. Quellen und Darstellungen zur Freimaurerfrage, Vol. 1. Berlin: Nordland Verlag, 1942.
Schiller, Friedrich. *Der Dreißigjährige Krieg*. München: Kindler, 1975.
Schilling, Heinz. *Religion, Political Culture and the Emergence of Early Modern Society*. Leiden: E. J. Brill, 1992.
Schmidt-Biggemann, Wilhelm. *Philosophia Perennis: Historische Umrisse abendländischer Spiritualität in Antike, Mittelalter und Früher Neuzeit*. Frankfurt am Main: Suhrkamp Verlag, 1998.
Schmitt, Charles B. (ed.). *The Cambridge History of Renaissance Philosophy*. Cambridge: Cambridge University Press, 1992.
Segal, Robert. "Critical Notice," *Journal of Analytical Psychology*, vol. 40, 1995, pp. 597-608.
Shamdasani, Sonu. *Cult Fictions: C. G. Jung and the Founding of Analytical Psychology*. London: Routledge, 1998.
Sheppard, H. J. "The Ouroboros and the Unity of Matter in Alchemy: A Study in Origins," *Ambix*, Vol. 10, No. 2, 1962, pp. 91-110.
Silberer, Herbert. *Probleme der Mystik und ihrer Symbolik*. Vienna: Hugo Deller & Co., 1914.
Smith, Henry Perry. *History of Addison County Vermont*. Syracuse, N.Y.: D. Mason & Co., 1886.
Srigley, Michael. *Images of Regeneration: A Study of Shakespeare's The Tempest and its Cultural Background*. Uppsala: Acta Universitatis Upsaliensis, 1985.
Stapleton, H. E. "The Antiquity of Alchemy," *Ambix*, Vol. 5, No. 1, 1953, pp. 9-15.
Steinmetz, Wiebke. *Heinrich Rantzau (1526-1598): Ein Vertreter des Humanismus in Nordeuropa und seine Wirkungen als Förderer der Künste*. Frankfurt am Main: Peter Lang, 1991.
Stevenson, David. *The Origins of Freemasonry: Scotland's Century, 1590-1710*. Cambridge: Cambridge University Press, 1988.

Stiehle, Hans. *Michael Maierus Holsatus (1569-1622): Ein Beitrag zur naturphilosophischen Medizin in seinen Schriften und zu seinem wissenschaftlichen Qualifikationsprofil.* Doctoral thesis, Zentralinstitut für Geschichte der Technik der Technischen Universität München, 1991.

Streich, Hildemarie. "Musikalische und psychologische Entsprechungen in der *Atalanta Fugiens* von Michael Maier." In *Correspondences in Man and World.* Eranos Yearbook, 1973. Leiden: E. J. Brill, 1975, pp. 361-426.

Strieder, Friedrich Wilhelm. *Grundlage zu einer Hessischen Gelehrten und Schriftsteller Geschichte Seit der Reformation bis auf Gegenwärtige Zeiten.* Vol. 6. Kassel: Göttingen: Barmeier, 1786.

Szydlo, Zbigniew. *Water which does not Wet Hands.* Warsaw: Polish Academy of Sciences, 1994.

Taylor, F. Sherwood. "The Visions of Zosimos," *Ambix,* Vol. 1, No. 1, May 1937, pp. 88-92.

Thomas, John D. "The Engine of Enlightenment: Samuel Hitchcock and the Creation of the University of Vermont Seal." Unpublished paper, an abstract of which is to be found in *The Center for Research on Vermont Newsletter,* Vol. 24, No. 1, April 1999.

Trunz, Erich. "Der deutsche Späthumanismus um 1600 als Standeskultur." In Alewyn, Richard (ed.). *Deutsche Barockforschung: Dokumentation einer Epoche.* Köln: Kiepenheuer und Witsch, 1966, pp. 147-181.

— "Späthumanismus und Manierismus im Kreise Kaiser Rudolfs II." In *Prag um 1600: Kunst und Kultur am Hofe Rudolfs II.* Freren: Luca-Verlag, 1988, pp. 57-60.

— *Wissenschaft und Kunst im Kreise Kaiser Rudolfs II. 1576-1612.* Neumünster: Karl Wachholtz Verlag, 1992.

Umminger, Walter. *Das Winterkönigreich.* Stuttgart: Klett-Cotta, 1994.

Volkmann, Ludwig. *Bilder-Schriften der Renaissance: Hieroglyphik und Emblematik in ihren Beziehungen und Fortwirkungen.* Leipzig: Karl W. Hiersemann, 1923.

Wahrig, Gerhard et. al. (eds.) *Brockhaus-Wahrig Deutsches Wörterbuch.* Vol. 4. Stuttgart: Deutsche Verlags-Anstalt, 1982.

Waite, Arthur Edward. *Azoth, or the Star in the East.* London: Theosophical Publishing, 1893.

— *Lives of the Alchemystical Philosophers.* London: George Redway, 1888.

— *The Brotherhood of the Rosy Cross.* London: Rider and Sons, 1924.

— *The Real History of the Rosicrucians, founded on their own manifestos, and on facts and documents collected from the writings of initiated brethren.* New York: J. W. Bouton, 1888.

— *The Secret Tradition in Alchemy.* New York: Alfred Knopf, 1926.

— (trans.). *The Turba Philosophorum, or the Assembly of Sages.* New York: Samuel Weiser, 1973.

Westman, Robert S. "Nature, Art and Psyche: Jung, Pauli and the Kepler-Fludd Polemic." In Vickers, Brian (ed.). *Occult and Scientific Mentalities in the Renaissance*. Cambridge: Cambridge University Press, 1984.

Whitney, Mark (dir.). *Matter of Heart*. Los Angeles: C. G. Jung Institute, 1983.

Wolter, F. A. *Geschichte der Stadt Magdeburg von ihrem Ursprung bis auf die Gegenwart*. Magdeburg: Faber, 1901.

Yarker, John. *The Arcane Schools; a Review of their Origin and Antiquity; with a General History of Freemasonry, and its Relation to the Theosophic, Scientific, and Philosophic Mysteries*. Belfast: William Tait, 1909.

Yates, Frances. *Giordano Bruno and the Hermetic Tradition*. Chicago: University of Chicago Press, 1991.

— *The Rosicrucian Enlightenment*. London: Routledge and Kegan Paul, 1972.

Index

Illustrations

Illustration sources:

Figures 1-6, 9-18, 20-32: Herzog August Bibliothek, Wolfenbüttel
Figures 8, 19: Niedersächsische Staats- und Universitätsbibliothek, Göttingen
Figure 7: Allgemeines Verwaltungsarchiv, Wien

TRES SCHOLA, TRES COESAR TITVLOS DE-
DIT; HÆC MIHI RESTANT,
POSSE BENE IN CHRISTO VIVERE, POSSE MORI.
MICHAEL MAIERVS COMES IMPERIALIS CON-
SISTORII etc. PHILOSOPH. ET MEDICINARVM
DOCTOR. P. C. C. NOBIL. EXEMPTVS FOR-OLIM
MEDICVS CÆS. etc.

1. Count Michael Maier (1569-1622).

2. Saturn tending to trees with flowers of gold and silver
(from the *Symbola Aureae Mensae*, 1617).

HENRICVS RANZOVIVS.
Ranzouiæ cui non est cognita gloria gentis?
Henrici cui non gloria Ranzouij?
Qui genus antiquum varijs virtutibus ornat,
Vates et medicus, miles et Astrologus.

31

3. Governor Heinrich Rantzau.

4. Emperor Rudolf II.

5. The title page of Maier's *Septimana Philosophica* (1620),
with the six days of creation represented in the
six circles on either side of the title.

6. The *ouroboros*, from Maier's *Atalanta Fugiens* (1617).

6.844

Allergnädigster Kayser, [es] sagt Avicenna der warhafft Hermetisch Philosophia in seiner Porta Elementorum, ein Adler, welcher fleuchet durch die lüfft, und ein Löw, welcher kreicht auf der erde, sein die Weisheyt; Da verstehet er durch den Adler den flüchtige theil des gemeinen Agent [...], durch den nidrigste [...] Löw, der fixen theil der erden, Von dieszen beiden ist zu prüren gezogen die Hermetisch Medicin und [...] der weiszen [...]

Dieweil den Allergnädigster Kayser E. May: mich mit minem [...] und andren gnädigst [...], und [...] das mein anbringen [...] Rom: Kay: May: nicht schlecht oder gemein ist, [...] guten [...] wendt, So ist mein [...] bitte Ihr May: wolle mir [...] solchem philoso-phischen Symbolo [...] gnädigsten helm [...] [...] und mir theilen; Ihn den dergleichen [...] helmen auf einem schild den von Adel [...] theile in Osterreich, auch etliche an andren örtern führen; Welche alle von E. May: [...] ihnen verbaten, oder Ihr May: selbst [...] und [...] darumb allergnädigsten Kayser, [...] mit [...] unser [...] und [...] Dienste gegen Ihr May: Vor prosten Ihr May: allergnädigst in den privilegio palatinal, auch de [...] armis ac galeis [...] [...] werdt, welches allso soll E. May: [...] mich, [...] und ehren

Mayer
1609

24

7. The first page of Maier's request to the emperor
for the symbol of Avicenna.

298

8. The title page of the *Arcana Arcanissima* (1614).

9. Figures and hieroglyphic inscriptions from the *Thesaurus Hieroglyphicorum* (c.1607) of Herwarth von Hohenburg; the ibis-headed deity is Thoth.

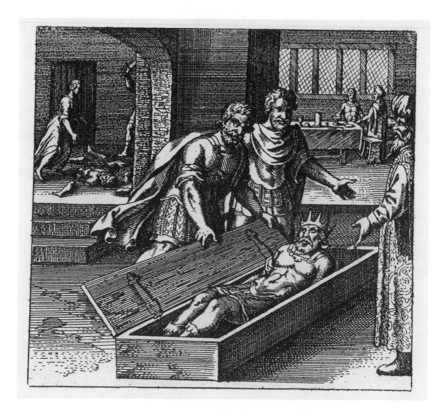

10. The resurrection of Osiris as depicted in the
44th emblem of the *Atalanta Fugiens*.

11. Moritz 'the Learned' of Hessen-Kassel.

12. The Elector Palatine, Prince Friedrich V.

13. Saturn regurgitating the *lapis* over Mt. Helicon, as shown in the 12th emblem of the *Atalanta Fugiens*.

14. Morienus in the *Symbola Aureae Mensae*: "When climbing without a ladder you will fall on your head."

15. The contemporary announcement of the wedding of Princess Elizabeth
to Prince Friedrich V, 1613.

TRIPVS AVREVS,

Hoc est,

TRES TRACTATVS

CHYMICI SELECTISSIMI,

Nempe

I. BASILII VALENTINI, BENEDICTINI ORDI-
nis monachi, Germani, PRACTICA vna cum 12. clauibus &
appendice, ex Germanico;

II. THOMÆ NORTONI, ANGLI PHILOSOPHI
CREDE MIHI feu ORDINALE, ante annos 140. ab authore scriptum, nunc ex Anglicano manuscripto in Latinum
translatum, phrasi cuiusque authoris vt & sententia retenta;

III. CREMERI CVIVSDAM ABBATIS WEST-
monasteriensis Angli Testamentum, hactenus nondum publicatum, nunc in diuersarum nationum gratiam editi, & figuris
cupro affabre incisis ornati operâ & studio

MICHAELIS MAIERI Phil. & Med. D. Com. P. &c.

FRANCOFVRTI
Ex Chalcographia Pauli Iacobi, impensis LVGÆ IENNIS.
Anno M. DC. XVIII.

16. The title page of the *Tripus Aureus* (1618), in which Basil Valentine,
Thomas Norton and Abbot Cremer are shown conferring in the laboratory.
The central furnace unites the library on the left (theory) and the workshop
on the right (practice).

183

TESTAMENTVM CRE-
MERI, ABBATIS WESTMONA-
STERIENSIS, ANGLI, OR-
dinis Benedictini.

TOMVS TERTIVS.

FRANCOFVRTI APVD JENNIS.

17. Abbot Cremer, as depicted in the *Tripus Aureus;* in the alchemist's vessel and within the earth itself metals are formed through the conjunction of mercury and sulphur.

18. "Join the brother with the sister, and offer them the cup of love."
Atalanta Fugiens, emblem 4.

19. The fish of the Philosophical sea, from Lambsprinck's
De Lapide Philosophico Libellus (1625).

20. The virgin Europe, from the *Septimana Philosophica*. According to Maier's accompanying explanation, the dark blemishes on the otherwise white face of Luna are "the reflected image of parts of the terrestrial globe, so that in Europe may be seen the idea of Europe, in Asia that of Asia, in Africa that of Africa, and in America that of America." Note that the moon's orbit is in the likeness of the *ouroboros*.

21. The seal of the Rosicrucian Fraternity, from the *Themis Aurea* (1618).

COLLOQVIVM RHODO-
STAVROTICVM.

Das ist:

Gespräch dreyer Personen/

von der vor wenig Jahren/ durch
die Famam & Confeßionem etlicher maſſen geoffenbarten

FRATERNITET
deß Roſen Creutzes;

Darinnen zu ſehen/

Was endlich von ſo vielen vnter-
ſchiedlichen in ihrem Namen publicirten
Schriefften/ vnd denn auch von der Brü-
derſchafft ſelbſten zu halten
ſey.

Allen trewhertzigen/ vnd aber durch ſo vielerhand Schreiben irzgemachten Chriſtlichen
Leſern zu lieb in druck ge-
geben.

Matth. 5. v. 16.

Laſſet ewer Liecht leuchten für den Leu-
then/ daß ſie ewre gute werck ſehen/ vnd
ewren Vatter im Himmel preiſen.

ANNO
M. DC. XXI.

22.The title page of the German edition of the
Colloquium Rhodo-Stauroticum (1621).

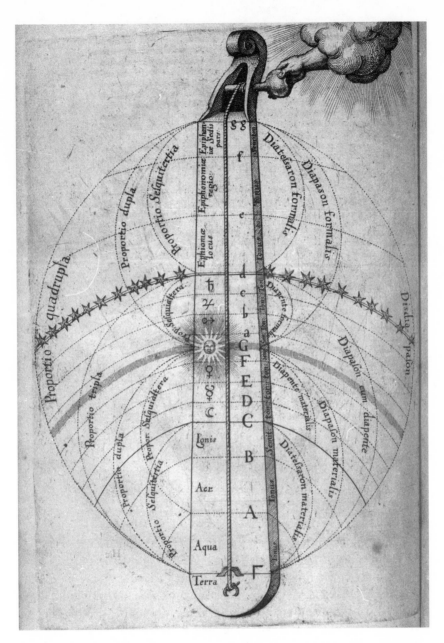

23. "If in the imagination a monochord is extended from the summit of the Empyrean heaven to the base of the earth itself, we shall perceive it to be divided into parts constituting consonances; and if the half part thereof were struck, it would produce the consonant diapason in the same manner as the instrumental monochord." Robert Fludd, *Utriusque Cosmi Maioris scilicet et Minoris Metaphysica, Physica, atque Technica Historia* (1617), p. 85.

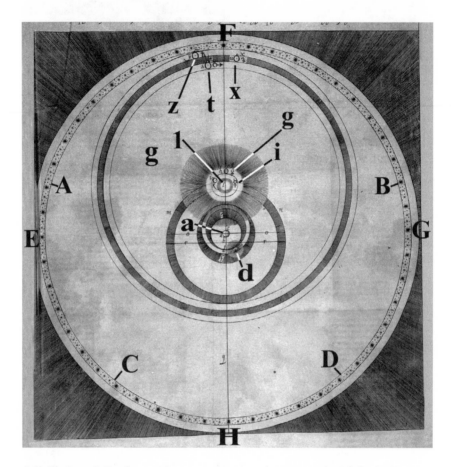

24. Christoph Rothmann's cosmology, as it appears in Maier's *Septim-ana Philosophica*: the moon (d) and the sun (l) orbit around the earth (a), and the planets revolve around the sun. The paths of the inner pla-nets, Mercury (i) and Venus (g) intersect with the sun's orbit around the earth, whilst the paths of the outer planets – Mars (t), Jupiter (x) and Saturn (z) – do not. A, B, C and D represent the sphere of the fixed stars, whilst E, F, G and H represent the *primum mobile*. This cosmology may be distinguished from that of Rothmann's contemporary, Tycho Brahe, by the fact that the orbit of Mars does not intersect with the solar orbit.

25. "Make a circle out of a man and a woman, derive from it a square, and from the square a triangle: make a circle [again] and you will have the Philosophers' Stone." *Atalanta Fugiens*, emblem 21.

26. The Defenestration of Prague.

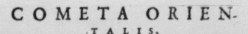

27. The comet of 1618, as depicted in Gotthard's *Cometa Orientalis* (1619); the caption is drawn from the warning in *2 Timothy* 3.1 that "in the last days perilous times will come."

28. The Star Palace of Friedrich V near the White Mountain.

29. Coral as the homologue of the *lapis philosophorum*:
Atalanta Fugiens, emblem 32.

30. The two 'stones' as eagles, from the
Atalanta Fugiens, emblem 46.

31. Magellan and the circumnavigation of the earth,
from Maier's *Viatorium* (1618).

32. Following in the footsteps of Nature;
Atalanta Fugiens, emblem 42.

■ Arbeiten zur Kirchengeschichte

23 x 15,5 cm. Leinen.

83 *Joachim Weinhardt*, Savonarola als Apologet. Der Versuch einer empirischen Begründung des christlichen Glaubens in der Zeit der Renaissance. 2003. XI, 296 S.

82 *Peter Gemeinhardt*, Die Filioque-Kontroverse zwischen Ost- und Westkiche im Frühmittelalter. 2002. XV, 644 S.

81 *Silke-Petra Bergjan*, Der fürsorgliche Gott. Der Begriff der ΠΡΟΝΟΙΑ Gottes in der apologetischen Literatur der Alten Kirche. 2002. XIII, 422 S.

80/1-2 *Hermann Geyer*, Verborgene Weisheit. Johann Arndts „Vier Bücher vom Wahren Christentum" als Programm einer spiritualistisch-hermetischen Theologie. 2001. 2 Bde. [Buch 1]: XXIX, 821 S. 1 Taf. [Buch 2]: IX, 545 S. 25 Abb.

79 *Volker Henning Drecoll*, Der Passauer Vertrag (1522). Einleitung und Edition. 2000. XII, 382 S.

78 *Wenrich Slenczka*, Heilsgeschichte und Liturgie. Studien zum Verhältnis von Heilsgeschichte und Heilsteilhabe anhand liturgischer und katechetischer Quellen des dritten und vierten Jahrhunderts. 2000. IX, 287 S.

77 *Lothar Vogel*, Vom Werden eines Heiligen. Eine Untersuchung der Vita Corbiniani des Bischofs Arbeo von Freising. 2000. XI, 542 S.

76 *Hans Georg Thümmel*, Die Memorien für Petrus und Paulus in Rom. Die archäologischen Denkmäler und die literarische Tradition. 1999. X, 102 S. 65 Taf.

75 *Hartmut Kühne*, Ostensio reliquiarum. Untersuchungen über Entstehung, Ausbreitung, Gestalt und Funktion der Heiltumsweisungen im römisch-deutschen Regnum. 2000. XIV, 967 S. 35 Abb.

74 *Wolfram Kinzig / Christoph Markschies / Markus Vinzent*, Tauffragen und Bekenntnis. Studien zur sogenannten „Traditio Apostolica", zu den „Interrogationes de fide" und zum „Römischen Glaubensbekenntnis". 1999. IX, 484 S.

73 *Ulrich Schneider*, Theologie als christliche Philosophie. Zur Bedeutung der biblischen Botschaft im Denken des Clemens von Alexandria. 1999. XV, 335 S.

72 *Joachim Mehlhausen*, Vestigia Verbi. Aufsätze zur Geschichte der evangelischen Theologie. 1999. X, 574 S.

71 *Friedrich Loofs*, Patristica. Ausgewählte Aufsätze zur Alten Kirche. Hrsg. v. Hanns Christof Brennecke und Jörg Ulrich. 1999. XIX, 453 S.

70 *Ulrich Löffler*, Lissabons Fall - Europas Schrecken. Die Deutung des Erdbebens von Lissabon im deutschsprachigen Protestantismus des 18. Jahrhunderts. 1999. XIII, 721 S.

69 *Jörg Lauster*, Die Erlösungslehre Marsilio Ficinos. Theologiegeschichtliche Aspekte des Renaissanceplatonismus. 1998. VIII, 268 S.

68 *Rochus Leonhardt*, Glück als Vollendung des Menschseins. Die beatitudo-Lehre des Thomas von Aquin im Horizont des Eudämonismus-Problems. 1998. VIII, 322 S.

67 *Heinz Ohme*, Kanon ekklesiastikos. Die Bedeutung des altkirchlichen Kanonbegriffs. 1998. XVII, 666 S.

66 *Andreas Mühling*, Karl Ludwig Schmidt. „Und Wissenschaft ist Leben". 1997. XI, 263 S.

65 *Christoph Strohm*, Ethik im frühen Calvinismus. Humanistische Einflüsse, philosophische, juristische und theologische Argumentationen sowie mentalitätsgeschichtliche Aspekte am Beispiel des Calvin-Schülers Lambertus Danaeus. 1996. XXI, 789 S.

64 *Knut Schäferdiek*, Schwellenzeit. Beiträge zur Geschichte des Christentums in Spätantike und Frühmittelalter. Hrsg. v. Winrich A. Löhr und Hanns Christof Brennecke. 1996. XIII, 546 S.